Progress in Mathematics
Vol. 40

Edited by
J. Coates and
S. Helgason

Birkhäuser
Boston · Basel · Stuttgart

Representation Theory of Reductive Groups

Proceedings of the University of Utah Conference 1982

P. C. Trombi, editor

1983

Birkhäuser
Boston · Basel · Stuttgart

Editor:

P.C. Trombi
Department of Mathematics
University of Utah
Salt Lake City, UT 84112

Library of Congress Cataloging in Publication Data

Representation theory of reductive groups.

(Progress in mathematics ; v. 40)
Papers presented at a conference held in Park City, Utah, Apr. 16-20, 1982.
1. Representations of groups—Congresses. I. Trombi, P. C. (Peter C.), 1942- . II. Series.
QA171.R43 1983 512'.2 83-15863
ISBN 0-8176-3135-6

CIP-Kurztitelaufnahme der Deutschen Bibliothek

Representation theory of reductive groups : proceedings of the Univ. of Utah conference 1982 / P. C. Trombi, ed. - Boston ; Basel ; Stuttgart : Birkhäuser, 1983.
(Progress in mathematics ; Vol. 40)
ISBN 3-7643-3135-6 (Basel, Stuttgart)
ISBN 0-8176-3135-6 (Boston)

NE: Trombi, Peter C. [Hrsg.]; University of Utah (Salt Lake City, Utah); GT

ISBN 0-8176-3135-6
ISBN 3-7643-3135-6
Printed in USA
9 8 7 6 5 4 3 2 1

PREFACE

This volume is the result of a conference on Representation Theory of Reductive Groups held in Park City, Utah, April 16-20, 1982, under the auspices of the Department of Mathematics, University of Utah. Funding for the conference was provided by the National Science Foundation.

The text includes a number of original papers together with expository articles on work already in print. It is hoped that the volume will be of use to both experts in the field and nonspecialists interested in obtaining some insight into the area.

Principal organizers of the conference were Henryk Hecht, Dragan Miličić, and Peter Trombi. They would like to express their thanks to the National Science Foundation for their support, to the speakers for their diligence in submitting their manuscripts, and to Carla Curtis, Karen Edge, and Katherine Ruth, for typing the manuscripts which were contributed.

CONTENTS

PARTICIPANTS

Dr. Jeff Adams, Department of Mathematics, Massachusetts Institute of Technology, Cambridge, Massachusetts 02139

Professor James Arthur, Department of Mathematics, University of Toronto, Toronto, Ontario, Canada M1C 1A4

Professor Lou Auslander, Mathematical Sciences Department, Research Division, I.B.M. - Box 218, Yorktown Heights, New York 10529

Professor Dan Barbasch, Department of Mathematics, Rutgers University, New Brunswick, New Jersey 08903

Professor William Barker, Department of Mathematics, Bowdoin College, Brunswick, Maine 04011

Professor Joseph Bernstein, Department of Mathematics, Harvard University, Cambridge, Massachusetts 02130

Dr. Brian Boe, Department of Mathematics, University of Utah, Salt Lake City, Utah 84112

Professor Christopher Brynes, Department of Mathematics, Harvard University, Cambridge, Massachusetts 02138

Professor William Casselman, Department of Mathematics, University of British Columbia, Vancouver, B.C., Canada V6T 1W5

David H. Collingwood, Department of Mathematics, University of Utah, Salt Lake City, Utah 84112

Professor Thomas Enright, Department of Mathematics, University of California, La Jolla, California 92093

Dr. Sal Friedburg, Department of Mathematics, University of California at San Diego, La Jolla, California 92093

Professor Kenneth Gross, Department of Mathematics, University of Wyoming, Laramie, Wyoming 82071.

Professor Henryk Hecht, Department of Mathematics, University of Utah, Salt Lake City, Utah 84112

Dr. Gerritt Heckman, Department of Mathematics, Massachusetts Institute of Technology, Cambridge, Massachusetts 02139

Professor Sigurdur Helgason, Department of Mathematics, Massachusetts Institute of Technology, Cambridge, Massachusetts 02139

Professor Rebecca Herb, Department of Mathematics, University of Maryland, College Park, Maryland 20742

Professor Roger Howe, Department of Mathematics, Yale University, New Haven, Connecticut 06520

Dr. Sheldon Katz, Department of Mathematics, University of Utah, Salt Lake City, Utah 84112

Thong-chai Kengmana, Department of Mathematics, Harvard University, Cambridge, Massachusetts 02139

Professor Harvey Keynes, Department of Mathematics, 127 Vincent Hall, University of Minnesota, Minneapolis, Minnesota 55455

Dr. David Keys, Department of Mathematics, University of Utah, Salt Lake City, Utah 84112

Professor Donald King, Department of Mathematics, University of California, La Jolla, California 92093

Professor Bertram Kostant, Department of Mathematics, Massachusetts Institute of Technology, Massachusetts 02139

Professor Ray A. Kunze, Department of Mathematics, University of California, Irvine, California 92717

Professor Phil Kutzko, Department of Mathematics, University of Iowa, Iowa City, Iowa 52242

Professor Ron Lipsman, Department of Mathematics, University of Maryland, College Park, Maryland 20742

Dr. David Manderscheid, Department of Mathematics, University of Utah, Salt Lake City, Utah 84112

Professor Roberto Miatello, Department of Mathematics, Rutgers University, New Brunswick, New Jersey 08903

Professor Dragan Miličić, Department of Mathematics, University of Utah, Salt Lake City, Utah 84112

Ivan Mirkovic, Department of Mathematics, University of Utah, Salt Lake City, Utah 84112

Dr. Rajagopalan Parthasarathy, Department of Mathematics, University of Utah, Salt Lake City, Utah 84112

Dr. Charles Patton, Department of Mathematics, University of Utah, Salt Lake City, Utah 84112

Professor Hugo Rossi, Department of Mathematics, University of Utah, Salt Lake City, Utah 84112

Professor Paul Sally, Department of Mathematics, University of Chicago, Chicago, Illinois 60637

Professor Wilfried Schmid, Department of Mathematics, Harvard University, Cambridge, Massachusetts 02138

Professor Allan Silberger, Department of Mathematics, Cleveland State University, Cleveland, Ohio 44115

Dr. Jedrzej Sniatycki, Department of Mathematics, University of Calgary, 2500 University Dr. N.W., Calgary, Alberta, Canada T2N 1N4

Professor Birgit Speh, Department of Mathematics, Cornell University, Ithaca, NY 14853

Professor Joseph Taylor, Department of Mathematics, University of Utah, Salt Lake City, Utah 84112

Professor Peter Trombi, Department of Mathematics, University of Utah, Salt Lake City, Utah 84112

Dr. Jerrold Tunnell, Department of Mathematics, Princeton University, Princeton, New Jersey 08544

Professor V. S. Varadarajan, Department of Mathematics, University of California, Los Angeles, California 90024

Professor Michele Vergne, Department of Mathematics, Massachusetts Institute of Technology, Cambridge, Massachusetts 02139

Professor David Vogan, Department of Mathematics, Massachusetts Institute of Technology, Cambridge, Massachusetts 02139

Professor Nolan Wallach, Department of Mathematics, Rutgers University, New Brunswick, New Jersey 08903

Dr. Norman Wildberger, Department of Mathematics, Yale University, New Haven, Connecticut 06520

Professor Joseph Wolf, Department of Mathematics, University of California, Berkeley, California 94720

Professor Gregg Zuckerman, Department of Mathematics, Yale University, New Haven, Connecticut 06520

MULTIPLIERS AND A PALEY-WIENER THEOREM FOR REAL REDUCTIVE GROUPS*

James Arthur

The classical Paley-Wiener theorem is a description of the image of $C_c^\infty(\mathbb{R})$ under Fourier transform. The Fourier transform

$$\hat{f}(\Lambda) = \int_{-\infty}^{\infty} f(x)e^{\Lambda x}\, dx$$

is defined a priori for purely imaginary numbers Λ, but if f has compact support $\hat{f}$ will extend to an entire function on the complex plane. The image of $C_c^\infty(\mathbb{R})$ under this map is the space of entire functions F with the following property - there exists a constant N such that

$$\sup_{\Lambda\in\mathbb{C}}\left(|F(\Lambda)\, e^{-N|\mathrm{Re}\,\Lambda|}(1 + |\mathrm{Im}\,\Lambda|)^n\right) < \infty$$

for every integer n. (There is a similar theorem which characterizes the image of the space of compactly supported distributions.)

Our purpose is to describe an analogous result for a reductive Lie group. We shall also discuss a closely related theorem on multipliers, a result whose statement is especially simple. Both results were proved in detail in the paper [1]. We will be content here to just describe some of the main ideas. In the case of groups of real rank 1, the theorems were proved by Campoli [2]. The new ingredients for higher rank are (a) a scheme for keeping track of multi-dimensional residues, reminiscent of Langlands' work on Eisenstein series [9(b), Chapter 7], [9(a), §10], and (b) a theorem of Casselman on partial matrix coefficients of induced representations.

A number of mathematicians have proved Paley-Wiener theorems for particular classes of groups. We mention the papers of Ephrenpreis and Mautner ([4(a)], [4(b)]), Helgason ([7(a)], [7(b)], [7(c)], [7(d)]),

Gangolli ([5]), Zelobenko ([10]), Delorme ([3]), and Kawazoe ([8(a)], [8(b)]) in addition to the thesis of Campoli cited above.

1. A MULTIPLIER THEOREM

Let G be a reductive Lie group, with Iwasawa decomposition

$$G = N_0 A_0 K.$$

We shall assume that G satisfies the general axioms of Harish-Chandra in [6(a)]. We shall denote the Lie algebras of Lie groups by lower case German script letters, and we will add a subscript $\mathbb{C}$ to denote complexification. Thus,

$$\mathfrak{g} = \mathfrak{n}_0 \oplus \mathfrak{a}_0 \oplus \mathfrak{k}.$$

Let

$$\mathcal{H} = C_c^\infty(G,K)$$

be the Hecke algebra. It is the space of functions in $C_c^\infty(G)$ whose left and right translates by K span a finite dimensional space; it becomes an algebra under convolution. We are interested in multipliers of $\mathcal{H}$. By this, we mean linear maps

$$C: \ \mathcal{H} \to \mathcal{H}$$

such that

$$C(f * g) = C(f) * g = f * C(g),$$

for every f and g in $\mathcal{H}$. (This condition is equivalent to saying that C commutes with the left and right action on $\mathcal{H}$ of the universal enveloping algebra of $\mathfrak{g}_{\mathbb{C}}$.)

Suppose that C is such a multiplier and that π belongs to $\Pi(G)$, the set of irreducible admissible representations of G. Then

$$\pi(C(f)) = C_\pi \pi(f), \qquad f \in \mathcal{H},$$

for a complex number C_π which is independent of f. The multiplier will be completely determined by the map

$$\pi \to C_\pi .$$

Because of Harish-Chandra's subquotient theorem, we can actually restrict our attention to the principal series. Recall that if M_0 is the centralizer of A_0 in K, the principal series

$$I(\sigma,\Lambda), \qquad \sigma \in \Pi(M_0), \qquad \Lambda \in \mathfrak{a}^*_{0,\mathbb{C}},$$

can be defined to act on a Hilbert space U_σ which is independent of Λ. It is irreducible for almost all Λ, so that $C_{I(\sigma,\Lambda)}$ is defined. As a function of Λ, $C_{I(\sigma,\Lambda)}$ is analytic and extends to an entire function on $\mathfrak{a}^*_{0,\mathbb{C}}$. If π is equivalent to a subquotient of $I(\sigma,\Lambda)$,

$$C_\pi = C_{I(\sigma,\Lambda)} .$$

Thus,

$$(\sigma,\Lambda) \to C_{I(\sigma,\Lambda)}, \qquad \sigma \in \Pi(M_0), \qquad \Lambda \in \mathfrak{a}^*_{0,\mathbb{C}},$$

is an entire function in Λ which completely determines C. It provides a very concrete way to realize any multiplier.

As an example, consider the center $\mathfrak{z}$ of the universal enveloping algebra of $\mathfrak{g}_\mathbb{C}$. If $z \in \mathfrak{z}$, then

$$C(f) = zf, \qquad f \in \mathcal{H},$$

is a multiplier of $\mathcal{H}$. To represent it as above, let $\mathfrak{a}_K$ be a Cartan subalgebra of $\mathfrak{m}_0$. Then

$$\mathfrak{h} = i\mathfrak{a}_K \oplus \mathfrak{a}_0$$

is a real vector space, and is a Cartan subalgebra of the split real form of $\mathfrak{g}_\mathbb{C}$. Its interest comes from the fact that it is invariant under the complex Weyl group W of $(\mathfrak{g}_\mathbb{C},\mathfrak{h}_\mathbb{C})$. Let γ_z be the W-invariant differential operator on $\mathfrak{h}$ obtained from z by the

Harish-Chandra map. We shall regard γ_Z as a W-invariant distribution on $\mathfrak{h}$ which is compactly supported. (It is in fact supported at the origin.) Its Fourier transform

$$\hat{\gamma}_Z(\nu), \qquad \nu \in \mathfrak{h}^*_{\mathbb{C}},$$

is a W-invariant polynomial on $\mathfrak{h}^*_{\mathbb{C}}$. If μ_σ is the linear functional in $i\mathfrak{a}^*_K$ which defines the infinitesimal character of a representation $\sigma \in \Pi(M_0)$,

$$C_{I(\sigma,\Lambda)} = \hat{\gamma}_Z(\mu_\sigma + \Lambda), \qquad \Lambda \in \mathfrak{a}^*_{0,\mathbb{C}}.$$

The multipliers from this last example are of course well known. They extend to the full convolution algebra $C_c^\infty(G)$. Since they are defined directly for any function f, it is not really necessary to look at the function $C_{I(\sigma,\Lambda)}$. It turns out, however, that there is a richer family of multipliers for H which do not in general extend to $C_c^\infty(G)$. These multipliers are intrinsically more algebraic, and can only be described by the functions $C_{I(\sigma,\Lambda)}$.

THEOREM 1. *Let γ be any compactly supported, W-invariant distribution on $\mathfrak{h}$. Then there is a unique multiplier C of H such that*

$$C_{I(\sigma,\Lambda)} = \hat{\gamma}(\mu_\sigma + \Lambda)$$

for all $\sigma \in \Pi(M_0)$ and $\Lambda \in \mathfrak{a}^*_{0,\mathbb{C}}$.

2. THE PALEY-WIENER THEOREM

Theorem 1 describes multipliers in terms of the Fourier transform on H. In order to prove it, we must characterize the image of H under Fourier transform. For any $f \in H$, set

$$\hat{f}(\sigma,\Lambda) = I(\sigma,\Lambda,f) = \int_G f(x)I(\sigma,\Lambda,x)dx,$$

with $\sigma \in \Pi(M_0)$ and $\Lambda \in \mathfrak{a}^*_{0,\mathbb{C}}$. Then $\hat{f}(\sigma,\Lambda)$ is an entire function of Λ which, for any σ, takes values in the space of operators on

U_σ. It is K-finite, in the sense that the space spanned by the functions

$$(\sigma,\Lambda) \to I(\sigma,\Lambda,k_1)\hat{f}(\sigma,\Lambda)I(\sigma,\Lambda,k_2),$$

indexed by k_1 and k_2 in K, is finite dimensional. There is a constant N, which depends in a simple way on the support of f, such that for every n,

$$\sup_{(\sigma,\Lambda)} (\|\hat{f}(\sigma,\Lambda)\| e^{-N\|\mathrm{Re}\,\Lambda\|}(1 + \|\mathrm{Im}\,\Lambda\|)^n) < \infty.$$

The function has another property, which comes from the various intertwining maps between principal series. Suppose there is a relation

$$\sum_{k=1}^m D_k(I(\sigma_k, \Lambda_k, x)u_k, v_k)) = 0 \ , \qquad (2.1)$$

valid for all $x \in G$, in which each D_k is a differential operator on $\mathfrak{a}^*_{0,\mathbb{C}}$ acting through Λ_k, and u_k, v_k are vectors in U_{σ_k}. Integrating this against the function f(x), we see that

$$\sum_{k=1}^m D_k(\hat{f}(\sigma_k, \Lambda_k)u_k, v_k) = 0.$$

Relations of this form are common, but are not easy to characterize explicitly. For example, there will be such a relation any time an irreducible representation occurs in two different ways as a composition factor of the principal series.

Let PW(G,K) be the space of functions

$$F: (\sigma,\Lambda) \to \mathrm{End}(U_\sigma), \qquad \sigma \in \Pi(M_0), \qquad \lambda \in \mathfrak{a}^*_{0,\mathbb{C}},$$

such that

(i) $F(\sigma,\Lambda)$ is entire in Λ.

(ii) F is K finite.

(iii) There is a constant N such that for any n,

$$\sup_{(\sigma,\Lambda)} (\|F(\sigma,\Lambda)\| e^{-N\|\mathrm{Re}\,\Lambda\|}(1 + \|\mathrm{Im}\,\Lambda\|)^n) < \infty.$$

(iv) Whenever a relation of the form (2.1) holds, we have

$$\sum_{k=1}^{m} D_k(F(\sigma_k, \Lambda_k)u_k, v_k) = 0. \qquad (2.2)$$

There are natural topologies which turn both H and PW(G,K) into Frechet spaces. Our Paley-Wiener theorem is

THEOREM 2. *The map*

$$f \to \hat{f}$$

is a topological isomorphism for H *onto* PW(G,K).

As we shall see in the next section, Theorem 1 is an easy consequence of Theorem 2. However, the proof of Theorem 2 is considerably harder.

3. PROOF OF THEOREM 1

Following an argument of Campoli, we shall derive the multiplier theorem as a corollary of Theorem 2. Suppose that γ is a compactly supported, W-invariant distribution on $\mathfrak{h}$, and that f belongs to H. Theorem 1 amounts to showing that

$$(\sigma,\Lambda) \to \hat{\gamma}(\mu_\sigma + \Lambda)\hat{f}(\sigma,\Lambda) \qquad (3.1)$$

is the Fourier transform of some other function in H. By Theorem 2, we need only show that this function belongs to PW(G,K). The first three conditions in the definition of PW(G,K) clearly hold. We must establish the less obvious fourth condition.

Now $\hat{\gamma}$ is an entire, W-invariant function on $\mathfrak{h}_{\mathbb{C}}^*$. Its Taylor series converges everywhere, and consists of polynomials on $\mathfrak{h}_{\mathbb{C}}^*$ which are W-invariant. It follows that

$$\hat{\gamma}(\nu) = \sum_{j=1}^{\infty} \hat{\gamma}_{z_j}(\nu), \qquad \nu \in \mathfrak{h}_{\mathbb{C}}^*,$$

for a sequence $\{z_j\}$ of elements in $\mathfrak{Z}$. But

$$\hat{\gamma}_{z_j}(\mu_\sigma + \Lambda)\hat{f}(\sigma,\Lambda) = (z_j f)^\wedge(\sigma,\Lambda).$$

If we have a relation (2.1), we can integrate it against $(z_j f)(x)$ to obtain

$$\sum_{k=1}^m D_k(\hat{\gamma}_{z_j}(\mu_{\sigma_k} + \lambda_k)\hat{f}(\sigma_k, \Lambda_k)u_k, v_k) = 0.$$

Since a convergent Taylor series can be differentiated term by term, the relation holds also for the function (3.1). So the function does belong to $PW(G,K)$ and γ does define a multiplier.

4. EISENSTEIN INTEGRALS

In the rest of this paper we shall try to give an idea of the proof of Theorem 2. It is almost immediate that the Fourier transform maps $\mathcal{H}$ into $PW(G,K)$. The problem is to show that the map is surjective. This amounts to being able to construct the inverse map from $PW(G,K)$ to $\mathcal{H}$.

It is convenient to work within Harish Chandra's framework of Eisenstein integrals. Let τ be a unitary two-sided representation of K on a finite dimensional Hilbert space V_τ. Theorem 2 has an equivalent formulation in this context. The Hecke algebra is replaced by the space $C_c^\infty(G,\tau)$ of smooth, compactly supported functions from G to V_τ which are τ spherical. The original Paley-Wiener space is replaced by a space $PW(G,\tau)$ of entire functions from $\mathfrak{a}_{0,\mathbb{C}}^*$ to the finite dimensional vector space

$$A_0 = C_c^\infty(M_0,\tau).$$

If $f \in C_c^\infty(G,\tau)$, let $\hat{f}$ be the function in $PW(G,\tau)$ such that

$$(\hat{f}(\Lambda), \phi) = \int_G (f(x), E_{P_0}(x,\phi, -\bar{\Lambda}))dx,$$

for any $\Lambda \in \mathfrak{a}_{0,\mathbb{C}}^*$ and $\phi \in A_0$. Here, $E_{P_0}(\cdot,\cdot,\cdot)$ is the Eisenstein integral associated to the minimal parabolic subgroup

$$P_0 = N_0A_0M_0.$$

It is essentially a matrix coefficient of the representation $I(\sigma,\Lambda)$.

Theorem 2 is equivalent to the assertion that for any τ,

$$f \to \hat{f}$$

is a topological isomorphism from $C_c^\infty(G,\tau)$ onto $PW(G,\tau)$.

Suppose that for $j = 0, 1, \ldots, n$, Λ_j is a point in $\mathfrak{a}_{0,\mathbb{C}}^*$ and S_j is a finite dimensional subspace of the symmetric algebra on $\mathfrak{a}_{0,\mathbb{C}}^*$. Suppose that F is a function in $PW(G,\tau)$. For any j, let

$$d_{S_j} F(\Lambda_j)$$

be the vector in

$$\mathrm{Hom}(S_j, A_0)$$

whose value at any $p \in S_j$ is the derivative

$$\partial(p) F(\Lambda_j).$$

After a little thought the reader will believe the following.

LEMMA 1. *There is a function* $g \in C_c^\infty(G,\tau)$ *such that*

$$d_{S_j} F(\Lambda_j) = d_{S_j} \hat{g}(\Lambda_j)$$

for $j = 0, 1, \ldots, n$.

See Lemma III.2.1 of [1].

This lemma is actually equivalent to the analogue of the condition (2.2) for $PW(G,\tau)$. It asserts that a function F in $PW(G,\tau)$ is locally the Fourier transform of a function in $C_c^\infty(G,\tau)$. The result we are trying to prove is that F is a Fourier transform globally (i.e., for all Λ).

5. CHANGE OF CONTOUR

The function $F \in PW(G,\tau)$ will be fixed from now on. We are attempting to construct a function $f \in C_c^\infty(G,\tau)$ whose Fourier transform is F. From Harish Chandra's Plancherel formula ([6(b)]) we know that any such f can be written uniquely as a sum of τ spherical Schwartz functions, indexed by the associativity classes of cuspidal parabolic subgroups. The only one of these functions which we can write down at the moment is the one which corresponds to the minimal parabolic subgroup. It equals

$$F^{\vee}_{P_0}(x) = \int_{i\mathfrak{a}_0^*} E_{P_0}(x, \mu(\Lambda)F(\Lambda),\Lambda)d\Lambda,$$

where $\mu(\Lambda)$ is the Plancherel density. We must somehow obtain from this a function of compact support.

Let a be a point in

$$A_0^+ = \exp \mathfrak{a}_0^+,$$

the positive chamber in A_0. Then

$$E_{P_0}(a, \mu(\Lambda)F(\Lambda), \Lambda) = \sum_{s\in W_0} \Phi(a, \mu(s\Lambda)F(s\Lambda), s\Lambda), \qquad (5.1)$$

where W_0 is the restricted Weyl group, and $\Phi(a, \mu(\Lambda)F(\Lambda), \Lambda)$ is a function defined by a convergent asymptotic series whose leading term is

$$(\mu(\Lambda)F(\Lambda))(1)e^{(\Lambda-\rho)(\log a)}.$$

As a function of Λ, $\Phi(a, \mu(\Lambda)F(\Lambda), \Lambda)$ is meromorphic. Its poles can be shown to lie along hyperplanes of the form

$$\langle\beta,\Lambda\rangle = r, \qquad r \in \mathbb{R},$$

for roots β of $(\mathfrak{g},\mathfrak{a}_0)$. Only finitely many of these singular hyperplanes intersect the negative chamber $-(\mathfrak{a}_0^*)^+$ in $\mathfrak{a}_0^*$.

Thus, for fixed $a \in A_0^+$, $F^{\vee}_{P_0}(a)$ is given by the integral over $\Lambda \in i\mathfrak{a}_0^*$ of a function which is asymptotic to

$$\sum_{s\in W_0} (\mu(s\Lambda)F(s\Lambda))(1)e^{(s\Lambda-\rho)(\log a)}.$$

The proof of the classical Paley-Wiener theorem suggests that we should change the contour of integration to $X + i\mathfrak{a}_0^*$, where X is some large vector in $\mathfrak{a}_0^*$. However, there is an immediate complication. While some of the terms in the integrand will be seen to be small after such a change of the contour, other terms will only blow up. It is necessary to first change variables. Let ε be a very small vector in $-(\mathfrak{a}_0^*)^+$. Then

$$F_{P_0}^{\vee}(a) = \int_{i\mathfrak{a}_0^*} E_{P_0}(a, \mu(\Lambda)F(\Lambda), \Lambda)d\Lambda$$

$$= \int_{\varepsilon+i\mathfrak{a}_0^*} \Big(\sum_{s\in W_0} \Phi(a, \mu(s\Lambda)F(s\Lambda), s\Lambda)\Big)d\Lambda.$$

With a change of variables we then see that $F_{P_0}^{\vee}(a)$ equals

$$\sum_{s\in W_0} \int_{s\varepsilon+i\mathfrak{a}_0^*} \Phi(a, \mu(\Lambda)F(\Lambda), \Lambda)d\Lambda. \tag{5.2}$$

Now, each integrand will be asymptotic to

$$(\mu(\Lambda)F(\Lambda))(1)e^{(\Lambda-\rho)(\log a)}.$$

If each contour of integration is replaced by $X + i\mathfrak{a}_0^*$, where X is a point in the negative chamber $-(\mathfrak{a}_0^*)^+$ which is far from the walls, we might expect the result to vanish for large $a \in A_0^+$. Incidentally, ε was introduced because the summands on the right of (5.1) could have singularities which meet $i\mathfrak{a}_0^*$, even though their sum is regular on $i\mathfrak{a}_0^*$.

If X is any point in $-(\mathfrak{a}_0^*)^+$ which is far from the walls, the integrand in (5.2) is analytic on $X + i\mathfrak{a}_0^*$. Define

$$F^{\vee}(a) = |W_0| \int_{X+i\mathfrak{a}_0^*} \Phi(a, \mu(\Lambda)F(\Lambda), \Lambda), \qquad a \in A_0^+.$$

<u>LEMMA 2.</u> <u>There is a number</u> N <u>such that</u> $F^{\vee}(a) = 0$ <u>whenever</u>

$\|\log a\| \geq N.$

See Theorem II.1.1 of [1].

Set $G_- = KA_0^+K$. It is an open dense subset of G. If

$$x = k_1 a k_2$$

is any point in $G\_$, define

$$f(x) = \tau(k_1)F^{\vee}(a)\tau(k_2).$$

The last lemma states that the function f has bounded support. It is our candidate for the inverse Fourier transform of F. It is not yet clear that f extends to a smooth function on G. However, we do know that $F^{\vee}(a)$ differs from (5.2) by a finite sum of residues. The main difficulty in the proof of Theorem 2 is to interpret these residues.

6. THE CASE OF REAL RANK 1

In order to get a feeling for what is required in general, we should recall Campoli's argument if G has real rank 1. This simply means that the integrals in (5.2) are over one dimensional spaces. The resulting residues will be evaluated at a finite number of points, $\Lambda_0, \Lambda_1, \ldots, \Lambda_n$, in the closure of $-(\mathfrak{a}_0^*)^+$. Then $F^{\vee}(a)$ equals the sum of $F^{\vee}_{P_0}(a)$ and a function

$$F^{\vee}_{cusp}(a) = \sum_{j=0}^{n} \operatorname*{Res}_{\Lambda=\Lambda_j} \Phi(a,\mu(\Lambda)F(\Lambda),\Lambda), \tag{6.1}$$

on A_0^+. (Of course, it is understood that the residues are taken with respect to some isomorphism of $\mathfrak{a}_0^*$ with $\mathbb{R}$.)

Let us illustrate the process with a diagram, in which $\mathfrak{a}_0^*$ is represented by a broken vertical line.

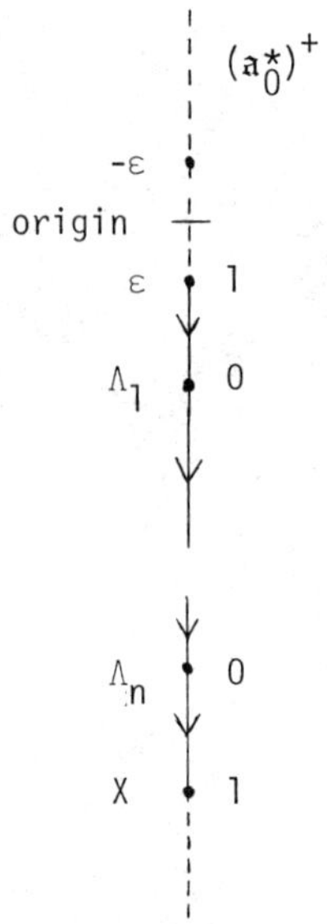

Each large dot stands for an integral over an imaginary space, of dimension 0 or 1, which lies above the dot. With the arrows, we have shown how to move the contour over the point ε to the contour over X. The contour over $-\varepsilon$ is moved the same way, except that there might also be a contribution from a residue at the origin.

We would like to show that $\check{F}_{cusp}$ extends to a τ spherical function on G which is a sum of matrix coefficients of discrete series. Consider (6.1) as a function of F. For each j there is a finite dimensional subspace S_j of the symmetric algebra on $\mathfrak{a}_{0,\mathbb{C}}^*$ such that (6.1) depends only on the vector

$$\bigoplus_{j=0}^{n} d_{S_j} F(\Lambda_j).$$

It follows from Lemma 1 that there is a function $g \in C_c^\infty(G,\tau)$ such that (6.1) equals

$$\sum_{j=0}^{n} \operatorname*{Res}_{\Lambda=\Lambda_j} \Phi(a,\mu(\Lambda)\hat{g}(\Lambda),\Lambda).$$

Now apply what we have shown so far to the function

$$G(\Lambda) = \hat{g}(\Lambda)$$

in $PW(G,\tau)$. Then

$$G^{\vee}(a) = G^{\vee}_{cusp}(a) + G^{\vee}_{P_0}(a)$$
$$= F^{\vee}_{cusp}(a) + G^{\vee}_{P_0}(a).$$

On the other hand, g is a Schwartz function, so that

$$g(x) = g_{cusp}(x) + G^{\vee}_{P_0}(x), \qquad x \in G,$$

for a uniquely determined function g_{cusp} which is a sum of matrix coefficients of discrete series. It follows that

$$F^{\vee}_{cusp}(a) - G^{\vee}(a) = g_{cusp}(a) - g(a)$$

for each $a \in A_0^+$. However, both $G^{\vee}(a)$ and $g(a)$ are of bounded support on A_0^+. This means that $F^{\vee}_{cusp}(a)$ equals $g_{cusp}(a)$ outside a bounded set. Since both functions are analytic, $F^{\vee}_{cusp}$ extends to a smooth, τ spherical function on G which is a sum of matrix coefficients of discrete series.

By its definition, $F^{\vee}_{P_0}(x)$ is a smooth, τ spherical function on G. Therefore the function

$$f(a) = F^{\vee}(a),$$

which we know equals

$$F^{\vee}_{cusp}(a) + F^{\vee}_{P_0}(a),$$

extends to a smooth, τ spherical function on G. Since it has bounded support on A_0^+, it belongs to $C_c^{\infty}(G,\tau)$. Moreover,

$$f(x) = F^{\vee}_{cusp}(x) + F^{\vee}_{P_0}(x)$$

must be the decomposition of f according to associativity classes of cuspidal parabolic subgroups. (If G is not cuspidal - that is, G has no discrete series - the function $F^{\vee}_{cusp}$ will of course be zero.) It follows without difficulty that

$$\hat{f}(\Lambda) = F(\Lambda).$$

This gives the proof of Theorem 2.

7. HIGHER RANK

If the real rank of G is greater than 1, it is considerably more difficult to interpret the residues. We will do nothing more than try to get a feeling for the main ideas by looking at the case of $SL(3, \mathbb{R})$.

For $G = SL(3, \mathbb{R})$, the space $\mathfrak{a}_0^*$ has dimension 2. For simplicity we will assume that for each positive root, the function

$$\Phi(a, \mu(\Lambda)F(\Lambda), \Lambda)$$

has exactly one associated singular hyperplane which meets the negative chamber $-(\mathfrak{a}_0^*)^+$. This leaves three singular hyperplanes to contend with, which we will represent in the diagram below by unbroken lines. The broken lines stand for the walls of the chambers in $\mathfrak{a}_0^*$. Each large dot stands for an integral over an imaginary space of dimension 0, 1 or 2, which lies above the dot.

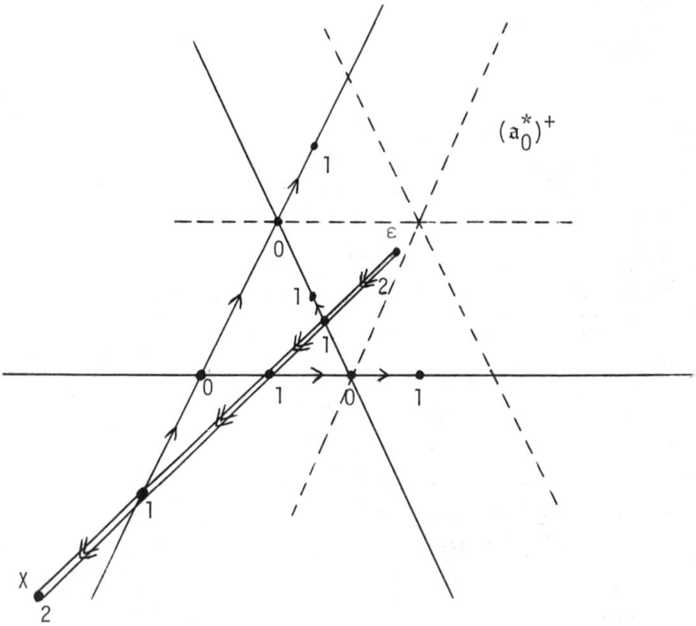

The diagram again illustrates what happens when we move the contour of integration from $\varepsilon + i\mathfrak{a}_0^*$ to $X + i\mathfrak{a}_0^*$. As we cross each of the three singular hyperplanes, we pick up a residue consisting of an integral over a space of dimension 1. We would expect these terms to give the contribution from induced discrete series (induced, that is, from maximal parabolic subgroups). Such representations are of course tempered, and can correspond only to the points on the singular hyperplanes which are *closest* to the origin. We must therefore move the contours of the 1-dimensional integrals to 1-dimensional imaginary spaces over these points. In so doing, we pick up further residues, at points on the diagram labelled with 0. We would expect the sum of these to give the contribution from the discrete series. Since $G = SL(3, \mathbb{R})$ has no discrete series, the sum should vanish.

It is clear that there will be some bookkeeping problems for general groups. However, it is possible to handle them with an induction hypothesis. Consider the 1-dimensional residues on the *horizontal* singular hyperplanes (of which there is just one in our diagram). Such residues are eventually moved over to the vertical line which passes through the origin. This vertical line corresponds to the Levi component of a maximal parabolic subgroup. In fact, the *geometry* of the 1-dimensional residues on the horizontal singular hyperplanes will be identical to the geometry of the 0-dimensional residues for the Paley-Wiener theorem for the Levi subgroup.

We assume inductively that Theorem 2 is true for the Levi component M of any proper parabolic subgroup of G. To exploit this, however, we need something more. We require a natural procedure for lifting functions from $M\_$ to functions on $G\_$ which generalizes the Eisenstein integral. Such a procedure is provided by a theorem of a Casselman.

8. THE THEOREM OF CASSELMAN

Suppose that J is a meromorphic function from $\mathfrak{a}_{0,\mathbb{C}}^*$ to A_0 such that the function

$$\Phi(a, J(\Lambda), \Lambda)$$

is analytic at $\Lambda = \Lambda_0$. Let $D = D_\Lambda$ be any differential operator on

$\mathfrak{a}^*_{0,\mathbb{C}}$. Define

$$\Psi(x) = \tau(k_1)(D_{\Lambda_0}\Phi(a,J(\Lambda_0), \Lambda_0))\tau(k_2)$$

for any point

$$x = k_1 a k_2, \qquad a \in A_0^+, \qquad k_1, k_2 \in K,$$

in $G\_$. Then Ψ is a $\mathfrak{Z}$ finite, τ spherical function from $G\_$ to V_τ. Let $A(G\_,\tau)$ be the space spanned by all functions obtained in this way. We would expect $A(G\_,\tau)$ to be the space of *all* $\mathfrak{Z}$ finite, τ spherical functions from $G\_$ to V_τ. However, I have not thought about this question. Let $A(G,\tau)$ be the subspace of functions in $A(G\_,\tau)$ which extend to smooth functions on G. Again, we would expect $A(G,\tau)$ to be the space of all $\mathfrak{Z}$ finite, τ spherical functions from G to V_τ.

Suppose that

$$P = NAM$$

is a parabolic subgroup of G. The Levi component M is reductive, so we can define the space $A(M\_,\tau)$ as above. (It consists of functions from $M\_$ to V_τ which are spherical with respect to the restriction of τ to $K \cap M$.) If ϕ belongs to the subspace $A(M,\tau)$ of $A(M\_,\tau)$, and

$$x = nmak, \qquad n \in N, \qquad m \in M, \qquad a \in A, \qquad k \in K,$$

is any point in G, define

$$\phi_P(x) = \phi(m)\tau(k).$$

We also write, as usual,

$$H_P(x) = \log a,$$

an element in the Lie algebra $\mathfrak{a}$ of A. Then the Eisenstein integral

$$E_P(x,\phi,\lambda) = \int_K \tau(k)^{-1}\phi_P(kx)e^{(\lambda+\rho)(H_P)kx))}dk,$$

as a function of x, belongs to $A(G,\tau)$. It depends analytically on $\lambda \in \mathfrak{a}_{\mathbb{C}}^*$.

THEOREM 3. (Casselman) The Eisenstein integral can be extended in a natural way to a linear map from $A(M\_,\tau)$ to $A(G\_,\tau)$, which depends *meromorphically* on a point $\lambda \in \mathfrak{a}_{\mathbb{C}}^*$.

The theorem seems quite remarkable to me. The map certainly cannot be defined by an integral as above, for the integral in general will not converge. However, the map turns out to be just what is needed. It allows one to identify the sum of 1-dimensional residues in §7 with a wave packet of Eisenstein integrals associated to the maximal parabolic subgroups. One can then identify the 0-dimensional residues with the discrete series of G by following the argument of §6.

This paper is an exposition of the results in [1]. The work was supported by an NSERC operating grant.

REFERENCES

[1] Arthur, J., A Paley-Wiener theorem for real reductive groups, to appear in Acta Math.

[2] Campoli, O., The complex Fourier transform on rank one semi-simple Lie groups, Thesis, Rutgers University, 1977.

[3] Delorme, P., Théorème de type Paley-Wiener pour les groupes de Lie semisimples réels avec une seule classe de conjugaison de sous-groupes de Cartan, preprint.

[4] Ehrenpreis, L., and Mautner, F. I., (a) Some properties of the Fourier transform on semisimple Lie groups I, Ann. of Math. 61 (1955), 406-439.

(b) Some properties of the Fourier transform on semisimple Lie groups, II, T.A.M.S. 84 (1957), 1-55.

[5] Gangolli, R., On the Plancherel formula and the Paley-Wiener theorem for spherical functions on semisimple Lie groups, Ann. of Math. 93 (1971), 150-165.

[6] Harish-Chandra, (a) Harmonic analysis on real reductive groups I, J. Funct. Anal. 19 (1975), 104-204.

(b) Harmonic analysis on real reductive groups III, Ann. of Math. 104 (1976), 117-201.

[7] Helgason, S., (a) An analog of the Paley-Wiener theorem for the Fourier transform on certain symmetric spaces, Math. Ann. 165 (1966), 297-308.

(b) A duality for symmetric spaces with applications to group representations, Advances in Math. 5 (1970), 1-154.

(c) The surjectivity of invariant differential operators on symmetric spaces I, Ann. of Math. 98 (1973), 451-479.

(d) A duality for symmetric spaces with applications to group representations II. Differential equations and eigenspace representations, Advances in Math. 22 (1976), 187-219.

[8] Kawazoe, T., (a) An analogue of Paley-Wiener theorem on SU(2,2), Tokyo J. Math.

(b) An analogue of Paley-Wiener theorem on semi-simple Lie groups and functional equations for Eisenstein integrals, preprint.

[9] Langlands, R. P., (a) Eisenstein series, Proc. Sympos. Pure Math., vol. 9, Amer. Math. Soc., Providence, R.I. (1966), 235-252.

(b) On the functional equations satisfied by Eisenstein series, Lecture Notes in Math., 544 (1976).

[10] Zelobenko, D. P., Harmonic analysis on complex semisimple Lie groups, Proc. Int. Cong. Math., Vancouver, 1974, Vol. II, 129-134.

WEYL GROUP REPRESENTATIONS AND NILPOTENT ORBITS

Dan Barbasch and David Vogan

1. INTRODUCTION

In [B-V2] and [B-V3] two related problems are studied for complex semisimple groups. One, is to classify the primitive ideals in the enveloping algebra. The other is to study Fourier inversion of unipotent orbital integrals.

This is carried out explicitly for regular integral infinitesimal character. The connection between the two problems is established via characters of irreducible admissible ($\mathfrak{g}$, K) modules and their wave front set or asymptotic support.

In these notes we would like to illustrate how the methods involved in [B-V2, 3] generalize to real rank groups in order to compute the cells (definition 2.5) and Fourier inversion for unipotent orbits. There are many technical complications and the results are far from complete. In order to keep the notation to a minimum and to be as clear as possible we will mainly restrict attention to $G = U(p,q)$ where the most complete results are known. (To give an idea how much more difficult the problem is for general groups, it is useful to compare the solution of the problem of classifying primitive ideals for type A_n, due to Joseph, to the solution of the same problem for an arbitrary semisimple Lie algebra).

The paper is organized as follows. In section 1 we introduce notation. In section 2 we parametrize the representations with a fixed regular integral infinitesimal character. We then study to coherent continuation representation and introduce the notion of a cell. In section 3 we review some results from [B-V1] on asymptotic support in order to calculate it for a special class of representations. In section 4 we apply the calculations in sections 1-3 to the case of U(p,q).

We consider G a connected reductive real group such that $G \subseteq G_c$, a complexification of G. Let $\mathfrak{g}_0$ be the Lie algebra of G and θ a Cartan involution. Let $\mathfrak{g}_0 = \mathfrak{k}_0 + \mathfrak{p}_0$ be the Cartan decomposition and $\mathfrak{g}, \mathfrak{k}, \mathfrak{p}$ the respective complexifications.

For $H \subseteq G$, a θ-stable Cartan subgroup, we write $\mathfrak{h}_0$ for its Lie algebra, $\mathfrak{h}$ for the complexification. Let $\Delta(\mathfrak{g}, \mathfrak{h})$ be the root system. We also write

$$H = TA = (H \cap K)(H \cap \exp \mathfrak{p}_0)$$

for the Cartan decomposition.

We make the following assumptions on G.

a) all Cartan subgroups are connected

b) rank $\mathfrak{g}$ = rank $\mathfrak{k}$.

The compact torus will be denoted by T. We will also use the notation $\mathfrak{h}_a$, $\Delta(\mathfrak{g}, \mathfrak{h}_a)$ etc. to denote the "abstract" Cartan subalgebra, root system and so on.

We will denote by W, the complex Weyl group of H, by $W^\theta(H) \subseteq W$, the θ-stable part of the Weyl group and by $W(H) \subseteq W^\theta(H)$ the real Weyl group of H.

2. THE COHERENT CONTINUATION REPRESENTATION

We need to parametrize all representations with fixed regular integral infinitesimal character. Without loss of generality we can assume that this infinitesimal character is ρ, in other words the same as the infinitesimal character of the trivial representation.

PROPOSITION 2.1 The set of equivalence classes of irreducible admissible representations with trivial infinitesimal character is in one-to-one correspondence with the set of K-conjugacy classes of positive systems $\Delta^+ \subseteq \Delta(\mathfrak{g}, \mathfrak{h})$ where $\mathfrak{h}$ is a θ-stable Cartan subalgebra.

PROOF. This is the Langlands classification applied to the case of a group G satisfying conditions a) and b) together with proposition 2.7 in [V2].

Given a regular integral $\lambda \in \hat{\mathfrak{h}}^1$, we will denote by $\pi(\lambda)$ the induced representation from a discrete series and call it the standard representation. We will denote by $\overline{\pi}(\lambda)$ the corresponding Langlands quotient. We let F be the group of virtual characters with trivial infinitesimal character. Then W_a acts on F in the following way.

Let $\Lambda \subseteq \mathfrak{h}_a^*$ be the integral lattice.

Definition 2.2. <u>A coherent family of virtual characters</u> $\{\Theta(\lambda)\}_{\lambda \in \Lambda}$ <u>is a set of virtual characters</u> $\Theta(\lambda)$ <u>with infinitesimal character</u> λ, <u>satisfying</u>

(2.2.1) <u>if</u> λ <u>is dominant for a fixed positive system</u> Δ_a^+, <u>then</u> $\Theta(\lambda)$ <u>is</u> 0 <u>or the character of an irreducible representation; and the latter is the case if</u> λ <u>is nonsingular</u>

(2.2.2) <u>if</u> F <u>is finite dimensional</u>,

$$\Theta(\lambda) \cdot \Theta(F) = \sum_{\mu \in \Delta(F)} \Theta(\lambda + \mu) .$$

Given any character of an irreducible representation there is a unique coherent family it belongs to.

Definition 2.3. <u>For</u> $w \in W_a$, <u>we define</u> $w\,\Theta(\lambda) = \Theta(w\lambda)$.

<u>This action of</u> W_a <u>on</u> F <u>is called the coherent continuation representation</u>.

We now decompose this representation. For any Θ-stable Cartan subgroup H we define a 1-dimensional representation of $W(H)$ in the following way. Let $\Delta^{i\mathbb{R}} \subseteq \Delta(\mathfrak{g},\mathfrak{h})$ be the subsystem of imaginary roots. Let $\mathfrak{h}_I = \text{lin span}\,\{H_\alpha \in \mathfrak{h}\colon \alpha \in \Delta^{i\mathbb{R}}\}$. Then $W(H) = \det \mathrm{Ad}w|_{\mathfrak{h}_I}$ for any $w \in W(H)$.

<u>PROPOSITION 2.4</u>

$$F \simeq \bigoplus_{\substack{H \text{ conjugacy} \\ \text{class of } \theta\text{-stable} \\ \text{Cartan subgroup}}} \mathrm{Ind}_{W(H)}^{W} \det{}_I$$

<u>PROOF</u>. We first describe $W(H)$ ([V3]proposition). Let $\Delta^{\mathbb{R}} \subseteq \Delta(\mathfrak{g},\mathfrak{h})$ be the system of real roots and fix positive systems

$\Delta^{\mathbb{R},+} \subseteq \Delta^+(\mathfrak{g},\mathfrak{h})$, $\Delta^{i\mathbb{R},+} \subseteq \Delta^+(\mathfrak{g},\mathfrak{h})$. Let

$$\rho^{i\mathbb{R}} = \tfrac{1}{2} \sum_{\alpha \in \Delta^{\mathbb{R},+}} \alpha$$

$$\rho^{\mathbb{R}} = \tfrac{1}{2} \sum_{\alpha \in \Delta^{i\mathbb{R},+}} \alpha$$

Then define

$$\Delta^q = \{\alpha \in \Delta(\mathfrak{g},\mathfrak{h}) \colon (\alpha,\rho^{i\mathbb{R}}) = 0\}$$

$$\Delta^f = \{\alpha \in \Delta \colon (\alpha,\rho^{\mathbb{R}}) = 0\}$$

$\Delta^{\mathbb{C}} = \Delta^q \cap \Delta^f$ and $W^{\mathbb{R}}$, $W^{\mathbb{C}}$, $W^{i\mathbb{R}}$ accordingly. Then

$$W(H) \simeq (W^{\mathbb{C}})^{\theta} \overset{W(H)}{\ltimes} (W^{\mathbb{R}} \times W(G^A,H))$$

where G^A is the centralizer of A in G and $W(G^A,H) \subseteq W^{i\mathbb{R}}$.

A natural basis for F is given by the characters of the standard representations $\pi(\gamma)$. We filter F according to dim A ,

$$F = F_0 \supseteq F_1 \supseteq \cdots \supseteq F_i \supseteq \cdots$$

where F_i is spanned by the $\pi(\gamma)$ such that γ is associated to a Cartan subgroup with split component of dimension greater than or equal to i . This is compatible with the action of W_a .

The discrete series character identities in [S] and the invariance of induced representations by $W^{\mathbb{R}}$ show that the coherent continuation representation on F_i/F_{i+1} coincides with $\det_I$ on $W^{\mathbb{R}} \times W(G^A,H)$. Remains to check the action of $(W^{\mathbb{C}})^{\theta}$. Suppose $\gamma = (\delta,\nu)$ where $\delta \in \mathfrak{t}^*$ corresponds to a discrete series parameter on G^A , $\nu \in \mathfrak{a}^*$. Then if $w \in (W^{\mathbb{C}})^{\theta}$, $w(\delta,\nu) = (\delta^1,\nu^1)$ in such a way that $\pi(\delta,\nu)$ is equivalent to $\pi(\delta^1,\nu^1)$. On ther other hand it can be seen that $\det_I w = 1$. Since also $\dim F_i/F_{i+1} = |W/W(H)|$, the result follows from the fact that any representaion of a finite group on a filtered vector space is equivalent to the representation on the associated graded vector space.

Definition 2.5. <u>We say</u> $\overline{\pi}(\gamma_1)$ <u>and</u> $\overline{\pi}(\gamma_2)$ <u>belong to the same cell and write</u> $\overline{\pi}(\gamma_1) \sim \overline{\pi}(\gamma_2)$ <u>if there are finite dimensional representations</u> F_1, F_2 <u>such that</u> $\overline{\pi}(\gamma_1)$ <u>is a composition factor of</u> $\overline{\pi}(\gamma_2) \otimes F_2$ <u>and</u> $\overline{\pi}(\gamma_2)$ <u>is a composition factor of</u> $\overline{\pi}(\gamma_1) \otimes F_1$. <u>We denote by</u> $C(\gamma)$ <u>the cell of</u> γ <u>and similar to [B-V2,3]</u>,

$$K(\gamma) = \{\gamma^1 : \text{there is } F^1 \text{ finite dimensional such that } \gamma^1 \text{ occurs in } \overline{\pi}(\gamma) \otimes F^1\}$$
$$K^+(\gamma) = \{\gamma^1 : \gamma^1 \in K(\gamma), \gamma^1 \notin C(\gamma)\} .$$

By abuse of notation we also denote the corresponding vector spaces generated by the characters by $K(\gamma)$ and $K^+(\gamma)$. Let

$$V(\gamma) = K(\gamma)/K^+(\gamma)$$

<u>PROPOSITION 2.6.</u> $V(\gamma)$ is stable under the action of W and has a basis formed of the characters $\overline{\pi}(\gamma)$ of $\gamma^1 \in C(\gamma)$.

<u>PROOF</u>. We refer to [BV-3], 2.8-2.12 for details.

3. NILPOTENT ORBITS AND REPRESENTATIONS

In this section, we review the notion of asymptotic support as defined in [B-V1]. As is apparent in [B-V2,3] in order to determine the cells one needs to know the induced nilpotent orbits. We define the appropriate notion and the representation that should give them.

Any character Θ_π can be lifted to an eigendistribution θ_π in a neighborhood of 0 in $\mathfrak{g}$. For $f \in C_c^\infty(\mathfrak{g})$ and $t > 0$ we let $f_t(x) = t^{-\dim \mathfrak{g}} f(t^{-1}x)$. Then $\theta_\pi(f_t)$ has an asymptotic expansion (like a Taylor series)

$$\theta_\pi(f_t) = \sum_{i=-r}^{\infty} t^i D_i(f) \quad \text{as} \quad t \to 0^+ .$$

The D_i are tempered homogeneous distributions. We define

$$AS(\pi) = \overline{\bigcup_i \operatorname{supp} \hat{D}_i} ,$$

the closure of the union of the supports of the Fourier transforms of the D_i . $AS(\pi)$ is a union of nilpotent orbits.

Let $\lambda \in i\mathfrak{t}^*$ be integral where $\mathfrak{t}$ is the compact Cartan subalgebra. We can associate to λ a θ-stable parabolic subalgebra $q = \ell + u$ by requiring that $\ell = \mathrm{Cent}_{\mathfrak{g}}\lambda$ and $\Delta(u,\mathfrak{t}) = \{\alpha \in \Delta(\mathfrak{g},\mathfrak{t}): \langle\alpha,\lambda\rangle > 0\}$. Then λ defines a character $\lambda: q \to \mathbb{C}$. We denote by $\pi^L(\lambda)$ this representation. In [V1] chapter 6 a general construction is given which in particular associates to λ an irreducible admissible module which we call $R_q(\lambda)$. It has the following property. Fix ψ_L , a positive root system in $\Delta(\ell,\mathfrak{t})$ and denote by $\{\Theta(\psi_L,\mu)\}$ the coherent family of characters determined by the discrete series character corresponding to ψ_L .

PROPOSITION 3.1 Let $\psi = \psi_L \cup \Delta(u)$. Then

$$\mathrm{ch}\, R_q(\lambda) = \frac{1}{|W(L \cap K)|} \sum_{w \in W(\ell)} (-1)^{\ell(w)} \Theta(\psi, w(\lambda + \rho(\psi)))$$

where $W(\ell)$ is the Weyl group of ℓ and $\rho(\psi) = \frac{1}{2} \sum_{\alpha \in \psi} \alpha$.

PROOF. This character identity follows from standard facts about $R_q(\lambda)$ in chapter 6 of [V1] and the following elementary identity for the character of the trivial representation π_0 (first observed by Hecht and Schmid)

$$\mathrm{ch}\, \pi_0 = \frac{1}{|W_K|} \sum_{w \in W} (-1)^{\ell(w)} \Theta(\psi, w\rho(\psi))$$

for any positive root system $\psi \subseteq \Delta(\mathfrak{g},\mathfrak{t})$. We omit the details.

We now consider the following sets

$$\mathfrak{t}^u \quad \{\lambda \in \mathfrak{t}^*: (\alpha,\lambda) = 0 \text{ for } \alpha \in \Delta(\ell)$$
$$(\alpha,\lambda) > 0 \text{ for any } \alpha \in \Delta(u)\}$$
$$\mathfrak{t}^\psi = \{\mu \in \mathfrak{t}^*: (\mu,\alpha) > 0 \text{ for } \alpha \in \psi \cup \Delta(u)\}$$

We define the following distributions for $f \in C_c^\infty(\mathfrak{g})$

$$\phi_f(\mu) = \prod_{(\alpha,\mu) > 0} (\alpha,\mu) \int_{G/T} f(x\mu x^{-1})\, dx \ , \ \mu \in \mathfrak{t}^\psi$$

$$\phi_f^u(\lambda) = \prod_{(\alpha,\lambda)>0} (\alpha,\lambda) \int_{G/L_0} f(x\lambda x^{-1})dx, \quad \lambda \in \mathfrak{t}^u$$

where $L_0 = \mathrm{Cent}_G\lambda$. The following properties of ϕ_f, ϕ_f^u follow from well known results of Harish - Chandra.

$f \to \phi_f(\mu)$, $\phi_f^u(\lambda)$ are tempered distribtuions and are Schwartz functions in μ and λ. (3.2.1)

Let $\omega_L = \prod_{\alpha \in \psi_L} \alpha$. Then there is a nonzero constant c such that

$$\lim_{\substack{\mu \to \lambda \\ \mu \in \mathfrak{t}^\psi}} \phi_f(\mu;\omega_L) = c\,\phi_f^u(\lambda) \tag{3.2.2}$$

(we use Harish - Chandra's notation $\partial(\omega)f(x) = f(x;\omega)$)

ϕ_f and ϕ_f^u have asymptotic expansions

$$\begin{array}{lll} \phi_f(\mu) \sim \Sigma\, c_i(\mu)E_i & \mu \to 0 & \mu \in \mathfrak{t}^\psi \\ \phi_f^u(\lambda) \sim \Sigma\, d_j(\lambda)F_j & \lambda \to 0 & \lambda \in \mathfrak{t}^u \end{array} \tag{3.2.3}$$

LEMMA 3.2 $\overline{\cup \operatorname{supp} F_i} = \{x\colon x = \lim_{i\to\infty} t_i \operatorname{Ad}x_i\,\lambda$ for some $x_i \in G$, $t_i \to 0^+\}$

PROOF. The proof is essentially the same as the ideas in 3.7 - 3.9 in [B-V1] where ϕ_f is replaced by ϕ_f^u. We omit the details.

We denote the set in lemma 3.2 by $\overline{\operatorname{Ind}_q^{\mathfrak{g}}(0)}$. This is motivated by the complex groups case where the set in question coincides with the usual notion of induction. As the notation suggests, it can be defined for any orbit in $\ell_0 = \ell \cap \mathfrak{g}_0$. We also note that it is a somewhat finer invariant than induction from a real parabolic subalgebra. For example in $s\ell(2,\mathbb{R})$ it is always the closure of just one real nilpotent orbit instead of two. Motivated by some more examples computed for real Lie algebras we make a conjecture.

3.3. CONJECTURE. $\overline{\operatorname{Ind}_q^{\mathfrak{g}}(0)}$ is the closure of exactly one real nilpotent orbit. We call it $\operatorname{Ind}_q^{\mathfrak{g}}(0)$, the Richardson orbit attached to q.

PROPOSITION 3.4

$$AS(R_q(\lambda)) = \overline{\mathrm{Ind}_q^{\mathfrak{g}}(0)} .$$

PROOF. By [Ro] we can write (up to constants)

$$\theta(\psi,\mu) \sim \sum_i c_i(\mu)E_i$$

Then

$$R_q(\lambda) \sim \sum_i \Big(\sum_{w \in W(\ell)} (-1)^{\ell(w)} c_i(\lambda+\rho(\psi))E_i$$

$$= \sum_i c_i^L (\lambda+\rho(\psi))E_i .$$

Then $\hat{E}_i$ is obtained from ϕ_f (up to constants) by the formula

$$\lim_{\substack{\mu \to 0 \\ (\alpha,\mu) > 0 \\ \alpha \in \psi}} \phi_f(\mu;\, c_i^L) = \hat{E}_i(f) .$$

By (3.2.1), (3.2.2)

$$\overline{\mathrm{Ind}_q^{\mathfrak{g}}(0)} \subseteq \bigcup_{c_i^L \neq 0} \operatorname{supp} \hat{E}_i$$

To show the converse inclusion we argue as follows. Since c_j^L is $W(\ell)$ - skew invariant, $c_j^L = \omega_L\, G_j$ where G_j is $W(\ell)$ invariant. Then

$$\phi_f(\mu) = \prod_{\alpha \in \Delta(u)} (\alpha,\mu) \int_{G/L_0} \phi^L_{f^{x_1}}(\mu)\, dx_1$$

where $f^{x_1}(X) = f(x_1 X x_1^{-1})$ and ϕ^L is the function ϕ_f defined relative to ℓ . Denoting by $\tilde{G}_j$ the invariant polynomial on ℓ corresponding to G_j under the Harish - Chandra isomorphism, we obtain up to a nonzero constant,

$$\phi_f(\mu;\, c_j^L) = \prod_{\alpha \in \Delta(u)} (\alpha,\mu) \int_{G/L_0} \phi_{\partial(\tilde{G}_j) f^{x_1}} (\mu;\, \alpha(\omega_L))dx_1$$

Letting $\mu \to 0$ we may assume that $\mu \in \mathfrak{t}^{u}$ (since ϕ_f extends as a C^∞ function to the closure of $\mathfrak{t}^{\psi} = \{\mu \in \mathfrak{t}^*: (\mu,\alpha) > 0 \text{ , } \alpha \in \psi\}$). This shows that $\operatorname{supp} \hat{E}_i \subseteq \overline{\operatorname{Ind}_q^{\mathfrak{g}}(0)}$.

This proves the proposition.

4. AN EXAMPLE.

In this section we compute the cells introduced in 2.5 for $G = U(p,q)$. We assume $p \geq q$ and write $n = p + q$. We use the standard realization of $U(p,q)$ as $n \times n$ matrices that leave $\sum_{i \leq p} |x_i|^2 - \sum_{j > p} |x_j|^2$ invariant.

Representatives of the θ-stable Cartan subgroups are given by $H^r = T^r \cdot A^r \quad 0 \leq r \leq q$ where

$$T^r = \operatorname{diag}(e^{i\phi_1},\dots,e^{i\phi_{p-r}},\, e^{i\phi_{p-r+1}},\dots,e^{i\phi_p},e^{i\phi_p},\dots,e^{i\phi_{p-r+1}},\, e^{i\phi_{p+r+1}} \dots e^{i\phi_n})$$

$$A^r = \operatorname{diag}(t^{x_{p-r+1}},\dots,t^{x_p}),\ t^{x_i} = \exp[x_i(E_{p-1,p+1} + E_{p+1,p-1})]$$

($E_{j,k}$ is the $n \times n$ matrix with 1 in the (j,k) entry and 0's everywhere else.)

Then

$$W(H) = S_{p-r} \times [(\mathbb{Z}/2\mathbb{Z})^r \ltimes S_r] \times S_{q-r}$$

Here S_m is the symmetric group in m letters and S_{p-r} permutes $(\phi_1,\dots,\phi_{p-r})$, S_{q-r} permutes $(\phi_{p+r+1},\dots,\phi_r)$, $(\mathbb{Z}/2\,\mathbb{Z})^r \ltimes S_r$ permutes $(\phi_{p-r+1},x_{p-r+1}),\dots(\phi_p,x_p)$ and changes the signs of the x_i . Then $\det_I$ = sign $\otimes$ trivial $\otimes$ sign we call $(\mathbb{Z}/2\,\mathbb{Z})^r \ltimes S_r = W(C_r)$, the Weyl group of type C_r.

The representations of S_m are parametrized by partitions of m or Young diagrams. For example S_4 has representations

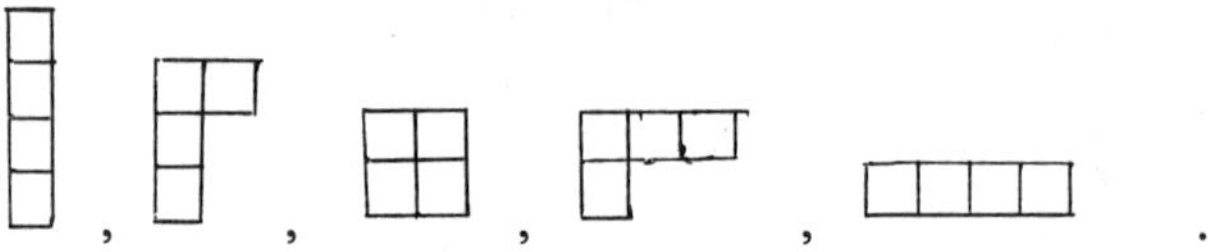

sign trivial

This is well known, A convenient reference is [R].

LEMMA 4.1. Let σ be a representation of S_ℓ . Then

a) $$\mathrm{Ind}_{S_\ell \times S_k}^{S_{\ell+k}} \sigma \otimes \mathrm{sign} = \bigoplus_{\sigma^1 \in \hat{S}_{\ell+k}} \sigma^1$$

where σ^1 are the diagrams obtained by adding k squares to σ so that no two are added to the same row.

b) $$\mathrm{Ind}_{W(C_r)}^{S_{2r}}(\mathrm{trivial}) = \bigoplus_{\sigma \in \hat{S}_{2r}} \sigma$$

where σ has even rows only. The multiplicities in a) and b) are all 1 .

PROOF. a) is well known. We refer to [R]. b) is proved by induction. An application of a) and a dimension computation shows that

$$\mathrm{Res}_{S_{2r-1}}^{S_{2r}} (\mathrm{Ind}_{W(C_r)}^{S_{2r}} (\mathrm{trivial})) = \mathrm{Ind}_{W(C_{r-1})}^{S_{2r-1}} (\mathrm{trivial}) \qquad (4.1.1)$$

and the right hand side is known by induction. It consists of $\sigma \in \hat{S}_{2r-1}$ with exactly one row of odd length, with multiplicity 1 . We have also used the fact that the restriction of $\sigma \in \hat{S}_{2r}$ to S_{2r-1} is the sum of all $\sigma^1 \in \hat{S}_{2r-1}$ obtained from σ by deleting one corner.

It follows that $\mathrm{Ind}_{W(C_r)}^{S_{2r}}$ (trivial) consists of σ's that have only even rows or σ's that have only two rows each of odd length. A descending induction on the length of the larger row shows that the latter cannot happen.

To compute the multiplicity of each σ we use (4.1.1) and the restriction formula.

Using lemma 4.1 and induction in stages we get the following procedure

Multiplicity of σ in F : Take p pluses and q minuses and place them alternately on each row starting with either a + or a - . The number of different ways in which this can be done is $m(\sigma,F)$. In this procedure two such "signed σ" are the same if they only differ by a permutation of equal rows.

For example, in $U(2,2)$ there are

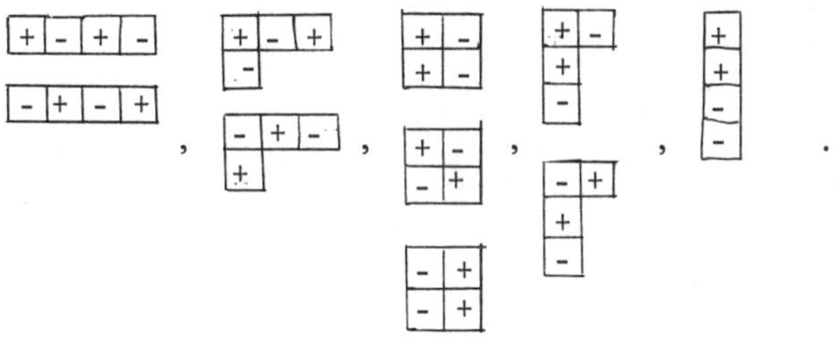

This procedure is set up so that each representation is in a one-to-one correspondence with the conjugacy classes of nilpotent orbits in $U(p,q)$ under the adjoint action of $U(p,q)$. The next theorem is the reason for this parametrization.

THEOREM 4.2. Let $G=U(p,q)$. The cells in F are in one-to-one correspondence with the set of nilpotent orbits in $\mathfrak{g}$.

1. This correspondence is such that the representations in the cell parametrized by $O(X)$ (the orbit of $X \in \mathfrak{g}$) have $\overline{O(X)}$ as their asymptotic support.

2. To each cell one can attach a, canonically defined, θ-stable parabolic subalgebra q such that $R_q(\lambda)$ is in the cell.

3. Each cell is an irreducible representation σ determined by the harmonic polynomial W_L (which transforms like the representation σ under W).

4. Let T_X be the canonical invariant measure determined by $O(X)$. Then it can be normalized in such a way that

$$\lim_{\substack{\mu \to 0 \\ (\mu,\alpha) > 0 \\ \alpha \in \psi}} \phi_f(\mu;\ \partial(\omega_L)) = T_X(f) .$$

PROOF. This is more or less straightforward given the results in 2, 3, 4. We describe the procedure for obtaining q from the nilpotent orbit and omit the other details. Suppose σ has k columns. Fill each column with λ_1's , $\lambda_2 \neq \lambda_1, \ldots, \lambda_k \neq \lambda_1, \ldots, \lambda_{k-1}$. Then the λ_i's labelled + are placed in the first p coordinates of $T = H^0$, the λ_i's labelled - in the others.

The authors were supported by the National Science Foundation.

REFERENCES

[B-V1] D. Barbasch and D. Vogan, "The local structure of characters" J. of Func. Analysis, vol 34, no 1, (1980) 27-55

[B-V2] D. Barbasch and D. Vogan, "Primitive ideals and orbital integrals in complex classical groups", to appear, Math. Annalen.

[B-V3] D. Barbasch and D. Vogan, "Primitive ideals and orbital integrals in complex exceptional groups", to appear, Comm. in Algebra.

[R] G. Robinson,"Representation theory of the symmetric group" University of Toronto Press, 1961.

[Ro] W. Rossmann,"Kirillov's character formula for reductive Lie groups" Inv. Math 48(1978) 207-220.

[S] W. Schmid, "Two character identities for semisimple Lie groups" Springer L N in Math., 587 Berlin 1977.

[V1] D. Vogan, "Representations of real reductive groups" Birkhauser 1981.

[V2] D. Vogan, "Irreducible characters of semisimple Lie groupsIII" preprint

[V3] D. Vogan, "Irreducible characters of semisimple Lie groups IV" preprint.

A GENERALIZATION OF CASSELMAN'S SUBMODULE THEOREM

Alexander Beilinson and Joseph Bernstein

1.

Let $G_{\mathbb{R}}$ be a real reductive Lie group, $\mathfrak{g}_{\mathbb{R}}$ its Lie algebra. Let M be an irreducible Harish-Chandra module. Using some fine analytic arguments, based on the study of asymptotic behavior of matrix coefficients, Casselman has proved that M can be imbedded into a principal series representation [2,3].

This statement can be formulated purely algebraically. Let $\mathfrak{g}$ be the complexification of $\mathfrak{g}_{\mathbb{R}}$ and let $\mathfrak{n}_0$ be a maximal nilpotent subalgebra of $\mathfrak{g}$, containing a maximal nilpotent subalgebra of $\mathfrak{g}_{\mathbb{R}}$. Then Casselman's theorem claims that the space $M_{\mathfrak{n}_0} = M/_{\mathfrak{n}_0}M$ is not equal to zero.

We want to generalize this statement and to prove it by purely algebraic methods. (Note that the first algebraic proof of Casselman's theorem is due to O. Gabber. It is based on Gabber's theorem on the integrability of the characteristic variety.) First of all, we drop the condition that M is a Harish-Chandra module. As a result we can forget about $G_{\mathbb{R}}$ and $\mathfrak{g}_{\mathbb{R}}$ and consider any $\mathfrak{g}$-module M and any maximal nilpotent subalgebra $\mathfrak{n}_0 \subset \mathfrak{g}$. We suppose M to be finitely generated, and we want to prove that $M_{\mathfrak{n}_0} \neq 0$. Of course, this is not true for any given subalgebra $\mathfrak{n}_0$ (see example in [5] where $M_{\mathfrak{n}_0} = 0$ although M is finitely generated even as an $\mathfrak{n}_0$-module). But it turns out that $M_{\mathfrak{n}_0} \neq 0$ for "almost all" $\mathfrak{n}_0 \subset \mathfrak{g}$. The set of all maximal nilpotent subalgebras of $\mathfrak{g}$ has a natural structure of an algebraic variety - its it the flag variety of $\mathfrak{g}$ and "almost all" means "contains an open dense subset in the Zariski topology."

So our aim is

THEOREM 1. *Let $\mathfrak{g}$ be a reductive Lie algebra over an algebraically closed field k of characteristic 0 and X the flag variety of $\mathfrak{g}$. Let M be a no zero finitely generated $\mathfrak{g}$-module. Then for almost all $x \in X$ (i.e. for all points x in some open dense subset $U \subset X$) the space $M_{\mathfrak{n}_x} = M/\mathfrak{n}_x M$ is not equal to 0.*

Let us check that Theorem 1 implies Casselman's result. Indeed suppose M is a Harish-Chandra module, i.e. a finitely generated $(\mathfrak{g},K)$-module, where K is the complexification of a maximal compact subgroup of $G_{\mathbb{R}}$. Consider the natural action of K on X. If points x,y belong to the same K-orbit, the spaces $M_{\mathfrak{n}_x}$ and $M_{\mathfrak{n}_y}$ are isomorphic, so $\dim M_{\mathfrak{n}_x}$ is constant along K-orbits. Since $\mathfrak{n}_0$ contains a maximal unipotent subalgebra of $\mathfrak{g}_{\mathbb{R}}$, the Iwasawa decomposition for $G_{\mathbb{R}}$ implies that the K-orbit of the corresponding point $x_0 \in X$ is open X. Hence, Theorem 1 implies that $M_{\mathfrak{n}_0} \neq 0$.

REMARK. N. Wallach explained to me that for $(\mathfrak{g},K)$-modules one can drop the condition that M is finitely generated (see [5]).

2.

For any point $x \in X$ we denote by $\mathfrak{n}_x$ and $\mathfrak{b}_x$ the corresponding nilpotent and Borel subalgebras ($\mathfrak{b}_x$ is the normalizer of $\mathfrak{n}_x$) and put $\mathfrak{h}_x = \mathfrak{b}_x/\mathfrak{n}_x$. We denote by $R_x \subset \mathfrak{h}_x^*$ the root system $\mathfrak{h}_x$ in $\mathfrak{g}$ and by R_x^+ the set of roots of $\mathfrak{h}_x$ in $\mathfrak{g}/\mathfrak{b}_x$. This ordering differs from the usual one by sign, because we study coinvariants $M_{\mathfrak{n}}$ instead of invariants $M^{\mathfrak{n}}$.

Note that all triples $(\mathfrak{h}_x, R_x, R_x^+)$ are canonically isomorphic. We will identify all these triples with an abstract Cartan triple

$(\mathfrak{h},R,R^+)$. The half-sum of positive roots we denote by ρ and the Weyl group of R by W.

Let M be a finitely generated $\mathfrak{g}$-module. We can assume that M has an infinitesimal character θ (for instance, M has an irreducible quotient M^1 and it is sufficient to prove that $M^1_{\mathfrak{n}} \neq 0$). Moreover, if $M_{\mathfrak{n}} = 0$, then for any finite-dimensional $\mathfrak{g}$-module V, $(V \otimes M)_{\mathfrak{n}} = 0$. Hence, decomposing in the usual way $V \otimes M$ with respect to infinitesimal characters, we can assume that the character θ is nondegenerate, i.e. corresponding W-orbit in $\mathfrak{h}^*$ consists of $\#W$ elements.

For any $x \in X$ the module $M_{\mathfrak{n}_x}$ has a natural structure of an $\mathfrak{h}_x = \mathfrak{h}$ - module. By the Harish-Chandra theorem, $M_{\mathfrak{n}_x}$ can be decomposed as

$$M_{\mathfrak{n}_x} = \bigoplus_{\chi \in \hat{\theta}} M^{\chi}_{\mathfrak{n}_x} ,$$

where $M^{\chi}_{\mathfrak{n}_x}$ consists of vectors of weight $\chi - \rho$ in $M_{\mathfrak{n}_x}$ and $\hat{\theta}$ is the W-orbit corresponding to θ. Fix a dominant weight χ_0 on the orbit, i.e. $\chi_0(h_\gamma) \neq 0, -1, -2, \ldots$, for any $\gamma \in R^+$ (here $h_\gamma \in \mathfrak{h}$ is the dual root). Then any weight $\chi \in \hat{\theta}$ can be written uniquely as $\chi = w\chi_0$ with $w \in W$. We put $\ell(\chi) = \ell(w)$; this is a distance from χ to χ_0. Note that $\ell(\chi)$ depends on the choice of a dominant weight χ_0. If χ is nonintegral, this choice is not unique.

We will prove

THEOREM 2. <u>Let</u> M <u>be a finitely generated</u> $\mathfrak{g}$-<u>module with a nondegenerate infinitesimal character</u> θ. <u>Then there exist a natural</u> ℓ <u>and a weight</u> $\psi \in \hat{\theta}$ <u>with</u> $\ell(\psi) = \ell$ <u>such that for almost all</u> $\mathfrak{n}$

$$M^{\chi}_{\mathfrak{n}} = 0 \ \ \underline{\text{for}}\ \ \ell(\chi) < \ell \ \ \underline{\text{and}}\ \ M^{\psi}_{\mathfrak{n}} \neq 0 .$$

3.

Fix a weight χ and let us study all spaces $M^{\chi}_{\mathfrak{n}_x}$ simultaneously. The key point is to understand the word "simultaneously". Studying these spaces simultaneously and separately is the same as studying the space $\prod_{x \in X} M^{\chi}_{\mathfrak{n}_x}$ - for sure this is the wrong way. Our key tool will be an algebraic object $\Delta_\chi(M)$ which contains all information about all spaces $M^{\chi}_{\mathfrak{n}_x}$. Roughly speaking, we consider the space M^0 of functions on X with values in M and put $\Delta(M) = M^0/\mathfrak{n}^0 M^0$, where $\mathfrak{n}^0$ is the algebra of functions $x \to \xi_x \in \mathfrak{n}_x$. Since there are very few global functions on X (we consider only regular functions), we should consider sheaves instead spaces of functions.

Now let us give precise definitions. Let $\mathcal{O}_X$ be the structure sheaf of the algebraic variety X. Quasicoherent sheaves of $\mathcal{O}_X$-modules we shall call simply $\mathcal{O}_X$-modules. Consider $\mathcal{O}_X$-modules

$$M^0 = \mathcal{O}_X \otimes_k M , \quad \mathfrak{g}^0 = \mathcal{O}_X \otimes_k \mathfrak{g} .$$

We shall consider sections of these sheaves as functions with values in M and $\mathfrak{g}$. Put

$$\mathfrak{n}^0 = \{f \in \mathfrak{g}^0 \mid f(x) \in \mathfrak{n}_x \text{ for all } x \in X\},$$
$$\mathfrak{h}^0 = \{f \in \mathfrak{g}^0 \mid f(x) \in \mathfrak{h}_x \text{ for all } x \in X\},$$
$$\Delta(M) = M^0/\mathfrak{n}^0 M^0.$$

It is clear that $\mathfrak{h}^0/\mathfrak{n}^0 = \mathcal{O}_X \otimes \mathfrak{h}$, so we have a natural imbedding $\mathfrak{h} \to \mathfrak{h}^0/\mathfrak{n}^0$, and hence an action of $\mathfrak{h}$ on $\mathcal{O}_X$-module $\Delta(M)$. We denote by $\Delta_\chi(M)$ the χ-component of $\Delta(M)$, i.e. the subsheaf of sections of weight $\chi - \rho$. The Harish-Chandra theorem implies that $\Delta(M) = \oplus \Delta_\chi(M)$, where $\chi \in \hat{\theta}$.

LEMMA. <u>The fiber of the $\mathcal{O}_X$-module $\Delta_\chi(M)$ at a point $x \in X$ is naturally isomorphic to $M^{\chi}_{\mathfrak{n}_x}$.</u>

Let us recall that the fiber of $\mathcal{O}_X$-module F at x is the linear space $F_x = F/m_x F$, where m_x is the maximal ideal of $\mathcal{O}_X$ consisting of functions f such that $f(x) = 0$. The proof is straightforward.

4.

The advantage of studying $\Delta_\chi(M)$ is that this sheaf has an additional structure - the structure of a $\mathfrak{g}$-module. Indeed, let us define actions of $\mathfrak{g}$ on M^0 and $\mathfrak{g}^0$ by the Leibnitz rule (we consider the adjoint action of $\mathfrak{g}$ on $\mathfrak{g}$ and the natural action of $\mathfrak{g}$ on $\mathcal{O}_X$). Since the subsheaves $\mathfrak{n}^0, \mathfrak{b}^0 \subset \mathfrak{g}^0$ are invariant under the action of the algebraic group G, corresponding to $\mathfrak{g}$, they are $\mathfrak{g}$-invariant. Hence $\Delta(M)$ is a $\mathfrak{g}$-module. Actions of $\mathfrak{g}$ and $\mathfrak{h}$ on $\Delta(M)$ commute, hence $\Delta_\chi(M)$ is also a $\mathfrak{g}$-module.

Let us describe more thoroughly operators acting on $\Delta_\chi(M)$. Consider the sheaf of algebras U^0 generated by $\mathfrak{g}$ and $\mathcal{O}_X$ with natural relations $[A,f] = A(f)$ for $A \in \mathfrak{g}$, $f \in \mathcal{O}_X$. As $\mathcal{O}_X$-module U^0 is isomorphic to $\mathcal{O}_X \otimes_k U(\mathfrak{g})$. Since $\mathfrak{n}^0$ is $\mathfrak{g}$-invariant, the ideal $\mathfrak{n}^0 U^0$ is two-sided, and we can put $\mathcal{D}_\mathfrak{h} = U^0/\mathfrak{n}^0 U^0$. The image of $\mathfrak{h}$ under the inclusion

$$\mathfrak{h} \to \mathfrak{b}^0/\mathfrak{n}^0 \to \mathcal{D}_\mathfrak{h}$$

belongs to the center of $\mathcal{D}_\mathfrak{h}$. Let us put

$$\mathcal{D}_\chi = \mathcal{D}_\mathfrak{h}/\{H - (\chi - \rho)(H) \mid H \in \mathfrak{h}\}\mathcal{D}_\mathfrak{h} .$$

It is clear that $\Delta_\chi(M)$ is a sheaf of $\mathcal{D}_\chi$- modules. We call a sheaf of $\mathcal{D}_\chi$-modules quasicoherent (or simply a "$\mathcal{D}_\chi$-module") if it is quasicoherent as an $\mathcal{O}_X$-module. The category of $\mathcal{D}_\chi$-modules we denote by $M(\mathcal{D}_\chi)$.

Consider the category of $\mathfrak{g}$-modules with the given infinitesimal character θ. If we put $U_\theta = U(\mathfrak{g})/\{Z - \theta(Z) \mid Z \in \text{Center of } U(\mathfrak{g})\}U(\mathfrak{g})$, then this category is the category $M(U_\theta)$ of U_θ -modules. We have constructed, for any $\chi \in \hat{\theta}$, the functor

$$\Delta_\chi : M(U_\theta) \to M(\mathcal{D}_\chi) .$$

We can define the right adjoint functor $\Gamma_\chi : M(\mathcal{D}_\chi) \to M(U_\theta)$ by

$$\Gamma_\chi(F) = \Gamma(X,F) .$$

5.

Let us discuss the structure of the sheaf $\mathcal{D}_X$.

LEMMA (i) The sheaf of algebras $\mathcal{D}_X$ is locally isomorphic to the sheaf $\mathcal{D}_X$ of differential operators on X.

(ii) $\mathcal{D}_\rho = \mathcal{D}_X$. More generally, let $\lambda \in \mathfrak{h}^*$ be an integral weight and $\mathcal{O}(\lambda)$ be the corresponding invertible sheaf of $\mathcal{O}_X$ -modules. Then there is a canonical isomorphism $\mathcal{D}_{\lambda+\rho} = \mathrm{Diff}(\mathcal{O}(\lambda))$ - the sheaf of differential operators in $\mathcal{O}(\lambda)$.

In other words, although we cannot define the sheaf $\mathcal{O}(\chi)$ for non-integral χ , we can define the sheaf $\mathrm{Diff}(\mathcal{O}(\chi))$.

PROOF. Fix $x \in X$ and the nilpotent subalgebra $\bar{\mathfrak{n}}$ opposite to $\mathfrak{n}_x$. Let $\bar{N}$ be the corresponding unipotent subgroup. Then, in a neighborhood of x , the variety X is isomorphic to $\bar{N}$ and $\mathcal{D}_X = \mathcal{O}_X \otimes_k U(\bar{\mathfrak{n}})$. This implies (i). The proof of (ii) is analogous.

PROPOSITION. Let F be a coherent (i.e. locally finitely generated) $\mathcal{D}_X$-module. Then the restriciton of F on some open dense subset $U \subset X$ is free as $\mathcal{O}_U$-module.

PROOF. Restrict F to some affine open subset $V \subset X$. Then we can replace F and $\mathcal{D}_X$ by their global sections: $F = F(V)$ and $D = \mathcal{D}_X(V) = D(V)$ - the algebra of differential operators on V . Consider the filtration $D^0 \subset D^1 \subset \ldots$ of D by the degree of differential operators, and put $\Sigma = \bigoplus_{n=0}^{\infty} D^n/D^{n-1}$. Then Σ is a **commutative** algebra, finitely generated over k , and $\mathcal{O}_X = D^0 \subset \Sigma$.

Fix generators $f_1,\ldots,f_k$ of F and consider the filtration $\{F^i = D^i f_1 + D^i f_2 + \ldots + D^i f_k\} \subset F$. Associated graded module $F_\Sigma = \oplus F^n_\Sigma$, where $F^n_\Sigma = F^n/F^{n-1}$, is a finitely generated Σ -module. Now, we have reduced the problem to the commutative case. General results from algebraic geometry imply that, after the restriction to some open dense subset $U \subset V$, F_Σ is a free $\mathcal{O}_U$-module (see [4, lecture 8, p.2^0]). Since F^n_Σ is a direct summand of F_Σ , it is a projective $\mathcal{O}_U$-module, and hence $F^n \approx F^{n-1} \oplus F^n_\Sigma$. This implies that $F \approx F^{\Sigma}$ as $\mathcal{O}_U$-modules, i.e. F is a free $\mathcal{O}_U$-module.

For a free $\mathcal{O}_X$-module the dimension of a fiber does not depend on a point. Hence, Theorem 2 is equivalent to the following statement about functors Δ_χ:

$$\operatorname{supp} \Delta_\chi(M) \neq X \quad \text{for} \quad \ell(\chi) < \ell$$

$$\operatorname{supp} \Delta_\psi(M) = X .$$

The following theorem describes the functor Δ_χ for dominant χ.

THEOREM (see [1]). _Suppose_ χ_0 _is a dominant regular weight. Then the functors_ Δ_{χ_0} _and_ Γ_{χ_0} _are mutually inverse and give an equivalence of categories._

$$M(U_\theta) \underset{\Gamma_{\chi_0}}{\overset{\Delta_{\chi_0}}{\rightleftarrows}} M(\mathcal{D}_{\chi_0}) .$$

In particular, if $M \neq 0$, then $\Delta_{\chi_0}(M) \neq 0$. If we denote the support of $\Delta_\chi(M)$ by S_χ this means that $S_{\chi_0} \neq \emptyset$. It is far from what we need (we need $S_\chi = X$), but at least it is something to start with.

7.

In order to prove Theorem 2 we will move from one weight χ to another in such a way that $\dim S_\chi$ will increase.

Let χ be a weight, α a simple root and $\phi = \sigma_\alpha \chi$. Suppose ϕ is α - dominant, i.e. $\phi(h_\alpha) \neq 0,-1,-2,\ldots$. We will construct the _intertwining functor_

$$I_{\chi,\phi} : M(\mathcal{D}_\phi) \to M(\mathcal{D}_\chi)$$

such that $\Delta_\chi = I_{\chi,\phi} \cdot \Delta_\phi : M(U_\theta) \to M(\mathcal{D}_\chi)$.

This functor will be described geometrically, as some operation with $\mathcal{D}$-modules. But firstly we shall describe how it changes the support of a sheaf.

Let us assign to a Borel subalgebra b_x the parabolic subalgebra $\mathfrak{p}_{x,\alpha}$ of type α by adding a root vector corresponding to α. This gives us a G-equivariant morphism $p_\alpha: X \to X_\alpha$, where X_α is an algebraic variety of parabolic subalgebras of type α. For any point $x \in X$ we denote by P_x the fiber of this morphism containing x, i.e. $P_x = p_\alpha^{-1} p_\alpha(x)$. As an algebraic variety P_x is isomorphic to projective line.

For any closed subset $S \subset X$ put

$$\mathrm{Env}_\alpha^+ (S) = \bigcup_{x \in S} P_x = p_\alpha^{-1} p_\alpha S .$$

We say that a fiber P of the morphism p_α is quasitransversal to S if it intersects S, all points of intersection are nonsingular in S and the morphism $p_\alpha|_S: S \to X_\alpha$ is an immersion at all these points.

We put $\mathrm{Env}_\alpha^-(S)$ = union of all fibers P quasitransversal to S.

STATEMENT. Let F be a $\mathcal{D}_\phi$-module and $S = \mathrm{Supp}\, F$. Then

(i) $\mathrm{Supp}\ I_{X,\phi}(F) \subset \mathrm{Env}_\alpha^+(S)$
(i) $\mathrm{supp}\ I_{X,\phi}(F) \supset \mathrm{Env}_\alpha^-(S)$.

We shall prove the statement in 11.

We shall derive Theorem 2 from Statement and the following geometric lemma.

LEMMA. Let S be a nonempty closed subset such that $\mathrm{Env}_\alpha^+ (S) = S$ for any simple root. Then $S = X$.

Indeed, let us identify X with G/B, where B is a Borel subgroup of G, and denote by $\bar{S}$ the preimage of S in G. The set $\bar{S}$ is invariant under (right) multiplication by B. The condition $\mathrm{Env}_\alpha^+(S) = S$ means that $\bar{S}$ is invariant under the multiplication by the parabolic subgroup P_α. Since the groups P_α for all simple roots α generate G, $\overline{S}$ is G-invariant, i.e. $\overline{S} = G$ and $S = X$.

8.

PROOF OF THEOREM 2. For any $\chi \in \hat{\theta}$ put $S_\chi = \mathrm{supp}\,(\Delta_\chi(M))$. If $\chi = \sigma_\alpha\phi$ and ϕ is α-dominant, we have $\Delta_\chi(M) = I_{\chi,\phi}(\Delta_\phi(M))$ and Statement 7. implies

$$\mathrm{Env}_\alpha^+ (S_\phi) \supset S_\chi \supset \mathrm{Env}_\alpha^- (S_\phi) .$$

In particular,

(i) $\dim S_\chi \leqslant \dim S_\phi + 1$

(ii) If $\dim S_\chi = \dim S_\phi + 1$, then any irreducible component S_χ^0 of maximal dimension of S_χ is a union of fibers P_χ.

Let $\ell = \mathrm{codim}\ S_{\chi_0}$. From (i) follows that $\mathrm{codim}\,(S_\chi) \leqslant \ell - \ell(\chi)$ for any $\chi \in \hat{\theta}$.. Let us prove by induction in i that for $i \leqslant \ell$ there exists a weight $\chi \in \hat{\theta}$ with $\ell(\chi) = i$ such that $\mathrm{codim}\ S_\chi = \ell - i$. Let ϕ be a corresponding weight with $\ell(\phi) = i-1$. Consider an irreducible component S of S_ϕ of the maximal dimension. Since $S \neq X$, the above lemma implies that there exists a simple root α such that $\mathrm{Env}_\alpha^+(S) \underset{\neq}{\supset} S$. Put $\chi = \sigma_\alpha\phi$

From (ii) we see that $\ell(\chi) = i$ and, in particular, ϕ is α-dominant. We want to prove that $\mathrm{codim}\ S_\chi = \ell - i$.

Condition $\mathrm{Env}_\alpha^+(S) \neq S$ means that $\dim p_\alpha(S) = \dim S$. Sard's lemma implies that for some dense subset $U \subset p_\alpha(S)$ the morphism p_α is an immersion on $p_\alpha^{-1}(U) \cap S$. Hence, $\mathrm{Env}_\alpha^-(S) \supset p_\alpha^{-1}(U)$.

Therefore, using the statement above, we obtain

$$S_\chi \supset \mathrm{Cl}(\mathrm{Env}_\alpha^- (S)) \supset \mathrm{Cl}(p_\alpha^{-1}(U)) = \mathrm{Env}_\alpha^+(S)$$

i.e.

$$\operatorname{codim} S_\chi = \operatorname{codim} S_\phi - 1 = \ell - i .$$

9.

In order to construct the functors $I_{\chi,\phi}$ we shall introduce some definitions and constructions from the theory of $\mathcal{D}$ - modules.

Let Y be a nonsingular algebraic variety, $\mathcal{O}_Y$ the structure sheaf of Y, $\mathcal{D}_Y$ the sheaf of differential operators on Y and $i : \mathcal{O}_Y \to \mathcal{D}_Y$ the standard inclusion.

DEFINITION. A twisted sheaf of differential operators (t.d.o for short) on Y is a pair $(i,\mathcal{D})$, where $\mathcal{D}$ is a sheaf of algebras on Y and $i: \mathcal{O}_Y \to \mathcal{D}$ is an inclusion of algebras; which is locally isomorphic to the standard pair $i: \mathcal{O}_Y \to \mathcal{D}_Y$.

A $\mathcal{D}$-module is a sheaf of (left) $\mathcal{D}$-modules, quasicoherent as a sheaf of $\mathcal{O}_Y$-modules. The category of $\mathcal{D}$-modules we denote by $\mathcal{M}(\mathcal{D})$.

Examples. 1. Let L be an invertible $\mathcal{O}_Y$-module and $\operatorname{Diff}(L)$ the sheaf of differential operators in L. Then $\operatorname{Diff}(L)$ is a t.d.o.

2. Let L be an invertible $\mathcal{O}_Y$-module and $\mathcal{D}$ a t.d.o. on Y. Consider the sheaf $L \otimes_{\mathcal{O}_Y} \mathcal{D}$ and put $\mathcal{D}^L = \mathcal{E}nd(\text{right } \mathcal{D}\text{-module } L \otimes_{\mathcal{O}_Y} \mathcal{D})$.

Then $\mathcal{D}^L$ is a t.d.o.

3. Let $\mathcal{D}$ be a t.d.o and $\mathcal{D}^0$ be the opposite algebra (i.e. the same sheaf with opposite multiplication). Then $\mathcal{D}^0$ is a t.d.o.

To prove this it is sufficient to verify that $(\mathcal{D}_Y)^0$ is a t.d.o. But it is easy to check that $(\mathcal{D}_Y)^0$ is canonically isomorphic to $\operatorname{Diff}(\Omega_Y)$, where Ω_Y is the sheaf of differential forms of the highest degree. The isomorphism is given by $\xi \to -\mathrm{Lie}_\xi$, where $\xi \in \mathcal{D}_Y$ is a vector field and Lie_ξ is the Lie derivative along ξ.

In the case of the flag variety X all sheaves $\mathcal{D}_\chi$ are t.d.o., $\mathcal{D}_\chi^{\mathcal{O}(\lambda)} = \mathcal{D}_{\chi+\lambda}$ and $(\mathcal{D}_\chi)^0 = \mathcal{D}_{-\chi}$.

Constructions.

1. Shift. Let L be an invertible $\mathcal{O}_Y$-module and $\mathcal{D}$ a t.d.o on Y. Then $L \otimes_{\mathcal{O}_Y} \mathcal{D}$ is a $\mathcal{D}^L$ - $\mathcal{D}$ -bimodule. Define the functor $L: M(\mathcal{D}) \to M(\mathcal{D}^L)$ by

$$L(F) = L \otimes_{\mathcal{O}_Y} F = (L \otimes_{\mathcal{O}_Y} \mathcal{D}) \otimes_{\mathcal{D}} F .$$

2. Inverse image. Let $\pi: Y \to Z$ be a morphism of nonsingular algebraic varieties and $\mathcal{D}$ a t.d.o on Z. Consider the sheaf of $\mathcal{O}_Y$-modules $\pi^*(\mathcal{D})$ - the inverse image of $\mathcal{O}_Z$-module $\mathcal{D}$ in the category of $\mathcal{O}$-modules and denote it by $\mathcal{D}_{Y\to Z}$. Recall that, by definition, $\pi^*(F) = \mathcal{O}_Y \otimes_{\pi^\circ \mathcal{O}_Z} \pi^\circ F$ where π° is the inverse image in the category of sheaves, i.e. locally, $\pi^*(F) = \mathcal{O}_Y \otimes_{\mathcal{O}_Z} F$.

Let us define the sheaf of algebras $\mathcal{D}^\pi$ on Y as a sheaf of differential endomorphisms of $\mathcal{O}_Y$-module $\pi^*(\mathcal{D})$ commuting with the right action of $\pi^\circ(\mathcal{D})$. It is easy to verify that the sheaf $(\mathcal{D}_Z)^\pi$ is canonically isomorphic to $\mathcal{D}_Y$. Hence, for any t.d.o $\mathcal{D}$ on Z the sheaf $\mathcal{D}^\pi$ is also a t.d.o.

Sheaf $\mathcal{D}_{Y \to Z}$ is a $\mathcal{D}^\pi$ - $\pi^\circ(\mathcal{D})$ - bimodule. Using it we define the functor of inverse image $\pi^+: M(\mathcal{D}) \to M(\mathcal{D}^\pi)$ by

$$\pi^+(F) = \mathcal{D}_{Y \to Z} \underset{\pi^\circ \mathcal{D}}{\otimes} \pi^\circ F$$

(i.e. locally $\pi^+(F) = \mathcal{D}_{Y \to Z} \otimes_{\mathcal{D}} F$). As $\mathcal{O}_Y$-module $\pi^+(F)$ is canonically isomorphic to $\pi^*(F)$.

3. Direct image. We want to define the functor of direct image $\pi_*: M(\mathcal{D}^\pi) \to M(\mathcal{D})$. In order to do this, we will construct a $\pi^\circ\mathcal{D}$ - $\mathcal{D}^\pi$ - bimodule $\mathcal{D}_{Z \leftarrow Y}$ and put

$$\pi_*(H) = \pi_\circ (\mathcal{D}_{Z \leftarrow Y} \otimes_{\mathcal{D}^\pi} H),$$

where $H \in M(\mathcal{D}^\pi)$ and $\pi_\circ$ is the direct image in the category of sheaves. The functor π_* has good properties only in the case of an affine morphism π (i.e. when the preimage of open affine subset $U \subset Z$ is affine).

For the general case this functor can be correctly defined only in derived categories. We will consider here only affine morphisms, because this is enough for our purposes. In this case the functor π_* is right exact.

By definition, we put

$$\mathcal{D}_{Z \leftarrow Y} = \Omega_Y \otimes_{\mathcal{O}_Y} \pi^*(\Omega_Z^{-1} \otimes_{\mathcal{O}_Z} \mathcal{D}^0).$$

This module has a natural structure of right $\pi^\circ(\mathcal{D}^0)$-module, i.e. of left $\pi^\circ\mathcal{D}$ - module. Now, we claim that the algebra of differential endomorphisms of $\mathcal{O}_Y$-module $\mathcal{D}_{Z \leftarrow Y}$ commuting with left action of $\mathcal{D}$ is canonically isomorphic to $(\mathcal{D}^\pi)^0$, i.e. $\mathcal{D}_{Z \leftarrow Y}$ has a canonical structure of a right $\mathcal{D}^\pi$- module.

Indeed, it is sufficient to consider the case $\mathcal{D} = \mathcal{D}_Z$. Then $\Omega_Z^{-1} \otimes_{\mathcal{O}_Z} \mathcal{D}^0 = \mathcal{D}_Z \otimes_{\mathcal{O}_Z} \Omega_Z^{-1}$ and hence $\pi^*(\Omega_Z^{-1} \otimes_{\mathcal{O}_Z} \mathcal{D}^0)$ is a left $\mathcal{D}^\pi = \mathcal{D}_Y$ - module. Therefore $\mathcal{D}_{Z \leftarrow Y}$ has the structure of a left $\mathcal{D}_Y^{\Omega_Y} = \mathcal{D}_Y^0$ - module, i.e. the structure of a right $\mathcal{D}^\pi = \mathcal{D}_Y$ - module. This structure does not depend on a local isomorphism $\mathcal{D} \tilde{\to} \mathcal{D}_Z$.

REMARK. The direct image of a sheaf is often denoted by $\int F$ because the functor π_* is an algebraic version of integration along fibers (see Example 1. below).

Examples. 1. Let $Y = A \times Z$, where A is an affine line and π the projection $\pi\colon\ Y \to Z$. We suppose Z to be affine and identify sheaves with their global sections. Then

$$\pi^+(F) = \mathcal{O}(A) \otimes_k F = k[t] \otimes_k F$$

$$\pi_*(H) = \Omega(A) \otimes_{\mathcal{O}_Y} H/\ \partial_t(\Omega(A) \otimes_{\mathcal{O}_Y} H) =$$

$$= H/\partial_t H \otimes_k k(dt)$$

where t is a linear parameter on A and $\partial_t = \dfrac{\partial}{\partial t}$.

2. Let $\pi\colon Y \to Z$ be a closed imbedding (i.e. Y is a closed subvariety of Z). Then π^+ is the usual restriction of $\mathcal{O}$-modules. Direct image π_* in this case is an exact functor. Locally, it

can be described as follows:

Let ℓ = codim Y and let $\partial_1, \ldots, \partial_\ell$ be vector fields transversal to Y . Then

$$\pi_*(F) = \{ \bigoplus_{n_1,\ldots,n_\ell \in \mathbb{Z}^+} \partial_1^{n_1} \partial_2^{n_2} \ldots \partial_\ell^{n_\ell} F^0 \}$$

where

$$F^0 = F \otimes_{\mathcal{O}_Y} \Omega_Y \otimes_{\mathcal{O}_Z} \Omega_Z^{-1}$$

The following technical theorem, due to Kashiwara, is often very useful.

THEOREM. Let $\pi: Y \to Z$ be a closed imbedding. Then π_* defines an equivalence of the category $M(\mathcal{D}^\pi)$ and the subcategory $M_Y(\mathcal{D}) \subset M(\mathcal{D})$ consisting of sheaves supported on Y .

10.

Now we can define intertwining functor $I_{\chi,\phi}$.

We have fixed simple root α and weights ϕ and $\chi = \sigma_\alpha \phi$ such that ϕ is α-dominant. Consider the projection $p_\alpha : X \to X_\alpha$ and put

$$N = \{(x,x^1) \in X \times X \mid p_\alpha(x) = p_\alpha(x^1),\ x \neq x^1\}$$

Denote by pr_1 , pr_2 : $N \to X$ projections of N on the first and second factor respectively. They both are G - equivariant fibrations with fibers isomorphic to the affine line A . Denote by L the invertible sheaf of $\mathcal{O}_N$ - modules corresponding to the tangent bundle to fibers of the projection pr_1 .

LEMMA. $\mathcal{D}_\chi^{pr_1}$ is canonically isomorphic to $(\mathcal{D}_\phi^{pr_2})^L$.

We will not prove the lemma, but explain it in the case when χ is integral. We want to check that

$$pr_2^*(\mathcal{O}(\phi - \rho)) = L \otimes pr_1^*(\mathcal{O}(\chi - \rho)) .$$

Since N is a homogeneous G - space, it is sufficient to prove the equality at one point $n = (x,y) \in N$. The stationary subgroup G_n is equal to $B_x \cap B_y$. Let us choose a Cartan subgroup $H \subset B_x \cap B_y$ and compare weights of the fibers of both sheaves at the point n . We identify H with a standard Cartan group using the subgroup B_y. If we use the subgroup B_x , we obtain weights changed by the automorphism σ_α.

$pr_2^*(\mathcal{O}(\phi - \rho))_n$ has a weight $\phi - \rho$,

$pr_1^*(\mathcal{O}(\chi - \rho))_n$ has a weight $\sigma_\alpha(\chi - \rho)$

L_n has a weight $\sigma_\alpha(-\alpha) = \alpha$ (recall that $\alpha \notin$ {roots of $\mathfrak{h}_x$ in $\mathfrak{n}_x$}).

The equality $(\phi - \rho) + \alpha = \sigma_\alpha(\chi - \rho)$ implies the lemma.

11.

DEFINITION. <u>Define the intertwining functor</u> $I_{\chi,\phi}: M(\mathcal{D}_\phi) \to M(\mathcal{D}_\chi)$ <u>by</u>

$$I_{\chi,\phi}(F) = (pr_1)_* (L \otimes pr_1^+ F) .$$

Informally

$$(I_{\chi,\phi}F)_x = \int_{P_x \setminus x} F|P_x ,$$

i.e. it really is intertwining.

The functor $I_{\chi,\phi}$ is right exact.

PROOF of Statement 7. Let F be a $\mathcal{D}_\phi$ -module, $S = \text{supp } F$. Put $F' = L \otimes pr_2^+(F)$, $S' = pr_2^{-1}(S)$. It is clear that $S' = \text{supp } F'$. We replace X by a small open subset Z and N by

$Y = Z \times A$, such that the natural morphism $\pi: Y \to Z$ is the projection pr_1 . We want to prove that

(i) supp $(\pi_*(F'))\subset (S')$

(ii) If $\pi|S': S' \to Z$ is an immersion, then supp $\pi_*(F') = \pi(S')$.

The assertion (i) is trivial and (ii) follows from Kashiwara's theorem, because F' is the direct image of a $\mathcal{D}_{S'}$-module F'' and hence $\pi_*(F') = (\pi|S')_*(F'')$ has support $\pi(S')$.

12.

THEOREM. $\Delta_\chi = I_{\chi,\phi} \cdot \Delta_\phi$.

We will sketch the proof of the theorem. (i) Fix a U_θ -module M and let us first prove that, for any point $x \in X$, the fibers $(\Delta_\chi(M))_x$ and $(I_{\chi,\phi}(\Delta_\phi(M)))_x$ are canonically isomorphic. It means that

$$(\Delta_\chi(M))_x = \int_{P_x \setminus x} (L \otimes \Delta_\phi(M)|P_x \setminus x) .$$

Consider the parabolic subalgebra $\mathfrak{p}_\alpha = \mathfrak{p}_{x,\alpha}$ (see 7) and its nilpotent radical $\mathfrak{n}_\alpha$ and put $\mathfrak{g}_\alpha = \mathfrak{p}_\alpha/\mathfrak{n}_\alpha$. The semisimple part of $\mathfrak{g}_a$ is isomorphic to $\mathfrak{sl}(2)$. The flag variety for $\mathfrak{g}_\alpha$ is naturally isomorphic to P_x .

Put $Q = M/\mathfrak{n}_\alpha M$. We will consider Q as an $\mathfrak{g}_\alpha$-module. It is easy to see that the restriction of the sheaf $\Delta_\chi(M)$ to P_x is naturally isomorphic to $\Delta_{\chi'}(Q)$, where $\chi' = \chi + (\rho - \rho(\mathfrak{g}_\alpha))$, and the same for ϕ . Using this fact we can (and will) reduce the problem to the case $\mathfrak{g} = \mathfrak{sl}(2)$, $X = \mathbb{P}^1$.

Let $x \in X = \mathbb{P}^1$, $A = X \setminus x$ is the affine line. We shall prove that $\Delta_\chi(M)_x = (M/\mathfrak{n}_x M)$ coincides with $\int_A (L \otimes \Delta_\phi(M))$.

Put $F = \Delta_\phi(M) \in M(\mathcal{D}_\phi)$, $H = F|_A$, F_* - the direct image of H on X . We have an exact sequence

$$0 \to K \to F \to F_* \to C \to 0$$

where $\mathcal{D}_\phi$-modules K and C are supported in x. Since ϕ is a dominant weight with respect to $\mathfrak{g}_\alpha$ we have the exact sequence

$$0 \to \Gamma(K) \to \Gamma(F) \to \Gamma(F_*) \to \Gamma(C) \to 0$$

and $\Gamma(F) = M$ (see 6). Using Kashiwara's theorem, one can verify that, for any $\mathcal{D}_\phi$ - module E supported in x, we have $H_0(\mathfrak{n}_x, \Gamma(E))^\chi = \Gamma(E)^\chi_{\mathfrak{n}_x} = 0$. Hence $M^\chi_{\mathfrak{n}_x} = \Gamma(F)^\chi_{\mathfrak{n}_x} = \Gamma(F_*)^\chi_{\mathfrak{n}_x}$.

Since $\Gamma(F_*) = \Gamma(A,H)$, we should prove

$$\int_A L \otimes H = \Gamma(A,H)^\chi_{\mathfrak{n}_x} .$$

Let e,h be generators of the Lie algebras $\mathfrak{n}_x$ and $\mathfrak{h} \subset \mathfrak{b}_x$ such that $[h,e] = -e$. Then there exists a unique linear coordinate t on $A = X \setminus x$ such that e and h act on A as ∂_t and $t\partial_t$. Then

$$\int_A L \otimes H = (\Omega(A) \otimes L \otimes H)/\partial_t(\Omega_A \otimes L \otimes H) = H/\partial_t H = \Gamma(A,H)_{\mathfrak{n}_x} .$$

Let us check that h acts on this space as multiplication by $(\chi - \rho)(h) = \chi(h) + \frac{1}{2}$. Indeed, h acts on H as $-t\partial_t - (\phi(h) + \frac{1}{2}) = -\partial_t t + 1 - \phi(h) - \frac{1}{2} = -\partial_t t + (\chi(h) + \frac{1}{2})$. Hence on the quotient space $H/\partial_t H$ the element h acts as $\chi(h) + \frac{1}{2}$.

ii) We have proved that the fibers of the sheaves $\Delta_\chi(M)$ and $I_{\chi,\phi}(\Delta_\phi(M))$ at any point x are canonically isomorphic. From this it follows that these sheaves are isomorphic in the case when M is a G-equivariant $\mathfrak{n}$-module and hence $\Delta_\chi(M)$ and $I_{\chi,\phi}(\Delta_\phi(M))$ are G-equivariant. In particular, these sheaves are canonically isomorphic for any free U_θ-module. Since both functors Δ_χ and $I_{\chi,\phi} \cdot \Delta_\phi$ are right exact, they are isomorphic for any U_θ - module M.

This finishes the proof of Theorem 12 and hence of Theorem 2.

13. SEVERAL REMARKS ON $\mathfrak{n}$-HOMOLOGY.

THEOREM. *The intertwining functor* $I_{\chi,\phi}$ *has homological dimension* $\leqslant 1$. *The corresponding derived functor* $L(I_{\chi,\phi}): D(\mathcal{M}(\mathcal{D}_\phi)) \to D(\mathcal{M}(\mathcal{D}_\chi))$ *is an equivalence of derived categories.*

COROLLARY. *Functors* Δ_χ *and* Γ_χ *have homological dimensions* $\leqslant \ell(\chi)$. *The corresponding derived functors*

$$L\Delta_\chi : D(\mathcal{M}(U_\theta)) \to D(\mathcal{M}(\mathcal{D}_\chi))$$

and

$$R\Gamma_\chi : D(\mathcal{M}(\mathcal{D}_\chi)) \to D(\mathcal{M}(U_\theta))$$

are mutually inverse and give an equivalence of derived categories.

COROLLARY. *Let* M *be a finitely generated* U_θ *-module and* $\ell = \operatorname{codim} \operatorname{supp} \Delta_{\chi_0}(M)$. *Then for almost all* $x \in X$

$$H_i(\mathfrak{n}_x, M)^\chi = 0 \quad \textit{for} \quad \ell(\chi) < \ell \quad \textit{and any} \quad i ,$$

$$H_i(\mathfrak{n}_x, M)^\chi = 0 \quad \textit{for} \quad \ell(\chi) = \ell \quad \textit{and} \quad i > 0$$

(*and, as we have seen, there exists* ψ *with* $\ell(\psi) = \ell$ *such that* $H_0(\mathfrak{n}_x, M)^\psi \neq 0$) .

The second author was supported by the National Science Foundation.

REFERENCES

[1] A. Beilinson, J.N. Bernstein, Localisation de $\mathfrak{g}$-modules, C.R. Acad. Sci. Paris, 292, (1981), 15-18.

[2] W. Casselman, Differential equations satisfied by matrix coefficients, preprint.

[3] D. Miličić, Notes on asymptotics of admissible representations of semi-simple Lie groups, Institute for Advanced Study, 1976.

[4] D. Mumford, Lectures on curves on an algebraic surface, Ann. of Math. Studies, Vol. 59, Princeton University Press, 1966.

[5] J.T. Stafford, N.R. Wallach, The restriction of admissible modules to parabolic subalgebras, Trans. Amer. Math. Soc. 272(1982), 333-350.

FOURIER TRANSFORMS OF ORBITS OF THE COADJOINT REPRESENTATION

Nicole Berline and Michele Vergne

1. INTRODUCTION.

Let G be a compact Lie group with Lie algebra $\mathfrak{g}$. Let $\mathcal{O} \subset \mathfrak{g}^*$ be an orbit of G under the coadjoint representation of maximal dimension 2n . For $f \in \mathcal{O}$, we denote by G(f) the stabilizer of f and $\underline{t} = \mathfrak{g}(f)$ the Lie algebra of G(f). Let W be the Weyl group of $(\mathfrak{g}, \underline{t})$. Recall that $\mathcal{O}$ is a symplectic manifold with a canonical 2-form σ. Let us denote the associated Liouville measure $\frac{\sigma^n}{n!}$ by dm. We have then; for $H \in \underline{t}$

$$\int_{\mathcal{O}} e^{i\langle \xi,H\rangle} \frac{dm(\xi)}{(2\pi)^n} = \sum_{w \in W} \frac{\varepsilon(w)e^{i(w\cdot f,H)}}{\prod_{\alpha>0} (\alpha,H)} .$$

This formula is closely related to the Weyl character formula for irreducible representations of G , and thus to the Atiyah-Bott fixed point formula [1]. Indeed, if H is a regular element of $\underline{t}$, the special points $\{w\cdot f;\ w \in W\}$ of the orbit $\mathcal{O}$, singled out in the right hand side of this formula are the zeros of the vector field H^* generated by the action of exp tH on $\mathcal{O}$. Inspired by the method of Bott in "Vector fields and characteristic numbers" [2], we will see that indeed this formula is a simple consequence of the following fact: the 2n-form $e^{i\langle\xi,H\rangle}\frac{\sigma^n}{n!}$ on $\mathcal{O}$ is an exact form $d\alpha_H$, except at the zeros of H^*, and we may compute this integral by Stokes theorem.

The same observation allows us to compute integrals $\int_M e^{iJ(\xi)} dm(\xi)$, where M is a compact symplectic manifold, J a function on M such that the corresponding Hamiltonian vector field generates a periodic action. These integrals, which appear in Kirillov's character formula [5], had been previously evaluated by Duistermaat-Heckman[3].

If $\mathcal{O}$ is a closed orbit of the coadjoint representation of a real algebraic group, the function

$$F_{\mathcal{O}}(X) = \int_{\mathcal{O}} e^{i\langle \xi, X\rangle} \frac{\sigma^d}{(2\pi)^d d!}$$

has a meaning as a generalized function. It is natural to predict from the Duistermaat-Heckman formula the value of this function whenever X is an elliptic element of $\mathfrak{g}$ (i.e. $\operatorname{ad}X$ has imaginary eigenvalues). We should have:

$$F_{\mathcal{O}}(X) = \sum_{\substack{f \in \mathcal{O} \\ f \text{ zeros of } X^*}} \frac{e^{i\langle f, X\rangle}}{D_f(X)} ,$$

where the denominator $D_f(X)$ will be defined in Section 2.

If $\mathfrak{g}$ is semi-simple and has discrete series, we can indeed prove this formula using again Stokes theorem, by proving that the remaining term at infinity tends to zero. We thank Masaki Kashiwara for helping us in the needed estimates. In particular, we reobtain Rossmann formula [8]. We wish to thank G. Heckman for many helpful discussions on these topics.

2. AN INTEGRAL FORMULA

2.1. Let M be a manifold. We denote by $\mathbf{a}(M) = \oplus\ \mathbf{a}^r(M)$ the graded ring of forms on the manifold M, d the exterior differentiation. If ξ is a vector field on M, we denote by $c(\xi)$ the contraction

$$(c(\xi)\cdot\omega)(\xi_1 \wedge \cdots \wedge \xi_{r-1}) = \omega(\xi \wedge \xi_1 \wedge \cdots \wedge \xi_{r-1})$$

if $\omega \in \mathbf{a}^r(M)$.

Let $L(\xi)$ be the Lie derivative. We recall the following properties:

a) d and $c(\xi)$ are skew-derivations of the ring $\mathbf{a}(M)$ and $d \circ d = 0$, $c(\xi) \circ c(\xi) = 0$

b) $L(\xi)$ is a derivation of $\mathfrak{a}(M)$ and

$$L(\xi) = d\circ c(\xi) + c(\xi)\circ d = (d + c(\xi))^2 \tag{2.1}$$

An element $\omega \in \mathfrak{a}(M)$ will be called a form on M, even if ω is not homogeneous.

2.2. Let T be a Lie group with Lie algebra $\underline{t}$. We suppose that T acts on M via a left action. For $X \in \underline{t}$, we denote by X^* the vector field on M generated by the action of T, i.e.

$$(X^*\phi)(m) = \frac{d}{d\varepsilon}\, \phi(\exp \varepsilon X\cdot m)\Big|_{\varepsilon = 0}\,.$$

We recall that $[X,Y]^* = -[X^*,Y^*]$. For $X \in \underline{t}$, let $\mathfrak{a}_X$ be the subring of forms ω on M such that $L(X^*)\omega = 0$. Let $Z(X) = \operatorname{Ker}(d + c(X^*))$. If $\omega \in Z(X)$, $L(X^*)\omega = 0$ by 2.1 b). So $Z(X)$ is a subring of $\mathfrak{a}_X$. We denote by $B(X) = (d + c(X^*))\, \mathfrak{a}_X$ and by $H(X)$ the ring $Z(X)/B(X)$. Let us remark that if $T = \{e\}$, the ring $H(0)$ is the usual cohomology ring of the manifold M.

2.3. If M' is a compact oriented submanifold of M and $\omega = \Sigma\, \omega^{[i]}$ we write $\int_{M'}\omega$ for $\int_{M'} \omega^{[\dim M']}$. If p is a point of M, we write $\omega(p)$ for $\omega^{[o]}(p)$.

2.4. Lemma. Suppose M' is a compact oriented submanifold of M invariant under $\exp tX$, and $\omega \in B(X)$. Then $\int_{M'}\omega = 0$. In particular, if p is a zero of the vector field X^*, then the map $\omega \to \omega(p)$ induces a map on $H(X)$, and (assuming M is compact oriented), the map $\omega \to \int_M \omega$ induces a map on $H(X)$.

PROOF. Let $\omega = (d + c(X^*))\alpha$, and let $r = \dim M'$. Then $\omega^{[r]} = d(\alpha^{[r-1]}) + c(X^*)\, \alpha^{[r+1]}$, and the second term vanishes on M'.

2.5 Let p be a zero of the vector field X^*. The map $L(X^*)$ induces a linear map $L_p(X^*)$ on the tangent space $T_p(M)$ of M. The vector field X^* will be called nondegenerate if $L_p(X^*)$ is an invertible transformation of $T_p(M)$ at all the zeros of X^*.

Suppose T is a compact Lie group. If $X \in \underline{t}$, at a zero p of X^* the map $L_p(X^*)$ can be represented by a skew-symmetric matrix Let $e_1, e_2, \ldots, e_{2n}$ be an oriented basis with

$$L_p(X^*)\, e_{2i-1} = \lambda_i e_{2i}$$

$$L_p(X^*)\, e_{2i} = -\lambda_i e_{2i-1},$$

we define $(\det L_p(X^*))^{1/2} = \lambda_1 \lambda_2 \ldots \lambda_n$.

2.6 Theorem: Let T be a compact Lie group acting on a compact oriented manifold M of dimension $2n$. Let $X \in \underline{t}$ such that X^* is a nondegenerate vector field on M. If $\omega \in H(X)$, then

$$\int_M \omega = (2\pi)^n \sum_{p \text{ zeros of } X^*} \frac{\omega(p)}{(\det L_p(X^*))^{1/2}}$$

PROOF. The proof of this theorem will be modelled on the argument of R . Bott in [2]. We will first prove an auxiliary lemma. Let α be a form of positive degree on M . Then $(1+\alpha)$ is invertible in the ring $\mathfrak{a}(M)$ with inverse

$$(1 + \alpha)^{-1} = 1 - \alpha + \cdots + (-1)^k \alpha^k + \cdots + \alpha^{2n} .$$

2.7. Lemma. Let M' be the complement of the zeros of the vector field X^* . Let π be a 1-form on M' such that $\pi(X^*) = 1$, $L(X^*)\pi = 0$. If $\omega \in \mathfrak{a}(M')$ is such that $(d + c(X^*))\omega = 0$ then:

$$c(X^*)(\omega - d(\pi(1 + d\pi)^{-1}\omega)) = 0 .$$

PROOF. We write

$$\begin{aligned} d(\pi(1 + d\pi)^{-1}\omega) &= d\pi(1 + d\pi)^{-1}\omega - \pi(1 + d\pi)^{-1}d\omega \\ &= d\pi(1 + d\pi)^{-1}\omega + \pi(1 + d\pi)^{-1}c(X^*)\omega . \end{aligned}$$

Now

$$c(X^*)\pi = 1$$
$$c(X^*)d\pi = -dc(X^*)\pi + L(X^*)\pi = 0$$

then

$$\begin{aligned} c(X^*)(d\pi(1 + d\pi)^{-1}\omega + \pi(1 + d\pi)^{-1}c(X^*)\omega) \\ = (d\pi)(1 + d\pi)^{-1}c(X^*)\omega + (1 + d\pi)^{-1}c(X^*)\omega \\ = (d\pi + 1)(1 + d\pi)^{-1}c(X^*)\omega = c(X^*)\omega . \end{aligned}$$

Let us consider our manifold M. We can choose on M a T-invariant metric $g(\ ,\ )$. Let $\pi(Y) = \frac{g(X^*,Y)}{g(X^*,X^*)}$, then π has the desired properties: $\pi(X^*) = 1$, $L(X^*)\pi = 0$. Let α be the $2n - 1$ form $(\pi(1 + d\pi)^{-1}\omega)^{[2n-1]}$. We obtain:

2.8. Corollary: Let $\omega \in Z(X)$, then $\omega^{[2n]} = d\alpha$ on M'.

PROOF. If μ belongs to the space of forms of top degree, the equation $c(X^*)\mu = 0$ implies $\mu = 0$ on M'. Thus the corollary follows from 2.7.

2.9 We may thus apply Stokes theorem to compute $\int_M \omega$. The zeros of X^* are isolated. Let M_ε be the complement of the union of small balls B^p_ε centered at each zero p of X^*. We may write, as $M_\varepsilon \subset M'$,

$$\int_M \omega = \lim_{\varepsilon\to 0} \int_{M_\varepsilon} \omega = \lim_{\varepsilon\to 0} \int_{M_\varepsilon} d\alpha = \lim_{\varepsilon\to 0} \int_{\partial(M_\varepsilon)} \alpha .$$

Now the boundary $\partial(M_\varepsilon)$ consists of unions of spheres S^p_ε centered at p. We may thus fix a point p and compute in a local chart around p, $\lim_{\varepsilon\to 0} \int_{S^p_\varepsilon} \alpha$.

Let g be a $L(X^*)$ invariant metric on M. We can scale our coordinates x_i in a neighborhood of $p = 0$ such that:

$$\frac{\partial}{\partial x_1}, \frac{\partial}{\partial x_2}, \ldots, \frac{\partial}{\partial x_{2n-1}}\ \frac{\partial}{\partial x_{2n}} \text{ is an oriented basis of } T_p(M)$$

$$X^* \sim \sum_{i=1}^{n} \lambda_i(x_{2i} \frac{\partial}{\partial x_{2i-1}} - x_{2i-1} \frac{\partial}{\partial x_{2i}})$$

$$g \sim \sum_{i=1}^{n} \lambda_i^{-2}(dx_{2i-1}^2 + dx_{2i}^2)$$

when $\sim$ denotes the equivalence modulo terms of higher order. Thus

$$g(X^*,X^*) \sim \sum_{i=1}^{2n} x_i^2$$

$$g(X^*,X^*)\pi \sim \sum_{i=1}^{n} \lambda_i^{-1}(x_{2i}dx_{2i-1} - x_{2i-1}dx_{2i}) \;.$$

We consider the ball B_ε given by $\|x\| \leqslant \varepsilon$. We denote by S_ε^+ the sphere $\{x;\ \|x\| = \varepsilon\}$ with its usual orientation, and S_ε^- the sphere S_ε with its reverse orientation. Thus the boundary of the complement of B_ε is the sphere S_ε^-.

If α is a $(2n-1)$-form on $\mathbb{R}^{2n} - \{0\}$,

$$\alpha = \Sigma\, \alpha_i\, dx_1 \wedge \ldots \wedge \widehat{dx_i} \wedge \ldots \wedge dx_{2n}$$

we have:

$$\lim_{\varepsilon\to 0} \int_{S_\varepsilon^+} \alpha = \sum_i \int_{S_1^+} (\lim_{\varepsilon\to 0} \varepsilon^{2n-1}\alpha_i(\varepsilon x))dx_1\wedge\ldots\wedge\widehat{dx_i}\wedge\ldots\, dx_{2n}.$$

Let $Q = \Sigma\, x_i^2$, $f = \sum_{i=1}^{n} \lambda_i^{-1}(x_{2i}dx_{2i-1} - x_{2i-1}dx_{2i})$, $\pi_1 = Q^{-1}f$,

so that π_1 is an approximation of π near 0. Let $\omega = \Sigma\, \omega^i$. As the ω^i are C^∞ at the point 0, it is easy to see that for $i + j = n - 1$, $j \neq 0$,

$$\lim_{\varepsilon\to 0} \int_{S_\varepsilon^+} \pi\ (d\pi)^i \omega^j = 0$$

while $\lim_{\varepsilon\to 0} \int_{S_\varepsilon^+} \pi(d\pi)^{n-1}\omega^0 = \omega^0(p) \int_{S_1^+} \pi_1(d\pi_1)^{n-1}$.

We now compute $\pi_1(d\pi_1)^{n-1}$. We have $\pi_1 = Q^{-1}f$ with f a 1-form, thus

$$d\pi_1 = Q^{-1}df - Q^{-2}\, dQ \wedge f$$
$$\pi_1 d\pi_1 = Q^{-2} f \wedge df$$
$$\pi_1 (d\pi_1)^{n-1} = Q^{-n} f \wedge (df)^{n-1}$$

As

$$f = \Sigma\, \lambda_i^{-1}(x_{2i}dx_{2i-1} - x_{2i-1}dx_{2i})$$
$$df = (-2)\, \Sigma\, \lambda_i^{-1}(dx_{2i-1} \wedge dx_{2i})$$
$$f \wedge (df)^{n-1} = (-2)^{n-1}(\lambda_1\lambda_2 \cdots \lambda_n)^{-1}\cdot(n-1)\,!\,\mu$$

with

$$\mu = \sum_i x_{2i}dx_1\wedge\ldots\wedge \widehat{dx_{2i}}\wedge\ldots\wedge dx_{2n} - x_{2i-1}dx_1\wedge\ldots\wedge \widehat{dx_{2i-1}}\wedge\ldots\wedge dx_{2n}).$$

Let σ be the volume form on S_1^+, we then have

$$\mu = -\sigma\ .$$

Thus, we finally obtain for $\alpha = (\pi(1 + d\pi)^{-1}\omega)^{[2n-1]}$

$$\lim_{\varepsilon\to 0} \int_{S_\varepsilon^-} \alpha = - \lim_{\varepsilon\to 0} \int_{S_\varepsilon^+} (-1)^{n-1}\pi_1(d\pi_1)^{n-1}\omega_0$$
$$= (n-1)!\ \mathrm{vol}(S_1^{2n-1})(2)^{n-1}(\lambda_1\lambda_2\ldots\lambda_n)^{-1}\omega_0(p)$$
$$= (2\pi)^n(\lambda_1\lambda_2\ \ldots\ \lambda_n)^{-1}\omega_0(p)$$

as $\mathrm{vol}\ S_1^{2n-1} = 2n\,\frac{\pi^n}{n!}$. q.e.d.

Let us first give an application of this theorem.

2.10. Let M be a symplectic manifold of dimension $2n$ with symplectic form σ and let T be a torus which acts on M in an Hamiltonian way. That is, there is given a linear map $X \to J_X$ from the Lie algebra $\underline{t}$ of T to the space of smooth functions on M, such that

a) For each $X \in \underline{t}$, the infinitesimal action of X on M is given by the Hamiltonian vector field of the function J_X.

b) The functions J_X are in involution.

We have the relation $c(X^*)\cdot\sigma + dJ_X = 0$. Thus, as $d\sigma = 0$, $c(X^*)J_X = 0$, the form $\omega = \sigma + J_X$ is an even form on M such that $(d + c(X^*))\omega = 0$. Recall that the Liouville measure dm on M is defined by $\frac{1}{n!}\sigma^n$. We thus may rewrite $\int_M e^{iJ_X}dm$ as $\frac{1}{i^n}\int_M e^{i(J_X+\sigma)}$. We obtain as corollary the following formula of Duistermaat-Heckman [3].

2.11. Corollary. If X^* is a nondegenerate vector field on M

$$\int_M e^{iJ_X}dm = \left(\frac{2\pi}{i}\right)^n \sum_p \frac{e^{iJ_X(p)}}{(\det L_p(X^*))^{1/2}}$$

3. FOURIER TRANSFORM OF ORBITS OF THE COADJOINT REPRESENTATION.

3.1. Recall [6],[7] that an important example of Hamiltonian action arises as follows:

Let G be a Lie group, $\mathfrak{g}$ its Lie algebra, $\mathcal{O} \subset \mathfrak{g}^*$ be an orbit of the coadjoint representation. For $\xi \in \mathcal{O}$, we denote by $G(\xi)$ the stabilizer of ξ and by $\mathfrak{g}(\xi)$ the Lie algebra of $G(\xi)$. For $X \in \mathfrak{g}$, we denote by X^* the vector field on $\mathcal{O}$ generated by the action of G, i.e. $(X^*)_\xi = X\cdot\xi$. The 2-form $\sigma_\xi(X\cdot\xi, Y\cdot\xi) = \xi([X,Y])$ determines a symplectic form σ on $\mathcal{O}$. The action of G on $\mathcal{O}$ is an Hamiltonian action: let $J_X(\xi) = -\langle \xi, X\rangle$. It is easy to verify that the function J_X on $\mathcal{O}$ satisfy the relation $dJ_X + c(X^*)\sigma = 0$, i.e. X^* is the Hamiltonian vector field of the function J_X.

3.2. In particular, let G be a compact Lie group with Lie algebra $\mathfrak{g}$ and Cartan subalgebra $\underline{t}$. Let $\lambda \in \mathfrak{g}^*$ such that $\mathfrak{g}(\lambda) = \underline{t}$ and $\mathcal{O} = G\cdot\lambda$. Let W be the Weyl group of $(\mathfrak{g},\underline{t})$, $\Lambda = i\lambda|\underline{t}$. Choose a system of positive roots such that Λ is dominant. For $H \in \underline{t}$, λ is a zero of H^* and $(\det L_\lambda(H^*))^{1/2} = \prod_{\alpha>0}(i\alpha(H))$.

Thus 2.11 implies the wellknown formula:

$$\int_{\mathcal{O}} e^{i(\xi,H)} \frac{\sigma^d}{(2\pi)^d d!} = \frac{\sum_{w\in W} \varepsilon(w)e^{(w\cdot\Lambda,\, H)}}{\prod_{\alpha>0}(\alpha,H)}$$

with $d = \frac{1}{2}\dim \mathcal{O}$.

We will now generalize this formula to the case where $\mathcal{O}$ is a closed orbit for a real semi-simple Lie group G having discrete series.

3.3. Let $\mathfrak{g}$ be the Lie algebra of G, with Cartan decompostion $\mathfrak{g} = \underline{k} + \underline{p}$. Let $\underline{t}$ be a Cartan subalgebra of $\underline{k}$ and of $\mathfrak{g}$. We write $\mathfrak{g} = \underline{t} \oplus [\underline{t},\mathfrak{g}]$ and we identify $\underline{t}^*$ with a subspace of $\mathfrak{g}^*$.

Let W be the normalizer of $\underline{t}$ in G, divided by its centralizer and let Δ be the set of roots of $\underline{t}^C$ in $\mathfrak{g}^C$. For $\lambda \in \underline{t}^*$, let $\Delta^+_\lambda = \{\alpha \in \Delta : (i\lambda, H_\alpha) > 0\}$, let $r(\lambda)$ be the number of non compact roots contained in Δ^+_λ, and let W_λ be the stabilizer of λ in W.

We denote by $\underline{t}_r$ the set of regular elements in $\underline{t}$ and by

$\mathfrak{g}_e = G.\underline{t}_r$ the open subset of regular elliptic elements in $\mathfrak{g}$.

Let $\mathcal{O}$ be a closed G-orbit in $\mathfrak{g}^*$ of dimension $2n$ and let σ be the canonical symplectic form on $\mathcal{O}$. Then

$$\int_{\mathcal{O}} e^{i(\xi,X)} \frac{\sigma^n}{(2\pi)^n n!}$$

defines a generalized function $F_{\mathcal{O}}$ on $\mathfrak{g}$, which belongs to $L^1_{loc}(\mathfrak{g})$ and is analytic on the regular set [4].

3.4. Theorem.

a) If $\mathcal{O} \cap \underline{t}^* = \emptyset$ then $F_{\mathcal{O}}|\mathfrak{g}_e = 0$.

b) If $\mathcal{O} = G.\lambda$ with $\lambda \in \underline{t}^*$, then for $H \in \underline{t}_r$

$$F_{\mathcal{O}}(H) = (-1)^{r(\lambda)} \sum_{W/W_\lambda} \frac{e^{i(w.\lambda,H)}}{\prod_{\alpha \in \Delta^+_\lambda} (w.\alpha,H)}$$

Remark. the function $\prod_{\alpha \in \Delta^+_\lambda} \alpha$ is indeed invariant under W_λ.

PROOF. Let ϕ be a C^∞-function on $\mathfrak{g}$ compactly supported on $\mathfrak{g}_e$, then by definition

$$\int_{\mathfrak{g}} F_{\mathcal{O}}(X)\, \phi(X) dX = \int_{\mathcal{O}} \left(\int_{\mathfrak{g}} e^{i(\xi,X)} \phi(X)\, dX\right) \frac{\sigma^n}{(2\pi)^n n!} \tag{3.5}$$

Fix a T-invariant positive definite quadratic form $Q(\xi)$ on $\mathfrak{g}^*$. For $c > 0$, denote

$$\mathcal{O}_c = \{\xi \in \mathcal{O};\ Q(\xi) \leqslant c\} \quad .$$

We may rewrite the right-hand side of (2.5) as

$$\lim_{c\to\infty} \int_{\mathcal{O}_c} \int_{\mathfrak{g}} e^{i(\xi,X)}\ \phi(X)\ dX)\frac{\sigma^n}{(2\pi)^n\ n!} =$$

$$\lim_{c\to\infty} \int_{\mathfrak{g}} (\int_{\mathcal{O}_c} e^{i(\xi,X)}\ \frac{\sigma^n}{(2\pi)^n n!})\ \ \phi(X)\ dX \ .$$

We will compute this in a way similar to 2.9.

3.6. Lemma. There exists a C^∞-map $X \to Q_X$ from $\mathfrak{g}_e$ to positive definite quadratic forms on $\mathfrak{g}^*$, such that Q_X is invariant under the action of the one parameter subgroup $\exp tX$.

PROOF. If $X = gH$ with $H \in \underline{t}_r$, set $Q_X(\xi) = Q(g^{-1}.\xi)$. Recall that $X \in \mathfrak{g}$ generates the vector field $X^*_\xi = X.\xi$ on $\mathfrak{g}^*$. Consider the 1-form π_X defined by

$$\pi_X(\eta)_\xi \ = \ \frac{Q_X(X^*_\xi,\ \eta_\xi)}{Q_X(X^*_\xi,\ X^*_\xi\ )}$$

on the open set $\{\xi \in \mathfrak{g}^*;\ X.\xi \neq 0\}$ and set

$$\alpha_X = \left(\pi_X(1 + d\pi_X)^{-1}\ \ e^{i(\xi,X)}\ -i\sigma\right)^{[2n-1]} \qquad (3.7)$$

Let $\mathcal{O}'_X$ be the complement in $\mathcal{O}$ of the zero-set of the vector-field X^*. Then, by 2.6 the forms

$$e^{i(\xi,X)}\ \frac{\sigma^n}{(2\pi)^n n!} \qquad \text{and} \qquad \frac{i^n}{(2\pi)^n}\ d\alpha_X$$

coincide on $\mathcal{O}'_X$.

Suppose $\mathcal{O} = G.\lambda$ with $\lambda \in \underline{t}^*$; then the zeros of H^* on $\mathcal{O}$ are the points $w.\lambda$, for $w \in W$. In particular, they are in finite number. It follows that, when X varies in a compact subset of $\mathfrak{g}_e$, the zeros of X^* on $\mathcal{O}$ lie in a compact subset of $\mathcal{O}$.

Let $f_{\mathcal{O}}$ be the G-invariant function on $\mathfrak{g}_e$, defined by

$$f_{\mathcal{O}}(H) = (-1)^{r(\lambda)} \sum_{W/W_\lambda} \frac{e^{i(w.\lambda,H)}}{\Pi_{\alpha \in \Delta_\lambda^+} (w.\alpha,H)} \quad \text{for } H \in \underline{t}_r .$$

Let c_0 be such that $\mathcal{O}'_X \subset \mathcal{O} \setminus \mathcal{O}_c$ for all X's in the support of ϕ and $c \geqslant c_0$. Arguing as in the proof of 2.6 we obtain

$$\int_{\mathcal{O}_c} e^{i(\xi,X)} \frac{\sigma^n}{(2\pi)^n n!} = f_{\mathcal{O}}(X) + \left(\frac{i}{2\pi}\right)^n \int_{\partial\mathcal{O}_c} \alpha_X$$

The sign $(-1)^{r(\lambda)}$ appears when one computes an oriented basis of the tangent space to $\mathcal{O}$ at λ as in 2.5.

In the case $\mathcal{O} \cap \underline{t}^* = \emptyset$, the vector field X^* does not vanish at any point of $\mathcal{O}$ and the function $f_{\mathcal{O}}$ is to be taken equal to zero.

Thus, to complete the proof of theorem 3.4 it is enough to show

$$\liminf_{c \to \infty} \left| \int_{\mathfrak{g}} \int_{\partial\mathcal{O}_c} \alpha_X \ \phi(X)\, dX \right| = 0$$

$$= \liminf_{c \to \infty} \left| \int_{\partial\mathcal{O}_c} \int_{\mathfrak{g}} \alpha_X \ \phi(X)\, dX \right| = 0 .$$

Set $\beta = \int_{\mathfrak{g}} \alpha_X \ \phi(X)\, dX$. It is enough to show that the integral

$$\int_{c_0}^{\infty} \left(\int_{\partial\mathcal{O}_c} \beta\right) dc$$

is convergent or, using Fubini theorem, that the integral

$$\int_{\mathcal{O} - \mathcal{O}_{c_0}} \beta \wedge dQ$$

is absolutely convergent.

Let (ξ_i) be a set of linear coordinates on $\mathfrak{g}^*$.

The form β is a linear combination of terms of the form

$$\phi_\alpha(\xi)(d\xi^{(\alpha)}|\mathcal{O})\wedge\sigma^j \qquad \text{with} \quad |\alpha| + 2j = 2n-1 .$$

Now

$$(d\xi^{(\alpha)}|\mathcal{O})\wedge\sigma^j\wedge(dQ|\mathcal{O}) = U_{\alpha,j}(\xi)\,\sigma^n$$

where $U_{\alpha,j}(\xi)$ is a polynomial in ξ.

Using the fact that the distribution on $\mathfrak{n}^*$ defined by σ^n is tempered, it therefore suffices to show that the functions $\phi_\alpha|_\mathcal{O}$ are rapidly decreasing at infinity.

We now compute the functions ϕ_α. Expanding (3.7) we see that β is a linear combination of terms of the form

$$\int_\mathfrak{n} e^{i(\xi,X)}\,\pi_X\wedge(d\pi_X)^{\ell-1}\wedge\sigma^j\quad\phi(X)\,dX$$

with $\ell+j = n$.

Set $D_X(\xi) = Q_X(X^*_\xi)$. Then $\pi_X = \Sigma\,\dfrac{l_{i,X}(\xi)\,d\xi_i}{D_X(\xi)}$ where $l_{i,X}(\xi)$ are linear forms in ξ. It follows that $\pi_X\,(d\pi_X)^{\ell-1}$ can be written as

$$\sum_{|\alpha| = 2\ell-1} D_X(\xi)^{-\ell}\,P_{\alpha,X}(\xi)\,d\xi^{(\alpha)}$$

where the $P_{\alpha,X}(\xi)$ are also linear in ξ. From this we obtain that β is a linear combination of forms $\phi_\alpha(\xi)(d\xi^{(\alpha)}|\mathcal{O})\wedge\sigma^j$ where

$$\phi_\alpha(\xi) = \int_\mathfrak{n} e^{i(\xi,X)}\,D_X(\xi)^{-\ell}\,P_{\alpha,X}(\xi)\quad\phi(X)\,dX$$

We will use the following fact:

3.8 LEMMA. Let C be a compact subset of $\mathfrak{g}_e$. There exists $c > 0$ and $a > 0$ such that for $X\in C$ and $\xi\in\mathcal{O}$ with $Q(\xi)\geqslant c$, one has

$$Q(\xi)\leqslant a\,D_X(\xi) .$$

PROOF. This inequality does not depend on the choice of the quadratic form Q. We consider the Cartan decomposition $\mathfrak{g} = \underline{k}\oplus\underline{p}$

and the dual decomposition $\mathfrak{g}^* = \underline{k}^* + \underline{p}^*$, we choose K-invariant scalar products on $\underline{k}^*$ and $\underline{p}^*$ such that the quadratic form on $\mathfrak{g}$ defined by

$$B(\xi) = \| \xi_0\|^2 - \| \xi_1\|^2 \quad \text{for} \quad \xi = \xi_0 + \xi_1 \ , \ \xi_0 \in \underline{k} \ , \ \xi_1 \in \underline{p} \ ,$$

is G-invariant. We take $Q(\xi) = \| \xi_0\|^2 + \| \xi_1\|^2$. There exists a compact subset $A \subset G$ such that any X in C is of the form $X = g\,H$ with $g \in A$ and $H \in \underline{t}_r$. Then

$$D_X(\xi) = Q(g^{-1} \cdot X\xi) = Q(H \cdot g^{-1}\xi)$$

so that $D_X(\xi) = 0$ if and only if $g^{-1}\xi \in \underline{t}^*$. Since B and Q coincide on $\underline{t}^*$, we have, if $Q(\xi) = 1$ and $D_X(\xi) = 0$ for some $X \in C$,

$$B(\xi) = B(g^{-1}\xi) = Q(g^{-1}\xi),$$

so that, for such ξ , $B(\xi)$ remains greater than a constant $2\varepsilon > 0$. Thus, the conditions $X \in C$, $B(\xi) \leqslant \varepsilon$, $Q(\xi) = 1$, imply $D_X(\xi) \neq 0$. As the function $B(\xi)$ is constant on the G-orbit $\mathcal{O}$, there exists c such that $B(\xi) \leqslant \varepsilon\, Q(\xi)$ for $\xi \in \mathcal{O}$ and $Q(\xi) \geqslant c$. This proves the lemma.

Finally, we prove that the functions $\phi_\alpha|_{\mathcal{O}}$ are rapidly decreasing at infinity. More precisely:

3.9.LEMMA. Let C be the support of the function ϕ and let c be as in Lemma 3.8. For every integer p, there exists a constant K_p such that

$$(1 + Q(\xi))^p \, |\phi_\alpha(\xi)| \leqslant K_p$$

for all $\xi \in \mathcal{O}$ such that $Q(\xi) \geqslant c$.

PROOF. Using integration by parts, it is enough to show that the partial derivatives with respect to the coordinates of X ,

$$\frac{\partial^p}{\partial_{x_1}^{p_1} \, \partial_{x_2}^{p_2} \cdots} \quad (D_X(\xi)^{-\ell} \; P_{\alpha,\,X}(\xi))$$

remain bounded as X varies in $\mathcal{C}$ and ξ in $\mathcal{O}$, with $Q(\xi) \geqslant c$. This expression is of the form

$$R_X(\xi)\ D_X(\xi)^{-(\ell+p)}$$

where $R_X(\xi)$ is a polynomial in ξ of degree $\leqslant 2(\ell+p)$, depending continuously on X. Thus there exists $a' > 0$ such that

$$|R_X(\xi)| \leqslant a'\ Q(\xi)^{(\ell+p)} \leqslant a'a^{(\ell+p)}\ D_X(\xi)^{(\ell+p)},$$

whenever $X \in C$, $\xi \in \mathcal{O}$ and $Q(\xi) \geqslant c$, q.e.d.

The second author was supported in part by the National Science Foundation.

REFERENCES

1 M. F. Atiyah and R. Bott. A Lefschetz fixed point formula for elliptic complexes, I. Ann. of Math. 86(1967) 374-407

2 R. Bott. Vector fields and characteristic numbers, Mich. Math. J. 14(1967) 231-244.

3 J. J. Duistermaat and G. Heckman. On the variation in the cohomology of the symplectic form of the reduced phase space. (To appear)

4. Harish-Chandra. Invariant eigendistributions on a semi-simple Lie algebra. I.H.E.S. Publ. Math. 27(1965) 457-508.

5. A. A. Kirillov. Character of unitary representations of Lie groups. Funct. Anal. and Appl. 2.2 (1968) 40-55.

6. A. A. Kirillov. Elements de la theorie des representations. Editions MIR, Moscou, 1974.

7. B. Kostant. Quantization and unitary representations. in "Modern analysis and applications". L.N. 170, Springer (1970) 87-207.

8. W. Rossmann. Kirillov's character formula for reductive groups. Inv. Math. 48(1978) 207-220.

$\mathbb{L}^2$- COHOMOLOGY FOR GROUPS OF REAL RANK ONE

W. Casselman

Let G be the group of real-valued points on a semi-simple algebraic group defined over $\mathbb{Q}$, which I will assume to be of rank one over both $\mathbb{Q}$ and $\mathbb{R}$. Further let

Γ = an arithmetic subgroup of G

K = a maximal compact subgroup

X = the symmetric space of G, which may be identified with G/K.

E = a finite-dimensional vector space over $\mathbb{C}$, on which G acts by a rational representation.

Let $\mathfrak{g},\mathfrak{k}$ be the complexified Lie algebras of G,K and $\mathfrak{s}$ the orthogonal complement of $\mathfrak{k}$ in $\mathfrak{g}$. Then E possesses a Hermitian metric preserved by K and with respect to which $\mathfrak{s}$ acts by Hermitian matrices. Associated to E and this choice of metric is a locally constant system $\mathcal{E}$ over $\Gamma\backslash X$ and an inner product on it. The $\mathbb{L}^2$-cohomology $H_{(2)}(\Gamma\backslash X,\mathcal{E})$ is defined to be the cohomology of the complex of C^∞ forms ω with values in $\mathcal{E}$ such that ω and $d\omega$ are both square-integrable. It is known (from Borel-Casselman [1983]) that it is finite-dimensional precisely when G possesses a compact Cartan subgroup, <u>which I assume to be the case from now on</u>. With this assumption, the dimension of X is known to be even.

The space $\Gamma\backslash X$ possesses a rather simple compactification $\overline{\Gamma\backslash X}$ obtained by adjoining to it a finite number of points parameterized by the Γ-conjugacy classes of proper rational parabolic subgroups of G. What I am going to do in this paper is to discuss a result due to Zucker [1982] in some cases and Borel in the rest: <u>the $\mathbb{L}^2$-cohomology $H_{(2)}(\Gamma\backslash X,\mathcal{E})$ may be identified with the middle intersection homology</u> $IH^\bullet(\overline{\Gamma\backslash X},\mathcal{E})$ (as defined by Goresky-MacPherson [1980],[1981]).

The only thing new in my treatment will be that instead of proceeding case-by-case for the crux of the argument, as Borel and Zucker do, I will prove a simple geometric lemma which I hope to be more satisfactory.

When X is a Hermitian symmetric space, $\overline{\Gamma\backslash X}$ is the Baily-Borel compactification of $\Gamma\backslash X$. When $\Gamma\backslash X$ is in addition a Shimura variety, the result above will presumably play a role in describing the Hasse-Weil ζ-function of $\overline{\Gamma\backslash X}$ (see Brylinski-Labesse [1982] for some results along these lines). I should also mention that even when G has real rank more than one, but X is Hermitian symmetric, Zucker has conjectured that the $\mathbb{L}^2$-cohomology and the middle intersection cohomology of the Baily-Borel compactification coincide. Borel has proven this for all groups of rational rank one.

1.

Let me begin with a few words about middle intersection (co) homology.

The result to be proven is perhaps best thought of as a generalization of the classical de Rham theorem. For this, beginning as naively as possible, one starts with a manifold M and triangulates it. Then one defines the homology of M (with coefficents in $\mathbb{R}$) in terms of the chain complex of this triangulation. Integration of forms over chains gives a map from the de Rham complex of C^∞ forms on M into the cochain complex, which is asserted to be an isomorphism. Thus the construction of the isomorphism is elementary. But the clearest and perhaps most satisfactory proof introduces sheaf theory. If $\Omega^\bullet$ is any complex of fine sheaves on M resolving $\mathbb{R}$, then the cohomomology of M with coefficients in $\mathbb{R}$ is just the cohomology of the complex $\Gamma(M,\Omega^\bullet)$. Given this very general fact, what is left in order to prove de Rham's theorem is that the sheaf of germs of C^∞ forms is fine (partition of unity) and resolves $\mathbb{R}$ (Poincaré Lemma).

The original definition of intersection (co)homology was in terms of triangulations, but eventually Goresky and MacPherson were able to characterize it much more elegantly in terms of sheaves. For our purposes, it suffices to consider just the simplest stiuation, where only point singularities occur. Thus, let V be a $2n$-dimensional manifold with a set V_0 of isolated singularities called cusps (and assuming as a regularity condition, say, that V may be triangulated with cusps included as vertices). Let $i: V - V_0 \to V$ be the inclusion map, and let E be a locally constant sheaf of finite-dimensional vector spaces over $\mathbb{C}$, defined on $V - V_0$.

1.1 Theorem (Goresky-MacPherson). Suppose $L^\bullet$ to be a non-negative complex of fine sheaves on V such that

(1) There exists an inclusion of $L^\bullet$ into $i_*(\Omega^\bullet(E))$ over all of V which induces an isomorphism $H^\bullet(L^\bullet) \cong E$ over $V - V_0$;

(2) At a cusp the cohomology of the stalk of $L^\bullet$ vanishes in dimension $\geqslant n$ and in dimensions $< n$ the inclusion of $L^\bullet$ into $i_*(\Omega^\bullet(E))$ induces an isomorphism of cohomology.

Then the cohomology of the complex $\Gamma(V,L^\bullet)$ may be identified with $IH^\bullet(V,E)$.

In other words, one does not have to know exactly what intersection cohomology is in order to recognize when one has it to hand.

In our case, take V to be $\Gamma\backslash X$. The sheaf $L^\bullet = L^\bullet_{(2)}(E)$ is to be defined in a somewhat complicated manner. Recall (from Borel-Wallach [1980], Section 2 of Chapter VII) that lifting forms along the canonical projection $pr: \Gamma\backslash G \to \Gamma\backslash X$ allows one to identify C^∞ forms on any open set $U \subseteq \Gamma\backslash X$ with elements of $\mathrm{Hom}_K(\Lambda^\bullet(\mathfrak{g}\backslash\mathfrak{k}), C^\infty(pr^{-1}(U)) \otimes E)$. For any open set $S \subseteq \Gamma\backslash G$ define $\mathbb{L}^{2,\infty}(S)$ to be the space of all functions F on S such that F and all its right derivatives $R_X F$ $(X \in U(\mathfrak{g}))$ are square-integrable. Then the subsheaf $L \subseteq i_*(\Omega^\bullet(E))$ is defined by the condition that $\omega \in \Gamma(U,L^\bullet)$ if and only if the corresponding element of $\mathrm{Hom}_K(\Lambda^\bullet(\mathfrak{g}\backslash\mathfrak{k}), C^\infty(pr^{-1}(U)) \otimes E)$ actually lies locally in $\mathrm{Hom}_K(\Lambda^\bullet(\mathfrak{g}\backslash\mathfrak{k}), \mathbb{L}^{2,\infty}(pr^{-1}(U)) \otimes E)$. The complex of global sections of $L^\bullet$ may be identified with the Lie algebra cohomology $H^\bullet(\mathfrak{g},K, \mathbb{L}^{2,\infty}(\Gamma\backslash G))$, and it is known (see Borel-Casselman [1983]) that this is the same as the $\mathbb{L}^2$-cohomology of E. For this sheaf, condition (1) of Theorem 1.1 is immediate. Hence, in order to prove the claim made in the introduction it suffices now to show that $L^\bullet$ is fine and that it satisfies condition (2) of Theorem 1.1.

In order to show $L^\bullet_{(2)}(E)$ to be fine, it suffices to find for each cusp functions f with support arbitrarily near the cusp, identically one near the cusp, which when lifted to $\Gamma\backslash G$ lie in

$\mathbb{L}^{2,\infty}(\Gamma\backslash G)$. This is done in Zucker [1982] (Proposition 4.4); it is somewhat technical, but not deep.

2.

It is condition (2) that is the crux of the matter. Suppose x to be a cusp of $\overline{\Gamma\backslash X}$, and say it corresponds to the rational parabolic P with Levi factorization $P = MN$. Let

A = The connected component of the maximal $\mathbb{Q}$-split torus in the center of M.

δ = The modulus character $|\det \mathrm{Ad}_{\mathfrak{n}}| : P \to \mathbb{R}^{pos}$ and for each $t > 0$ let

$$P^+(t) = \delta^{-1}(t,\infty)$$

$$A^+(t) = A \cap P^+(t), \text{ etc.}$$

Then as a basis of neighborhoods of x in $\overline{\Gamma\backslash X}$ one may take the images of the sets

$$X_P^+(t) = \Gamma \cap P\backslash P^+(t)/K \cap P$$

in $\Gamma\backslash X$, adjoined to $\{x\}$, for $t \gg 0$.

Since $X = G/K$ is also $P/K\cap P$, a form ω on $\Gamma\backslash X$ can be lifted to one on $\Gamma\backslash P$, and one on $X_P^+(t)$ to one on $\Gamma \cap P\backslash P^+(t)$, and these to an element of $\mathrm{Hom}_{K_P}(\Lambda^\bullet(\mathfrak{p}\backslash \mathfrak{k}_P), C^\infty(\Gamma\cap P\backslash P^+(t))\otimes E)$. If it corresponds to a section of $L^\bullet$, then it induces an element of

$$\mathrm{Hom}_{K_P}(\Lambda^\bullet(\mathfrak{p}\backslash\mathfrak{k}_P), \mathbb{L}^{2,\infty}_{\mathrm{left}}(\Gamma \cap P \backslash P^+(t')) \otimes E).$$

for $t' > t$. Here the "left" refers to a measure on $\Gamma \cap P\backslash P$ induced by a left-invariant Haar measure on P. Since a function f on $\Gamma \cap P\backslash P$ lies in $\mathbb{L}^2_{\mathrm{left}}$ if and only if $f\,\delta^{-1/2}$ lies in $\mathbb{L}^2_{\mathrm{right}}$ this corresponds in turn to an element of

$$\mathrm{Hom}_{K_P}(\Lambda^\bullet(\mathfrak{p}\backslash\mathfrak{k}_P), \mathbb{L}^{2,\infty}_{\mathrm{right}}(\Gamma \cap P\backslash P^+(t')) \otimes E \otimes \delta^{1/2}).$$

This is just the Koszul complex of the $(\mathfrak{p},K_P)$-module $\mathbb{L}^{2,\infty}_{\mathrm{right}} \otimes E \otimes \delta^{1/2}$. Since in considering condition (2) of Theorem 1.1 we are looking at the stalk of $L^{\bullet}$, we are only interested in the direct limit of cohomology as $t \to \infty$, and it can be verified without too much trouble that what remains to be done is to prove:

2.1. Proposition. Let $2n = \dim X$, $t > 0$.

(1) <u>The cohomology</u>

$$H^{\bullet}(\mathfrak{p},K_P, \mathbb{L}^{2,\infty}_{\mathrm{right}}(\Gamma \cap P\backslash P^+(t)) \otimes E \otimes \delta^{1/2}$$

<u>vanishes in dimensions</u> $\geq n$, <u>and</u>

(2) <u>The map of cohomology from this to</u>

$$H^{\bullet}(\mathfrak{p},K_P, C^{\infty}_{*} (\Gamma \cap P\backslash P^+(t)) \otimes E \otimes \delta^{1/2})$$

<u>induced by the natural inclusion is an isomorphism in dimensions</u> $< n$. Here C^{∞}_{*} denotes functions which are the restrictions of functions which are C^{∞} on all $\Gamma \cap P\backslash P$.

Let for the moment V be either of the two $(\mathfrak{p},K_P)$-modules $\mathbb{L}^{2,\infty}_{\mathrm{right}}(\Gamma \cap P\backslash P^+(t))$ or $C^{\infty}_{*}(\Gamma \cap P\backslash P^+(t))$. Then by Hochschild-Serre there exists a spectral sequence converging to $H^{\bullet}(\mathfrak{p},K_P,V \otimes E \otimes \delta^{1/2})$ with E_2-term

$$H^{\bullet}(\mathfrak{m},K_M,H^{\bullet}(\mathfrak{n},V \otimes E \otimes \delta^{1/2})).$$

2.2 Lemma (1) <u>The inclusion of</u> V^N <u>into</u> V <u>induces an isomorphism of</u> $\mathfrak{n}$-<u>cohomology</u> $H^{\bullet}(\mathfrak{n},V^N \otimes E) \cong H^{\bullet}(\mathfrak{n},V \otimes E)$;

(2) <u>The space</u> $\mathbb{L}^{2,\infty}_{\mathrm{right}} (\Gamma \cap P\backslash P^+(t))^N$ (resp. $C^{\infty}_{*}(\Gamma \cap P\backslash P^+(t))^N$) <u>may be identified with</u> $\mathbb{L}^{2,\infty}(\Gamma_M\backslash M^+(t))$ (resp. $C^{\infty}_{*}(\Gamma_M\backslash M^+(t))$.

Here Γ_M is the image in M of $\Gamma \cap P$. Since G has real rank one, this is at most a finite group, and may be taken to be trivial if we pass to at worst a subgroup of finite index in Γ. This is harmless, so <u>I assume</u> $\Gamma_M = \{1\}$.

Part (2) of this is straightforward. Part (1) is of the type of result first proven by Nomizu [1954] and van Est [1958]. A proof is given in Section 1 of Brylinski-Labesse [1982]. Something equivalent can be found in Zucker [1982] (Proposition 4.24) and Borel has also proven a similar result.

2.3 Corollary. There exists a spectral sequence converging to

$$H^{\bullet}(\mathfrak{p}, K_P, \mathbb{L}^{2,\infty}_{right}(\Gamma \cap P \backslash P^+(t)) \otimes E \otimes \delta^{1/2})$$

with E_2-term

$$\mathrm{Ext}^{\bullet}_{(\mathfrak{m}, K_M)}(H_{\bullet}(\mathfrak{n}, \hat{E}) \otimes \delta^{-1/2}, \mathbb{L}^{2,\infty}(M^+(t)))$$

Similarly for $H^{\bullet}(\mathfrak{p}, K_P, C^{\infty}_{*}(\Gamma \cap P\backslash P^+(t)) \otimes E \otimes \delta^{1/2})$.

Here $\hat{E}$ is the contragredient of E.

Since G has real rank one, $M \cong K_M \times A$ and this E_2-term can be simplified even further to

$$\mathrm{Ext}^{\bullet}_{\mathfrak{a}}(H_{\bullet}(\mathfrak{n}, \hat{E}) \otimes \delta^{-1/2}, \mathbb{L}^{2,\infty}(A^+(t))).$$

and similarly for C^{∞}_{*} instead of $\mathbb{L}^{2,\infty}$.

The action of A on $H(\mathfrak{n}, \hat{E})$ is semi-simple, hence a sum of characters χ: $A \to \mathbb{C}^*$. Therefore, Proposition 2.1 follows from the results:

2.4 Lemma. Let χ be any character: $A \to \mathbb{C}^*$. Then

(a) if $|\chi| > 1$ on $A^+(1)$,

$$\mathrm{Ext}^{\bullet}_{\mathfrak{a}}(\chi, \mathbb{L}^{2,\infty}(A^+(t))) = 0;$$

(b) if $|\chi| = 1$ on $A^+(1)$ then $\mathrm{Ext}^0 = 0$ while Ext^1 is infinite-dimensional;

(c) if $|\chi| < 1$ on $A^+(1)$ then $\mathrm{Ext}^1 = 0$ while $\mathrm{Ext}^0 = \mathbb{C}$.

Furthermore,

$$\mathrm{Ext}^{M}_{\mathfrak{a}}(\chi, C^{\infty}(A^{+}(t))) = \begin{cases} \mathbb{C}, & m=0 \\ 0, & m=1. \end{cases}$$

for all χ.

2.5 Proposition. Let χ be an eigencharacter of $H_m(\mathfrak{n},\hat{E}) \otimes \delta^{-1/2}$. Then χ is never unitary, and $|\chi| < 1$ on $A^{+}(1)$ precisely when $m < n$.

The first result will be the concern of the next section.

As for the second, note that $X \cong AN$, since $G = PK$ and $P = ANK_M$. Therefore, the dimension of $\mathfrak{n}$ is $2n - 1$, and the condition $m < n$ is equivalent to $m < 1/2(\dim \mathfrak{n})$.

It is illuminating to follow Zucker and look first at the most elementary case, $G = SO(2n,1)$ and $E = \mathbb{C}$. Then $H_\bullet(\mathfrak{n},\mathbb{C}) \cong \Lambda^\bullet\mathfrak{n} \cong \Lambda^\bullet(\mathbb{C}^{2n-1})$, $A \cong \mathbb{R}^{pos}$ acts as a^m on H_m, $\delta = a^{2n-1}$, and the Proposition is clear. Note that if n were odd then A would act on the middle dimensional homology exactly as $\delta^{1/2}$, and thus by 2.4 the local $L^\bullet$-cohomology would be infinite-dimensional.

Continuing case-by-case is not too difficult since there are only a few cases to be dealt with, but I prefer something else. The following is somewhat stronger than is needed here, but provides perhaps some insight into the mechanism of Zucker's conjecture.

2.6 Proposition. Let G be an arbitrary semi-simple Lie group, and

P = maximal proper parabolic subgroup of G with real Levi decomposition $P = MN$

δ_P = modulus character of P

$M(1) = M \cap \ker(\delta_P)$

E = a finite-dimensional complex representation of G isomorphic to its own complex contragredient.

Thus $M \cong M(1) \times A$ with $A \cong \mathbb{R}^{pos}$. Let σ be an irreducible M-constituent of $H_m(\mathfrak{n},E)$ whose restriction to $M(1)$ is isomorphic to its own complex contragredient, and let ε be the character by which

A act on σ. Then the restriction of $|\varepsilon|$ to $A^+(1)$ is

$$>\ ,\ =\ ,\ \text{or}\ <\ \delta_P^{1/2}$$

according to whether m is

$$>\ ,\ =\ ,\ \text{or}\ <\ 1/2(\dim \mathfrak{n}).$$

In the case at hand the condition on σ is automatic since $M(1) = K_M$ is compact, and that on E is automatic since we have assumed G to possess a compact Cartan. But the more general result stated here is tailored as closely as possible to prove many other cases of Zucker's conjecture when G has rational, but not necessarily real, rank one.

The proof is almost a matter of geometry, given Kostant's well-known result on the structure of $H_\bullet(\mathfrak{n},E)$.

Choose a Borel subgroup B of $G(\mathbb{C})$ contained in $P(\mathbb{C})$ and a maximal torus $T \subseteq M(\mathbb{C}) \cap B$. Let $T(1)$ be the Zariski closure of $M(1) \cap T$.

It is easy to see from the hypothesis on E that since σ is a constituent of $H_m(\mathfrak{n},E)$, $\overline{\sigma}^\wedge \otimes \delta_P$ is one of $H_{n-m}(\mathfrak{n},E)$, where now (for the moment) $n = \dim \mathfrak{n}$ and $\overline{\sigma}^\wedge$ is the complex contragredient of σ. Let χ be the lowest weight of σ (for (B,T)), τ that of $\overline{\sigma}^\wedge \otimes \delta_P$. Then again by hypothesis, χ and τ have the same restriction to $T(1)$. Or: $\chi = \tau\delta_P^s$ for some $s \in \mathbb{R}$. (Here we have $\mathbb{R}$ and not $\mathbb{C}$ because $T/T(1)$ is a $\mathbb{Q}$-split torus).

Let $X(T)$ be the lattice of holomorphic characters of T. In the vector space $X(T) \otimes \mathbb{R}$ let C be the interior of the cone of weights anti-dominant with respect to B. Thus $\delta_B^{-1/2}$ lies in B. For χ to be a lowest weight with respect to $M(1) \cap B$ means that $\chi\delta_P^{-t}$ lies in $\overline{C}$ for $t >> 0$.

There are three cases now to be distinguished: $s > 0$, $s = 0$, and $s < 0$. Since $\delta_P > 1$ on $A^+(1)$ these correspond respectively to $|\chi| > |\tau|, |\chi| = |\tau|$, or $|\chi| < |\tau|$ on $A^+(1)$. Since τ is a weight of $\overline{\sigma}^\wedge \otimes \delta_P$, the restriction of τ to A is $\varepsilon^{-1}\delta_P$, where ε is that of χ to A. So these conditions are in turn equivalent to $|\varepsilon|\ \delta_P^{-1/2} > 1$, $= 1$, or < 1 on $A^+(1)$.

Say for example that $s < 0$. Then $\chi \neq \tau$ at least, and the line from τ through χ continues on to intersect $\overline{C}$. This line shifted by $\delta_B^{-1/2}$, that is to say the line from $\tau\delta_B^{-1/2}$ through $\chi\delta_B^{-1/2}$, will meet not only $\overline{C}$ but even C.

What we now need from Kostant's results on the structure of $H_{\bullet}(\mathfrak{n},E)$ are these: (1) the characters $\chi\delta_B^{-1/2}$ and $\tau\delta_B^{-1/2}$ are regular; (2) if $\chi \neq \tau$ they lie in different Weyl chambers; (3) the number m, the dimension of the homology in which χ occurs, is the same as the number of root hyperplanes separating χ from C. Similarly for τ. In other words, if χ lies in wC with w in the complex Weyl group, then $m = \ell(w)$.

Because χ lies on a line between τ and C, any hyperplane which separates χ and C must also separate τ and C, so by (3) we have $(n-m) \geqslant m$. But by (2) there must exist at least one hyperplane separating τ from C but not χ from C. So in fact $n-m > m$ or $m < \frac{1}{2}(\dim \mathfrak{n})$.

The cases $\delta = 0$, $\delta < 0$ give no new trouble.

Q.E.D.

Given Proposition 2.6, all that remains in order to prove 2.5 is the claim that unitary characters never occur. This is not at all trivial—it is one of the main results of Borel-Casselman [1983].

3.

This section will be spent on Lemma 2.4. I will give two proofs. The first will follow Zucker (Proposition 2.39 of Zucker [1982]) and is entirely elementary. The second is much more complicated, but illustrates what I believe to be an important technique.

First proof. Since Ext^0 is Hom and χ is square-integrable on $A^+(t)$ if and only if $|\chi| < 1$ on $A^+(1)$, all the assertions about Ext^0 are trivial.

As for Ext^1, I use the explicit isomorphism

$$\begin{aligned}\mathrm{Ext}^1_{\mathfrak{a}}(\chi, V) &\cong H^1(\mathfrak{a}, \chi^{-1} \otimes V) \\ &\cong V/(\alpha - d\chi(\alpha))V\end{aligned}$$

where α is a generator of $\mathfrak{a}$. If χ is a character of A, then identifying A with $\mathbb{R}^{pos}$ we have

$$\chi(x) = x^s$$

for some $s \in \mathbb{C}$. The three cases of Lemma 2.5 correspond to the trichotomy $Re(s) > 0$, $Re(s) = 0$, $Re(s) < 0$. The differential $d\chi$ takes $\alpha = xd/dx$ to s. Thus describing Ext^1 is related to solving the differential equation

$$x\frac{d\phi}{dx} - s\phi = f$$

given $f \in \mathbb{L}^{2,\infty}$.

First of all say $Re(s) > 0$. Then for any $f \in \mathbb{L}^{2,\infty}$ we can choose

$$\phi(x) = -x^s \int_x^\infty u^{-s} f(u)(du/u) \quad (x > t)$$

(as we tell our students in the first week of D.E.'s). The integral makes sense since du/u is multiplicatively invariant and both x^{-s} and $f(x)$ are square-integrable. But why does ϕ lie in $\mathbb{L}^{2,\infty}$? For ϕ itself, note that the above integral is the convolution of the $\mathbb{L}^2$ function f with the $\mathbb{L}^1$ function β:

$$\beta(x) = \begin{cases} x^s & x \leqslant 1 \\ 0 & x > 1 \end{cases}$$

and hence is itself $\mathbb{L}^2$. I leave it as an exercise to check the property for all the derivatives $(xd/dx)^n\phi$.

For 6.1(c), given $f \in \mathbb{L}^{2,\infty}(A^+(t))$ define

$$\phi(x) = x^s \int_t^x u^{-s} f(u)(du/u).$$

This is the convolution of f with a new β:

$$\beta(x) = \begin{cases} x^s & x \geqslant 1 \\ 0 & x < 1 \end{cases}$$

So the same reasoning applies.

As for 6.1(b), we do not really need it, and I leave it also as as an exercise. (Hint: one may as well assume $s = 0$.)

To conclude the proof of 2.4 all that remains are the assertions about $C_*^\infty(A^+(t))$. But these are clear, after applying the second integral above.

This concludes my first proof of Lemma 2.4.

The second proof will illustrate a principle I hope will play a role in many different situations involving cohomology and automorphic forms. The point is that from the considerations above it is more or less clear that calculating Ext-groups is closely related to solving differential equations, and as is well known one technique in doing this is to apply the Fourier transform.

What I am interested in is a characterization of the functions in $\mathbb{L}^{2,\infty}(A^+(t))$ in terms of their multiplicative Fourier transforms. It will do no harm to set $t = 1$, and it will simplify notation to work with the additive group of $\mathbb{R}$ rather than the multiplicative group $\mathbb{R}^{pos}$. This means only that I must choose a new coordiante by exponentiation. In other words, I will look at $\mathbb{L}^2(0,\infty)$ with respect to the measure dx.

The starting point is a classical result of Paley-Wiener (I refer to Chapter 3, Section 3.4 of Dym-McKean [1972] for a simplified proof). Given $f \in \mathbb{L}^2(0,\infty)$ its Fourier transform

$$\hat{f}(s) = \int_0^\infty e^{-sx} f(x)\,dx$$

is defined and holomorphic in the region $\mathrm{Re}(s) > 0$. The boundary value of $\hat{f}(s)$ along $i\mathbb{R}$ is the usual $\mathbb{L}^2$ Fourier transfrom of f. The content of the theorem of Paley-Wiener is that the Fourier transforms $F(s)$ of all of $\mathbb{L}^2(0,\infty)$ are characterized by these two properties:

(a) $F(s)$ is analytic for $\mathrm{Re}(s) > 0$;

(b) There exists a common bound for all the integrals

$$\int_{\sigma - i\infty}^{\sigma + i\infty} |F(s)|^2 d|s| \qquad (\sigma > 0).$$

This upper bound may be taken as the $\mathbb{L}^2$-norm of the ordinary transform of f. Such functions are called Hardy functions.

The subspace $\mathbb{L}^{2,\infty}(0,\infty)$ may be topologized by the $\mathbb{L}^2$-norms of its derivatives. Call $H^{2,\infty}$ its topological dual: this, rather than $\mathbb{L}^{2,\infty}$, is the space I really want to look at. Since truncation in $(-\infty,0)$ gives a continuous $\mathfrak{a}$-morphism from the Schwartz space $S(\mathbb{R})$ into $\mathbb{L}^{2,\infty}(0,\infty)$, the space $H^{2,\infty}$ may be considered as a subspace of that of tempered distribution with support on $[0,\infty)$. Hence any $\Phi \in H^{2,\infty}$ also possesses as Fourier transform a function $F(s)$ analytic for $Re(s) > 0$ (and whose boundary value on $i\mathbb{R}$ is a tempered distribution, the usual transform of Φ).

There are two kinds of derivatives of a function in $\mathbb{L}^{2,\infty}$. On the one hand if $f \in \mathbb{L}^{2,\infty}$ then by definition so do all the $(d/dx)^n f$, again considered as functions on $(0,\infty)$. But f may also be considered as a distribution, and its derivative as such is not the same. It is easy to see that any function in $\mathbb{L}^{2,\infty}$ is in the neighborhood of 0 the restriction of a C^∞ function on all of $\mathbb{R}$, and as a distribution the derivative of f is $f' + f(0)\,\delta_0$, its second derivative $f'' + f(0)\,\delta_0' + f'(0)\,\delta_0$, etc. In other words the $\mathfrak{a}$-module $\mathbb{L}^{2,\infty}(0,\infty)$ ($\mathfrak{a}$ acting by the first differentiation) is not self-dual.

For this reason, the Fourier transforms of functions in $\mathbb{L}^{2,\infty}$ are difficult to characterize: the Laplace transform of f' is $s\hat{f}(s) - f(0)$. But those of $H^{2,\infty}$ are no problem.

3.1 Proposition. A function $F(s)$ in $Re(s) > 0$ is the Fourier transform of some $\Phi \in H^{2,\infty}$ if an only if $(1 + s)^{-n}F(s)$ is a Hardy function for some $n \geqslant 0$.

Proof. Let $AC^1(0,\infty)$ be the space of all $f \in \mathbb{L}^2(0,\infty)$ which are absolutely continuous and such that f' also lies in $\mathbb{L}^2(0,\infty)$. Let D be the operator $f \longrightarrow f'$ with domain $AC^1(0,\infty)$. Define $AC^n (n > 1)$ inductively: $f \in AC^n$ if and only if $f \in AC^1$ and Df lies in AC^{n-1}. Thus $\mathbb{L}^{2,\infty} = \cap\, AC^n$ $(n > 0)$.

3.2 Lemma. For any $\lambda \in \mathbb{C}$ with $Re(\lambda) > 0$, $(D - \lambda)$ is a bijection of $AC^1(0,\infty)$ and $\mathbb{L}^2(0,\infty)$.

In other words, the spectrum of D has no points in the right half-plane. The proof is trivial: we clearly have no kernel, and

$$(D - \lambda)^{-1} f(x) = - \int_x^\infty e^{-\lambda(t-x)} f(t)dt.$$

Composition with the truncation map gives a diagram

$$S(\mathbb{R}) \longrightarrow AC \xrightarrow{n(D-\lambda)^n} \mathbb{L}^2$$

and dual to this is

$$\mathbb{L}^2 \xrightarrow{(-d/dx-\lambda)^n} \text{dual of } AC^n \rightarrow \text{tempered distributions}$$

Applying the Lemma n times, one sees that the dual of AC^n consists of all tempered distributions which can be written as $(d/dx + \lambda)^n$ applied to some $f \in \mathbb{L}^2$. Since the dual of $\mathbb{L}^{2,\infty}$ is just the union of the duals of the AC^n, and since under Fourier transformation d/dx corresponds to multiplication by s, this proves the Proposition.

Precisely because d/dx corresponds to multiplication by s under Fourier transformation, this Proposition presents a fairly clear picture of $H^{2,\infty}$ as an $\mathfrak{a}$-module. In particular:

<u>3.3 Proposition.</u> <u>The operator</u> $d/dx - \lambda$, <u>for</u> $Re(\lambda) \neq 0$, <u>is an injection of</u> $H^{2,\infty}$ <u>into itself with closed image.</u>

<u>3.4 Corollary.</u> <u>For</u> $Re(\lambda) \neq 0$ <u>the operator</u> $d/dx - \lambda$ <u>is a surjection from</u> $\mathbb{L}^{2,\infty}$ <u>onto itself.</u> <u>In other words,</u> $Ext^1_{\mathfrak{a}}(\chi, \mathbb{L}^{2,\infty}(0,\infty)) = 0$ <u>for</u> $|\chi| \neq 1$.

The reasoning used here is hardly a simple proof of Lemma 2.4. But Proposition 3.3 strikes me as interesting in its own right. Similar results in other contexts will always have cohomological significance. I summarize it by saying that $H^{2,\infty}$ is a <u>Paley-Wiener module</u> with respect to $\mathfrak{a}$ over the spectrum $\mathbb{C} - i\mathbb{R}$. (For another cohomological application of a type of Paley-Wiener theorem, see Casselman [1983]).

4. SOME FINAL REMARKS.

The method used by Borel to prove Zucker's conjecture for all rational rank one groups are along the same lines used above, except in one very interesting case. Suppose D is a central devision algebra, say of degree d, over a quadratic imaginary extension of $\mathbb{Q}$. Let τ be the involution of D which amounts to conjugation of matrix coefficients on $D_{\mathbb{R}} \cong M_d(\mathbb{C})$. Let $\mathbb{Q}$ be the Hermitian form $xx^{\tau} - yy^{\tau}$ on D^2, and let $G = SU(Q)$. The corresponding real group is $SU(n,n)$, but the rational rank of G is one. The Baily-Borel compactification is obtained by adding cusps, and the corresponding parabolic subgroups P have $N \cong$ {Hermitian dxd matrices}, $M \cong GL_d(\mathbb{C})$. In this case, Borel tells me, one needs the very precise vanishing theorems of Enright [1980] in order to prove Zucker's conjecture. This strongly suggests an important role for vanishing theorems when the rational rank is more than one.

Another open question is a more direct construction of the isomorphism of $\mathbb{L}^2$- cohomology and $IH^{\bullet}$. For example, Cheeger [1980] was able to integrate $\mathbb{L}^2$-cocycles over almost all the chains satisfying the suitable perversity condition. Can something similar be done here? Along the same lines, one knows that certain $\mathbb{L}^2$-cohomology arises from residues of Eisenstein's series. Can one relate these residues to specific cycles on $\Gamma\backslash X$?

Supported by the National Science and Engineering Research Council of Canada.

REFERENCES

[1] A. Borel and W. Casselman, L^2-cohomology of locally symmetric manifolds of finite volume, preprint, 1983.

[2] A. Borel and N. Wallach, Continuous cohomology, discrete subgroups, and representations of reductive groups, Ann. of Math. Studies 94, Princeton University Press, Princeton, 1980.

[3] J.L. Brylinski and J.P. Labesse, Cohomologie d'intersection et fonctions L de certaines variétés de Shimura, preprint, 1982.

[4] W. Casselman, Automorphic forms and a Hodge theory for congruence subgroups of $SL_2(\mathbb{Z})$, preprint, 1983.

[5] J. Cheeger, Geometry of the Laplace operator, in Proc. Symp. Pure Math. XXXVI, A.M.S., Providence, 1980.

[6] J. Cheeger, M. Goresky, R. MacPherson, L^2-cohomology and intersection homology of singular algebraic varieties, in Seminar on Differential Geometry, Ann. of Math. Studies, Princeton University Press, Princeton, 1982.

[7] H. Dym and H.P. McKean, Fourier series and integrals, Academic Press, New York, 1972.

[8] T. Enright, Relative Lie algebra cohomology and unitary representations of complex Lie groups, Duke Math. J. 46(1979), 513-525.

[9] W.T. van Est, A generalization of the Cartan-Leray spectral sequence II, Proc. Koninkl. Ned. Ak. v. Wet. Amsterdam, series A, 61(1958), pp. 406-413.

[10] M. Goresky and R. MacPherson, Intersection homology theory, Topology 19 (1980), pp. 135-162.

[11] M. Goresky and R. MacPherson, Intersection Homology II, Invent. Math. 72(1983), 77-129.

[12] K. Nomizu, On the cohomology of compact homogeneous spaces of nilpotent Lie groups, Ann. of Math. 59(1954), pp. 531-538.

[13] M. Reed and B. Simon, Methods of modern mathematical physics I., Academic Press, New York, 1972.

[14] S. Zucker, L^2-cohomology of warped products and arithmetic groups, Invent. Math. 70(1982), 169-218.

CHARACTER RELATIONS BETWEEN SINGULAR HOLOMORPHIC REPRESENTATIONS

Heather Willow Chang

This note is a complement to [EHW] and [Hol] in this volume.

For the goups $G = SU_{p,q}$, $Sp_{2n}(\mathbb{R})$, and SO^*_{2n}, it has been shown in [EHW] that all unitary holomorphic representations arise by embedding G (or more precisely by embedding $G = U_{p,q}$, $\tilde{S}p_{2n}(\mathbb{R})$, and O^*_{2n}) as one member of a dual pair (G,G') in some symplectic group where G' is compact, and decomposing the restriction of the oscillator representation. If we fix G and let G' vary, then we obtain various families of holomorphic representations of G. For G' very small, we obtain singular holomorphic representations of G, of some fixed Gelfand-Kirillov dimension. For G' large, we obtain holomorphic discrete series, which are repeated over and over as G' increases in size. Together these families exhaust the holomorphic unitary representations of G.

On the other hand, we can reverse our viewpoint and fix G'. Then to each representation σ' of G' we can associate, for all sufficiently large G, a holomorphic representation σ of G. In other words, associated to σ' we have a family of pairs (G,σ) where G is the other member of some dual pair containing G', and σ is a holomorphic representation of G. It is natural to ask whether there is some relation, some family resemblance, among the various σ associated to a fixed σ', and whether this resemblance can be expressed directly, without any explicit mention of σ. The answer to both these questions is yes. One connection between these σ is that they have in some sense the "same" K-spectra (K being the maximal compact subgroup of G). This is described precisely in [Hol]. Here we want to use the results of [Hol] to express the relationship between the various σ in an even more direct way: one can describe the character of one σ in terms of that of another.

Thus if (G_1,σ_1) and (G_2,σ_2) are two pairs of groups - with - representation associated to σ', we will give a formula relating the characters of σ_1 and σ_2. We emphasize this is a character relation, not a character formula. The character of neither σ_1 nor σ_2 is given explicitly. Rather a formula is given such that if we know that character of σ_1, we can compute that of σ_2. In particular, it will follow that the character of every unitary holomorphic representation can be computed if one knows those of maximal Gelfand-Kirillov dimension. Explicit character formulas have been given by Parthasarathy [P] for unitary holomorphic representations of non-singular infinitesimal character, and by Rawnsley, Schmid and Wolf [RSW] for the set of representations they construct, which includes most holomorphic unitary representations. Hence the character relations described here will do little to further explicit knowledge of character values. However, the author feels these relations are of intrinsic interest in that they demonstrate a close connection between representations of different groups of the same type, a connection which might not immediately force itself on one after a perusal of the character formulas, which are moderately complicated.

Since the results of [Hol] are stated for $U_{p,q}$ we will restrict the discussion here also to that family of groups. Similar results for $\tilde{S}p_{2n}(\mathbb{R})$ and O^*_{2n} are obtainable by analogous procedures.

We follow the notation of [Hol],§4. In particular, we label a representation of U_p by a pair of Young's diagrams D_1 and D_2; thus a typical representation of U_p is denoted $\sigma_p(D_1,D_2)$. The Young's diagrams must satisfy $\text{rk } D_1 + \text{rk } D_2 \leqslant p$, where $\text{rk } D$ is the number of non-zero rows of D. The polynomial representations of U_p are those for which $D_2 = \emptyset$, the empty diagram, with no non-zero rows. These representations will simply be specified by their first Young's diagram; thus we write $\sigma_p(D_1, \emptyset) = \sigma_p(D_1)$. Also we allow ourselves the flexibility, at a cost of some redundancy, of twisting representations by $\det_p$, the determinant representation of U_p. Thus sometimes we will denote a representation of U_p by $\det_p^\ell \otimes \sigma_p(D_1,D_2)$, where $\ell \in \mathbb{Z}$, instead of modifying D_1 and D_2 in order to incorporate the factor $\det_p^\ell$.

The basis for our computation is the fact that, given a Young's diagram D, and $p,q \geq \mathrm{rk}\, D$, there is a direct relation between the characters of $\sigma_p(D)$ and $\sigma_q(D)$. We will describe this relation which is a formal consequence of the Weyl character formula.

Let $T_p = T$ the standard diagonal torus in U_p. Denote a typical element $t \in T$ by the p-tuple of its diagonal elements:

$$t = (Z_1, Z_2, \ldots, Z_p) \qquad Z_i \in \mathbb{C},\ |Z_i| = 1 \tag{1}$$

For a Young's diagram D with rows of length a_i, and $\mathrm{rk}\, D \leq p$, define a character e_p^D of T_p by

$$e_p^D(t) = \prod_i Z_i^{a_i} \tag{2}$$

Define also a character $\delta_p = \delta$ by

$$\delta_p(t) = \prod_i Z_i^{p-i} \tag{3}$$

The symmetric group S_p is the Weyl group of U_p. It acts on T by permuting the coordinates of t. We will need the action of S_p on functions on T by precomposition:

$$\nu^*(f)(t) = f(\nu^{-1}(t)) \tag{4}$$

for $\nu \in S_p$ and f a function on T.

Let $\chi_p(D)$ denote the character of $\sigma_p(D)$. It is a conjugation invariant function on U_p, so is determined by its restriction to T. For a character λ of T, define

$$\Delta(\lambda) = \sum_{\nu \in S_p} (\mathrm{sgn}\ \nu)\ \nu^*(\lambda) \tag{5}$$

where sgn is the usual signum character of S_p. Then for a Young's diagram D of rank $\leq p$ set

$$\Delta_p(D) = \Delta(e_p^D \delta_p) \tag{6}$$

Then

$$\Delta_p(\emptyset) = \Delta(\delta_p) = \prod_{i<j}(Z_i - Z_j) \tag{7}$$

is Weyl's denominator for U_p. The Weyl character formula says that, as functions on T one has

$$\Delta_p(\emptyset)\chi_p(D) = \Delta_p(D) \tag{8}$$

Now take $p \geqslant q \geqslant \text{rk } D$. We identify T_q with the subgroup of T_p whose elements have their last $p-q$ coordinates equal to 1. We denote by T'_{p-q} the subgroup of T_p whose elements have their first q coordinates equal to 1. We obviously have a direct sum decomposition:

$$T_p \cong T_q \times T'_{p-q} \tag{9}$$

Let $\pi_{p,q} = \pi$ be projection onto the first factor of this decomposition. Let $\pi'_{p,q} = \pi'$ be the projection onto the second factor. We identify T'_{p-q} with T_{p-q} in the obvious way, by decreasing the index on each of its coordinates by p. For any object associated to T_{p-q} the analogous object on T'_{p-q} will be denoted by adding a prime to it. Thus δ_{p-q} becomes δ'_{p-q} and so on. Given a function f on T_q, we write

$$\pi^*(f) = f \circ \pi \tag{10}$$

even though this notation is not quite consistent with (4). Observe that the subgroup $S_q \times S'_{p-q}$ of S_p commutes with the decomposition (9) and hence with the maps π and π'.

With the conventions just made, the following formula is a trivial consequence of definition (3)

$$\delta_p = \pi^*(\delta_q \det_q{}^{p-q})(\delta'_{p-q} \circ \pi') \tag{11}$$

In the formulas to come, we will write the coset space

$S_p/(S_p \times S'_{p-q}) = C_{p,q} = C$. We now compute, for our Young's diagram D of rank $\leqslant q$, the sum

$$\Delta_p(D) = \sum_{\nu \in S_p} (\operatorname{sgn} \nu)\, \nu^*(e_p^D \delta_p)$$

$$= \sum_{\eta \in C} (\operatorname{sgn} \eta)\eta^*\Big(\sum_{\lambda \in S_q} \sum_{\mu \in S'_{p-q}} (\operatorname{sgn} \lambda\mu)\lambda^*\mu^* (\pi^*(e_q^D \delta_q \det_q{}^{p-q})(\delta'_{p-q} \circ \pi'))$$

$$= \sum_{\eta \in C} (\operatorname{sgn} \eta)\eta^*\Big(\sum_{\lambda \in S_q} (\operatorname{sgn} \lambda)\lambda^*(\pi^*(e_q^D \delta_q \det_q^{p-q})) \Big(\sum_{\mu \in S'_{p-q}} (\operatorname{sgn} \mu)\mu^*(\delta'_{p-q} \circ \pi') \qquad (12)$$

$$= \sum_{\eta \in C} (\operatorname{sgn} \eta)\eta^*((\pi^*\Delta_q(D))(\pi^*(\det_q))^{p-q} (\Delta'_{p-q}(\emptyset) \circ \pi'))$$

$$= \sum_{\eta \in C} (\operatorname{sgn} \eta)\eta^*(\Delta'_{p-q}(\emptyset) \circ \pi')(\eta^*\pi^*(\det_q))^{p-q} \eta^*\pi^*(\Delta_q(D))$$

Thus if we define for a function f on T_q the function $\tilde{R}_{p,q}(f)$ on T_p by the formula

$$\tilde{R}_{p,q}(f) = \sum_{\eta \in C} (\operatorname{sgn} \eta)\eta^*(\Delta'_{p-q}(\emptyset) \circ \pi')(\eta^*\pi^*(\det_q))^{p-q} \eta^*\pi^*(f) \qquad (13)$$

then the computation (12) shows

$$\Delta_p(D) = \tilde{R}_{p,q}(\Delta_q(D)) \qquad (14)$$

Combining this with the Weyl character formula gives

$$\Delta_p(\emptyset)\chi_p(D) = \tilde{R}_{p,q}(\Delta_q(\emptyset)\chi_q(D)) \qquad (15)$$

In other words the linear map

$$R_{p,q}: f \to \Delta_p(\emptyset)^{-1}\tilde{R}_{p,q}(\Delta_q(\emptyset)f) \tag{16}$$

from functions on T_q to functions on T_p takes irreducible characters of polynomial representations to irreducible characters, and preserves the parametrization of these characters by Young's diagrams.

For the correspondences associated to dual pairs, we will need a slight variant of the map $R_{p,q}$. Specifically, for any $r \in \mathbb{Z}$, we will want a map that takes the character of $\det_q{}^{r/2} \otimes \sigma_q(D)$ to the character of $\det_p{}^{r/2} \otimes \sigma_p(D)$. Evidently this is accomplished by the map

$$R^r_{p,q}: f \to \det_p{}^{r/2} R_{p,q}(\det_q{}^{-r/2} f) \tag{17}$$

Of course, strictly speaking, when we deal with half-integer powers of $\det_p$, we are not actually working on T_p, but on a two-fold cover $\tilde{T}_p$ of T_p.

We will also need the complex conjugates of the map $R^r_{p,q}$. These are defined by

$$\overline{R}^r_{p,q}(f) = (R^r_{p,q}(\overline{f}))^- \tag{18}$$

Here $\overline{f}$ is the complex conjugate of the function f. Evidently one has $\overline{R}_{p,q}(\overline{\chi}_q(D)) = \overline{\chi}_p(D)$, and an analogous relation for $\overline{R}^r_{p,q}$. Note that $\overline{\chi}_q(D)$ is the character of $\sigma_q(D)^*$, the contragredient of $\sigma_q(D)$.

Consider now the dual pair $(U_{p,q}, U_r)$ and the associated correspondence of representations. This is in fact a correspondence between representations of $\tilde{U}_{p,q}$ and $\tilde{U}_r$ where $\tilde{U}_r$ is the two-fold cover of U_r on which $\det_r^{\frac{1}{2}}$ is a well-defined function, and similarly for $\tilde{U}_{p,q}$. Thus a representation of $\tilde{U}_r$ can be represented in the form $\det_r^{\ell/2} \otimes \sigma_r(D_1, D_2)$.

Denote by $\rho^r_{p,q}(D_1, D_2)$ the holomorphic representation of $\tilde{U}_{p,q}$ which corresponds to the representation $\det_r^{\frac{p-q}{2}} \otimes \sigma_r(D_1, D_2)$ of $\tilde{U}_r$.

(This is not the notation of [Hol] ; but we adopt it to emphasize the role of D_1 and D_2) . In order for $\rho^r_{p,q}(D_1,D_2)$ to exist one needs $p \geq \operatorname{rk} D_1$ and $q \geq \operatorname{rk} D_2$. In particular, if $p,q \geq r$, (the stable range) then all representations $\sigma_r(D_1,D_2)$ of U_r give rise to representations $\rho^r_{p,q}(D_1,D_2)$ of $\tilde{U}_{p,q}$.

The maximal compact subgoup of $\tilde{U}_{p,q}$ is covered twice by $\tilde{U}_p \times \tilde{U}_q$. The representations of $\tilde{U}_p \times \tilde{U}_q$ which occur in the (pull back of the) restrictions of the representations $\rho^r_{p,q}(D_1,D_2)$ have the form

$$\begin{aligned} &\det_p^{r/2} \otimes \sigma_p(D_3,\emptyset) \otimes \det_q^{-r/2} \sigma_q(\emptyset,D_4) \quad \text{(outer tensor product)} \\ &\quad = \det_p^{r/2} \sigma_p(D_3) \otimes (\det_q^{r/2} \sigma_q(D_4))^* \end{aligned} \tag{19}$$

where $(\det_q{}^{r/2}\sigma_q(D_4))^*$ is the representation contragredient to $\det_q^{r/2} \sigma_q(D_4)$. Here D_3 and D_4 must satisy

$$\operatorname{rk} D_3 \leq \min(p,r) \qquad \operatorname{rk} D_4 \leq \min(q,r)$$

Hence for $p,q \geq r$ (the stable range), the Young's diagrams D_3 and D_4 occurring in (19) are all those of rank at most r , independently of p and q .

Let $m(D_3,D_4;\, D_1,D_2)$ be the multiplicity with which the representation (19) of $\tilde{U}_p \times \tilde{U}_q$ occurs in $\rho^r_{p,q}(D_1,D_2)$. Proposition 4.1 of [Hol] shows this multiplicity is independent of p and q so long as $p,q \geq r$, and so justifies the omission of p and q from the notation. Now the formal or "K-character" of $\rho^r_{p,q}(D_1,D_2)$ is

$$\sum_{\operatorname{rk} D_3 \leq r \geq \operatorname{rk} D_4} m(D_3,D_4;D_1,D_2) \det_p^{r/2} \chi_p(D_3) \otimes (\det_q^{r/2} \chi_q(D_4))^{-} \tag{20}$$

where $^-$ indicates complex conjugate. The independence of multiplicity from p and q , and the formulas (14) through (18) suggest the following result.

THEOREM 1: Suppose $p' \geq p \geq r$ and $q' \geq q \geq r$. Let $\operatorname{ch}\rho_{p,q}(D_1,D_2)$ denote the character of $\rho^r_{p,q}(D_1,D_2)$, for Young's diagrams such that $\operatorname{rk} D_1 + \operatorname{rk} D_2 \leq r$, regarded as a smooth function on the regular points of $\tilde{U}_{p,q}$; and likewise for $\tilde{U}_{p',q'}$. Then, as a function on the regular elements of the compact torus $\tilde{T}_{p'} \times \tilde{T}_{q'} \subseteq \tilde{U}_{p'} \times \tilde{U}_{q'}$, one has the formula

$$\operatorname{ch}\rho^r_{p',q'}(D_1,D_2) = R^r_{p',p} \otimes \overline{R}^r_{q',q}\,(\operatorname{ch}\rho^r_{p,q}(D_1,D_2)) \tag{21}$$

The proof of theorem 1 depends on the following observation.

THEOREM 2: The holomorphic representations $\rho^r_{p,q}(D_1,D_2)$ of $\tilde{U}_{p,q}$ extend from $\tilde{U}_{p,q}$ to a subsemigroup with interior of the complexification $\tilde{GL}_{p,q}(\mathbb{C})$ of $\tilde{U}_{p,q}$. The map $g \to \rho^r_{p,q}(D_1,D_2)(g)$ is holomorphic on the interior of this subsemigroup, and the elements of the interior are sent to trace class operators.

REMARKS: a) A consequence of theorem 2, the main one as far as the proof of Theorem 1 is concerned, is that $\operatorname{ch}\rho^r_{p,q}(D_1,D_2)$ continues to a holomorphic function on an open subset of $\tilde{GL}_{p,q}(\mathbb{C})$ bordering on $\tilde{U}_{p,q}$. This phenomenon was exploited by Hecht [He] in his study of characters of holomorphic representations, and indeed Harish-Chandra in his original study [HC] of holomorphic discrete series makes use of essentially this fact.

b) Theorem 2 is by no means restricted to $U_{p,q}$; it is valid for arbitrary holomorphic representations of groups with Hermitian symmetric structure. The proof we will give is somewhat <u>ad hoc</u>, but it is convenient in our present context, and extends immediately to $Sp_{2n}(\mathbb{R})$ and O^*_{2n}. A general <u>a priori</u> proof, valid even for Eudidean Lie algebras is given in [RW].

PROOF of theorem 2: (sketch) Theorem 2 is a simple consequence of a formula for the operators of the oscillator representation. Unfortunately, the author does not know where to find this formula in the required form in the literature, and does not wish to derive it here, although it is not especially difficult to do so. Therefore we will simply state here the formula we need; it is taken from unpublished work of R. Howe (c.f.[Ho2] for the finite field analogue, for which the proof is quite similar).

The members of the dual pair $(U_{p,q}, U_r)$ belong to $Sp_{2r(p+q)}(\mathbb{R})$, which acts on $\mathbb{R}^{2r(p+q)}$, to be denoted W, preserving a symplectic form which we will denote $<,>$. Let ω denote the oscillator representation of $\tilde{S}p(W)$, the two-fold cover of $Sp(W)$. Let $\mathcal{Y}$ be the space of ω, and let $\mathcal{Y}^\infty \subseteq \mathcal{Y}$ be the subspace of smooth vectors for $\omega(\tilde{S}p(W))$. According to [Ho3] the operators on $\mathcal{Y}^\infty$ can be regarded as distributions on W. The distributions associated to elements of $\omega(\tilde{S}p(W))$ all have the form

$$e^{iB(v,v)}dv$$

where $V \subseteq W$ is a linear subspace, dv is a Haar measure on V, and B is a symmetric bilinear form on V. More precisely, for those $g \in Sp$ with no fixed vectors in W, one has the formula

$$\omega(\tilde{g}) = ch\omega(\tilde{g})\, e^{(1/2)\pi \, < C(g)W,W>} dw \tag{22}$$

where $\tilde{g}$ is one of the inverse images of g in $\tilde{S}p(W)$, and

$$C(g) = \frac{g+1}{g-1} \tag{23}$$

is the Cayley transform from $Sp(W)$ to its Lie algebra $\mathfrak{sp}(W)$, and $ch\omega(\tilde{g})$ is the character of ω at $\tilde{g}$. A detailed description of $ch\omega(\tilde{g})$ is given in [T]. We note

$$|ch\omega(\tilde{g})| = |\det_W(1-g)|^{-\frac{1}{2}} \tag{24}$$

where $\det_W$ is the determinant of a linear transformation on W.

The form

$$B_g(W_1,W_2) = <C(g)W_1,W_2> \qquad w_i \in W$$

is a symmetric bilinear form on W. If in formula (22) we allow ourselves to replace B_g with a complex-valued bilinear form with positive definite imaginary part, then we obtain the semigroup with the desired properties. Since the functions

$$e^{i(B_1(W,W) + iB_2(W,W))} \tag{25}$$

where B_i are symmetric bilinear forms and B_2 is positive definite, are Schwartz class functions, the operators T_{B_1,B_2} to which they give rise are certainly trace class. One can check directly from the convolution formula in [Ho3] that the composition of two of the operators T_{B_1,B_2} is up to multiples a third one, so that we have a semigroup. Furthermore, the same computation, together with formula (23) serves to verify that the law of composition of the T_{B_1,B_2} is just a complexification of the group law of Sp. This is how one proves the Theorem 2 for $\tilde{Sp}$. To deal with $\tilde{U}_{p,q}$ one simply restricts attention to the appropriate subsemigroup. This concludes our discussion of Theorem 2.

REMARKS: The semigroup of the T_{B_1,B_2}, or rather an appropriate enlargement of it, is the real analogue of the "oscillator semigroup" for finite fields discussed in [Ho2]. The famous "heat semigroup", the fundamental solution to the heat equation

$$\frac{\partial\phi}{\partial t} = \Delta\phi$$

where $\phi \in C^{\infty}(\mathbb{R}^n)$ and Δ is the Laplacian, is a one-parameter subsemigroup of this extended "oscillator semigroup".

PROOF of theorem 1: Consider the compact Cartan subgroup $\tilde{T}_p \cdot \tilde{T}_q$ of $\tilde{U}_{p,q}$. Let $S_{p,q}$ denote the complex subsemigroup of the "oscillator semigroup" generated by $\tilde{T}_p \cdot \tilde{T}_q$. The group $T_p \cdot T_q \simeq T_{p+q}$ is a product of circles T_i, $1 \leqslant i \leqslant p+q$, corresponding to the elements of T_{p+q} which have only the i-th coordinate (as in equation (1) not equal to 1. The 2-fold cover $\tilde{T}_i$ of this is again a circle, and it is straightforward to verify that the complex subsemigroup generated by $\tilde{T}_i$ is just a complex disk Δ_i, with $\tilde{T}_i$ as the boundary. The product of the Δ_i maps surjectively with finite fibres onto $S_{p,q}$.

The functions $\det_p^{r/2}\chi_p(D_3) \otimes (\det_q^{r/2}\chi_q(D_4))^-$ in the sum (20) extend to holomorphic functions on $S_{p,q}$. Similar remarks apply with p',q' in place of p,q . Also it is clear that the formula

$$\det{}_{p'}^{r/2}\chi_{p'}(D_3) \otimes (\det{}_{q'}^{r/2}\,\chi_{q'}(D_4))^{-} =$$

$$R^{r}_{p',p} \otimes R^{r}{}_{q',q}\ (\det{}_{p}^{r/2}\,\chi_p(D_3) \otimes (\det{}_{q}^{r/2}\,\chi_q(D_4))^{-}) \qquad (26)$$

is valid as an identity of holomorphic functions on $S_{p',q'}$. But on the interior of $S_{p',q'}$, the partial sums of expression (20) converge absolutely and uniformly on compacta to a holomorphic function, which will certainly equal $\mathrm{tr}\rho^{r}_{p,q}(D_1,D_2)$ (s), for s in the interior of $S_{p,q}$. By a continuity argument, which we omit, this is just the continuation into all of $S_{p,q}$ of $\mathrm{ch}\rho^{r}_{p,q}$. Taking boundary values, theorem 1 follows.

REFERENCES

[EHW] T. Enright, R. Howe, and N. Wallach, A classification of unitary highest weight modules, this volume.

[HC] Harish-Chandra, Representations of semisimple Lie groups, IV, Am J. Math. 77(1955), 743-777; V. Am. J. Math, 78 (1956), 1-41.

[He] H. Hecht, The Caracters of some Representations of Harish-Chandra, Math.Ann. 219, 213-226 (1976).

[Ho1] R. Howe, Reciprocity laws in the theory of dual pairs, this volume.

[Ho2] R. Howe, Invariant theory and duality for classical groups over finite fields, preprint

[Ho3] R. Howe, Quantum Mechanics and Partial Differential Equations, J. Fun. Anal, 38 (1980), 188-254.

[P] R. Parthasarathy, Criteria for the unitarizability of some highest weight modules, Proc. Ind. Acad. Sci. 89 (1980), 1-24.

[RSW] J. Rawnsley, W. Schmid and J. Wolf, Singular unitary representations and indefinite harmonic theory, preprint.

[RW] A. Rocha-Caridi and N. Wallach, to appear.

[T] P. Torasso, Sur le caractere de la representation de Shale-Weil de Mp (n, $\mathbb{R}$) et Sp (n,$\mathbb{C}$), Math. Ann. 252 (1980), 53-86.

A CLASSIFICATION OF UNITARY HIGHEST WEIGHT MODULES

Thomas Enright, Roger Howe and Nolan Wallach

1. INTRODUCTION

Let G be a simply connected, connected simple Lie group with center Z. Let K be a closed maximal subgroup of G with K/Z compact and let g be the Lie algebra of G. A unitary representation (π,H) of G such that the underlying $(\mathfrak{g},K)$ - module is an irreducible quotient of a Verma module for $\mathfrak{g}_{\mathbb{C}}$ is called a unitary highest weight module. Harish-Chandra ([4],[5]) has shown that G admits non-trivial unitary highest weight modules precisely when (G,K) is a Hermitian symmetric pair. In this paper we give a complete classification of the unitary highest weight modules.

The classification question for unitary highest weight modules has been studied by many authors and its history would make this introduction long and rather cumbersome. Some of the more pertinent references here are [4], [5], [17], [15], [9], [10], [11], [14], [16], and [3]. This list is by no means complete and we apologize to those authors who have not been cited.

An essential point of our classification is that highest weights are given explicitly in terms of easily computed invariants of the pair (G,K). The precise statement is given in section two. Although the results are stated in a uniform manner, the proof involves a variety of techniques. There are three basic ingredients in our arguments. The first is a criterion (due to Parthasarathy) for the unitarizability of a highest weight module in terms of its K- structure. The second is Jantzen's formula for the determinant of the contravariant form on a generalized Verma module. The third is Howe's theory of dual pairs where one group in the pair is compact. The proof of the classification depends partly on general principles developed in sections three through six, and partly on case-by-case analysis, given in sections seven through thirteen.

From the classification we find that for the groups $SO^*(2n)$, $SU(p,q)$ and the double covering of $Sp(2n,\mathbb{R})$, although not their covering groups, all unitary highest weight modules are realized in the formalism of reductive dual pairs [7]. For $SU(p,q)$ and $SP(2n,\mathbb{R})$ this was conjectured in [14] and proven in [2].

The results of this paper were obtained while all three authors were in La Jolla during winter quarter of 1981. The last two authors wish to thank the University of California, San Diego for its hospitality during this period. We all thank the organizers at the University of Utah for the wonderful conference which produced this volume.

CONTENTS

2. NOTATION AND STATEMENT OF RESULTS

Assume G is simple and (G,K) is a Hermitian symmetric pair. Let $\mathfrak{g}_0$ (resp. $\mathfrak{k}_0$) be the Lie algebra of G (resp. K) and let $\mathfrak{g}_0 = \mathfrak{k}_0 \oplus \mathfrak{p}_0$ be a Cartan decomposition. Let $\mathfrak{t}_0 \subseteq \mathfrak{k}_0$ be a Cartan subalgebra (CSA). Our assumptions on G imply that $\mathfrak{t}_0$ is a CSA of $\mathfrak{g}_0$ also. By convention we delete the subscript 0 to denote complexifications of Lie algebras.

Fix a Borel subalgebra $\mathfrak{b}$ containing $\mathfrak{t}$. Let Δ denote the roots of $(\mathfrak{g},\mathfrak{t})$ and Δ^+ the positive **roots** determined by $\mathfrak{b}$. Since (G,K) is a Hermitian symmetric pair, we may assume $\mathfrak{b}$ is chosen so that $\mathfrak{q} = \mathfrak{k} + \mathfrak{b}$ is a parabolic subalgebra of $\mathfrak{g}$. In the terminology of [4], Δ^+ is then a totally positive system of roots. Let Δ_c be the roots of $(\mathfrak{k},\mathfrak{t})$, the compact roots, and let Δ_n be the remaining roots of Δ, the noncompact roots.

Define highest weight modules as follows. For $\lambda \in \mathfrak{t}^*$, the algebraic dual of $\mathfrak{t}$, let $\mathbb{C}_\lambda$ denote the one dimensional $\mathfrak{h}$-module where elements H in $\mathfrak{t}$ act by $\lambda(H)$ and elements in the nilradical act by zero. Put $\Delta_c^+ = \Delta_c \cap \Delta^+$. If λ is Δ_c^+-dominant integral, let $F(\lambda)$ be the irreducible $\mathfrak{k}$-module with highest weight λ. By letting the nilradical act by zero, $F(\lambda)$ is also a module for the parabolic $\mathfrak{q}$. Now put:

$$M(\lambda) = U(\mathfrak{g}) \underset{U(\mathfrak{h})}{\otimes} \mathbb{C}_\lambda, \qquad N(\lambda) = U(\mathfrak{g}) \underset{U(\mathfrak{q})}{\otimes} F(\lambda). \tag{2.1}$$

Let $L(\lambda)$ denote the irreducible quotient of both $M(\lambda)$ and $N(\lambda)$. The main result of this article **determines** those $L(\lambda)$ which correspond to unitary representations of G.

Let $\mathfrak{t}_1^*$ be the span of Δ_c. By our assumptions on G, $\mathfrak{t}_1^*$ has comdimension one in $\mathfrak{t}^*$; i.e., $\mathfrak{k}$ has one dimensional center. Let β denote the unique maximal noncompact root of Δ^+. For any $\alpha \in \Delta$ and $\lambda \in \mathfrak{t}^*$, we write λ_α for $\frac{2\langle\lambda,\alpha\rangle}{\langle\alpha,\alpha\rangle}$. Now choose $\zeta \in \mathfrak{t}^*$ so that

$$\zeta \text{ is orthogonal to } \Delta_c \text{ and } \zeta_\beta = 1. \tag{2.2}$$

Then $\mathbb{C}\cdot\zeta$ is a complement to $\mathfrak{t}_1^*$ in $\mathfrak{t}^*$. Next we introduce a collection of special lines in $\mathfrak{t}^*$. Every line of the form $\lambda + z\zeta$, $z \in \mathbb{C}$, can be expressed uniquely in the form

$$\lambda_0 + z\zeta, \quad z \in \mathbb{C}, \quad \text{with } \langle\lambda_0 + \rho,\beta\rangle = 0, \quad \rho = \frac{1}{2}\sum_{\alpha\in\Delta^+} \alpha. \tag{2.3}$$

We shall write λ for a general point on the line $\lambda_0 + z\zeta$.

A $\mathfrak{g}$-module $L(\lambda)$ will be called unitarizable if it is equivalent to the $\mathfrak{g}$-module of $\mathfrak{k}$-finite vectors in a unitary representation of G. An obvious necessary condition is that the highest weight be a unitary character of T, the Lie subgroup of K with Lie algebra $\mathfrak{t}_0$. So, if $L(\lambda)$ is unitarizable, then $\lambda = \lambda_0 + z\zeta$ with $z \in \mathbb{R}$. Also the $\mathfrak{k}$-finiteness implies that λ must be Δ_c^+-dominant integral. For these reasons, we shall consider only the real part of the lines above, that is only real values of z, and we assume λ_0 is Δ_c^+-dominant integral.

We now describe the main results:

<u>THEOREM 2.4. The set of real numbers z with $L(\lambda_0 + z\zeta)$ a unitarizable $\mathfrak{g}$-module is given by the diagram</u>:

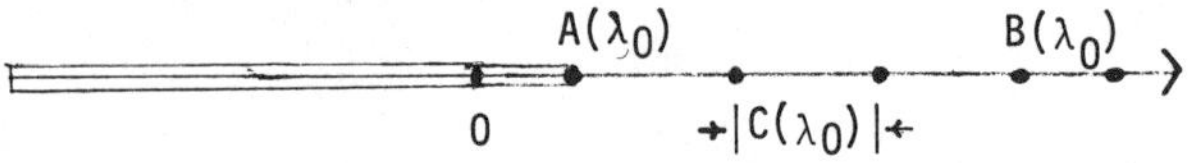

a) The set includes the half line ending at $A(\lambda_0)$.

b) The discrete series representations of G correspond to values $z < 0$ and the limit of discrete series corresponds to $z = 0$.

c) The smallest value z with $N(\lambda_0 + z\zeta)$ reducible is $z = A(\lambda_0)$. We call $A(\lambda_0)$ the first reduction point.

d) In addition to the half line there are a number of equally spaced points in the set. These points are spaced at an interval of length $C(\lambda_0)$. They begin at $A(\lambda_0)$ and end at $B(\lambda_0)$.

Next we shall give formulae for the constants $A(\lambda_0)$, $B(\lambda_0)$ and $C(\lambda_0)$. To do this we associate root systems to the line $\lambda_0 + z\zeta$. These root systems measure, to some degree, the singularity of the highest weight with respect to the compact roots. Let $\Delta_c(\lambda_0) = \{\alpha \in \Delta_c \mid \langle\lambda_0,\alpha\rangle = 0\}$ and recall the definition of β, the maximal noncompact root. Let $\{\pm\beta,\Delta_c(\lambda_0)\}$ be the sub root system of Δ generated by $\pm\beta$ and $\Delta_c(\lambda_0)$. Decomposing this root system into a disjoint union of simple root systems, let $Q(\lambda_0)$ be the simple root system which contains β. If Δ has two root lenghts, if there are short compact roots α not orthogonal to $Q(\lambda_0)$ with $\lambda_{0_\alpha} = 1$, then let Ψ be the root system generated by $\pm\beta,\Delta_c(\lambda_0)$ and all such α. Let $R(\lambda_0)$ be the simple component of Ψ which contains β. If Δ has only one root length or if no such α exists then let $R(\lambda_0) = Q(\lambda_0)$. Since these root systems are subsystems of Δ, each has compact and noncompact root and each is the root system of a Hermitian symmetric pair.

We now describe an algorithm for computing the root systems $Q(\lambda_0)$ and $R(\lambda_0)$. We begin with the Dynkin diagram of $\mathfrak{g}_0$. We illustrate with su (p,q). Draw the Dynkin diagram circling the unique noncompact simple root.

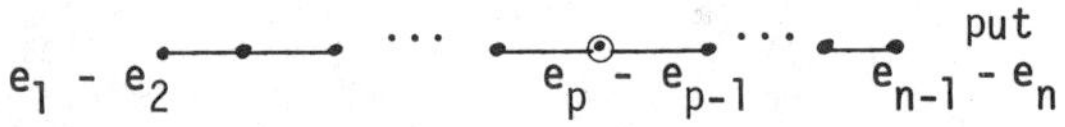

put $n = p + q$

Next omit the noncompact root and adjoin a node corresponding to $-\beta$, the negative of the maximal root. Connect $-\beta$ by the usual rules, as when constructing the extended Dynkin diagram. We obtain:

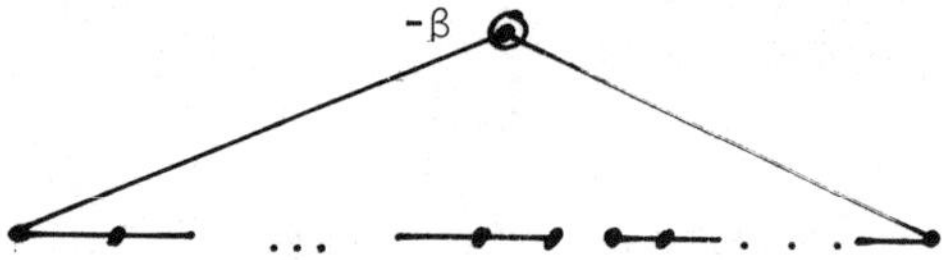

(2.5)

Now take the maximal connected subdiagram of (2.5) containing $-\beta$ and so that every compact simple root is orthogonal to λ_0. This subdiagram is the diagram of $Q(\lambda_0)$. The following table shows the possible systems obtained as $Q(\lambda_0)$.

TABLE 2.6

$\mathfrak{g}_0$	POSSIBLE $Q(\lambda_0)$
$SU(p,q)$	$SU(p',q')$ with $p' \leqslant p$ and $q' \leqslant q$
$Sp(n,\mathbb{R})$	$Sp(n',\mathbb{R})$ with $n' \leqslant n$
$SO^*(2n)$	$SU(1,m)$ with $m < n$ or $SO^*(2m)$ with $m \leqslant n$
$SO(2, 2n-2)$	$SU(1,m)$ with $m < n$ or $SO(2, 2n-2)$
$SO(2, 2n-1)$	$SU(1,m)$ with $m < n$ or $SO(2, 2n-1)$
E III	$SU(1,m)$ with $m \leqslant 5$, $SO(2,8)$ or E III
E VII	$SU(1,m)$ with $m \leqslant 6$, $SO(2,10)$ or E VII

There are only two cases where $Q(\lambda_0) \neq R(\lambda_0)$. We now describe these. For $Sp(n,\mathbb{R})$, if $Q(\lambda_0) \neq R(\lambda_0)$ then $Q(\lambda_0) = sp(n', \mathbb{R})$ and $R(\lambda_0) = sp(n'', \mathbb{R})$ with $n' < n'' \leqslant n$. The remaining case of $SO(2, 2n-1)$ is somewhat special and so we treat it in detail.

Following Bourbaki [1], write:

$$\Delta_c^+ = \{e_i \pm e_j \mid 2 \leqslant i < j \leqslant n\} \cup \{e_i \mid 2 \leqslant i \leqslant n\}$$

$$\Delta_n^+ = \{e_1 \pm e_j \mid 2 \leqslant j \leqslant n\} \cup \{e_1\}.$$

Write $\lambda_0 = (\lambda_1, \ldots, \lambda_n)$. Since λ_0 is Δ_c^+-dominant integral, $\lambda_i - \lambda_j \in \mathbb{N}$ for $2 \leqslant i < j \leqslant n$ and $2\lambda_n \in \mathbb{N}$. In this case $\zeta = e_1$

and $\beta = e_1 + e_2$. If $Q(\lambda_0) \neq R(\lambda_0)$ then $Q(\lambda_0)$ has diagram

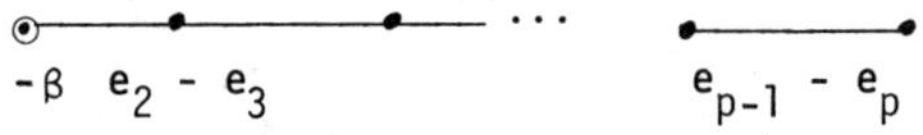

Then $\lambda_2 = \lambda_3 = \ldots = \lambda_p \neq \lambda_{p+1}$. But there exists a short compact root α not orthogonal to $Q(\lambda_0)$ with $(\lambda_0)_\alpha = 1$. Then $\alpha = e_i$ for $2 \leqslant i \leqslant p$; and so, $\lambda_2 = \ldots = \lambda_p = 1/2$. But $\lambda_p - \lambda_{p+1} \in \mathbb{N}$ and $\lambda_n \geqslant 0$. So we have $p = n$ and λ_0 has form:

$$\lambda_0 = (\lambda_1, 1/2, 1/2, \ldots, 1/2). \tag{2.7}$$

This proves that if $\mathfrak{g}_0 = SO(2, 2n-1)$ and if $Q(\lambda_0) \neq R(\lambda_0)$ then $Q(\lambda_0) = SU(1, n-1)$ and $R(\lambda_0) = SO(2, 2n-1)$.

We are now prepared to determine $B(\lambda_0)$. Let $\Delta^+_{c,1} = \Delta^+_c \cap Q(\lambda_0)$ and $\Delta^+_{c,2} = \Delta^+_c \cap R(\lambda_0)$. Let $\rho_{c,1}$ (resp. $\rho_{c,2}$) be half the sum of roots in $\Delta^+_{c,1}$ (resp. $\Delta^+_{c,2}$).

THEOREM 2.8. a) *If* $\mathfrak{g}_0 = so(2, 2n-1)$ *and* $Q(\lambda_0) \neq R(\lambda_0)$ then

$$B(\lambda_0) = 1 + (\rho_{c,2})_\beta.$$

b) *In all other cases*

$$B(\lambda_0) = 1 + (\rho_{c,1} + \rho_{c,2})_\beta.$$

The constants $C(\lambda_0)$ only depend on $\mathfrak{g}_0$ and are given by the table:

TABLE 2.9

$\mathfrak{g}_0$	SU(p,q)	Sp(n,ℝ)	SO*(2n)	SO(2,2n-2)	SO(2,2n-1)	E III	E VII
$C(\lambda_0)$	1	1/2	2	n - 2	n - 3/2	3	4

These constants are multiplicities associated with certain strongly orthogonal roots. See section five for more details.

THEOREM 2.10. *The first reduction point* $A(\lambda_0)$ *is given by:*

$$A(\lambda_0) = B(\lambda_0) - (\text{split rank } Q(\lambda_0) - 1) \cdot C(\lambda_0).$$

Theorems 2.4, 2.8 and 2.10 describe completely the unitarizable highest weight modules for $\mathfrak{g}_0$. These theorems are proved in section fourteen by combining the general results of sections three through six with several case by case verifications given in sections seven through thirteen. Also, in sections seven through thirteen these results are expressed in coordinates for each Lie algebra $\mathfrak{g}_0$. Theorems 7.4, 8.4, 9.4, 10.4, 11.4, 12.4 and 13.4 summarize the results for each case.

Finally the reader should observe that isolated values of z in (2.4) need not be isolated in the unitary dual of the group. For example, in E III consider the first reduction point μ on the line containing the trivial representation. Then no component of $N(\mu)$ is isolated in the unitary dual. But one such component corresponds to an isolated parameter on a different line.

3. THE FIRST REDUCTION POINT

Let notations be as in section two. Let $\lambda = \lambda_0 + z\zeta$, $z \in \mathbb{R}$. Let a be the smallest real number with $N(\lambda_0 + a\zeta)$ reducible. We call a the first reduction point.

PROPOSITION 3.1. a) *For* $z < 0$ (*resp.* $z = 0$), $L(\lambda) = N(\lambda)$ *and these modules are (resp. this module is) infinitesimally equivalent to (resp. a limit of) holomorphic discrete series representations.*

b) *Assume* $N(\lambda)$ *is irreducible. Then* $N(\lambda)$ *is unitarizable if and only if* $z < a$.

c) *For* $z = a$, $L(\lambda)$ *is unitarizable.*

PROOF. For all $\alpha \in \Delta_n^+$, $\alpha = \beta$ minus a sum of roots in Δ_c^+. So, by our normalization (2.3), for $z \leqslant 0$,

$$\langle\lambda + \rho, \beta\rangle \leqslant 0; \text{ and thus, } \langle\lambda + \rho,\alpha\rangle \leqslant 0 \quad \text{for} \quad \alpha \in \Delta_n^+.$$

This implies $N(\lambda)$ is irreducible (cf. [12] Lemma 2) for $z \leqslant 0$. Let $\mathfrak{n}^+$ (resp. $\mathfrak{n}^-$) be the sum of the root spaces for positive (resp. negative) roots. Then $\mathfrak{g} = \mathfrak{n}^- \oplus \mathfrak{t} \oplus \mathfrak{n}^+$. Let P denote the projection $U(\mathfrak{g}) \to U(\mathfrak{t})$ which sends $\mathfrak{n}^- U(\mathfrak{g}) + U(\mathfrak{g})\mathfrak{n}^+$ to zero. Let σ be the conjugate linear involutive antiautomorphism of $U(\mathfrak{g})$ which equals -1 on the real form $\mathfrak{g}_0$ of $\mathfrak{g}$. Then the Verma module $M(\lambda)$ admits a sesquilinear form $\langle\cdot,\cdot\rangle$ defined by:

$$\langle x \otimes 1, y \otimes 1\rangle = \langle P(\sigma y \cdot x),\lambda\rangle, \quad x,y \in U(\mathfrak{g}). \tag{3.2}$$

This form has the maximal submodule of $M(\lambda)$ as its radical; and so, induces forms on $N(\lambda)$ and $L(\lambda)$. We shall use $\langle\ ,\ \rangle$ to denote this form on any of these modules. These forms satisfy $\langle x\cdot m, m'\rangle = \langle m,\sigma(x)m'\rangle$ for all m, m' in the module and $x \in U(\mathfrak{g})$. Forms satisfying this identity will be called contravariant. It is easy to prove (cf. [13]) that $\langle\cdot,\cdot\rangle$ is the unique contravariant form on $M(\lambda)$, $N(\lambda)$ or $L(\lambda)$ (up to scalar multiple). Also, since the form is nonzero and $L(\lambda)$ is irreducible, the form is nondegenerate on $L(\lambda)$.

Let $\mathfrak{p}^+$ (resp. $\mathfrak{p}^-$) be the sum of the root spaces $\mathfrak{g}_\alpha$ for $\alpha \in \Delta_n^+$ (resp. $-\alpha \in \Delta_n^+$). Both $\mathfrak{p}^+$ and $\mathfrak{p}^-$ are $\mathfrak{k}$-modules under the adjoint action and we have $\mathfrak{k}$-module isomorphisms:

$$N(\lambda) \simeq S(\mathfrak{p}^-) \otimes F(\lambda) \simeq S(\mathfrak{p}^-) \otimes F(\lambda_0) \otimes \mathbb{C}_{z\zeta}. \tag{3.3}$$

By fixing a basis for $S(\mathfrak{p}^-) \otimes F(\lambda_0)$ we may consider the family of $\mathfrak{g}$-modules $N(\lambda)$ as being defined on a fixed vector space where the actions of elements of $U(\mathfrak{g})$ are given by operators which depend polynomially on z. Similarly the canonical forms $\langle\ ,\ \rangle$ on $N(\lambda)$ will define a family of forms $\langle\ ,\ \rangle_z$ on $S(\mathfrak{p}^-) \otimes F(\lambda_0)$ which depend polynomially on z. For $z < a$ these forms are nondegenerate. The contravariance implies that distinct weight spaces are orthogonal and of course finite dimensional. On any fixed weight space of $S(\mathfrak{p}^-) \otimes F(\lambda_0)$, the restricted forms remain nondegenerate for $z < a$. Therefore the signature cannot change. So for $z < a$, these modules are either all unitarizable or all not unitarizable. The results of

Harish-Chandra [5] prove the second part of a). By construction, the holomorphic discrete series are unitary. Thus $N(\lambda)$ is unitary for $z < a$. To prove part c, we note that the forms $< >_z$ for $z < a$ are all nondegenerate and positive definite. Therefore at $z = a$ the form $< >_a$ is positive semidefinite on $N(\lambda_0 + a\zeta)$ and induces a positive definite form on $L(\lambda_0 + a\zeta)$. This proves a), c) and half of b).

To complete the proof of b) we will need two preliminary results. We shall describe a connection between the $\mathfrak{k}$-structure of $L(\lambda)$ and unitarity. This connection was observed by Parthasarathy ([15] Corollary 2.8 and Proposition 5.1). His arguments are based on the formal Dirac operator. We give a similar result using only the Casimir. Define Casimir operators

$$\Omega = \sum H_i^2 + \sum_{\alpha\in\Delta} X_{-\alpha}X_{+\alpha},\ \Omega_c = \sum H_i^2 + \sum_{\alpha\in\Delta_c} X_{-\alpha}X_{+\alpha} \tag{3.4}$$

Then

$$\Omega - \Omega_c = 2\sum_{\alpha\in\Delta_n^+} X_{-\alpha}X_{+\alpha} + \sum_{\alpha\in\Delta_n^+} t_\alpha \tag{3.5}$$

where $t_\alpha \in \mathfrak{t}$ and $\forall\nu \in \mathfrak{t}^*$, $<\nu,\alpha> = \nu(t_\alpha)$

<u>LEMMA 3.6. Let</u> v <u>be a</u> Δ_c^+ <u>highest weight vector in</u> $N(\lambda)$ <u>of weight</u> μ. <u>Then</u>

$$(\|\lambda+\rho\|^2 - \|\mu+\rho\|^2)< v,v> = -2\sum_{\alpha\in\Delta_n^+} <X_\alpha \cdot v,\ X_\alpha \cdot v>.$$

<u>Proof</u>. Let $\rho_c = \frac{1}{2}\sum_{\alpha\in\Delta_c^+}\alpha$, $\rho_n = \frac{1}{2}\sum_{\alpha\in\Delta_n^+}\alpha$. Since $\mathfrak{q}$ is a parabolic, ρ_c and ρ_n are orthogonal. Ω acts by $\|\lambda+\rho\|^2 - \|\rho\|^2$ while Ω_c acts on v by $\|\mu+\rho_c\|^2 - \|\rho_c\|^2$. An easy computation gives $\|\mu+\rho\|^2 - \|\rho\|^2 = \|\mu+\rho_c\|^2 - \|\rho_c\|^2 + 2<\mu,\rho_n>$. So evaluating $<(\Omega-\Omega_c)v,v>$ we obtain:

$$(\|\lambda+\rho\|^2 - \|\mu+\rho\|^2 + 2<\mu,\rho_n>)\ <v,v> \tag{3.7}$$

For any noncompact root $\alpha, \sigma X_{-\alpha} = -X_\alpha$; and so, evaluating the action of the right hand side of (3.5) on v gives

$$<(\Omega-\Omega_c)v,v> = \left| -2 \sum_{\alpha\in\Delta_n^+} <X_\alpha v, X_\alpha v> + 2<\mu,\rho_n> \right| <v,v> \quad (3.8)$$

Now (3.7) and (3.8) combine to give (3.6).

PROPOSITION 3.9. $L(\lambda)$ is unitarizable if and only if for all $\mathfrak{k}$-modules $F(\mu)$ occuring in $L(\lambda)$ with $\mu \neq \lambda$, $\|\mu+\rho\| > \|\lambda+\rho\|$.

PROOF. Let $E = N(\lambda)$ or $L(\lambda)$ and introduce a grading on E by putting E^i equal to the sum of the weight spaces of E of weight ν where $<\nu,\zeta> = <-i\beta + \lambda,\zeta>$, $i \in \mathbb{N}$. In the case $E = N(\lambda)$ and $S^i(\mathfrak{p}^-)$ is the usual grading of the symmetric algebra then following (3.3), $E^i \approx S^i(\mathfrak{p}^-) \otimes F(\lambda)$. Observe that each E^i is a $\mathfrak{k}$-module and for all $\alpha \in \Delta_n^+$, $X_\alpha E^i \subseteq E^{i-1}$. If the inequality (3.9) holds and if the restriction of the form to $L^j(\lambda)$ for $j < i$ is positive definite, then by (3.6) the form on $L^i(\lambda)$ is positive definite. So, by induction on i, $L(\lambda)$ is unitarizable.

Conversely if $L(\lambda)$ is unitarizable then the canonical form must be definite. So, again by (3.6), $\|\mu+\rho\|^2 - \|\lambda+\rho\|^2$ is positive. This proves (3.9).

We now complete the proof of (3.1). Let $\nu = \lambda_0 + a\zeta$. Then ν is the first reduction point for $N(\nu)$. Let μ be a highest weight of the maximal submodule of $N(\nu)$. Then $M(\nu)$ and $M(\mu)$ must have the same central character; i.e., $\nu + \rho$ and $\mu + \rho$ lie in the same Weyl group orbit. So

$$\|\nu+\rho\| = \|\mu+\rho\| . \quad (3.10)$$

Also, $F(\mu)$ occurs in $N(\nu)$ and then by (3.3),

$$F(\mu+z\zeta) \to N(\nu+z\zeta), \quad z \in \mathbb{R}. \quad (3.11)$$

Assume $N(\nu+ z\zeta)$ is irreducible and unitarizable. Then by (3.9) and (3.11), $\|\mu+\rho+z\zeta\| > \|\nu+\rho+z\zeta\|$. Using (3.10) this ineqaulity becomes:

$$z<\mu-\nu,\zeta> > 0. \quad (3.12)$$

Clearly, this is satisfied only for positive z or negative z. But by (3.1)a, for large negative values of z, $L(\nu+z\zeta)$ is unitary. So, by (3.12), z is negative. This completes the proof of (3.1)b.

As a corollary to the above proof we have:

LEMMA 3.13. Let $\nu = \lambda_0 + a\zeta$ be the first reduction point for $N(\lambda)$ and let μ be a highest weight of the maximal submodule of $N(\nu)$. Assume $L(\nu + t\zeta)$ is unitarizable with $t \geq 0$.

Then $F(\mu + t\zeta)$ does not occur in $L(\nu + t\zeta)$.

PROOF. The inequality $\|\mu+\rho+t\zeta\|^2 > \|\nu+\rho+t\zeta\|^2$ is equivalent to $t\langle\mu-\nu,\zeta\rangle > 0$. For large negative values of s, $L(\nu + s\zeta)$ is unitarizable and so, by (3.9) $F(\mu + t\zeta)$ does not occur in $L(\nu + t\zeta)$.

Recall from above the grading $N^i(\lambda)$ of $N(\lambda)$. Any submodule of $N(\lambda)$ is the direct sum of finite dimensional **weight spaces.** It follows that any submodule J of $N(\lambda)$ is a graded submodule; i.e., $J = \sum_{i\geq 0} J^i$, $J^i = J \cap N^i(\lambda)$.

DEFINITION 3.14. Assume $N(\lambda)$ is reducible and J is the maximal submodule. Define the level of reduction in $N(\lambda)$ to be the maximal index i with $J^i \neq 0$. For convenience we abbreviate this term to level of $N(\lambda)$ and write level $N(\lambda)$. Since $N^0(\lambda) = F(\lambda)$ and this $\mathfrak{k}$-module is cyclic, the level of $N(\lambda)$ is greater than or equal to one.

PROPOSITION 3.15. Let μ be Δ_c^+-dominant integral and $\nu = \mu + t\zeta$ for some $t > 0$. Assume both $N(\mu)$ and $N(\nu)$ are reducible and $L(\mu)$ and $L(\nu)$ are unitarizable. Then

level $N(\nu) <$ level $N(\mu)$.

PROOF. Let ξ be a highest weight vector for the maximal submodule of $N(\mu)$. Then $\|\mu+\rho\| = \|\xi+\rho\|$ and **since** $\langle\mu-\xi,\zeta\rangle > 0$ $\|\nu+\rho\| > \|\xi+t\zeta+\rho\|$. Since $L(\nu)$ is unitary, (3.13) implies that $F(\xi+t\zeta)$ occurs in the maximal submodule J of $N(\nu)$. Let $a =$ level $N(\nu)$. Any Δ_c^+ highest weight vector of J^a is a highest weight vector for Δ^+. So if it has weight χ then $\chi + \rho$ and $\nu + \rho$ are in the same Weyl group orbit. In particular, they have the same norm. Therefore, $\|\nu+\rho\| > \|\xi+t\zeta+\rho\|$ implies that $F(\xi+t\zeta)$ must occur in J^{a+b} for some $b \geq 1$. Now

level of $N(\mu) = 2\,\frac{\langle\mu-\xi,\zeta\rangle}{\langle\beta,\beta\rangle}$

$$= 2\,\frac{\langle\nu-(\xi+t\zeta),\zeta\rangle}{\langle\beta,\beta\rangle} = a + b.$$

This proves (3.15).

COROLLARY 3.16. *Let* $z = a$ *be the first reduction point and let* ℓ *be the level of reduction of* $N(\lambda_0+a\zeta)$. *Then the number of unitarizable* $L(\lambda_0+t\zeta)$ *with* $t > a$ *is bounded by* $\ell-1$.

PROOF. By (3.15) the level of reduction must drop on passing through each z with $N(\lambda_0+z\zeta)$ reducible and $L(\lambda_0+z\zeta)$ unitarizable. The level of reduction is $\geqslant 1$; so, the estimate follows.

In the light of (3.1), the values where $N(\lambda)$ is reducible will be critical. We include here a preliminary result for reduction.

LEMMA 3.17. Write $\lambda = \lambda_0+z\zeta$ as usual. Now

i) λ is integral precisely when $z \in \mathbb{Z}$

ii) if Δ has one root length and $N(\lambda)$ is reducible then $z \in \mathbb{Z}$.

iii) if Δ has two root lengths and $N(\lambda)$ is reducible then $2z \in \mathbb{Z}$.

PROOF. By normalization λ_0 is integral. Also, since $\mathfrak{p}^+$ is irreducible $\mathfrak{k}$-module $t\zeta (t\in\mathbb{C})$ is integral if and only if $t\in\mathbb{Z}$. This proves i). If $N(\lambda)$ is reducible then for some $\alpha\in\Delta_n^+$, $(\lambda+\rho)_\alpha\in\mathbb{N}^*$ by Lemma 2 in [13]. If Δ has only one root length then $\zeta_\alpha = 1$ for all $\alpha\in\Delta_n^+$. If α has two root lengths then $\zeta_\alpha = 1$ for $\alpha\in\Delta_n^+$ and α long and $\zeta_\alpha = 2$ for $\alpha\in\Delta_n^+$ and α short. So if $(\lambda+\rho)_\alpha \in\mathbb{N}^*$ then $z\in\mathbb{Z}$ if α is long and $2z\in\mathbb{Z}$ if α is short. This proves ii) and ii).

4. AN UPPER BOUND FOR $B(\lambda_0)$.

Proposition 3.9 gives a necessary and sufficient condition for $L(\lambda)$ to be unitarizable in terms of the $\mathfrak{k}$-structure of $L(\lambda)$. In this section, we obtain some precise informaiton on this $\mathfrak{k}$-structure; and in turn, we obtain a sharp upper bound for the constant $B(\lambda_0)$ in Theorem 2.4

LEMMA 4.1. Let $\lambda\in\mathfrak{t}^*$ be Δ_c^+-dominant integral and let $\alpha\in\Delta_n^+$. Assume $\lambda+\rho-\alpha$ is Δ_c-regular but not Δ_c^+-dominant. Then there exists a unique simple root $\gamma\in\Delta_c^+$ with

i) $\lambda_\alpha = 0$

ii) $\alpha_\gamma = 2$

ii) $s_\gamma(\lambda+\rho-\alpha) = \lambda+\rho-\alpha+\gamma$ is Δ_c^+-dominant.

Moreover, in this case Δ must have two root lengths and α is long and γ is short.

PROOF. By assumption we can choose $\gamma \in \Delta_c^+$ with $(\lambda+\rho-\alpha)_\gamma < 0$. Then $(\lambda+\rho)_\gamma < \alpha_\gamma$. However, the root system G_2 does not occur for our groups; and so, $\alpha_\gamma \leqslant 2$. Thus we have:

$$\lambda_\gamma = 0, \quad \rho_\gamma = 1 \quad \text{and} \quad \alpha_\gamma = 2. \tag{4.2}$$

This implies γ is simple and $\|\alpha\|^2 = 2\|\gamma\|^2$. Now (4.2) implies $(\lambda+\rho-\alpha)_\gamma = -1$; and so the identity in iii) holds. This completes the proof except for the uniqueness of γ and the second assertion in iii).

Let t be the unique element of the Weyl group of Δ_c, W_c, such that $t(\lambda+\rho-\alpha)$ is Δ_c^+-dominant. Then, by (4.2), $-t^{-1}\Delta_c^+ \cap \Delta_c^+ = \{\gamma_1, \ldots, \gamma_p\}$ is a set of simple roots of Δ^+ each satisfying (4.2). Since **the** set is the intersection of two positive systems it follows that the simple roots γ_i must be mutually orthogonal. Then $t = s_{\gamma_1} \circ \ldots \circ s_{\gamma_p}$; and so, by (4.2) we obtain:

$$t\alpha - \alpha = -2(\gamma_1 + \ldots + \gamma_p). \tag{4.3}$$

Since γ_i are compact and α is noncompact, $\langle\alpha_i,\zeta\rangle = 0$ and $\langle\alpha,\zeta\rangle \neq 0$. Therefore α and $\gamma_1 + \ldots + \gamma_p$ cannot be multiples. Now applying the triangle inequality to (4.3), we obtain using (4.2),

$$\|\alpha\|^2 > \|\gamma_1 + \ldots + \gamma_p\|^2 = p\|\gamma_1\|^2 = \frac{p}{2}\|\alpha\|^2. \tag{4.4}$$

This proves $p = 1$ and proves the uniqueness of γ. Also $t = s_\gamma$ which proves the second part of iii). This completes the proof of (4.1).

LEMMA 4.5. Let $\lambda \in \mathfrak{t}^*$ be Δ_c^+-dominant integral and let $\alpha \in \Delta_n^+$. Assume $\lambda-\alpha$ is Δ_c^+-dominant. Then $\mathrm{Hom}_{\mathfrak{k}}(F(\lambda-\alpha), \mathfrak{n}^- \otimes F(\lambda))$ $= 0$ if and only if there exists a simple root γ in Δ_c^+ with

i) $\lambda_\gamma = 0$

ii) $\alpha_\gamma = 0$

iii) $\alpha + \gamma \in \Delta_n^+$.

Note that ii) and iii) imply that Δ_n^+ contains roots of two lengths. In this case, both α and γ are short roots.

PROOF. We proceed by expanding the character of the tensor product. Let $D = e^{\rho_n} \sum_{s\in W_c} \det(s) e^{s\cdot\rho_c}$. Then, letting ch denote character and recalling that Δ_n^+ is W_c-stable,

$$D \cdot \mathrm{ch}(\mathfrak{p}^- \otimes F(\lambda)) = \sum_{\xi\in\Delta_n^+} \sum_{s\in W_c} \det(s)\, e^{s(\lambda+\rho-\xi)}. \tag{4.6}$$

Now the multiplicity of $F(\lambda-\alpha)$ in $\mathfrak{p}^- \otimes F(\lambda)$ is equal to the coefficient of $e^{\lambda+\rho-\alpha}$ in (4.6).

First suppose the coefficient of $e^{\lambda+\rho-\alpha}$ in (4.6) is zero. Then there exists $t \in W_c$, $t \neq 1$ and $\chi \in \Delta_n^+$ with $t(\lambda+\rho-\chi) = \lambda + \rho - \alpha$. Since $\lambda + \rho - \alpha$ is Δ_c-regular, so is $\lambda + \rho - \chi$ and we may apply (4.1). This gives a simple root γ in Δ_c^+ with $\lambda_\gamma = 0$, $\chi_\gamma = 2$ and $s_\gamma(\lambda+\rho-\chi) = \lambda + \rho - \chi + \gamma$ Δ_c^+-dominant integral. Then $\lambda + \rho - \chi + \gamma$ and $\lambda + \rho - \alpha$ are both dominant and in the W_c-orbit of $\lambda + \rho - \chi$. So, they are equal, $t = s_\gamma$ and thus $\gamma + \alpha = \chi$. Since $2 = \chi_\gamma = \gamma_\gamma + \alpha_\gamma = 2 + \alpha_\gamma$, $\alpha_\gamma = 0$. This proves properties i), ii) and iii).

We now prove the converse. In general the coefficient of $e^{\lambda+\rho-\alpha}$ is the sum $\sum \det(t)$ taken over pairs $(\chi,t) \in \Delta_n^+ \times W_c$ such that $t(\lambda+\rho-\chi) = \lambda + \rho - \alpha$. Since $\lambda + \rho - \alpha$ is regular, for each $\chi \in \Delta_n^+$ there is at most one pair (χ,t) in this sum. But the argument in the previous paragraph proves that if $t \neq 1$ and $t(\lambda+\rho-\chi) = \lambda + \rho - \alpha$, then t is a simple reflection. But the sum $\sum \det(t)$ is a multiplicity hence is nonnegative. This implies the sum is taken over the identity alone giving multiplicity one or over the identity and one simple reflection giving multiplicity zero. If γ exists satisfying i) ii) and iii) in (4.5) then letting $\chi = \alpha + \gamma$, we have by the previous paragraph, $s_\gamma(\lambda+\rho-\chi) = \lambda + \rho - \alpha$. So, in this case the sum is over two elements and the multiplicity is zero. This completes the proof of (4.5).

PROPOSITION 4.7. <u>Let $\lambda \in \mathfrak{t}^*$ be Δ_c^+ dominant integral and let $\alpha \in \Delta_n^+$. Assume $\lambda-\alpha$ is Δ_c^+ dominant and assume there does not exist any simple root γ in Δ_c^+ with $\lambda_\gamma = \alpha_\gamma = 0$ and $\gamma + \alpha \in \Delta_n^+$. Then,</u>

if $L(\lambda)$ is unitarizable, λ satisfies:

$$(\lambda+\rho)_\alpha \leqslant 1.$$

Note that if Δ has only one root length then such γ never exist.

PROOF. We shall use the notation of section three. In particular, let $N^i(\lambda)$ be the grading of $N(\lambda)$ defined there. By (4.5) and our assumptions, $F(\lambda-\alpha)$ occurs in $N^1(\lambda)$. If $F(\lambda-\alpha)$ does not occur in $L(\lambda)$ then $F(\lambda-\alpha)$ is contained in the maximal submodule J of $N(\lambda)$. Since $\mathfrak{p}^+$ maps $N^1(\lambda)$ into $N^0(\lambda)$ and $N^0(\lambda) \simeq F(\lambda)$, any Δ_c^+-highest weight vector v in $N^1(\lambda) \cap J$ must be a highest weight vector of J. So, if $F(\lambda-\alpha)$ does not occur in $L(\lambda)$ then the Verma module $M(\lambda-\alpha)$ imbeds in $M(\lambda)$. But then $\lambda + \rho$ and $\lambda - \alpha + \rho$ lie in the same Weyl group orbit; and so, $\|\lambda+\rho-\alpha\|^2 = \|\lambda+\rho\|^2$. This gives $(\lambda+\rho)_\alpha = 1$.

Now assume that $F(\lambda-\alpha)$ occurs in $L(\lambda)$. Then by (3.9), $\|\lambda+\rho-\alpha\| > \|\lambda+\rho\|$ and the same computation as above gives $1 > (\lambda+\rho)_\alpha$. This proves (4.7).

COROLLARY 4.8. Assume $F(\lambda-\alpha)$ occurs in $\mathfrak{p}^- \otimes F(\lambda)$. Then, if $L(\lambda)$ is unitarizable, $(\lambda+\rho)_\alpha \leqslant 1$.

PROOF. Combine (4.7) and (4.5).

Next we shall use the root systems $Q(\lambda_0)$ and $R(\lambda_0)$ of section two, to determine a unique choice of α for the above inequalities. Let notation be as in section two with λ_0 satisfying (2.3).

LEMMA 4.9. Assume $Q(\lambda_0) = R(\lambda_0)$. Then there exists a unique long noncompact root α in $R(\lambda_0)$ such that $\lambda_0-\alpha$ is Δ_c^+-dominant. For this root α, $F(\lambda_0+z\zeta-\alpha)$ occurs in $\mathfrak{p}^- \otimes F(\lambda_0+z\zeta)$ for all $z \in \mathbb{R}$.

PROOF. For convenience write λ for $\lambda_0 + z\zeta$. Write R for $R(\lambda_0)$ and put $R^+ = R \cap \Delta^+$, $R_c = R \cap \Delta_c$, $R_n = R \cap \Delta_n$, $R_n^+ = R \cap \Delta_n^+$ and $R_c^+ = R \cap \Delta_c^+$. Then R and R_c are the root system of a Hermitian symmetric pair of Lie algebras $(\mathfrak{g}_1,\mathfrak{k}_1)$ with $\mathfrak{g}_1$ simple. As we have done for $(\mathfrak{g},\mathfrak{k})$, write $\mathfrak{g}_1 = \mathfrak{p}_1^- \oplus \mathfrak{k} \oplus \mathfrak{p}_1^+$ and observe that $\mathfrak{k}_1$ acts irreducibly on $\mathfrak{n}_1^+$ and $\mathfrak{n}_1^-$. For an irreducible finite dimensional representation, the extreme weights form one orbit for the Weyl group. Therefore, the long roots in R_n^+ form one orbit for $W_{\mathfrak{k}_1}$, the Weyl group of $\mathfrak{k}_1$. Now since λ_0 is orthogonal to elements of R_c, if α exists it must be the unique long R_c^+-antidominant element of R_n^+. This proves uniqueness.

Now let α be the unique R_c^+-antidominant element of R_n^+. Then, if $\gamma \in R_c^+$, $(\lambda-\alpha)_\gamma \geqslant 0$. If $\gamma \in \Delta_c^+$ but $\notin R_c$, then $\lambda_\gamma \in \mathbb{N}^*$. So, if $(\lambda-\alpha)_\gamma < 0$ then $\alpha_\gamma \geqslant 2$. This implies that γ is short. Moreover, since G_2 cannot appear in a Hermitian symmetric pair, $\alpha_\gamma = 2$ and $\lambda_\gamma = 1$. But $\alpha \in Q(\lambda_0)$, so γ is a short compact root not orthogonal to $Q(\lambda_0)$ with $\lambda_\gamma = 1$. Then $\gamma \in R(\lambda_0)$, contradicting our assumption that $Q(\lambda_0) = R(\lambda_0)$. This implies that $\lambda-\alpha$ is Δ_c^+-dominant. Since α is a long root, (4.5) implies that $F(\lambda-\alpha)$ occurs in $\mathfrak{n}^- \otimes F(\lambda)$. This completes the proof of (4.9).

Let $\rho_{c,1}$ equal half the sum of the elements in the positive system $Q(\lambda_0) \cap \Delta_c^+$. Recall that β is the maximal root in Δ^+.

PROPOSITION 4.10. Let notation be as in (2.3) and assume $Q(\lambda_0) = R(\lambda_0)$. If $L(\lambda_0+z\zeta)$ is unitarizable then

$$z \leqslant 1 + (2\rho_{c,1})_\beta .$$

PROOF. Let notation be as in the proof of (4.9). The element α given in (4.9) is the unique R_c^+-antidominant element in R_n^+. But β is the unique dominant element in R_n^+; and so, if w_0 is the longest element in the Weyl group $W_{\mathfrak{k}_1}$, then $\alpha = w_0\beta$ and $w_0 = w_0^{-1}$. Combining (4.9) and (4.8), we find that if $L(\lambda_0+z\zeta)$ is unitarizable then $(\lambda_0+\rho+z\zeta)_\alpha \leqslant 1$. Using $\zeta_\alpha = 1$ and $w_0\lambda_0 = \lambda_0$ we have: $(\lambda_0+\rho+z\zeta)_\alpha = (\lambda_0+w_0\rho)_\beta + z = (w_0\rho-\rho)_\beta + z$, by (2.3). Since λ_0 is Δ_c^+-dominant and $\mathfrak{q}$ is a parabolic, $\mathfrak{t} + \mathfrak{k}_1$ is the reductive part of a parabolic of $\mathfrak{g}$ containing $\mathfrak{h}$. This implies that $w_0\rho - \rho = w_0\rho_{c,1} - \rho_{c,1} = -2\rho_{c,1}$. This gives $z \leqslant 1 + (2\rho_{c,1})_\beta$ completing the proof.

LEMMA 4.11. Assume that $Q(\lambda_0) \neq R(\lambda_0)$. Then there exists a unique short root α in $R(\lambda_0)$ such that $\lambda_0 - \alpha$ is Δ_c^+-dominant and $F(\lambda_0+z\zeta-\alpha)$ occurs in $\mathfrak{n}^- \otimes F(\lambda_0+z\zeta)$, for all $z \in \mathbb{R}$.

PROOF. Since there must be two root lengths in Δ we have only two cases to check.

Case 1. $\mathfrak{g}_0 \simeq Sp(n,\mathbb{R})$. Lemma 3.4 in [2] gives the existence of α. The fact that there are only three short roots in $R(\lambda_0)$ with $\lambda_0 - \alpha$ Δ_c^+-dominant, (4.5) and a short computation gives the uniqueness of α.

Case 2. $\mathfrak{g}_0 \simeq SO(2, 2n-1)$. By (2.7) we know that $\lambda_0 = (\lambda_1, 1/2, 1/2, \ldots, 1/2)$. Also, there is only one short noncompact root e_1. If $F(\lambda_0 - e_1)$ does not occur in $\mathfrak{n}^- \otimes F(\lambda_0)$ then by (4.5) there exists a short compact root γ with $(\lambda_0)_\gamma = 0$. But the short compact roots are the e_i, $2 \leqslant i \leqslant n$, and $(\lambda_0)_{e_i} = 1$, $2 \leqslant i \leqslant n$. This proves (4.11) in the second case and completes the proof.

We now have the analogue of (4.10). Let $\rho_{c,1}$ (resp. $\rho_{c,2}$) be half the sum of elements in $Q(\lambda_0) \cap \Delta_c^+$ (resp. $R(\lambda_0) \cap \Delta_c^+$).

PROPOSITION 4.12. Assume $Q(\lambda_0) \neq R(\lambda_0)$. If $L(\lambda_0 + z\zeta)$ is unitarizable, then

$$z \leqslant 1 + (\rho_{c,1} + \rho_{c,2})_\beta \quad \text{for } sp(n,\mathbb{R})$$
$$z \leqslant 1 + (\rho_{c,2})_\beta \quad \text{for } so(2, 2n-1).$$

PROOF. Let α be the unique short noncompact root given by (4.11). Let w_1 (resp. w_2) be the maximal element in the Weyl group of $Q(\lambda_0) \cap \Delta_c$ (resp. $R(\lambda_0) \cap \Delta_c$). A short computation shows that $2\alpha = w_1\beta + w_2\beta$ for $Sp(n,\mathbb{R})$ and $2\alpha = \beta + w_2\beta$ for $SO(2,2n-1)$. We now calculate $(\lambda+\rho)_\alpha$ for $Sp(n,\mathbb{R})$.

$$(\lambda+\rho)_\alpha = (\lambda+\rho)_{w_1\beta} + (\lambda+\rho)_{w_2\beta}.$$

Now, exactly as in the proof of (4.10), $(\lambda+\rho)_{w_1\beta} = -(2\rho_{c,1})_\beta + z$. The element w_2 does not fix λ_0. However, $(w_2\lambda_0)_\beta = (\lambda_0)_\beta - 1$; and so, the same computation now yields:

$$(\lambda+\rho)_{w_2\beta} = -(2\rho_{c,2})_\beta - 1 + z.$$

By (4.11) and (4.8), if $L(\lambda)$ is unitarizable then $(\lambda+\rho)_\alpha \leqslant 1$. With the above identities this becomes: $2z - 1 - 2(\rho_{c,1}+\rho_{c,2})_\beta \leqslant 1$. Simplifying, we have $z \leqslant 1 + (\rho_{c,1}+\rho_{c,2})_\beta$.

A similar computation with $2\alpha = \beta + w_2\beta$ yields $z \leqslant 1 + (\rho_{c,2})_\beta$.

5. THE ONE DIMENSIONAL CYCLIC $\mathfrak{k}$-TYPE CASE

In this section we summarize the results of the third author for highest weight modules generated by a one dimensional $\mathfrak{k}$-type [17]. We also include a corollary concerning the value of the first reduction point.

Following Harish-Chandra define a collection of orthogonal roots as follows: Let γ_1 be the least element of Δ_n^+, and inductively, let γ_k be the least element of Δ_n^+ which is orthogonal to $\gamma_1, \ldots, \gamma_{k-1}$. Let $\gamma_1, \ldots, \gamma_r$ be the maximal collection obtained. Then r is the split rank of $\mathfrak{g}_0$. Let H_{γ_i} be dual to γ_i and let $\mathfrak{h}^-$ equal the span of H_{γ_i}, $1 \leqslant i \leqslant 1$. For $1 \leqslant i \leqslant r$, let c_j be the number of compact positive roots α with $\alpha|_{\mathfrak{h}^-} = \frac{1}{2}(\gamma_j-\gamma_i)$, $i < j$. Note that $c_1 = 0$. A case by case check shows that $c_j = 2(j-1)c$ with c given by the table:

$\mathfrak{g}_0$	SU(p,q)	Sp(n,$\mathbb{R}$)	SO*(2n)	SO(2,2n-2)	SO(2,2n-1)	EIII	EVII
c	1	1/2	2	n-2	n-3/2	3	4

Theorem 5.10 in [17] can now be rephrased as:

THEOREM 5.2. $L(z\zeta)$ *is unitarizable if and only if* $z < -(r-1)c$ *or* $z = -(j-1)c$ *for some* integer j, $1 \leqslant j \leqslant r$.

The normalization in (5.2) has $z = 0$ corresponding to the trivial representation. This is not our normalization. By (2.3) we normalize this line by $\lambda_0 + z\zeta$ where $\lambda_0 = (-\rho_\beta)\zeta$.

LEMMA 5.3. *For the case of one dimensional cyclic* $\mathfrak{k}$-*type the maximal* z *with* $L(\lambda_0+z\zeta)$ *unitary is given by equality in 4.10. In particular*, $z = 1 + (2\rho_c)_\beta = \rho_\beta$.

PROOF. Let w be the maximal element of W_c, the Weyl group of Δ_c. Then $w\beta$ is the unique root given by (4.9). Since β is the maximal root, $w\beta$ is the minimal root in Δ_n^+; and so, $w\beta$ is a simple root in Δ^+. Then the inequality (4.8) gives $\lambda_{w\beta} \leq 0$. Clearly $\lambda = 0$ is the unique point on the line where $\lambda_{w\beta} = 0$. But the limiting value of z in (4.10) was obtained by combining (4.9) and (4.8). So $z = 1 + (2\rho_c)_\beta$ corresponds to $\lambda = 0$ which in turn gives $z = \rho_\beta$. This proves the lemma.

6. JANTZEN'S REDUCIBILITY CRITERIA

The maximal proper submodule of $N(\lambda)$ is precisely the radical of the canonical contravariant form on $N(\lambda)$. Therefore $N(\lambda)$ is reducible if and only if this form is degenerate. Jantzen has computed the determinant of the form on each weight space [12] and given several useful criteria for irreducibility of $N(\lambda)$. We list several of these criteria here. Recall that W_c is the Weyl group of Δ_c^+ and, for $\lambda \in \mathfrak{t}^*$, define $\chi'(\lambda+\rho) = \sum_{w \in W_c} \det(w)\, \mathrm{ch}\, M(w(\lambda+\rho)-\rho)$. For all $\gamma \in \Delta_n^+$, following Jantzen, we put $\Delta_\gamma = (\mathbb{Q}\Delta_c + \mathbb{Q}\cdot\gamma) \cap \Delta$ and $\Delta_\gamma^+ = \Delta_\gamma \cap \Delta^+$. In our case, since $\mathfrak{p}^+$ is a simple $\mathfrak{k}$-module $\Delta_\gamma = \Delta$ and $\Delta_\gamma^+ = \Delta^+$. Jantzen's Satz 3 [12] becomes:

<u>THEOREM 6.1</u>. $N(\lambda)$ <u>is irreducible if and only if the sum of</u> $\chi'(s_\alpha(\lambda+\rho))$ <u>with</u> $\alpha \in \Delta_n^+$ <u>and</u> $(\lambda+\rho)_\alpha \in \mathbb{N}^*$ <u>is equal to zero</u>.

<u>COROLLARY 6.2</u>. <u>If</u> $N(\lambda)$ <u>is irreducible and for some</u> $\alpha \in \Delta_n^+$, $(\lambda+\rho)_\alpha \in \mathbb{N}^*$ <u>then</u> $\lambda+\rho$ <u>is singular</u>.

This result is a reformulation of Corollary 2 [12].

<u>COROLLARY 6.3</u>. <u>Assume for any</u> $\alpha \in \Delta_n^+$ <u>with</u> $(\lambda+\rho)_\alpha \in \mathbb{N}^*$, <u>there is</u> $\gamma \in \Delta$ <u>with</u> $(\lambda+\rho)_\gamma = 0$ <u>and</u> $s_\alpha(\gamma) \in \Delta_c$. <u>Then</u> $N(\lambda)$ <u>is irreducible.</u> Note that since $\mathfrak{p}$ is a $\mathfrak{k}$-module, $s_\gamma(\alpha) \in \Delta_c$ implies that γ as well as α is noncompact.

This is a reformulation of Corollary 3[12].

THEOREM 6.4. *If* $\mathfrak{g}$ *is of type* A_n *then the condition of (6.3) is necessary and sufficient for* $N(\lambda)$ *to be irreducible.*

Recall the notion of level introduced in Definition 3.14.

THEOREM 6.5. *Assume* $N(\lambda)$ *is reducible. For* $n \in \mathbb{N}^*$, *let* $C(n)$ *equal the sum of* $\chi'(s_\alpha(\lambda+\rho))$ *with* $\alpha \in \Delta_n^+$ *and* $(\lambda+\rho)_\alpha = n$ *and let* $a = \min\{n \mid C(n) \neq 0\}$. *Then* $a = \text{level } N(\lambda)$.

PROOF. Let C equal the sum of $\chi'(s_\alpha(\lambda+\rho))$ with $\alpha \in \Delta_n^+$ and $(\lambda+\rho)_\alpha \in \mathbb{N}^*$. Then $C = \sum_{n \geq 1} C(n)$. By (6.1), $C \neq 0$; and so, a is well defined. Jantzen's proof of Satz 3 in [12] or (6.1) above proves the following: Let J be the maximal submodule of $N(\lambda)$ and let $j \in \mathbb{N}^*$. Then $C(i) = 0$ for $1 \leq i \leq j$, if and only if $J \cap N^i(\lambda) = 0$ for $1 \leq i \leq j$. This proves $a = \text{level } N(\lambda)$.

7. Su(p,q)

We begin with the standard coordinate expressions of the root system. Put $n = p + q$

$\Delta \sim A_{n-1}$ diagram 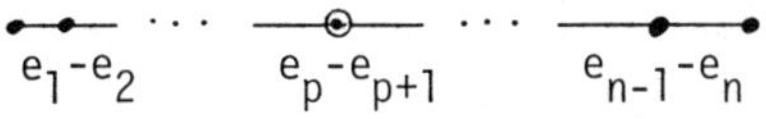

$$\Delta_c^+ = \{e_i - e_j \mid 1 \leq i < j \leq p \quad \text{or} \quad p+1 \leq i < j \leq n\}$$

$$\Delta_n^+ = \{e_i - e_j \mid 1 \leq i \leq p,\ p+1 \leq j \leq n\}$$

$$\beta = e_1 - e_n, \quad 2\rho = (n-1,\ n-3,\ \ldots,\ -n+3,\ -n+1).$$

Write $\lambda = \lambda_0 + z\zeta$ with $\lambda_0 = (\lambda_1, \lambda_2, \ldots, \lambda_n)$, $\lambda_1 \geq \lambda_2 \cdots \geq \lambda_p$, $\lambda_{p+1} \geq \cdots \geq \lambda_n$ and $\lambda_i - \lambda_j \in \mathbb{Z}$, $1 \leq i < j \leq p$ or $p+1 \leq i < j \leq n$. Put $a = \frac{q}{n}$, $b = \frac{-p}{n}$ then $\zeta = (a, a, \ldots, a, b, \ldots, b)$ with p copies of a and q of b. By the normalization $(\lambda_0+\rho)_\beta = 0$ we have: $\lambda_1 - \lambda_n + n - 1 = 0$.

Now consider the root system $Q(\lambda_0)$. $Q(\lambda_0)$ is of type $Su(p',q')$ and we have simple roots for $Q^+(\lambda_0)$ and diagram:

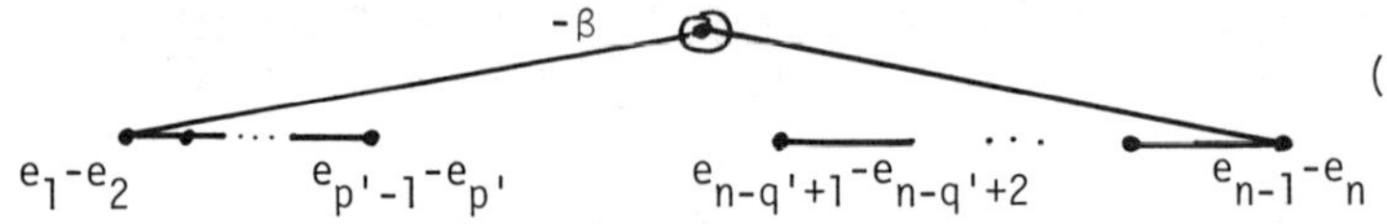

(7.1)

Put $n' = p' + q'$. Then
$2\rho_{c,1} = (p'-1, \ldots, -p'+1, 0, \ldots, 0, q'-1, \ldots, -q'+1)$. By Proposition 4.10, we obtain:

LEMMA 7.2. *If* $L(\lambda_0+z\zeta)$ *is unitarizable then*

$$z \leqslant 1 + (2\rho_{c,1})_\beta = p' + q' - 1.$$

LEMMA 7.3. *The first reduction point is* $z = \max\{p',q'\}$. *Moreover, at this value the level of reduction is* $\min\{p',q'\}$.

PROOF. Assume $p' \geqslant q'$. The other case is proved in essentially the same way. Assume $z \leqslant p'-1$ and let $\alpha \in \Delta_n^+$ be such that $(\lambda+\rho)_\alpha = a \in \mathbb{N}^*$. Write $\alpha = e_i-e_j$, $i \leqslant p < j$. We claim that $i+a \leqslant p'$. To see this write $a = (\lambda+\rho)_\alpha = (\lambda_0+\rho)_\alpha + z \leqslant (\lambda_0+\rho)_\alpha + p'-1$. Then we use the normalization $(\lambda_0+\rho)_\beta = 0$, $\beta = e_1-e_n$ and note that $\langle\lambda_0+\rho, e_\ell\rangle \geqslant \langle\lambda_0+\rho, e_{\ell+1}\rangle + 1$ for all $\ell \neq p-1$. This proves the claim. But then if $\gamma = e_{i+a}-e_j$, $\gamma \in \Delta_n$, $(\lambda+\rho)_\gamma = 0$ and $s_\alpha(\gamma) \in \Delta_c$. So, by (6.4), $N(\lambda)$ is irreducible for $z \leqslant p'-1$. Thus the first possible reduction point is the integer $z = p'$ by (3.13).

Let $z = p'$. Then $\langle\lambda+\rho, e_{p'}-e_n\rangle = 1$ and $\langle\lambda+\rho, e_i-e_n\rangle \neq 0$ for all i, $1 \leqslant i \leqslant p$. Likewise, $\langle\lambda+\rho, e_{p'-q'+1}-e_{n-q'+1}\rangle = 1$ and $\langle\lambda+\rho, e_{p'-q'+1}-e_j\rangle \neq 0$ for all j, $p+1 \leqslant j \leqslant n$. So let $\alpha = e_{p'-q'+1}-e_n$. Then $(\lambda+\rho)_\alpha = q' \in \mathbb{N}^*$ but there does not exist $\gamma \in \Delta_n$ with $(\lambda+\rho)_\gamma = 0$ and $s_\alpha(\gamma) \in \Delta_c$. So by (6.4), $N(\lambda)$ is reducible. Using (6.5) a short computation shows that level $N(\lambda) = q'$. This proves (7.3).

THEOREM 7.4. *With notation as above,* $L(\lambda_0+z\zeta)$ *is unitarizable if and only if* $z \leqslant \max\{p',q'\}$ *or* z *is an integer and* $z \leqslant p'+q-1$.

PROOF. By (7.3) the first reduction point occurs at $z = \max\{p',q'\}$. So by (3.1) and (3.13), if $z \notin \mathbb{Z}$ then $L(\lambda)$ is unitarizable if and only if $z \leqslant \max\{p',q'\}$. For any value z we have, $z \leqslant p' + q' - 1$ by (7.2). However, for these integer values Kashiwara and Vergne [14] have shown these modules are unitarizables (see also Enright-Parthasarathy [2]). This proves (7.4).

8. $Sp(n,\mathbb{R})$

$\Delta \sim C_n$ diagram

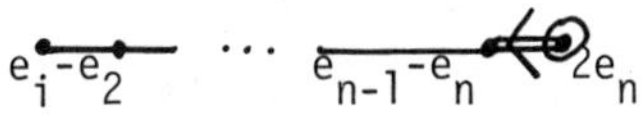

$\Delta_c^+ = \{e_i - e_i \mid 1 \leqslant i < j \leqslant n\}$

$\Delta_n^+ = \{e_i + e_i \mid 1 \leqslant i \leqslant j \leqslant n\}$

$\beta = 2e_1 \qquad \rho = (n, \ldots, 1)$

$\lambda = \lambda_0 + z\zeta, \quad \lambda_0 = (\lambda_1, \ldots, \lambda_n)$ and $\zeta = (1,1,,\ldots,1)$.

Since λ_0 is Δ_c^+-dominant integral $\lambda_i - \lambda_j \in \mathbb{N}$, $i < j$. By the normalization, $(\lambda+\rho)_\beta = 0$ we have: $\lambda_1 = -n$.

Now consider the root systems $Q(\lambda_0)$ and $R(\lambda_0)$. The only possibilities are $Q(\lambda_0) = sp(q, \mathbb{R})$ and $R(\lambda_0) = sp(r, \mathbb{R})$ with $r \geqslant q$. The diagrams are:

$Q(\lambda_0)$

$R(\lambda_0)$

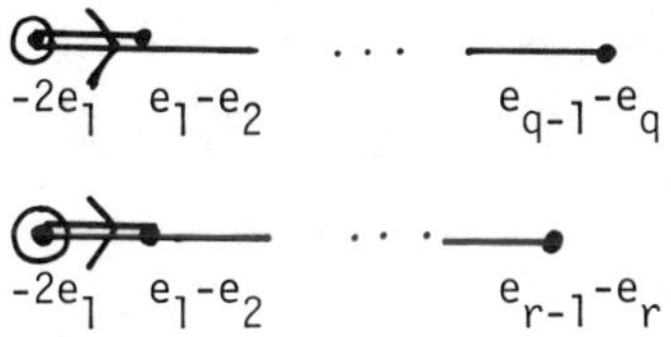

(8.1)

Then $2\rho_{c,1} = (q-1, q-3, \ldots, -q+1, 0, \ldots, 0)$

$2\rho_{c,2} = (r-1, r-3, \ldots, -r+1, 0, \ldots, 0)$.

By Propositions 4.10 and 4.12, we obtain:

LEMMA 8.2. *If $L(\lambda)$ is unitarizable, then*

$$z \leqslant 1 + (\rho_{c,1} + \rho_{c,2})_\beta = \frac{1}{2}(q+r).$$

LEMMA 8.3. The first reduction point is $z = \frac{1}{2}(r+1)$. Moreover, at this point level $N(\lambda) = q$.

The idea of the proof is essentially the same as that for (7.3). However, the criteria (6.4) is not available in this case and so we must use (6.1) directly. The verification is cumbersome but straightforward. We omit the calculations. These same computations give level $N(\lambda) = q$ by (6.5).

THEOREM 8.4. $L(\lambda_0+z\zeta)$ is unitarizable if and only if $z \leqslant \frac{1}{2}(r+1)$ or $2z \in \mathbb{Z}$ with $z \leqslant \frac{1}{2}(q+r)$.

PROOF. By (8.3) the first reduction point occurs at $z = \frac{1}{2}(r+1)$. So, by (3.1) and (3.13), if $2z \notin \mathbb{Z}$ then $L(\lambda)$ is unitarizable if and only if $z \leqslant \frac{1}{2}(r+1)$. For any value of z, we have $z \leqslant \frac{1}{2}(q+r)$ by (8.2). But by the work of Kashiwara and Vergne [14] (see also Enright-Parthasarathy [2]) these half integer values correspond to unitarizable $L(\lambda)$. This proves (8.4).

9. $SO^*(2n)$

$\Delta \sim D_n$ diagram

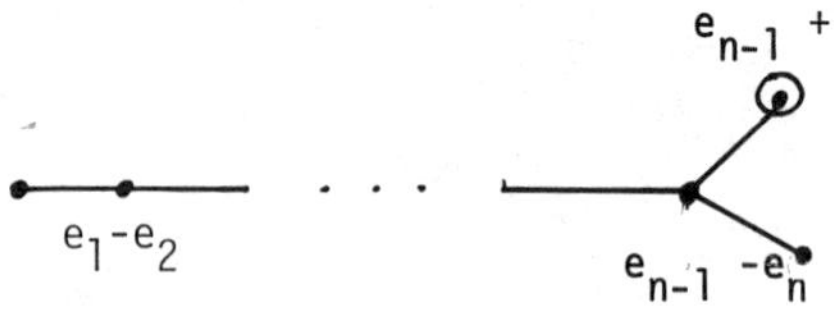

$\Delta_c^+ = \{e_i-e_j \mid 1 \leqslant i < j \leqslant n\}$

$\Delta_n^+ = \{e_1+e_2 \mid 1 \leqslant i < j \leqslant n\}$

$\beta = e_1 + e_2 \qquad \rho = (n-1, \ldots, 1, 0)$

$\lambda = \lambda_0 + z\zeta$, $\lambda_0 = (\lambda_1, \ldots, \lambda_n)$ and $\zeta = \frac{1}{2}(1, 1, \ldots, 1)$.

Since λ_0 is Δ_c^+-dominant integral, $\lambda_i - \lambda_j \in \mathbb{N}$ for $i \leqslant j$. Also, by the normalization $(\lambda_0+\rho)_\beta = 0$, we have: $\lambda_1 + \lambda_2 = -2n + 3$.

Now consider the root system $Q(\lambda_0) = R(\lambda_0)$. The only possibilities are: $Q(\lambda_0) = su(1, q)$, $1 \leqslant q \leqslant n-1$, and $SO^*(2p)$, $3 \leqslant p \leqslant n$. The diagrams are:

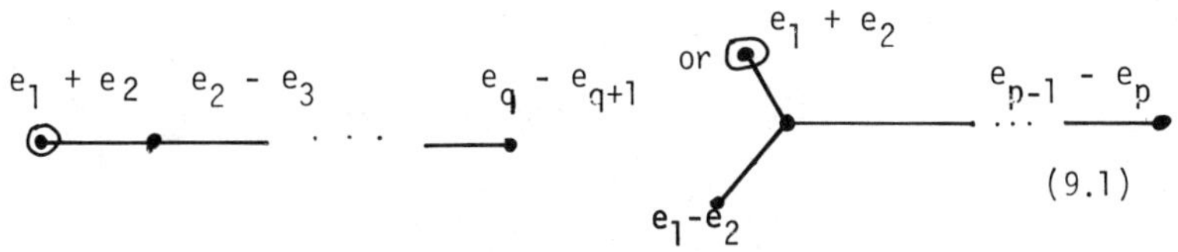

(9.1)

For these two cases

$$2\rho_{0,1} = (0,\ q-1,\ q-3,\ \ldots,-q+1,\ 0\ \ldots\ 0)$$

or $$(p-1,\ p-3,\ \ldots\ ,\ -p+1,\ 0\ \ldots\ 0)$$

From Proposition 4.10, we obtain:

<u>LEMMA 9.2.</u> <u>If</u> $L(\lambda)$ <u>is unitarizable then</u>

$$z \leqslant 1 + (2\rho_{c,1})_\beta = \begin{cases} q & \text{if } Q(\lambda_0) = su(1,q) \\ 2p-3 & \text{if } Q(\lambda_0) = so^*(2p) \end{cases}$$

<u>LEMMA 9.3.</u> <u>The first reduction point is</u>:

$$z = \begin{cases} q & \text{if } Q(\lambda_0) = su(1,q) \\ p-1 & \text{if } Q(\lambda_0) = so^*(2p)\ ,\ p \text{ even} \\ p & \text{if } Q(\lambda_0) = so^*(2p)\ ,\ p \text{ odd} \end{cases}$$

Moreover, at this value

$$\text{level } N(\lambda) = \begin{cases} 1 & \text{if } Q(\lambda_0) = su(1,q) \\ [\frac{p}{2}] & \text{if } Q(\lambda_0) = so^*(2p) \end{cases}$$

<u>PROOF</u>: First consider the case $Q(\lambda_0) = su(1,q)$. Then $\lambda_0 + \rho$ has the form $(a,\ -a,\ -a-1,\ \ldots,\ -a-q+1,\ -a-q-b\ ,\ldots,\ )$ with $a > 0$ and $b > 0$. By (6.1), we verify that the first reduction occurs at $z = q$. Also, by (6.5) we verify that level $N(\lambda) = 1$ at this point.

In the case $Q(\lambda_0) = so^*(2p)$ then

$$\lambda_0 + \rho = (a,\ a-1,\ a-2,\ \ldots\ ,\ a-p+1,\ a-p-b\ldots) \text{ with } a = \frac{1}{2},\ b < 0$$

By (6.1) and (6.5) we verify that the first reduction occurs at $z = p-1$ for p even and $z = p$ for p odd.

Also, the level of $N(\lambda)$ is $[\frac{p}{2}]$ at this point.

THEOREM 9.4. i) *For* $\mathfrak{Q}(\lambda_0) = su(1,q)$ *then* $L(\lambda)$ *is unitarizable if and only if* $z \leq q$.

ii) *For* $\mathfrak{Q}(\lambda_0) = so^*(2p)$ *then* $L(\lambda)$ *is unitarizable if and only if either*

a) $z \leq \begin{cases} p-1 & \text{if } p \text{ is even} \\ p & \text{if } p \text{ is odd} \end{cases}$

or

b) $z = 2p-3-2j$ for some integer j, $0 \leq j \leq [\frac{p}{2}] - 2$.

The proof of (9.4) will be given in several parts. First, (9.2), (9.3) and (3.1) imply i) of (9.4). Likewise in case ii), (9.2), (9.3) and (3.1) imply that (9.4) ii) will follow as soon as we determine the unitarizability or non unitarizability of $L(\lambda)$ for $z = 2p-3-k$ with k an integer $0 \leq k \leq 2[\frac{p}{2}] - 3$. We must show that for such k, $L(\lambda)$ is unitarizable if and only if k is even. The level of $N(\lambda)$ at the first reduction point is $[\frac{p}{2}]$. Therefore, by (3.16) the number of integers k, $0 \leq k \leq 2[\frac{p}{2}] - 3$, with $L(\lambda)$ unitarizable for $z = 2p-3-k$ is bounded by $[\frac{p}{2}] - 1$. This value is precisely the number of even k in this range. So to prove $L(\lambda)$ is unitarizable if and only if k is even in this range, we need only prove the following proposition.

Proposition 9.5. *Assume* $\mathfrak{Q}(\lambda_0) = so^*(2p)$. *Then* $L(\lambda)$ *is unitarizable for* $z = 2p-3-2j$, $0 \leq j \leq [\frac{p}{2}] - 2$, $j \in \mathbb{N}$.

We will use the second named author's theory of dual reductive pairs to prove (9.5). For details of this theory the reader should consult "Remarks on classical invariant theory" [7]. Consider the dual pair $(O^*(2\ell), Sp(k)) \subseteq Sp(2\ell k, \mathbb{R})$ where $O^*(2\ell)$ is given as in [6], p.340, and $Sp(k)$ is the $k \times k$ quaternionic unitary group. Let ω be the oscillator representation of the two fold covering of $Sp(2\ell k, \mathbb{R})$ and let ω^0 denote the space of finite vectors for the double cover of the maximal compact subgroup $U(2\ell k)$ of $Sp(2\ell k, \mathbb{R})$. Consider this representation as given on the polynomial functions on $\mathbb{C}^{2\ell k}$ which will be looked upon as $2k$ by ℓ matrices.

We take for coordinates z_{ij} and w_{ij}, $1 \leq i \leq k$, $1 \leq j \leq \ell$. Then the complexified Lie algebra of $Sp(k)$ acts as the differential operators:

$$m_{ab} = \sum_j z_{aj} \frac{\partial}{\partial z_{bj}} - w_{bj} \frac{\partial}{\partial w_{aj}} ,$$

$$n_{ab} = \sum_j z_{aj} \frac{\partial}{\partial w_{bj}} + z_{bj} \frac{\partial}{\partial w_{aj}} ,$$

$$\overline{n}_{ab} = \sum_j w_{aj} \frac{\partial}{\partial z_{bj}} + w_{bj} \frac{\partial}{\partial z_{aj}} .$$

The complexified Lie algebra of $O^*(2\ell)$ acts by the operators

$$k_{cd} = \sum_i z_{ic} \frac{\partial}{\partial z_{id}} + w_{ic} \frac{\partial}{\partial w_{id}} + \delta_{cd} k,$$

$$p_{cd} = \sum_i z_{ic} w_{id} - z_{id} w_{ic}$$

$$\overline{p}_{cd} = \sum_i \frac{\partial^2}{\partial z_{ic} \partial w_{id}} - \frac{\partial^2}{\partial z_{ic} \partial w_{id}}$$

The complex span of the k_{cd} is the Lie algebra of the maximal compact subgroup $U(\ell)$ of $O^*(2\ell)$. Let $\mathfrak{k}$ denote this Lie algebra. The span of the p_{cd} (resp. $\overline{p}_{cd}$) is $\mathfrak{n}^+$ (resp. $\mathfrak{n}^-$).

The operators m_{ab} span the complexified Lie algebra $\mathfrak{t}'$ of a maximal torus of $Sp(k)$ and the operators k_{cc} span the complexified Lie algebra $\mathfrak{t}$ of a compact Cartan subgroup of $O^*(2\ell)$. Let $\mathfrak{n}' = \text{span}\{m_{ab} \mid a < b\} + \text{span}\ \{n_{ab}\}$. Then $\mathfrak{b}' = \mathfrak{t}' \oplus \mathfrak{n}'$ is a Borel subalgebra of $Sp(k)$. A Borel subalgebra for $\mathfrak{k}$ is given by span $\{k_{cd} \mid c \leq d\}$ and denoted $\mathfrak{b}_{\mathfrak{k}}$. Let $\mathfrak{b} = \mathfrak{b}_{\mathfrak{k}} \oplus \mathfrak{n}^-$. Then $\mathfrak{b}$ is a Borel subalgebra of $\mathfrak{g}$, the Lie algebra of $O^*(2\ell)$. Now consider the roots. For $H \in \mathfrak{t}$, we write $H = \sum_{c=1}^{\ell} \beta_c k_{cc}$.

Then the roots of $\mathfrak{b}$ are $\pm \beta_c - \beta_d$, $c < d$.

<u>LEMMA 9.6.</u> <u>Let</u> $r = \min\{k, \ell\}$ <u>and define</u> $\eta_1 = z_{11}$,

$$\eta_2 = \det \begin{bmatrix} z_{11} & z_{12} \\ z_{21} & z_{22} \end{bmatrix}, \ \ldots, \ \eta_r = \det \begin{bmatrix} z_{11} & z_{12} & \cdots & z_{1r} \\ \vdots & & \ddots & \\ z_{r1} & & & z_{rr} \end{bmatrix} .$$

Then, for $1 \leqslant i \leqslant r$,

$$\mathfrak{n}' \cdot \eta_i = \mathfrak{n}_k \cdot \eta_i = \mathfrak{p}^- \cdot \eta_i = 0 .$$

The proof is a direct calculation and is omitted.

Since the operators m_{ab}, n_{ab} and k_{cd} are first order operators without constant term for $a \neq b$, the products of the η_i are also annihilated by $\mathfrak{n}'$ and $\mathfrak{n}_k$. The $\overline{p}_{cd}$ are first order in the z_{ij} without constant term so the same result holds for $\mathfrak{p}^-$ also. We obtain:

LEMMA 9.7. Let $\underline{q}$ be a multi index $\underline{q} = (q_1,\ldots,q_r) \in (\mathbb{N}^*)^r$. Let $v(\underline{q}) = \eta_1^{q_1} \ldots \eta_r^{q_r}$. Then

$$\mathfrak{n}' \cdot v(\underline{q}) = \mathfrak{n}_k \cdot v(\underline{q}) = \mathfrak{p}^- \cdot v(\underline{q}) = 0 .$$

From our formulas, a short computation gives:

LEMMA 9.8. The vector $v(\underline{q})$ has weight

$$\sum_{c=1}^{r} \left(\sum_{i=c}^{r} q_i\right)\beta_c + k \sum_{c=1}^{\ell} \beta_c$$

The vectors $v(\underline{q})$ generate unitary highest weight modules. From (9.8), these highest weights have the form:

$$(w_1 + k,\ w_2 + k,\ldots,w_r + k,\ k,\ldots,k) \quad \text{with} \qquad (9.9)$$
$$w_1 \geqslant w_2 \geqslant \ldots \geqslant w_r \geqslant 0 , \quad r = \min\{k,\ell\}.$$

These are highest weights with respect to the positive root system $\Delta_c^+ \cup -\Delta_n^+$. Let s_0 be the maximal element of W_c . Then $-s_0(\Delta_c^+ \cup -\Delta_n^+) = \Delta^+$. Applying the corresponding automorphism to $\mathfrak{g}$, the highest weight modules above become highest weight modules with respect to Δ^+ having highest weights:

$$(-k,-k,\ldots,-k,-k-w_r,\ldots,-k-w_1) \quad \text{with}$$
$$0 \geqslant -w_r \geqslant -w_{r-1} \geqslant \ldots \geqslant -w_1 \text{ and } r = \min\{k,\ell\}.$$

We now prove (9.5). Recall the notation at the beginning of this section. For $Q(\lambda_0) = so^*(2p)$, $\lambda_1 = \lambda_2 = \ldots = \lambda_p$. Since $\lambda_1 + \lambda_2 = -2n + 3$, $\lambda_i = -n + 3/2$, $1 \leq i \leq p$. The i th coordinate of λ for $z = 2p-3-2j$ is $-n+p-j$ for $1 \leq i \leq p$. Now put $\ell = n$, $r = n-p+j$. If j satisfies the hypotheses of (9.5) then $r \leq n$. Let $k = r$. Then λ has the form given in (9.10); and so $L(\lambda)$ is unitarizable. This proves (9.5); and inturn, completes the proof of (9.4).

10. so(2, 2n-2)

$\Delta \sim D_n$ diagram

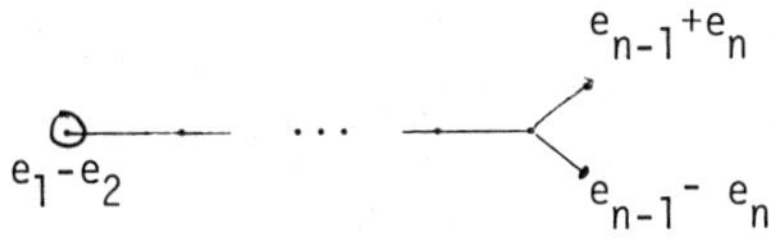

$$\Delta_c^+ = \{e_i \pm e_j \mid 2 \leq i < j \leq n\}$$

$$\Delta_n^+ = \{e_1 \pm e_j \mid 2 \leq j \leq n\}$$

$$\beta = e_1 + e_2 \qquad \rho = (n-1, \ldots, 0)$$

$$\lambda = \lambda_0 + z\zeta, \quad \lambda_0 = (\lambda_1, \ldots, \lambda_n) \text{ and } \zeta = (1,0,\ldots,0)$$

Since λ_0 is Δ_c^+ dominant integral, $\lambda_2 \geq \lambda_3 \geq \ldots \geq \lambda_{n-1} \geq |\lambda_n|$ and $\lambda_i - \lambda_j \in \mathbb{N}$ for $2 \leq i < j \leq n$. By the normalization $(\lambda_0 + \rho)\beta = 0$, $\lambda_1 + \lambda_2 = -2n + 3$.

There are three possibilities for the root system $Q(\lambda_0)$: su(1,p), so(2,2n-2) or su(1,n-1). The diagrams are:

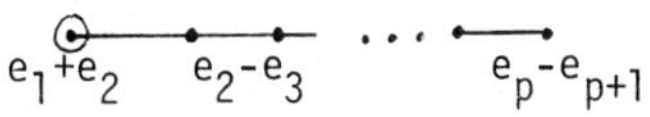

(p<n) or

(10.1)

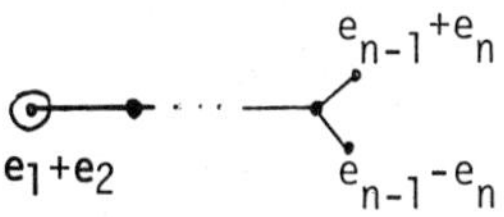

or

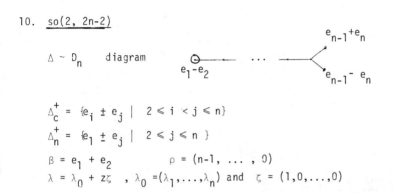

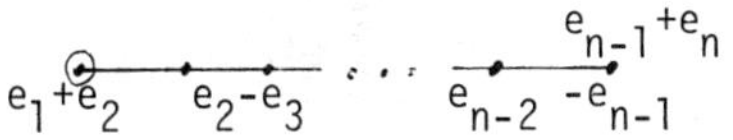

There exists an automorphism of $\mathfrak{g}$ which takes e_n to $-e_n$ and fixes e_i, $1 \leq i < n$. This automorphism interchanges the third case with the first for $p = n-1$. Thus the solution of the third case will follow easily from the solution of the first. We must consider the cases:

Case I, p: $\quad Q(\lambda_0) = R(\lambda_0) = su(1,p)$, $1 \leq p \leq n-1$, and
Case II : $\quad Q(\lambda_0) = R(\lambda_0) = so(2,2n-2)$. Then

$$\rho_{c,1} = \begin{cases} 1/2\ (0,\ p-1,\ p-3,\ldots,-p+1,\ 0,\ldots 0) & \text{in Case I, p} \\ (0,\ n-2,\ n-3,\ldots\qquad ,0) & \text{in Case II} \end{cases}$$

From Proposition (4.12) we obtain:

LEMMA 10.2 If $L(\lambda)$ is unitarizable then

$$z \leq 1 + 2(\rho_{1,c})_\beta = \begin{cases} p & \text{in Case I, p} \\ 2n-3 & \text{in Case II} \end{cases}.$$

LEMMA 10.3 The first reduction point is

$$z = \begin{cases} p & \text{in Case I , p} \\ n-1 & \text{in Case II} \end{cases}$$

Moreover, at this value,

$$\text{level } N(\lambda) = \begin{cases} 1 & \text{in Case I , p} \\ 2 & \text{in Case II} \end{cases}$$

PROOF: Using (6.1) the reader may verify that $N(\lambda)$ is irreducible for z less than the values above. Then by (3.1) and (5.2), reduction must occur at these values. This proves the first assertion. The level of $N(\lambda)$ can be verified using (6.5). We give the verification only in Case II. Consider the $2 \times (n-1)$ matrix with entries $a_{1,i} = (\lambda + \rho)_\alpha$, $\alpha = e_1 + e_{i+1}$ and $a_{2,i} = (\lambda + \rho)_\alpha$, $\alpha = e_1 - e_{i+1}$, $1 \leq i \leq n-1$. In Case II, $\lambda_0 = (-2n+3,\ 0,\ 0,\ldots,0)$ and $\lambda_0 + \rho = (-n+2,\ n-2,\ n-3,\ldots,1,0)$. The matrix is:

$$\begin{pmatrix} z & z-1 & . & . & . & . & z-n+3 & z-n+2 \\ z-2n+4 & . & . & . & . & . & z-n+1 & z-n+2 \end{pmatrix}$$

Applying (6.5) with $z = n-1$, we find that $C(1) = 0$ and $C(2) \neq 0$. This proves level $N(\lambda) = 2$.

Finally, combining (10.2), (10.3), (3.1), and (3.16) we obtain:

THEOREM 10.4 $L(\lambda)$ is unitaizable if and only if either $z \leqslant p$ in Case I, p or $z \leqslant n-1$ or $z = 2n-3$ in Case II. The value $z = 2n-3$ in Case II corresponds to the trivial representation of $\mathfrak{g}$.

11. SO(2, 2n-1)

$\Delta \sim B_n$ diagram

$\Delta_c^+ = \{e_i \pm e_j \;|2 \leqslant i < j \leqslant n\} \cup \{e_j | 2 \leqslant j \leqslant n\}$

$\Delta_n^+ = e_1 \pm e_j \;|2 \leqslant j \leqslant n\} \cup \{e_1\}$

$\beta = e_1 + e_2$ $\qquad \rho = (n - 1/2, n - 3/2, \ldots , 1/2)$

$\lambda = \lambda_0 + z\zeta$, $\lambda_0 = (\lambda_1,\ldots,\lambda_n)$ and $\zeta = (1,0,\ldots, 0)$.

Since λ_0 is Δ_c^+ - dominant integral $\lambda_2 \geqslant \ldots \geqslant \lambda_n \geqslant 0$, $\lambda_i - \lambda_j \in \mathbb{Z}$, and $2\lambda_i \in \mathbb{N}$ for all i, j, $2 \leqslant i, j \leqslant n$. By the normalization $(\lambda_0 + \rho)_\beta = 0$ we have: $\lambda_1 + \lambda_2 = -2n + 2$.

As discussed in section two, there are three cases to consider. Case I, p: $Q(\lambda_0) = R(\lambda_0) = su(1,p)$, Case II: $Q(\lambda_0) = R(\lambda_0) = SO(2,2n-1)$ and Case III: $Q(\lambda_0) = su(1,n-1)$ and $R(\lambda_0) = SO(2,2n-1)$. The diagrams for $Q(\lambda_0)$ and $R(\lambda_0)$ in these cases are:

Case I, p $\qquad 1 \leqslant p < n$

Case II $\qquad$ (11.1)

Case III

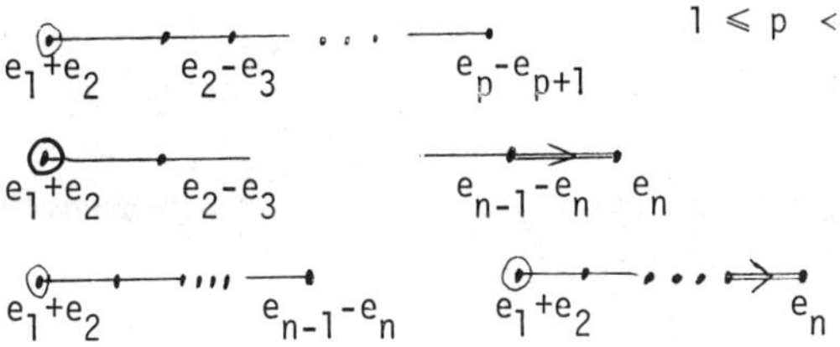

Then

$$\rho_{1,c} = \begin{cases} 1/2(0,p-1,\; p-3,\ldots,-p+1,\; 0\ldots0) & \text{Case I, p} \\ (0,\; n-3/2,\ldots\; 3/2,\; 1/2) & \text{Case II} \\ 1/2(0,n-2,\; n-4,\; \ldots,\; -n+2) & \text{Case III} \end{cases}$$

$$\rho_{2,c} \quad \begin{cases} \rho_{1,c} & \text{Case I or Case II} \\ (0,\ n-3/2,\ \ldots\ 3/2\ ,\ 1/2) & \text{Case III} \end{cases}$$

From Propositions (4.10) and (4.12), we obtain:

LEMMA 11.2 *If* $L(\lambda)$ *is unitarizable then*

$$z \leqslant \begin{cases} 1 + (\rho_{1,c} + \rho_{2,c})_\beta & \text{in Case I or II} \\ 1 + (\rho_{2,c})_\beta & \text{in Case III} \end{cases} = \begin{cases} p & \text{in Case I, p} \\ 2n-2 & \text{in Case II} \\ n-1/2 & \text{in Case III.} \end{cases}$$

LEMMA 11.3 *The first reduction point is*

$$z = \begin{cases} p & \text{in Case I, p} \\ n-1/2 & \text{in Case II or Case III} \end{cases}$$

Moreover, at this value

$$\text{level } N(\lambda) = \begin{cases} 1 & \text{in Case I, p and Case III} \\ 2 & \text{in Case II} \end{cases}$$

PROOF: Using (6.1), the reader may verify the irreducibility of $N(\lambda)$ for z less than the values above. By (3.1), (5.2) and (11.2), these values are reduction points for $N(\lambda)$. Using (6.5) as in the proof of (10.3), the reader may verify the formula for level $N(\lambda)$.

Combining (11.2), (11.2), (3.1) and (3.16) for Case I, p and Case III and (5.2) for Case II we have:

THEOREM 11.4 $L(\lambda)$ *is unitarizable if and only if either* $L(\lambda)$ *is the trivial representation or*

$$z \leqslant \begin{cases} p & \text{in Case I, p} \\ n-1/2 & \text{in Case II or Case III} \end{cases} .$$

The trivial representaion corresponds to the value $z = 2n-2$.

12. E III

$\Delta \sim E_6$ diagram 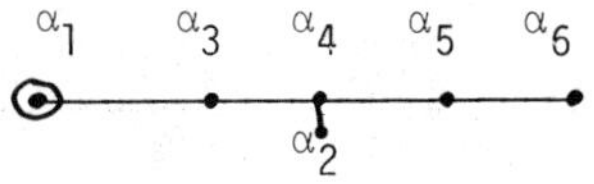

$\alpha_2 = e_1 + e_2\,,\quad \alpha_i = e_{i-1} - e_{i-2} \quad (3 \leqslant i \leqslant 6)$

$\alpha_1 = 1/2(e_1 - e_2 - e_3 - \dots - e_6 - e_7 + e_8)$

$\Delta_c^+ = \{\pm e_i + e_j \mid 1 \leqslant i < j \leqslant 5\}$

$$\Delta_n^+ = \{1/2(\sum_{i=1}^{5} (-1)^{\nu(i)} e_i - e_6 - e_7 + e_8) \mid \sum_{i=1}^{5} \nu(i) \text{ is even}\}$$

The maximal root β has the form:

$$\beta = 1/2(e_1 + e_2 + e_3 + e_4 + e_5 - e_6 - e_7 + e_8)$$
$$= \alpha_1 + 2\alpha_3 + 2\alpha_2 + 3\alpha_4 + 2\alpha_5 + \alpha_6 .$$

Also

$$\zeta = (0, 0, 0, 0, 0, -2/3, -2/3, 2/3)$$
$$\rho = (0, 1, 2, 3, 4, -4, -4, 4) .$$

Write $\lambda = \lambda_0 + z\zeta$ with $\lambda_0 = (\lambda_1, \dots, \lambda_8)$. Since λ_0 is Δ_c^+-dominant intergral, $|\lambda_1| \leqslant \lambda_2 \leqslant \dots \leqslant \lambda_5$, $\lambda_i - \lambda_j \in \mathbb{Z}$, $2\lambda_i \in \mathbb{Z}$, $i, j \leqslant 5$. The normalization $(\lambda_0 + \rho)_\beta = 0$ gives: $(\lambda_0)_\beta = -11$.

The root system $Q(\lambda_0) = R(\lambda_0)$ is either $su(1,p)$, $1 \leqslant p \leqslant 5$, $SO(2,8)$ or E III. We shall refer to these as CaseI, p $(1 \leqslant p \leqslant 5)$, Case II and Case III respectively. Case I, 4 occurs in two forms; either with diagram 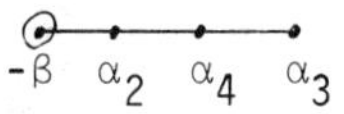

or 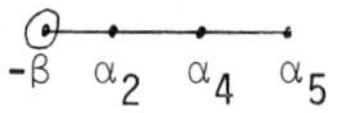

. The

The diagram for Case II is

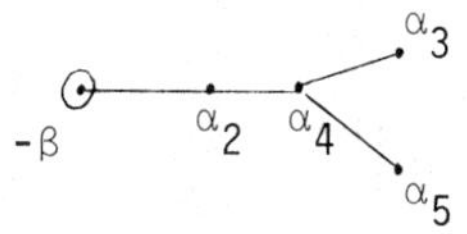

(12.1)

Applying Proposition (4.10), we obtain

<u>LEMMA 12.2</u> <u>If</u> $L(\lambda)$ <u>is unitarizable then</u>

$$z \leqslant 1 + 2(\rho_{c,1})_\beta \quad = \begin{cases} p & \text{in Case I, } p \\ 7 & \text{in Case II} \\ 11 & \text{in Case III} \end{cases}$$

<u>LEMMA 12.3</u> <u>The first reduction point is given by:</u>

$$z = \begin{cases} p & \text{in Case I, } p \\ 4 & \text{in Case II} \\ 8 & \text{in Case III} \end{cases} .$$

For Case I, p , if $z < p$, $\alpha \in \Delta_n^+$ and $(\lambda + \rho)_\alpha \in \mathbb{N}^*$ then $\alpha \in Q(\lambda_0)$. Then the computation in the proof of (7.3) shows that by (6.2), $N(\lambda)$ is irreducible. With (12.2) and (3.1) this implies that $z = p$ is the first reduction point.

For Case II, if $z \leqslant 4$, $\alpha \in \Delta_n^+$ and $(\lambda + \rho)_\alpha \in \mathbb{N}^*$ then $\alpha \in Q(\lambda_0)$. Now using (6.1) exactly as in the proof of (10.3), the reader may verify that the first reduction occurs at $z = 4$. In Case III if we combine (5.2) and (3.1) , we conclude that the first reduction point occurs at $z = 11 - 3 = 8$. This proves (12.3).

<u>THEOREM 12.4</u> $L(\lambda)$ <u>is unitarizable if and only if</u>

a) $z \leqslant p$ in Case I,p

b) $z \leqslant 4$ or $z = 7$ in Case II

c) $z \leqslant 8$ or $z = 11$ in Case III .

PROOF. For a), we combine (3.1),(12.2) and (12.3). For c), we combine (5.2) and (3.1). Now consider b). For $z \leqslant 4$, (3.1) and (12.3) imply that $L(\lambda)$ is unitarizable. For $z = 4$, $\alpha \in \Delta_n^+$ and $(\lambda + \rho)_\alpha \in \mathbb{N}^*$ then $\alpha \in Q(\lambda_0)$. Then exactly as in the proof of (10.5), $N(\lambda)$ has reduction level two at $z = 4$. So, by (3.16), there is <u>at most</u> one value $z > 4$ with $L(\lambda)$ unitarizable. To complete the proof of (12.4), we need only show that $L(\lambda)$ is unitarizable for $z = 7$ in Case II. The remainder of this section is devoted to this verification.

Assume we are in Case II. Then $(\lambda_0)_{\alpha_i} = 0$, $2 \leq i \leq 5$. Let $a = (\lambda_0)_{\alpha_6}$. Then $a \in \mathbb{N}^*$ and $\lambda_0 = (0, 0, 0, 0, a, -b', -b', b')$.

By our normalization $(\lambda_0 + \rho)_\beta = 0$; and so, $a + 3b' = -22$. We are interested in the point $\lambda = \lambda_0 + 7\zeta = (0, 0, 0, 0, a, -b, -b, b)$ with $a + 3b = -8$. For the remainder of this section assume λ has this form.

PROPOSITION 12.5 The $\mathfrak{k}$-spectrum of $L(\lambda)$ is multiplicity free and $F(\mu)$ occurs in $L(\lambda)$ if and only if μ has form $\lambda - n_1\gamma_1 - n_2\gamma_2$, $n_1 \geq n_2 \geq 0$, $n_i \in \mathbb{N}$.

Assume for the moment (12.5) is true.

COROLLARY 12.6 $L(\lambda)$ is unitary.

PROOF: A direct calculation shows that $\|\lambda+\rho-n_1\gamma_1-n_2\gamma_2\|^2-\|\lambda+\rho\|^2 = 3(n_1-n_2) + a(n_1+n_2) + n_1^2+n_2^2$. Since $n_1 \geq n_2$ and a is positive the basic criterion (3.9) implies $L(\lambda)$ is unitarizable.

This corollary completes the proof of (12.4). We now prove (12.5) through a series of lemmas.

The strongly orthogmal roots are:

$$\gamma_1 = 1/2(1, -1, -1, -1, -1, -1, -1, 1)$$

$$\gamma_2 = 1/2(-1, 1, 1, 1, -1, -1, -1, 1)$$

Put $\mathfrak{h}^- = \mathbb{C}H_{\gamma_1} + \mathbb{C}H_{\gamma_2}$. Set R equal to the set of $\alpha \in \Delta$ such that $\alpha|_{\mathfrak{h}^-}$ is not of the form $\pm 1/2\, \gamma_i$, $i = 1,2$. Then R is a root system. Set $R^+ = R \cap \Delta_n^+$ and $R_c^+ = R \cap \Delta_c^+$ and $R_c^+ = R \cap \Delta_c^+$. We write Q in place of $Q(\lambda_0)$, and put $Q^+ = Q \cap \Delta^+$, $Q_n^+ = Q \cap \Delta_n^+$ and $Q_c^+ = Q \cap \Delta_c^+$.

LEMMA 12.7 Δ_n^+ equals the disjoint union of R_n^+ and Q_n^+ Furthermore, $\alpha \in R_n^+$ (resp. Q_n^+) if and only if the fifth coordinate is $-1/2$ (resp $+1/2$).

PROOF. Let W_c^0 be the Weyl group of R_c^+. By Lemma 2.2 [17], R is a simple root system and being Hermitian symmetric the noncompact positive root vectors span an irreducible module for the compact subalgebra. But since there is only one length of root vector, $W_c^0 \cdot \alpha_1 = R_n^+$(note $\alpha_1 = \gamma_1$). By a short computation the reader may verify that R_c^+ has simple roots α_i, $2 \leqslant i \leqslant 5$; and so, elements of W_c^0 fix the fifth coordinate. Since α_1 has fifth coordinate $-1/2$ we obtain the result for R_n^+.

The same argument applies to Q_n^+ since W_c^0 is also the Weyl group for Q_c^+. So $Q_n^+ = W_c^0 \cdot \beta$ and thus elements of Q_n^+ have fifth coordinate $+1/2$. This also implies $Q_n^+ \cap R_n^+ = \emptyset$. Both sets contain eight elements while Δ_n^+ contains sixteen. Therefore $\Delta_n^+ = Q_n^+ \cup R_n^+$.

LEMMA 12.8 Put $\gamma = 1/2(-1, -1, -1, -1, 1, -1, -1, 1)$. Then $\mathfrak{p}^- \otimes F(\lambda) = F(\lambda - \alpha_1) \oplus F(\lambda - \gamma)$.

PROOF. This follows easily from (4.5) since we are in the equal root length case.

Let Z denote the maximal proper submodule of $N(\lambda)$

LEMMA 12.9 Put $\delta = 1/2(1,1,1,-1,-1,-1,-1,1)$. The following $\mathfrak{k}$-modules $F(\mu)$ occur in Z:

a) $\mu = \lambda - \gamma - n_1\gamma_1 - n_2\gamma_2$, $n_1 \geqslant n_2 \geqslant 0$, $n_i \in \mathbb{N}$.
b) $\mu = \lambda - \gamma - \delta - n_1\gamma_1 - n_2\gamma_2$, $n_1 \geqslant n_2 \geqslant 0$, $n_i \in \mathbb{N}$.

PROOF. $(\lambda + \rho)_\gamma = 1$ so $\lambda + \rho$ and $\lambda - \gamma + \rho$ have the same norm. Then by (3.6), $\lambda - \gamma$ is a highest weight of Z. Let z be a vector in Z of weight $\lambda - \gamma$. Let $u_1 \in U(\mathfrak{p}^-)^{\mathfrak{n}_\mathfrak{k}}_{-\gamma_1}$ and $u_2 \in U(\mathfrak{p}^-)^{\mathfrak{n}_\mathfrak{k}}_{-\gamma_1-\gamma_2}$. Then it is well known ([17] Corollary 3.2) that

$U(\mathfrak{p}^-)^{\mathfrak{n}_k} = \mathbb{C}[u_1,u_2]$. Since $N(\lambda)$ is free as a $U(\mathfrak{p}^-)$-module, $u_1^{n_1-n_2} u_2^{n_2} z \neq 0$. This proves a).

To prove b) consider the map $N(\lambda - \gamma) \to Z$ induced by $1 \otimes 1 \to z$. Using (4.5) as in (12.8), we find that $F(\lambda - \gamma - \delta) \to N(\lambda - \gamma)$. If this $\mathfrak{k}$-module was contained in the maximal proper submodule of $N(\lambda - \gamma)$ then exactly as above, $\lambda - \gamma - \delta$ would be a highest weight of the maximal submodule. But then

$$\|\lambda - \gamma - \delta + \rho\| = \|\lambda - \gamma + \rho\|.$$

Then $(\lambda - \gamma + \rho)_\delta = 1$. However by evaluation, $(\lambda - \gamma + \rho)_\delta = -a \neq 1$. So, $F(\lambda - \gamma - \delta)$ occurs in $L(\lambda - \gamma)$ and thus in Z. Again as above, if w is a Δ_c^+-highest weight vector in Z of weight $\lambda - \gamma - \delta$ then $u_1^{n_1-n_2} u_2^{n_2} \cdot w$ is a non-zero Δ_c^+-highest weight vector with weight of the form b). This proves b).

For $\mu \in \mathfrak{t}^*$, let $q(\mu)$ denote the number of ways μ can be expressed as a sum of elements of Δ_n^+. We call q the partition function of Δ_n^+. Let q^0 (resp. q^V) be the partition of R_n^+ (resp. Q_n^+).

<u>LEMMA 12.10</u>. (1) <u>If</u> $\lambda - \mu$ <u>is</u> Δ_c^+<u>-dominant integral then</u>

$$\dim \operatorname{Hom}_{\mathfrak{k}} (F(\lambda-\mu), N(\lambda)) = \sum_{s \in W_c} \det(s)\, q(s(\lambda+\rho) - (\lambda-\mu+\rho))$$

$$= \sum_{s \in W_c} \det(s)\, q(\lambda+\rho-s(\lambda-\mu+\rho)).$$

(2) <u>For</u> $\xi \in \mathfrak{t}^*$, $q(\xi) = \sum_\nu q^0(\xi-\nu) q^V(\nu)$.

PROOF: (1) is the usual multiplicity formula for generalized Verma modules. The second identity in (1) follows since Δ_n^+ is stable under W_c. Identity (2) follows from (12.7).

<u>LEMMA 12.11</u>. <u>Let</u> $s \in W_c$, $\alpha \in \Delta_n^+$, $n_1 \geq n_2 \geq 0$, $n_i \in \mathbb{N}$. <u>If</u> $q(\lambda+\rho- s(\lambda+\rho-\alpha-n_1\gamma_1-n_2\gamma_2)) \neq 0$ <u>then</u> $s \in W_c^0$.

PROOF: The root system Δ_c is D_5. In our coordinates for $s \in W_c$, the action of s can be given by first multiplying the ith coordinate $(1 \leq i \leq 5)$ by $\eta_i, \eta_i = \pm 1$ and $\Pi \eta_i = 1$ and then permuting the first five coordinates. The element s lies in W_c^0 if and only if $\eta_5 = 1$ and the permutation fixes the fifth coordinate.

We now verify (12.11). Set $\mu = \lambda+\rho-\alpha-n_1\gamma_1-n_2\gamma_2 n_1 \geq n_2 \geq 0, n_i \in \mathbb{N}$. The fifth coordinate of μ is $a+4+1/2(n_1+n_2) \pm 1/2$. If the permutation takes 5 to i, $i < 5$, then the ith coordinate of $\lambda+\rho-s\mu$ is:

$$i-1-\eta_5(a+4+1/2(n_1+n_2) \pm 1/2). \qquad (12.12)$$

By assumption $q(\lambda+\rho-s(\mu)) \neq 0$ and since all $\nu \in \Delta_n^+$ satisfy $\zeta\nu = 1$, $\lambda+\rho-s(\mu)$ must be a sum of $n_1 + n_2 + 1$ elements in Δ_n^+. But any such sum will have i^{th} coordinate with absolute value $\leq 1/2(n_1 + n_2 + 1)$. This contradicts (12.12); and so, the permutation must leave the fifth coordinate fixed. Now assume the permutation leaves the fifth coordinate fixed and $\eta_5 = -1$. Then the fifth coordinate of $\lambda+\rho-s\mu$ is $2a + 8 + 1/2(n_1+n_2 \pm 1)$. But arguing as above this value is too large for the fifth coordinate of any sum of n_1+n_2+1 elements of Δ_n^+. Finally we conclude that $\eta_5 = 1$ and s fixes the fifth coordinate. This means $s \in W_c^0$ which proves (12.11).

PROOF of (12.5) We shall proceed by induction. $L(\lambda)$ is graded. The graded form of (12.5) is:

(12.13j) The $\mathfrak{k}$-spectrum of $L^j(\lambda)$ is multiplicity free and $F(\mu)$ occurs in $L^j(\lambda)$ if and only if μ has the form $\lambda-n_1\gamma_1-n_2\gamma_2$, $n_1 \geq n_2 \geq 0$, $n_1 \in \mathbb{N}$ and $n_1+n_2 = j$.

Clearly, (12.13j) is true for $j = 0$. Now assume $j \geq 1$ and (12.13i) is true for $i \leq j - 1$.

Let z be a Δ_c^+-highest weight vector in $L^j(\lambda)$ of weight ν. Since $\mathfrak{p}^+ \cdot z \neq 0$, there exists $\alpha \in \Delta_n^+$ with $\nu+\alpha$ a Δ_c^+-highest weight of $L^{j-1}(\lambda)$. By the induction hypothesis, $\nu+\alpha = \lambda - n_1\gamma_1 - n_2\gamma_2$, $n_1 \geq n_2 \geq 0$, $n_i \in \mathbb{N}$, and $n_1 + n_2 = j - 1$.

<u>LEMMA 12.14</u>. <u>Let</u> $\mu \in \mathfrak{t}^*$ <u>be integral</u>.

a) <u>Assume</u> $\alpha \in R_n^+$, $q^\vee(\mu) \neq 0$, $s \in W_c^\circ$. <u>If</u> $q^\circ(s(\lambda+\rho) - (\lambda+\rho-n_1\gamma_1-n_2\gamma_2-\alpha)-\mu) \neq 0$ <u>then</u> $\mu = 0$.

b) <u>Assume</u> $\alpha \in Q_n^+$, $q^\vee(\mu) \neq 0$, $s \in W_c^\circ$. <u>If</u> $q^\circ(s(\lambda+\rho) - (\lambda+\rho-n_1\gamma_1-n_2\gamma_2-\alpha)-\mu) \neq 0$. <u>Then</u> $\mu \in Q_n^+$. <u>Moreover, in this case</u> $q^\vee(\mu) = 1$.

<u>PROOF</u>: Since $s \in W_c^\circ$, $s(\lambda+\rho) - (\lambda+\rho) = s\rho-\rho$ which is a sum of elements in $-R_c^+$. Also $(s\rho-\rho+n_1\gamma_1+n_2\gamma_2)_{\mathfrak{h}^-} = e\gamma_1+f\gamma_2$ with $e+f=n_1+n_2$.

If $q^{\vee}(\mu) \neq 0$ and $2\langle\mu,\zeta\rangle = k\langle\beta,\beta\rangle$ then $\mu|_{\mathfrak{h}^-} = c\gamma_1+d\gamma_2$ with $c+d = \frac{k}{2}$. If $q^{\circ}(\nu) \neq 0$ and $2\langle\nu,\zeta\rangle = r\langle\beta,\beta\rangle$, then $\nu|_{\mathfrak{h}} = u\gamma_1+v\gamma_2$ with $u+v = r$. These last assertions are verified easily using basic properties of the strongly orthogonal roots. The reader should consult section two of [17]. We write $(s(\lambda+\rho)-(\lambda+\rho-n_1\lambda_1-n_2\lambda_2-\alpha)-\mu)|_{\mathfrak{h}^-} = s\gamma_1+t\gamma_2$. Now applying the identies above under the hypotheses of a) we compute $s+t$ in two ways. We obtain $n_1+n_2+1-\frac{k}{2} = n_1+n_2+1-k$. This implies $k=0$; and so, $\langle\mu,\zeta\rangle = 0$. But this contradicts $q^{\vee}(\mu) \neq 0$ unless $\mu=0$. This proves a). Under the hypotheses of b) we evaluate $s+t$ in two ways. This gives $k=1$ and, since $q^{\vee}(\mu) \neq 0, \mu \in Q_n^+$ and $q^{\vee}(\mu) = 1$. This proves b).

<u>LEMMA 12.15.</u> <u>Assume</u> $\alpha \in R_n^+$, $n_1 \geqslant n_2 \geqslant 0$, $n_i \in \mathbb{N}$ <u>and</u> $\lambda-n_1\gamma_1-n_2\gamma_2-\alpha$ <u>is</u> Δ_c^+<u>-dominant integral</u>. <u>Put</u>

$$p= \sum_{s\in W_c} \det(s)q(s(\lambda+\rho)-(\lambda+\rho-n_1\gamma_1-n_2\gamma_2-\alpha)).$$

<u>Then</u> $p \neq 0$ <u>if and only if</u> $n_1\gamma_1+n_2\gamma_2+\alpha = n_1\gamma_1+m_2\gamma_2$ <u>with</u> $m_1 \geqslant m_2 \geqslant 0$, $m_i \in \mathbb{N}$. <u>Moreover, in this case</u> $p = 1$.

<u>PROOF.</u> By (12.11) and (12.10)(2), $p=\sum_{W_c^{\circ}} \det(s)q(s(\lambda+\rho)-(\lambda+\rho-n_1\gamma_1-n_2\gamma_2-\alpha)) = \sum_{\mu}\sum_{s\in W_c^{\circ}} \det(s)q^{\circ}(s\rho-\rho+n_1\gamma_1+n_2\gamma_2+\alpha-\mu)q^{\vee}(\mu)$. Now applying (12.14)(a) $p = \sum_{s\in W_c^{\circ}} \det(s)q^{\circ}(s\rho-\rho+n_1\gamma_1+n_2\gamma_2+\alpha))$. This last expression is precisely the multiplicity of the $\mathfrak{k}^{\circ}$-module with highest weight $n_1\gamma_1+n_2\gamma_2+\alpha$(in $S(\overline{\mathfrak{p}}^{\circ})$, where $\mathfrak{k}^{\circ}+\mathfrak{p}^{\circ}=\mathfrak{g}^{\circ}$ is the Cartan decomposition of the Hermitian symmetric pair with root sytem R. Then the results of Schmid (cf.[17] Section 3) for the decomposition of $S(\overline{\mathfrak{p}}^{\circ})$ give (12.15).

<u>LEMMA 12.16.</u> <u>Assume</u> $\alpha \in Q_n^+$, $n_1 \geqslant n_2 \geqslant 0$, $n_i \in \mathbb{N}$ <u>and</u> $\lambda-n_1\gamma_1-n_2\gamma_2-\alpha$ is Δ_c^+<u>-dominant integral</u>. <u>Then, with p as in</u> (12.15) $p = 1$.

<u>PROOF.</u> Arguing as in the proof of (12.15) but using (12.14)(b) instead of (12.14)(a), $p = \sum_{\mu\in Q_n^+} p_\mu$ with $p_\mu = \sum_{s\in W_c^{\circ}} \det(s)$ $q^{\circ}(s\rho-\rho+n_1\gamma_1+n_2\gamma_2+\alpha-\mu)$. If $\mu=\alpha$ then p_α is the multiplicity of the

$\mathfrak{k}^\circ$-module with highest weight $-n_1\gamma_1-n_2\gamma_2$ in $S(\bar{\mathfrak{p}}^\circ)$ (notation as in the proof of (12.15)) which is one. So to complete the proof we must show $p_\mu = 0$ if $\mu \in Q_n^+$, $\alpha \neq \mu$.

Since $\rho-n_i\gamma_1-n_2\gamma_2-\alpha$ is Δ_c^+-dominant integral and regular and since we are in the equal root length case, $\rho-n_1\gamma_1-n_2\gamma_2-\alpha+\mu$ is Δ_c^+-dominant. If this element is Δ_c^- singular then $p_\mu = 0$. So we may assume it is Δ_c^+ -dominant integral and regular. But then from the proof of (12.15), if $p_\mu \neq 0$ then $-n_1\gamma_1 - n_2\gamma_2 - \alpha+\mu = -m_1\gamma_1-m_2\gamma_2$ with $m_1 \geqslant m_2 \geqslant 0$, $m_i \in \mathbb{N}$. Now choose k,ℓ in $\{1,2\}$ with $\alpha|_{\mathfrak{h}^-} = \frac{1}{2}\gamma_i, \mu|_{\mathfrak{h}^-} = \frac{1}{2}\gamma_j$. Since $n_1\gamma_1+n_2\gamma_2+\alpha=m_1\gamma_1+m_2\gamma_2+\mu$, they are equal when restricted to $\mathfrak{h}^-$. This gives $k = \ell$, $n_i = m_i, i = 1, 2$; and in turn, $\alpha = \mu$. This completes the proof of (12.16).

<u>LEMMA 12.17.</u> <u>Let</u> $n_i \in \mathbb{N}$ <u>with</u> $n_1 \geqslant n_2 \geqslant 0$ <u>and let</u> $\alpha \in \Delta_n^+$ <u>be such that</u> $-n_1\gamma_1-n_2\gamma_2-\alpha$ <u>is</u> Δ_c^+<u>-dominant integral</u>. <u>Then either</u>

a) $n_1 = n_2$ and $\alpha = \gamma_1$ or γ (γ as in (12.8)

<u>or</u>

b) $n_1 > n_2$ and $\alpha = \gamma_1, \gamma, \gamma_2, \delta_1, \delta_2$ where $\delta_1 = \frac{1}{2}(-1,1,1,-1,1,-1,-1,1), \delta_2 = \frac{1}{2}(-1,1-1,-1,-1,-1,-1,1)$.

The proof of (12.17) is by a direct calculation. We omit the details.

We now return to the notation prior to (12.14). In particular $\nu = \lambda-n_1\gamma_1-n_2\gamma_2-\alpha$. By (12.17), α is given by a) or b). If $n_1 = n_2$ then $\alpha = \gamma_1$ or γ and by (12.15) or (12.16), $F(\nu)$ occurs in $N(\lambda)$ with multiplicity one. If $n_1 > n_2$ then $\alpha = \gamma_1, \gamma, \gamma_2, \delta_1$ or δ_2. But $\gamma, \delta_1 \in Q_n^+$ and $\gamma_1, \gamma_2, \delta_2 \in R_n^+$; and so by (12.16) and (12.15), $F(\nu)$ occurs in $N(\lambda)$ with multiplicity one for $\alpha = \gamma$, δ_1, γ_1 and γ_2 and with multiplicity zero for $\alpha = \delta_2$.

Now recall (12.9) and observe that $\gamma+\delta = \gamma_1+\delta_1$. This shows $F(\nu)$ occurs in $Z(\lambda)$ for $\alpha = \gamma$ and also for $\alpha = \delta_1$ if $n_1 > n_2$. Since by the preceeding paragraph the multiplicity of $F(\nu)$ is at most one in $N(\lambda)$, we conclude that since ν was chosen with $F(\nu) \hookrightarrow L(\lambda)$, $\alpha = \gamma_1$ if $n_1 = n_2$ and $\alpha = \gamma_1$ or γ_2 if $n_1 > n_2$. This completes the proof of (12.13j); and so the induction step is complete. In turn, this proves (12.5).

13. <u>E VII</u>

$\Delta \sim E_7$ diagram 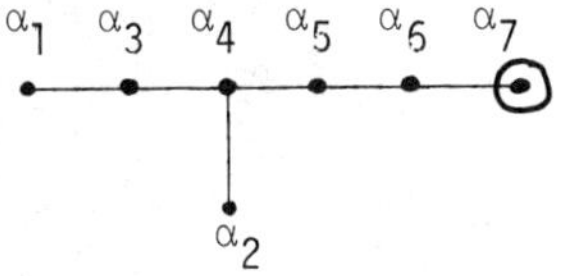

Δ_c^+ equals the full set of positive roots for E_6 as in Section 12.

$$\Delta_n^+ = \{\pm e_i + e_6\}_{1\leqslant i\leqslant 5} \cup \{e_8 - e_7\}$$
$$\cup\{\tfrac{1}{2}(\textstyle\sum_{1\leqslant i\leqslant 5}(-1)^{\nu(i)}e_i + e_6 - e_7 + e_8) \mid \Sigma\nu(i) \text{ is odd}\}$$

Let α_i, $1 \leqslant i \leqslant 6$, be as in Section 12 and put $\alpha_7 = e_6 - e_5$. Now the maximal root is $\beta = e_8 - e_7 = 2\alpha_1+2\alpha_2+3\alpha_3+4\alpha_4+3\alpha_5+2\alpha_6+\alpha_7$. Then $\zeta = e_6 + \tfrac{1}{2}(e_8-e_7) = (0,0,0,0,0,1,-\tfrac{1}{2},\tfrac{1}{2})$, $\rho = (0,1,2,3,4,5,-{}^{17}/2, {}^{17}/2)$ Write $\lambda = \lambda_0 + z\zeta$ with $\lambda_0 = (\lambda_1, \ldots, \lambda_8)$ and $\lambda_7 = -\lambda_8$. Since λ_0 is Δ_c^+-dominant integral, $|\lambda_1| \leqslant \lambda_2 \leqslant \ldots \leqslant \lambda_5$, $\lambda_i - \lambda_j \in \mathbb{Z}$, $2\lambda_i \in \mathbb{Z}$, $1 \leqslant i \leqslant j \leqslant 5$, and $(\lambda_0)_{\alpha_1} \in \mathbb{N}$. The normalization $(\lambda_0+\rho)_\beta = 0$ gives: $(\lambda_0)_\beta = -17$ or $\lambda_8 = -\frac{17}{2}$.

The root system $Q(\lambda_0) = R(\lambda_0)$ is either $su(1,p)$, $1 \leqslant p \leqslant 6$, $so(2,10)$ or EVII. We refer to these as Case I,p $(1 \leqslant p \leqslant 6)$, Case II and Case III respectively. Case I, 5 occurs in two forms; either with diagram 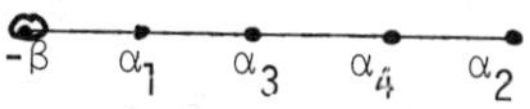 or

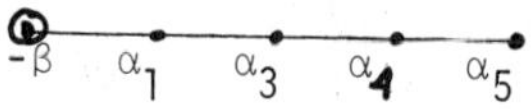 . The diagram for Case II is:

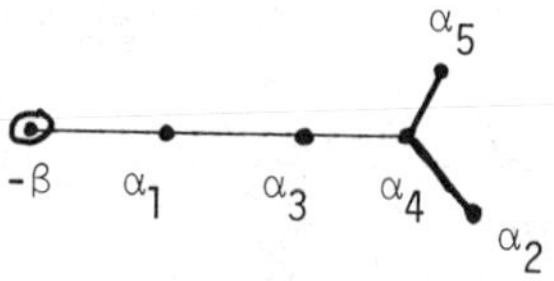

(13.1)

Applying Proposition (4.10), we obtain:

LEMMA 13.2. If $L(\lambda)$ is unitarizable then

$$z \leqslant 1 + 2\,(\rho_{c,1})_\beta = \begin{cases} p & \text{in Case I,p} \\ 9 & \text{in Case II} \\ 17 & \text{In Case III} \end{cases}$$

LEMMA 13.3. The first reduction point is given by:

$$z = \begin{cases} p & \text{in Case I,p} \\ 5 & \text{in Case II} \\ 9 & \text{in Case III.} \end{cases}$$

For Case I,p, if $z < p$, $\alpha \in \Delta_n^+$ and $(\lambda+\rho)_\alpha \in \mathbb{N}^*$ then $\alpha \in Q(\lambda_0)$. Then the computation in the proof of (7.3) shows by (6.2) that $N(\lambda)$ is irreducible. With (13.2) and (3.1) this implies that $z = p$ is the first reduction points.

For Case II, if $z \leqslant 5$, $\alpha \in \Delta_n^+$ and $(\lambda+\rho)_\alpha \in \mathbb{N}^*$ then $\alpha \in Q(\lambda_0)$. Now using (6.1) exactly as in the proof of (10.3), the reader may verify that the first reduction point occurs at $a = 5$. In Case III, (13.3) follows from (3.1) and (5.2).

THEOREM 13.4. $L(\lambda)$ is unitarizable if and only if

a) $z \leqslant p$ in Case I,p

b) $z \leqslant 5$ or $z = 9$ in Case II

c) $z \leqslant 9$ or $z = 13$ or $z = 17$ in Case III.

PROOF. For a) we merely combine (3.1), (13.2) and (13.3). For c) we combine (5.2) and (3.1). Now consider b). For $z \leqslant 5$, (3.1) and (13.3) imply that $L(\lambda)$ is unitarizable. For $z = 5$ $\alpha \in \Delta_n^+$ and $(\lambda+\rho)_\alpha \in \mathbb{N}^*$ one can check that $\alpha \in Q(\lambda_0)$. Then exactly as in the proof of (10.5), $N(\lambda)$ has level of reduction two at $z = 5$. Then, by (3.16), there is at most one value $z > 5$ with $L(\lambda)$ unitarizable. Therefore to complete the proof of (13.4), we need only show $L(\lambda)$ is unitarizable for $z = 9$ in Case II. The remainder of this section is devoted to this verification.

Recall the set $\gamma_1 < \gamma_2 < \ldots < \gamma_r$ of strongly orthogonal roots for $\mathfrak{g}$ introduced in Section 5. The last unitarizable point before the trivial representation, occurs at $\lambda = -c\zeta$. We shall account for the remaining unitarizable representations of $\mathfrak{g}$ by analyzing $L(-c\zeta) \otimes L(-c\zeta)$.

LEMMA 13.5. As a $\mathfrak{k}$-module, $L(-c\zeta)$ is isomorphic to $\bigoplus_{k=0}^{\infty} \mathbb{C}_{-c\zeta} \otimes F(-k\gamma_1)$.

This lemma is proved in [17]. See the last two lines of the proof of Theorem 5.10.

LEMMA 13.6. $L(-c\zeta) \otimes L(-c\zeta) = \bigoplus_{k=0}^{\infty} L(-2c\zeta-k\gamma_1)$.

PROOF. Write $M = M(-c\zeta)$, $L = L(-c\zeta)$ and let Z be the maximal submodule of M. We first decompose $M \otimes L$. Since $N = U(\mathfrak{g}) \otimes_{U(\mathfrak{q})} \mathbb{C}_{-c\zeta}$

$$M \otimes L \simeq U(\mathfrak{g}) \otimes_{U(\mathfrak{q})} (\mathbb{C}_{-c\zeta} \otimes L). \tag{13.7}$$

Let $L_j = \bigoplus_{0 \leq k \leq j} F(-c\zeta - k\gamma_1)$. Then, clearly $\mathfrak{p}^+ L_j \subseteq L_{j-1}$ and so, L_j is a flag of $\mathfrak{q}$-submodules of L with $L_j/L_{j-1} \simeq F(-c\zeta - j\gamma_1)$. This filtration of L induces from $\mathfrak{q}$ to $\mathfrak{g}$ to give a filtration of $N \otimes L$ with

$$(N \otimes L)_i = U(\mathfrak{g}) \underset{U(\mathfrak{q})}{\otimes} (\mathbb{C}_{-c\zeta} \otimes L_i) \text{ and } \tag{13.8}$$

$$(N \otimes L)_i \,/\, (N \otimes L)_{i-1} \simeq N(-2c\zeta - i\gamma_1)$$

We now claim:

$$N \otimes L = \bigoplus_{k=0}^{\infty} N(-2c\zeta - k\gamma_1). \tag{13.9}$$

The value of the Casimir on $N(-2c\zeta - k\gamma_1)$ is $\|-2c\zeta - k\gamma_1 + \rho\|^2 - \|\rho\|^2 = \|-2c\zeta + \rho\|^2 - \|\rho\|^2 + k(k+2c-1)\,\|\gamma_1\|^2$. This value is strictly increasing in k, $k \geq 0$, $2c \geq 1$; and so, writing $N \otimes L$ as a sum of generalized eigenspaces for the Casimir operator and applying (13.8) we obtain the direct sum (13.9).

From Theorem 3.1 [17] and (13.5), $F(\mu)$ occurs in Z if and only if $\mu = -c\zeta - k_1\gamma_1 - k_2\gamma_2 ,,, -k_r\gamma_r$ with $k_1 \geq k_2 \geq \ldots \geq k_r$ and $k_2 > 0$. Then any $F(\xi)$ which occurs in $Z \otimes L$ must have the form $\xi = \mu +$ (weight of L). But then $\xi = -2c\zeta - \sum_{1 \leq i \leq r} k_i\gamma_i - Q$ where Q is a sum of elements in Δ_n^+ (with multiplicity) and $k_2 \geq 1$. We cannot write $-2c\zeta - k\gamma_1$ in this form (since γ_1 is a simple root). This implies that no factor $N(-2c\zeta - k\gamma_1)$ in (13.9) is mapped to zero under the natural projection $N \otimes L \to L \otimes L$. Also, $L \otimes L$ is the tensor product of unitarizable highest weight modules and so is the direct sum of irreducible submodules. Therefore, the image of $N(-2c\zeta - k\gamma_1)$ in $L \otimes L$ is precisely $L(-2c\zeta - k\gamma_1)$. This proves (13.6).

We now complete the proof of (13.4). In Case II, $(\lambda_0)\alpha_i = 0$, $i=1,2,\ldots,5$. Let $(\lambda_0)\alpha_6 = k$. Then $\lambda_0 = (0,0,0,0,k,-k-17,{}^{17}/2,{}^{-17}/2)$ and $\lambda_0 + 9\zeta = (0,0,0,0,k,-k-8,4,-4)$. Put $c=4, \gamma_1 = \alpha_7 = e_6 - e_5$. So $-2c\zeta = (0,0,0,0,0,-8,4,-4)$, and thus, $\lambda_0 + 9\zeta = -2c\zeta - k\gamma_1$. By (13.6), $z=9$ corresponds to a unitarizable representation. This completes the proof of (13.4).

In our original proof of the theorem we gave the complete $\mathfrak{k}$-spectrum of these $L(\lambda)$ for $z=9$. Since this is possibly of some independent interest we state the result here.

LEMMA 13.10. *The $\mathfrak{k}$-multiplicities of* $L(-8\zeta-k\gamma_1)$ *are either zero or one*. $F(\mu)$ *occurs in* $L(-8\zeta-k\gamma_1)$ *if and only if* $\mu = -8\zeta-k\gamma_1-n_1\gamma_1-n_2\gamma_2-r\delta$ *with* $\delta=\alpha_7+\alpha_6$, $n_1 \geq n_2 \geq 0$ *and* $0 \leq r \leq k$.

14. CONCLUDING REMARKS

Here we collect the results from earlier sections to prove Theorem 2.4, 2.8 and 2.10. Proposition 3.1 proves parts a), b) and c) of (2.4). Theorem 7.4, 8.4, 9.4, 10.4, 11.4, 12.4 and 13.4 combine to prove Theorem 2.8 and 2.10 and part d) of Theorem 2.4.

The authors were supported by the National Science Foundation.

BIBLIOGRAPHY

1. N. Bourbaki, "Groupes et Algèbres de Lie," Chap. IV,V,VI, Act. Sci. Ind. 1337, Hermann, Paris, 1968.

2. T. J. Enright and R. Parthasarathy, A proof of a conjecture of Kashiwara and Vergne, "Non Commutative Harmonic Analysis and Lie Groups" Lecture Notes in Mathematics, 880, Springer Verlag, 1981.

3. H. Garland and G. Zuckerman, On unitarizable highest weight modules of Hermitian pairs, J. Fac. Sci. Tokyo, 28 (1982), 877-889.

4. Harish-Chandra, Representations of semisimple Lie groups, IV, Amer. J. Math., 77 (1955), 743-777.

5. ______, Representations of semisimple Lie groups V, Amer. J. Math., 78 (1956), 1-41.

6. S. Helgason, "Differential Geometry and Symmetric Spaces", Academic Press, New York, 1962.

7. R. Howe, Remarks on Classical Invariant Theory, preprint.

8. ______, On a notion of rank for unitary representation of classical groups, Proceedings Cime Conference on Non Abelian Harmonic Analysis, Cortona, July, 1980.

9. H. Jakobsen, On singular holomorphic representations, Inv. Math. 62(1980), 67-78.

10. ______, The last possible place of unitarity for certain highest weight modules, preprint.

11. H. Jakobsen, Hermitian symmetric spaces and their unitary highest weight modules, preprint.

12. J. C. Jantzen, Kontravariante Formen auf induzierten Darstellungen halbeinfacher Lie-Algebren, Math. Ann. 226 (1977), 53-65.

13. ______, "Moduln mit einem höchsten Gewicht", Lecture Notes in Mathematics, No. 750, Springer-Verlag, Berlin/Heidelberg/New York, 1979.

14. M. Kashiwara and M. Vergne, On the Segal-Shale-Weil representations and harmonic polynomials, Inv. Math. 44 (1978), 1-47.

15. R. Parthasarathy, Criteria for the unitarizability of some highest weight modules, Proc. Indian Acad. Sci. 89 (1980), 1-24.

16. J. Rawnsley, W. Schmid and J. Wolf, Singular unitary representations and indefinite harmonic theory, preprint, 1981.

17. N. R. Wallach, The analytic continuation of the discrete series I, II, T.A.M.S. 251 (1979), 1-17, 19-37.

THE RANGE OF THE RADON TRANSFORM ON A SYMMETRIC SPACE

Sigurdur Helgason

1. INTRODUCTION

Let G be a connected semisimple Lie group with finite center, $G = KAN$ an Iwasawa decomposition. Let

$$X = G/K, \quad \Xi = G/MN$$

denote, respectively, the symmetric space X associated with G and the space Ξ of the horocycles in X. (Here M is the centralizer of A in K). Let o be the origin in X and $\xi_o = N \cdot o$ the origin in Ξ. Fixing Haar measure dg, dk, da, dn and dm on the groups above, the Radon transform $f \to \hat{f}$ and its dual $\phi \to \check{\phi}$ can be defined as follows:

$$\hat{f}(g\cdot\xi_o) = \int_N f(gn\cdot o)dn, \tag{1}$$

$$\check{\phi}(g\cdot o) = \int_K \phi(gk\cdot\xi_o)dk \tag{2}$$

Then $f \to \hat{f}$ maps the space $\mathcal{D}(X)$ into $\mathcal{D}(\Xi)$ and $\phi \to \check{\phi}$ maps $\mathcal{E}(\Xi)$ into $\mathcal{E}(X)$. (As usual, $\mathcal{D} = C_c^\infty$, and $\mathcal{E} = C^\infty$.) Since

$$\int_X f(x)\check{\phi}(x)dx = \int_\Xi \hat{f}(\xi)\phi(\xi)d\xi, \tag{3}$$

where dx and $d\xi$ are certain fixed invariant measures we define the operations $\wedge$ and $\vee$ on distributions as follows. Let $\mathcal{D}'(Z)$ denote the space of all distributions on a manifold Z, $\mathcal{E}'(Z)$ the subspace of distributions of compact support. If $S \in \mathcal{E}'(X)$, $\tau \in \mathcal{D}'(\Xi)$ we define $\hat{S} \in \mathcal{E}'(\Xi)$, $\check{\tau} \in \mathcal{D}'(X)$ by

$$\hat{S}(\phi) = S(\check{\phi}), \qquad \phi \in \mathcal{E}(\Xi), \tag{4}$$

$$\check{\tau}(f) = \tau(\hat{f}), \qquad f \in \mathcal{D}(X). \tag{5}$$

In this note we describe some new results about the ranges $\mathcal{D}(X)^{\wedge}$ and $\mathcal{E}'(X)^{\wedge}$.

2. PALEY-WIENER THEOREMS FOR THE FOURIER TRANSFORM ON X.

Let $\mathfrak{g}$, $\mathfrak{k}$, $\mathfrak{m}$, $\mathfrak{a}$, $\mathfrak{r}$, denote the Lie algebras of the groups considered above. If $g \in G$ we write its Iwasawa decomposition $g = k \exp H(g)n$ where $H(g) \in \mathfrak{a}$ and then put $A(gK,kM) = -H(g^{-1}k)$. If f is a function on X, (for example $f \in \mathcal{D}(X)$) its Fourier transform is defined [3b] by

$$\tilde{f}(\lambda,b) = \int_X f(x)e^{(-i\lambda+\rho)(A(x,b))}dx. \tag{6}$$

Here $\lambda \in \mathfrak{a}_c^*$ (the complex dual of $\mathfrak{a}$), $b \in B = K/_M$ and ρ is half the sum of the roots of X with multiplicity. We shall need a description of the range $\mathcal{D}(X)^{\sim}$ as well as a more explicit description of the range $\mathcal{D}_o(X)^{\sim}$ where $\mathcal{D}_o(X)$ is the space of K-finite elements in $\mathcal{D}(X)$.

THEOREM 1. [3d] The range $\mathcal{D}(X)^{\sim}$ consists of the functions $\psi(\lambda,b)$ entire in $\lambda \in \mathfrak{a}_c^*$ of exponential type (uniformly in $b \in B$) and satisfying

$$\int_B \psi(\lambda,b)e^{(i\lambda+\rho)(A(x,b))}db \quad \text{is W-invariant in } \lambda.$$

Here db is the K-invariant measure on B and W the Weyl group.

Let δ be an irreducible unitary representation of K on a vector space V_δ and let V_δ^M denote the space of vectors $v \in V_\delta$ fixed under $\delta(M)$. Let $d(\delta) = \dim V_\delta$, $\ell(\delta) = \dim V_\delta^M$, and let $\check{\delta}$ be the representation of K contragredient to δ. We consider the generalized spherical function

$$\Phi_{\lambda,\delta}(x) = \int_K e^{(i\lambda+\rho)(A(x,kM))}\delta(k)dk, \; x \in X, \; \lambda \in \mathfrak{a}_c^*, \tag{7}$$

and let $\mathcal{D}_{\check{\delta}}(X)$ denote the set of K-finite functions in $\mathcal{D}(X)$ of type $\check{\delta}$. For functions $f \in \mathcal{D}_{\check{\delta}}(X)$ the Fourier transform as defined by (6) essentially reduces to the following definition:

$$\tilde{f}(\lambda) = d(\delta)\int_X f(x)\Phi_{\bar{\lambda},\delta}(x)^* dx, \tag{8}$$

where * denotes the adjoint of an operator on V_δ. Then the Fourier transform $\tilde{f}$ of a function $f \in \mathcal{D}_{\check{\delta}}(X)$ is an element of the topological space $\mathcal{H}(\mathfrak{a}^*, \mathrm{Hom}(V_\delta, V_\delta^M))$ of holomorphic functions on $\mathfrak{a}_c^*$ of exponential type with values in the space $\mathrm{Hom}(V_\delta, V_\delta^M)$. Let $Q^\delta(\lambda)$ denote the $\ell(\delta) \times \ell(\delta)$ matrix with polynomial entries defined in [3e], §6; it is a modification of matrices defined in [5] §4, and [4]. We then consider the topological vector space

$$\mathcal{H}^\delta(\mathfrak{a}^*) = \{F \in \mathcal{H}(\mathfrak{a}^*, \mathrm{Hom}(V_\delta, V_\delta^M)) : (Q^{\check{\delta}})^{-1} F \ \ W\text{-invariant}\}.$$

With this notation Theorem 1 can be stated for K-finite f in a more specific form.

<u>THEOREM 2</u>. ([3e], p. 204.) <u>The mapping</u> $f \to \tilde{f}$ <u>where</u>

$$\tilde{f}(\lambda) = d(\delta)\int_X f(x)\Phi_{\bar{\lambda},\delta}(x)^* dx$$

<u>is a homeomorphism of</u> $\mathcal{D}_{\check{\delta}}(X)$ <u>onto</u> $\mathcal{H}^\delta(\mathfrak{a}^*)$.

<u>Remark</u>. The case when δ is the trivial representation was settled in [3a], [2] and [3e] p. 37. On the other hand, ranges for the Fourier transform of functions $f \in \mathcal{D}(G)$, K-finite on both sides, have been discussed by several people. For an account of this see Arthur's paper [1] where the most general result is given.

3. <u>RANGE OF THE RADON TRANSFORM ON</u> X.

The Fourier transform $\tilde{f}$ on X and the Radon transform $\hat{f}$ on X are related by the formula

$$\tilde{f}(\lambda, kM) = \int_A \hat{f}(ka \cdot \xi_o) e^{(-i\lambda+\rho)(\log a)} da,$$

where da is a Haar measure on A. Thus Theorem 1 leads to a description of the range $\{\hat{f}: f \in \mathcal{D}(X)\}$ (cf. [3d], Theorem 8.4). Although this description is not very transparent it leads to the following modest consequence which turns out to be quite useful in obtaining the characterization of $(\mathcal{E}'(X))^{\wedge}$.

PROPOSITION 3. *The range* $\mathcal{D}(X)^{\wedge}$ *is a closed subspace of* $\mathcal{D}(\Xi)$ *even in the weak topology* $\sigma(\mathcal{D}(\Xi), \mathcal{E}(\Xi))$.

Here $\sigma(\mathcal{D},\mathcal{E})$ denotes as usual the weakest topology for which the maps

$$m_\phi: f \in \mathcal{D}(\Xi) \to \int_\Xi f(\xi)\phi(\xi)d\xi$$

are continuous $(\phi \in \mathcal{E}(\Xi))$.

Now let N denote the kernel of the dual transform:

$$N = \{\phi \in \mathcal{E}(\Xi): \check{\phi} = 0\}.$$

It is then obvious from (4) that each $\phi \in \mathcal{E}'(X)^{\wedge}$ vanishes identically on N. Using Proposition 3 and the inversion formula for the Radon transform we can also prove the converse.

THEOREM 4. *The Radon transform* $S \to \hat{S}$ *is a bijection of* $\mathcal{E}'(X)$ *onto*

$$\{\sigma \in \mathcal{E}'(\Xi): \sigma(N) = 0\}.$$

We can also use Theorem 2 to describe the range of the Radon transform on the K-types. Let $f \in \mathcal{D}(X)$ and put

$$f^\delta(x) = d(\delta)\int_K f(k^{-1}\cdot x)\delta(k)dk$$

so that

$$f(x) = \sum_{\delta \in \hat{K}_M} \operatorname{Tr}(f^\delta(x)).$$

Here $\hat{K}$ is the unitary dual of K and $\hat{K}_M = \{\delta \in \hat{K}: V^M \neq 0\}$. We put

$$\hat{f}^{\delta}(\xi) = \int_{\xi} f^{\delta}(x)d\sigma(x) \qquad (\xi \in \Xi)$$

and since $\hat{f}^{\delta}(k\cdot\xi) = \delta(k)\hat{f}^{\delta}(\xi)$ the function $\hat{f}^{\delta}$ is determined by its restriction to $A \cdot \xi_0$. Let $Q^{\delta}(D)$ denote the $\ell(\delta) \times \ell(\delta)$ differential operator matrix obtained by replacing the polynomial entries in $Q^{\delta}(\lambda)$ by the corresponding constant coefficient differential operators on A. Now Theorem 2 implies the following results.

THEOREM 5. *Fix* $\delta \in \hat{K}_M$. *As* f *runs through* $\mathcal{D}(X)$ *the functions* $\hat{f}^{\delta}$ *on* $A \cdot \xi_0$ *run through the set of functions of the form*

$$F(a) = e^{-\rho(\log a)}\,(\check{Q}^{\delta}(D)H)(a) \qquad (a \in A)$$

where $H \in \mathcal{D}(A, \mathrm{Hom}(V_{\delta}, V_{\delta}^{M}))$ *is invariant under* W.

Examples. Let X be the non-Euclidean disk $|z| < 1$ with the Riemannian structure

$$ds^2 = \frac{dx^2+dy^2}{(1-x^2-y^2)^2}\,.$$

Here the horocycles are the circles tangential to the boundary $|z| = 1$. Let $\xi_{t,\theta}$ be the horocycle through $e^{i\theta}$, having (non-Euclidean) distance t from the origin; here t is taken negative if the origin is inside the horocycle. Here Theorem 5 specializes to the following result.

THEOREM 6. *The range* $\mathcal{D}(X)^{\wedge}$ *consists of the function* $\psi \in \mathcal{D}(\Xi)$ *which when expanded (in a Fourier series in* θ)

$$\psi(\xi_{t,\theta}) = \sum_{n\in\mathbb{Z}} \psi_n(t)e^{in\theta}$$

have the property: *For each* $n \in \mathbb{Z}$,

$$\psi_n(t) = e^{-t}\left(\frac{d}{dt} - 1\right) \cdots \left(\frac{d}{dt} - 2|n| + 1\right)\phi_n(t),$$

where $\phi_n \in \mathcal{D}(\mathbb{R})$ *is even*.

It is of some interest to compare this with the range of the Radon transform on $\mathbb{R}^2$. By definition this is the mapping $f \to \hat{f}$ where

$$\hat{f}(\omega,p) = \int_{(x,\omega)=p} f(x)d\sigma(x).$$

Here ω is a unit vector, $p \in \mathbb{R}$, $(\ , \ )$ the inner product and $d\sigma$ the measure on the line $(x,\omega) = p$.

If we now work out the modification of Theorem 6 for X of constant curvature $-\varepsilon$ and then let $\varepsilon \to 0$ we are led to expect the following result:

PROPOSITION 7. The range $\mathcal{D}(\mathbb{R}^2)^\wedge$ consists of the functions $\psi \in \mathcal{D}(S^1 \times \mathbb{R})$ which when expanded in a Fourier series

$$\psi(e^{i\theta},p) = \sum_n \psi_n(p)e^{in\theta}$$

have the property: For each $n \in \mathbb{Z}$

$$\psi_n(p) = \frac{d^{|n|}}{dp^{|n|}} \phi_n(p)$$

where $\phi_n \in \mathcal{D}(\mathbb{R})$ is even.

This characterization of the range is indeed true because it is readily seen to be equivalent to the standard characterization: $\psi \in \mathcal{D}(\mathbb{R}^2)^\wedge$ if and only if $\psi \in \mathcal{D}(S^1 \times \mathbb{R})$ and if for each $k \in \mathbb{Z}^+$, $\int_{\mathbb{R}} \psi(\omega,p)p^k dp$ is a homogeneous k^{th} degree polynomial in ω_1, ω_2 ([3a]).

The author was supported by the National Science Foundation.

REFERENCES

[1] J. Arthur, A Paley-Wiener theorem for real reductive groups (preprint).

[2] R. Gangolli, On the Plancherel formula and the Paley-Wiener theorem for spherical functions on semisimple Lie groups. Ann. of Math. 93(1971), 150-165.

[3] S. Helgason, a) A duality in integral geometry; some generalizations of the Radon transform. Bull. Amer. Math. Soc. 70(1964), 435-446.

b) Radon-Fourier transforms on symmetric spaces and related group representations. Bull. Amer. Math. Soc. 71(1965), 757-763.

c) An analog of the Paley-Wiener theorem for the Fourier transform on certain symmetric spaces. Math. Ann. 165(1966), 297-308.

d) The surjectivity of invariant differential operators on symmetric spaces I. Ann. of Math. 98(1973), 451-479.

e) A duality for symmetric spaces with applications to group representations I, II. Advan. Math. 5(1970), 1-154; 22(1976), 187-219.

[4] B. Kostant, On the existence and irreducibility of certain series of representations. Bull. Amer. Math. Soc. 75(1969), 627-642.

[5] K. R. Parthasarathy, R. Ranga Rao and V. S. Varadarajan, Ann. of Math. 87(1967), 383-429.

WEIGHTED ORBITAL INTEGRALS

Rebecca A. Herb

Let G be a reductive Lie group of Harish-Chandra class, K a maximal compact subgroup of G, and θ the corresponding Cartan involution. Suppose initially that rank G = rank K so that G has discrete series representations. Then Harish-Chandra has proved the following theorem relating orbital integrals of matrix coefficients and characters for discrete series representations.

Let $\pi \in \mathcal{E}_2(G)$, the set of equivalence classes of discrete series representations of G. Let Θ_π denote the character of π as a function on G', the regular set of G. For any $f \in \mathcal{C}(G)$, the Schwartz space of G, let $\langle\Theta_\pi, f\rangle = \int_G f(x)\overline{\Theta_\pi(x)}\, dx$. Let $T = T_I T_R$ be a θ-stable Cartan subgroup of G where $T_I = T \cap K$ and T_R is split. For $h \in T' = T \cap G'$ and $f \in C_c^\infty(G)$, the integral of f over the orbit of h is defined by $r_f(h) = \int_{T_R \backslash G} f(x^{-1}hx)d\dot{x}$ where $d\dot{x}$ is a G-invariant measure on the quotient. It is well-known that the distribution $r(h): f \to r_f(h)$ is tempered, that is extends continuously to $f \in \mathcal{C}(G)$.

Now suppose that f is a K-finite matrix coefficient of π. Then, in 1966, Harish-Chandra proved in [2a] that for $h \in T'$,

$$r_f(h) = \begin{cases} \langle\Theta_\pi, f\rangle\Theta_\pi(h) & \text{if} \quad \{1\} = T_R \\ 0 & \text{if} \quad \{1\} \subsetneq T_R. \end{cases} \tag{1}$$

If h is an elliptic element, (1) relates the integral of f over the orbit of h and the value of the character of π at h. For arbitrary h, (1) can be interpreted as giving the Fourier inversion formula for the distribution $r(h)$ restricted to the space of cusp forms on G.

In 1976 Arthur [1a] proved the following beautiful generalization of Harish-Chandra's formula. Let A be a special vector subgroup of G, that is, the split component of a parabolic subgroup. For any $P \in \mathcal{P}(A)$, the set of parabolic subgroups of G with A as split component, G can be decomposed as $G = MANK$ where MAN is the Langlands decomposition of P. For $x \in G$, write $x = m \exp(H_P(x))nk$ where $m \in M$, $n \in N$, $k \in K$, and $H_P(x) \in \underline{a}$, the Lie algebra of A. For a fixed Euclidean measure on $\underline{a}$, let $v_A(x)$ be the volume in $\underline{a}$ of the convex hull of $\{H_P(x): P \in \mathcal{P}(A)\}$. Then v_A is left-invariant by $L = MA$. Thus if T is a Cartan subgroup of G with $A \subseteq T_R$ so that $T \subseteq L$, v_A is well-defined on the quotient $T_R\backslash G$ and can be used to define a weighted orbital integral

$$r_f^A(h) = \int_{T_R\backslash G} f(x^{-1}hx)v_A(x)d\dot{x} \quad \text{for} \quad h \in T', \; f \in C_c^\infty(G).$$

Arthur proved that the distributions $r^A(h)\colon f \to r_f^A(h)$ are tempered and have many properties analogous to those of ordinary orbital integrals.

Such weighted orbital integrals occur in the Selberg trace formula for the case of non-compact quotient and thus, as for the case of ordinary orbital integrals, it is important to know their Fourier inversion formulas as tempered distributions. Ordinary orbital integrals can be recovered as a special case of the weighted orbital integrals when A is the split component of G and the weight v_A is by convention equal to 1.

Arthur's generalization of (1) is as follows. Let f be a K-finite matrix coefficient of a discrete series representation π. Let T be a Cartan subgroup of G with $A \subseteq T_R$. Then for $h \in T'$

$$r_f^A(h) = \begin{cases} (-1)^p < \theta_\pi, f > \theta_\pi(h) & \text{if} \quad A = T_R \\ 0 & \text{if} \quad A \subsetneq T_R \end{cases} \tag{2}$$

where $p = \dim A$.

Arthur's formula can be interpreted as relating the character of π on any regular element h to a suitably weighted integral of any matrix coefficient over the orbit of h. It also gives the Fourier inversion formula for the distributions $r^A(h)$ on the space of cusp forms. Note that (2) shows that on the cusp forms $r^A(h)$ is an invariant distribution, even though $r^A(h)$ is not invariant on the full Schwartz space of G.

It is natural to ask if there is an analogue of formula (2) for induced representations. Again, results of Harish-Chandra for orbital integrals provide important motivation. We now drop the assumption that rank G = rank K and let $P = MAN$ be a cuspidal parabolic subgroup of G. For each $\omega \in \mathcal{E}_2(M)$ and $\nu \in \mathcal{F} = \underline{a}^*$, the real dual of the Lie algebra of A, let $\pi_{\omega,\nu}$ be the unitary representation of G induced from $\omega \otimes e^{i\nu} \otimes 1$ on P. Let $\theta_{\omega,\nu}$ denote the character of $\pi_{\omega,\nu}$ considered as a function on G'.

For ψ any $(K \cap M)$-finite matrix coefficient of ω on M, the Eisenstein integral $E(P:\psi:\nu)$ defined in [1b] can be regarded as a matrix coefficient for $\pi_{\omega,\nu}$. It is not a Schwartz class function on G. Thus it is necessary to consider wave packets ϕ_α, $\alpha \in C_c^\infty(\mathcal{F})$, defined by

$$\phi_\alpha(x) = \int_{\mathcal{F}} \alpha(\nu)E(P:\psi:\nu:x)\mu(\omega:\nu)d\nu \quad \text{where} \quad \mu(\omega:\nu)d\nu \quad \text{is}$$

the Plancherel measure corresponding to $\pi_{\omega,\nu}$. Then $\phi_\alpha \in C(G)$, and Harish-Chandra proves in [1c] that for $h \in T'$ when T is a Cartan subgroup of G with $\dim T_R \geqslant \dim A$,

$$r_{\phi_\alpha}(h) = \begin{cases} [W(\omega)]^{-1}\int_{\mathcal{F}} \langle\theta_{\omega,\nu},\phi_\alpha\rangle\theta_{\omega,\nu}(h)d\nu & \text{if } \dim T_R = \dim A \\ 0 & \text{if } \dim T_R > \dim A \end{cases} \tag{3}$$

where $W(\omega) = \{s \in N_G(A)/MA \mid s\omega = \omega\}$.

Formula (3) relates the characters of the induced representations with the orbital integral of a wave packet for h in a fundamental Cartan subgroup of $L = MA$. Because the individual matrix coefficients for the $\pi_{\omega,\nu}$ are not Schwartz class, it is not possible to isolate one representation as was done in (1). It also gives the Fourier inversion formula for the distribution $r(h)$, $h \in T'$, on the space $C_A(G)$ spanned by wave packets coming from some $P \in \mathcal{P}(A)$, but only in case $\dim T_R \geqslant \dim A$. When $\dim T_R < \dim A$, formulas for $r_f(h)$, $f \in C_A(G)$, are known, but are much more complicated (see [3a]).

There are now two possible ways in which formula (2) can be generalized to the setting of induced representations. The first would be to find a formula relating the characters $\theta_{\omega,\nu}(h)$ for h in conjugacy classes other than that of the fundamental Cartan subgroup of L, to certain weighted orbital integrals of wave packets. The second would be to find a Fourier inversion formula for Arthur's weighted orbital integrals on the spaces $C_A(G)$ of wave packets. Unfortunately, it is not possible in this situation to combine these two aspects in one formula.

Because of the two roles that split components of parabolic subgroups play, we will now denote the cuspidal parabolic subgroups from which we induce representations $\pi_{\omega,\nu}$ by $P_1 = M_1A_1N_1$.

Let A be a special vector subgroup of M_1. It is possible to associate to P_1 and A a weighting function $v(P_1:A)$ which is left-invariant by $C_G(AA_1)$ and satisfies the following. Let $f = \phi_\alpha \in C_{A_1}(G)$ be a wave packet coming from $\omega \in E_2(M_1)$ and let $h \in T'$ where $AA_1 \subseteq T_R$. Then

$$\int_{T_R\backslash G} f(x^{-1}hx)v(P_1:A:x)d\dot{x} = \begin{cases} (-1)^p[W(\omega)]^{-1}\int_F <\theta_{\omega,\nu},f>\theta_{\omega,\nu}(h)d\nu & \text{if } AA_1 = T_R \\ 0 & \text{if } AA_1 \subsetneq T_R \end{cases} \tag{4}$$

where $p = \dim A$. Since it is well-known that the characters $\theta_{\omega,\nu}$ are non-zero only on conjugacy classes with representatives in $L_1 = M_1A_1$, the above formula relates the character $\theta_{\omega,\nu}$ on any conjugacy class in its support to a suitably weighted orbital integral of a wave packet.

Formula (4) is an easy consequence of techniques of Harish-Chandra relating analysis on G and M_1 and Arthur's formula (2) for the representation ω of M_1. The weighting function $v(P_1:A)$ is defined in terms of Arthur's weight function v_A on M_1. (See [3b] for details.)

The Fourier inversion problem for Arthur's original distributions, $r^A(h)$, is much more difficult. Even for orbital integrals, there is a simple formula for $r_f(h)$ only in certain cases. Recall that for $f \in C_{A_1}(G)$ and $h \in T'$, $r_f(h) = 0$ if $\dim A_1 < \dim T_R$, $r_f(h)$ is possibly non-zero but still given by a simple formula when $\dim A_1 = \dim T_R$, and $r_f(h)$ is complicated when $\dim A_1 > \dim T_R$.

The weighted orbital integral $r^A(h)$ is defined only for $A \subseteq T_R$.

When $A = T_R$, the distribtuion $r^A(h)$ is nontrivial on the space of cusp forms, which in our notation in $\mathcal{C}_{\{1\}}(G)$. In this case we can expect that the Fourier inversion formula will be very complicated for $f \in \mathcal{C}_{A_1}(G)$, $\dim A_1 > 0$. However, if $A \subsetneq T_R$ so that $r^A(h)$ is trivial on the space of cusp forms, it is reasonable to expect that $r_f^A(h)$ may have a simple formula for $f \in \mathcal{C}_{A_1}(G)$, A_1 of sufficiently small dimension.

In fact we can obtain the following formula. Suppose $\dim A_1 \leqslant \dim T_R - \dim A$. Let $f \in \mathcal{C}_{A_1}(G)$ be a wave packet coming from $\omega \in \mathcal{E}_2(M_1)$. Then there is a "weighted character" $\theta^A_{\omega,\nu}$ so that for $h \in T'$

$$r_f^A(h) = \begin{cases} (-1)^P[W(\omega)]^{-1}\int_F <\theta_{\omega,\nu}, f>\theta^A_{\omega,\nu}(h)d\nu & \text{if } \dim T_R = \dim A_1 + \dim A. \\ 0 & \text{if } \dim T_R > \dim A_1 + \dim A. \end{cases} \quad (5)$$

The function $\theta^A_{\omega,\nu}$ on T' is called a weighted character because its formula is similar to the formula giving the induced character $\theta_{\omega,\nu}(h)$, $h \in T'$, as a sum of terms of the form $(\theta_\omega \otimes e^{i\nu})(xhx^{-1})$ where θ_ω is the character of ω on M_1', and the xhx^{-1} vary over distinct L_1 conjugacy classes in the G-orbit of h. The only difference in the formula for $\theta^A_{\omega,\nu}$ is that constants depending on A have been inserted in the sum. Formulas for the functions $\theta^A_{\omega,\nu}$ including explicit values for these weighting constants are given in [3c].

The proof of formula (5) given in [3c] is an extension of Arthur's proof of (2) and uses all of his results giving boundary values, growth conditions, and differential equations for the weighted orbital integrals on arbitrary Schwartz class functions. The idea is to show that both sides of the equation have the same properties, and that these properties are enough to characterize them completely.

The problem of finding a complete Fourier inversion formula for the distributions $r^A(h)$ is still open and appears to be very difficult. It is not completely understood even when $G = SL(2,R)$. It is of course complicated by the fact that these distributions are not invariant, although Arthur has shown in [1b] that the problems can in theory be reduced to the study of certain associated invariant distributions.

The author was supported by the National Science Foundation.

REFERENCES

[1] J. Arthur, (a) The characters of discrete series as orbital integrals, Inv. Math. 32 (1976), 205-261.
(b) On the invariant distributions associated to weighted orbital integrals, preprint.

[2] Harish-Chandra, (a) Discrete series for semisimple Lie groups II, Acta Math. 116 (1966), 1-111.
(b) Harmonic analysis on real reductive groups, I, J. Funct. Anal. 19 (1975), 104-204.
(c) Harmonic analysis on real reductive groups III, Ann. of Math 104 (1976), 117-201.

[3] R. Herb, (a) Discrete series characters and Fourier inversion on semisimple real Lie groups, to appear Trans. AMS.
(b) Characters of induced representations and weighted orbital integrals, to appear Pacific J. Math.
(c) An inversion formula for weighted orbital integrals, to appear Compositio Math.

RECIPROCITY LAWS IN THE THEORY OF DUAL PAIRS

Roger Howe

1. RECIPROCITY FOR SEE-SAW PAIRS.

Let $Sp_{2n}(\mathbb{R}) = Sp$ be the real symplectic group in 2n variables (of rank n), and let $\widetilde{Sp}$ be its two-fold (metaplectic) covering group. For any subgroup G of Sp, we denote the inverse image of G in $\widetilde{Sp}$ by $\tilde{G}$.

Let (G_1, G_1') be a reductive dual pair in Sp. That is, G_1 and G_1' are reductive subgroups of Sp, and G_1' is the (full) centralizer of G_1 in Sp, and vice versa. Let (G_2, G_2') be a second such pair. Following Kudla [Ku] we call these two pairs see-saw pairs if $G_1 \subseteq G_2$ and (hence) $G_2' \subseteq G_1'$.

Let ω be the oscillator representation of $\widetilde{Sp}$ [S], [W]. We want to formulate a relationship between representations of $\tilde{G}_1$ and of $\tilde{G}_2'$ occurring in the restriction of ω to these groups In this section we will give a general nonsense version of this relation, and in further sections we will look at variants and special cases.

Let R be a reductive Lie group. Let $\mathcal{R}(R)$ denote the set of infinitesimal equivalence classes of irreducible admissible representations of R, and choose $\sigma \in \mathcal{R}(R)$. Let η be any smooth representation of R, on a space $\mathcal{H}$. Set

$$I_\sigma = \cap I$$

where I denotes any closed R-submodule of $\mathcal{H}$ such that $\mathcal{H}/I$ is irreducible and in σ. Set further

$$(\mathcal{H})_\sigma = \mathcal{H}/I_\sigma \qquad (1.1)$$

We may describe $(H)_\sigma$ as the "σ-isotypic quotient" of H-the largest quotient of H on which R acts by a multiple of σ.

Let Y denote the Hilbert space on which the oscillator representation ω of $\tilde{S}p$ acts. Let $Y^\infty \subseteq Y$ denote the subspace of smooth vectors for $\tilde{S}p$. We consider Y^∞ to have its natural Frechet topology. Let ω^∞ denote the action of $\tilde{S}p$ on Y^∞.

Choose representations $\sigma \in R(\tilde{G}_1)$ and $\tau' \in R(\tilde{G}_2')$. Consider $(Y^\infty)_\sigma$. Since $\tilde{G}_2'$ commutes with $\tilde{G}_1$, it is evident from the definition of $(Y^\infty)_\sigma$ that it is a $\tilde{G}_2'$-quotient of Y^∞ as well as a $\tilde{G}_1$-quotient. Hence we may consider the τ'-isotypic $\tilde{G}_2'$ quotient $((Y^\infty)_\sigma)_{\tau'}$. We can also reverse the roles of G_1 and $\tilde{G}_2'$ and consider $((Y^\infty)_{\tau'})_\sigma$. On the other hand, the tensor product $\sigma \otimes \tau'$ defines an element of $R(\tilde{G}_1 \times \tilde{G}_2')$. It is clear that

$$((Y^\infty)_\sigma)_{\tau'} = (Y^\infty)_{\sigma \otimes \tau'} = ((Y^\infty)_{\tau'})_\sigma \qquad (1.2)$$

The formula (1.2) of course expresses a relation that holds far more generally than the context of dual pairs-one simply needs two groups acting on a vector space and commuting with each other. In our situation we have some extra structure as follows. If we use $\tilde{G}_1'$ in place of $\tilde{G}_2'$, we have a more precise picture [Ho1], namely

$$(Y^\infty)_\sigma \simeq \sigma \otimes \sigma_1' \qquad (1.3)$$

as $\tilde{G}_1 \otimes \tilde{G}_1'$-module, where σ_1' is an admissible, finitely generated, quasi-simple $\tilde{G}_1'$-module. (It is also shown in [Ho1] that σ_1' has a unique irreducible quotient σ', but we emphasize that it is σ_1', not σ', that intervenes here. Of course, generically $\sigma' = \sigma_1'$.) In similar fashion we have

$$(Y^\infty)_{\tau'} \simeq \tau_1 \otimes \tau' \qquad (1.4)$$

as $\tilde{G}_2 \times \tilde{G}_2'$ - module. Using (1.3) and (1.4) we may refine (1.2) to

$$\sigma \otimes (\sigma_1'|\tilde{G}_2')_{\tau'} \simeq (Y^\infty)_{\sigma \otimes \tau'} \simeq (\tau_1|\tilde{G}_1)_\sigma \otimes \tau' \qquad (1.5)$$

Here of course $\sigma_1'|\tilde{G}_2'$ indicates the restriction of σ_1' to $\tilde{G}_2'$.

The formula (1.5) is the relationship we had in mind. It may be loosely interpreted as an equality of multiplicities, viz, the multiplicity of τ' in $\sigma_1'|\tilde{G}_2'$ equals the multiplicity of $\sigma \otimes \tau'$ in $\omega|\tilde{G}_1 \times \tilde{G}_2'$ equals the multiplicity of σ in $\tau_1|\tilde{G}_1$. This formulation must be interpreted with some caution, however. We have been speaking of infinitesimal equivalence classes of some representations. However $\sigma_1'|\tilde{G}_2'$ will not generally be admissible, but will have a complicated spectrum with continuous and discrete parts. It is conceivable that different elements of the infinitesimal equivalence class σ_1' could look rather different when restricted to $\tilde{G}_2'$. Thus to use equation (1.5) properly, the representative of σ_1' must be taken to be the explicit representative that intervenes in the isomorphism (1.3). Similar remarks of course apply to $\tau_1|\tilde{G}_1$. We note that an alternate formulation of this phenomenon is possible in terms of $(\mathfrak{g},K)$-modules, as in [Hol]; such a formulation would obviate this subtlety, and would further allow a precise translation of formulas (1.5) into an equality of certain Hom-spaces.

2. AN L^2 VERSION.

One can also work directly with the Hilbert space Y to formulate a variant of (1.5). This can doubtless be done for the entire spectrum using appropriate almost-everywhere constructions. Here we will consider only the discrete spectrum.

For a locally compact group R, let $\hat{R}$ denote the unitary dual of R - the set of equivalence classes of irreducible unitary representations of R. Given a unitary representation of R on a Hilbert space H, and $\sigma \in \hat{R}$, let $H(\sigma)$ denote the direct sum of all subspaces of H which are R-invariant and on which R acts irreducibly by a representation of class σ. The space $H(\sigma)$ is called the <u>σ-isotypic</u> subspace, or component, of H. The space $H(\sigma)$ will be the orthogonal direct sum of a certain number of irreducible subspaces. This number is the multiplicity of σ in H.

Now consider Y, the Hilbert space on which ω is defined Choose $\sigma \in (\tilde{G}_1)^\wedge$ and $\tau' \in (\tilde{G}_2')^\wedge$. Then we have the obvious analogue of (1.2):

$$y(\sigma)(\tau') = y(\sigma \otimes \tau') = y(\tau')(\sigma) \tag{2.1}$$

The L^2-version of the duality theorem for dual pairs ([Hol],§6) tells us that

$$y(\sigma) \simeq \sigma \otimes \sigma' \tag{2.2}$$

as $\tilde{G}_1 \times \tilde{G}_1'$ representation, where $\sigma' \in (\tilde{G}_1')^{\wedge}$. Similarly

$$y(\tau') \simeq \tau \otimes \tau' \tag{2.3}$$

as $\tilde{G}_2 \times \tilde{G}_2'$ representation, with $\tau \in (\tilde{G}_2)^{\wedge}$. Thus (2.1) may be written

$$\sigma \otimes (\sigma'|\tilde{G}_2')(\tau') \simeq y(\sigma \otimes \tau') \simeq (\tau|\tilde{G}_1)(\sigma) \otimes \tau' . \tag{2.4}$$

From (2.4), the equality of the multiplicities, in the sense of unitary representations as defined above, of τ' in σ', of $\sigma \otimes \tau'$ in ω, and of σ in τ, follows directly.

3. MULTIPLICITIES OF K-TYPES.

Let (G,G') be a reductive dual pair in Sp. Let K and K' be the maximal compact subgroups in G and G'. A main observation used in [Hol] was that each of K and K' belongs to a dual pair. Thus we can find groups $M \supseteq G$ and $M' \supseteq G'$ such that if we arrange goups in order by containment as follows

$$\begin{array}{ccccc} K & \subseteq & G & \subseteq & M \\ M' & \supseteq & G' & \supseteq & K' \end{array} \tag{3.1}$$

then the vertical pairs of groups are dual pairs. The possibilities for G, K and M for irreducible pairs (G,G') are listed in [Hol]. In particular we have the see-saw pairs (G,G') and (M,K'). If we let (G,G') play the role of (G_1,G_1') in §2, and (M,K') play that of (G_2,G_2'), then the formula (2.4) becomes a statement about multiplicities of K'-types in representations of G'. We make this explicit.

PROPOSITION 3.1. Let $(G,G') \subseteq Sp$ be a reductive dual pair. Let K' be the maximal compact subgroup of G'. Consider $\sigma \in (\tilde{G}')^\wedge$ and $\tau' \in (\tilde{K}')^\wedge$. Let $m(\tau',\sigma')$ denote the multiplicity with which τ' occurs in $\sigma'|\tilde{K}'$. Suppose $\sigma \in (\tilde{G})^\wedge$ is such that $\sigma \otimes \sigma'$ is a summand of $\omega|\tilde{G}\cdot\tilde{G}'$. Let M be the centralizer of K' in Sp, so that (M,K') form a dual pair in Sp. Suppose $\tau \in (\tilde{M})^\wedge$ is such that $\tau \otimes \tau'$ occurs in $\omega|\tilde{M}\cdot\tilde{K}'$. Then

$$m(\tau',\sigma') = m(\sigma,\tau) \qquad (3.2)$$

where $m(\sigma,\tau)$ is the multiplicity of σ in $\tau|\tilde{G}$.

REMARKS. a) Although the construction of M appears to depend on G' (through K'), inspection of the table in [Hol], §5 shows that in fact, if (G,G') is simple, than so long as G' is non-compact, the group M is independent of G', and so may be considered as intrinsically attached to G. Thus equation (3.2) is an equation between quantities associated to G' and quantities associated to G.

b) Since K' is by definition compact, the group M is Hermitian symmetric or compact. Also, the representation τ will always have finite multiplicity when restricted to G.

c) An interesting feature of formula (3.2), in view of the independence of M from G', is that as G' varies among the possible groups for which (G,G') will be a dual pair, there is a way of parametrizing the representations of $\tilde{G}'$ (that occur in the representation of $\tilde{G}'$ associated to (G,G')), and a way of parametrizing the representations of $\tilde{K}'$ in such a way that the multiplicities of $\tilde{K}'$-types in the $\tilde{G}'$ representations involved is independent of $\tilde{G}'$.

4. AN EXAMPLE: THE PAIRS $(U_p,U_{r,s})$

We will illustrate formula 3.1 with the pairs $(U_p,U_{r,s})$. The representations of $U_{r,s}$ which arise from this pair are all holomorphic, and it is known [EHW], [EP], [Jk] that all holomorphic unitary representations of $SU_{r,s}$ occur in this way as p varies. Somewhat more precisely, the representations of maximal Gelfand-Kirillov dimension rs will come from pairs $(U_p,U_{r,s})$ with

$p \geq \min(r,s)$, while for $p < \min(r,s)$ (the stable range), the methods of [Ho2] show that all holomorphic representations of $SU_{r,s}$ of Gelfand-Kirillov dimension $p(r+s-p)$ arise from the pair $(U_p, U_{r,s})$.

To label representations, we will use the classical notation involving Young's diagrams, By a Young's diagram D, formally we mean a sequence $a_1, a_2, \ldots, a_r, \ldots$ of non-negative integers, such that i) $a_i \geq a_{i+1}$, and ii) $a_i = 0$ for all sufficiently large i. If $a_r \neq 0$ but $a_{r+1} = 0$, then r is the rank of D, denoted rk D. To this sequence of integers one is to quietly associate an array of square boxes, arranged in horizontal rows of length a_i, one under the other, proceeding to the right from some fixed vertical axis. Thus (4,3,1,0,... corresponds to the array

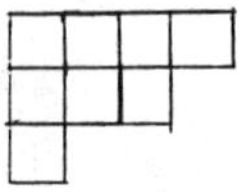

Representations of U_p may be associated with Young's diagrams and vice versa. Let T be the standard diagonal Cartan subgroup of U_p. Denote a typical element t of T by the p-tuple of its diagonal coordinates:

$$t = (Z_1, Z_2, \ldots, Z_p) \qquad Z_i \in \mathbb{C},\ |Z_i| = 1$$

An irreducible representation σ of U_p will have highest weight (with respect to the ordering for which $Z_i Z_{i+1}^{-1}$, are the fundamental positive roots)

$$t \to Z_1^{\alpha_1} \; Z_2^{\alpha_2} \; \ldots \; Z_p^{\alpha_p}$$

where the α_i are (not necessarily positive) integers satisfying $\alpha_i \geq \alpha_{i+1}$. Suppose $\alpha_r \geq 0 \geq \alpha_{r+1}$. Then we associate to σ the two Young's diagrams

$$D_1 = (\alpha_1, \alpha_2, \ldots, \alpha_r, 0, 0 \ldots$$
$$D_2 = (-\alpha_p, -\alpha_{p-1}, \ldots, -\alpha_{r+1}, 0, 0 \ldots$$

We write $\sigma = \sigma_p(D_1,D_2)$. This produces a 1-1 parametrization of the representations of U_p by pairs (D_1,D_2) of Young's diagrams satisfying $\mathrm{rk}\, D_1 + \mathrm{rk}\, D_2 \leq p$.

The determinant representation $\det_p$ of U_p has highest and only weight

$$t \to Z_1 Z_2 \dots Z_p$$

We will use a redundant but somewhat more flexible scheme for labeling representations by twisting our original labeling with powers of $\det_p$. Thus we will denote representations by $(\det_p)^m \otimes \sigma_p(D_1,D_2)$, for $m \in \mathbb{Z}$.

Now turn to consideration of the pair $(U_p,U_{r,s})$. It is convenient to label the representations of $\tilde{U}_p$ which arise from this pair by $(\det_p)^{\frac{r-s}{2}} \otimes \sigma_p(D_1,D_2)$. If we do so, then the Young's diagrams D_1, D_2 which appear (c.f. [KV]) are those such that $\mathrm{rk}\, D_1 \leq r$, $\mathrm{rk}\, D_2 \leq s$, and of course $\mathrm{rk}\, D_1 + \mathrm{rk}\, D_2 \leq p$.

The maximal compact subgroup of $U_{r,s}$ is $U_r \times U_s$, and its centralizer in Sp is $U_p \times U_p$. The U_p of the pair $(U_p,U_{r,s})$ is the diagonal subgroup of $U_p \times U_p$. The correspondence between representations of $U_r \times U_s$ and $U_p \times U_p$ is

$$\begin{aligned}(\det_p{}^{r/2} \otimes \sigma_p(D_1,\emptyset)) \otimes (\det_p{}^{-s/2} \otimes \sigma_p(\emptyset,D_2)) \quad \leftrightarrow \\ (\det_r{}^{p/2} \otimes \sigma_r(D_1,\emptyset)) \otimes (\det_s{}^{-p/2} \otimes \sigma_s(\emptyset,D_2))\end{aligned} \tag{4.1}$$

Here $\emptyset$ denotes the empty Young's diagram, all of whose rows have length zero. The Young's diagrams D_i must satisfy $\mathrm{rk}\, D_1 \leq \min(p,r)$ and $\mathrm{rk}\, D_2 \leq \min(p,s)$.

The correspondence between representations of U_p and of $U_{r,s}$ is easily seen (c.f.[KV]) to take the representation $\det_p^{\frac{r-s}{2}} \otimes \sigma_r(D_1,D_2)$ to the holomorphic representation whose "lowest K-type" in the obvious sense of that term is

$$(\det_r{}^{p/2} \otimes \sigma_r(D_1,\emptyset)) \otimes (\det_s{}^{-p/2} \otimes \sigma_s(\emptyset,D_2)) \tag{4.2}$$

Since the U_p centralizing $U_{r,s}$ is just the diagonal subgroup of the $U_p \times U_p$ centralizing $U_r \times U_s$, the restriction of the (outer) tensor product representation

$$(\det_p^{r/2} \otimes \sigma_p(D_1,\emptyset)) \bigotimes (\det_p^{-s/2} \otimes \sigma_p(\emptyset,D_2))$$

of $U_p \times U_p$ to U_p is simply the (inner) tensor product

$$(\det_p^{\frac{r-s}{2}}) \otimes (\sigma_p(D_1,\emptyset) \otimes \sigma_p(\emptyset,D_2)) \tag{4.3}$$

If we combine the correspondences described in formulas (4.1) and (4.2) with formula (3.2), we obtain a formula for the multiplicity of a $(\tilde{U}_r \times \tilde{U}_s)$-type in a holomorphic representation of $\tilde{U}_{r,s}$. Both of the representations involved in the U_p side of the formula may be seen to involve a factor $\det_p(\frac{r-s}{2})$. Clearly this factor can be cancelled from both without affecting the relevant multiplicity. Let us denote a holomorphic representation of $\tilde{U}_{r,s}$ with lowest $(\tilde{U}_r \times \tilde{U}_s)$-type $\mu \otimes \nu$, $\mu \in (\tilde{U}_r)^\wedge$, $\nu \in (\tilde{U}_s)^\wedge$, by $\rho(\mu,\nu)$ Let us abbreviate $\sigma_r(D,\emptyset) = \sigma_r(D)$. Also, note that $\sigma_s(D_1,D_2) = \sigma_s(D_2,D_1)^*$, where $*$ indicates contragredient. Hence we have $\sigma_s(\emptyset,D_2) = \sigma_s(D_2)^*$. With these conventions we may state our formula

$$\begin{aligned} &m(\det_r{}^{p/2}\sigma_r(D_1) \bigotimes (\det_s{}^{p/2}\ \sigma_s(D_2))^*, \\ &\qquad \rho(\det)_s{}^{p/2}\ \sigma_r(D_3),\ (\det_s{}^{p/2}\sigma_s(D_1))^*) \\ &= m(\sigma_p(D_3,D_4),\ \sigma_p(D_1) \otimes \sigma_p(D_2)^*) \end{aligned} \tag{4.4}$$

Here the D_i are Young's diagrams satisfying

$$\operatorname{rk}(D_i) \leqslant p\ ,\quad \operatorname{rk} D_1 \leqslant r \geqslant \operatorname{rk} D_3\ ,\quad \operatorname{rk} D_2 \leqslant s \geqslant \operatorname{rk} D_4\ ,$$

$$\operatorname{rk} D_3 + \operatorname{rk} D_4 \leqslant p$$

The formula (4.4) of course reduces the problem of computing the multiplicities of $(\tilde{U}_r \times \tilde{U}_s)$-types in holomorphic $\tilde{U}_{r,s}$-modules to the classical problem of computing multiplicities in the decomposition of tensor products. For this there is a standard formula available [Hu], [Jc] . If we employ it we obtain

$$m(\det_r{}^{p/2}\sigma_r(D_1) \otimes (\det_s{}^{p/2}\sigma_s(D_2))^*,$$

$$\rho(\det_r{}^{p/2}\sigma_r(D_3),\ (\det_s{}^{p/2}\sigma_s(D_4))^*) \tag{4.5}$$

$$= \sum_{\mu,\nu \in S_p} \operatorname{sgn}(\mu,\nu) P(\mu(D_1+\delta_p) - \nu(W_0D_2 - \delta_p) - (D_3 - W_0D_4 + 2\delta_p))$$

In this formula, S_p is the symmetric group on p letters; P is the usual partition function on the root lattice of the maximal torus in U_p; the D_i are regarded as p-tuples by deleting all their entries after the p th (these are all zero); W_0 is the "longest element" in S_p, the one which switches i and $p-i$ for each i; and $2\delta_p = (p-1, p-3, \ldots -(p-3), -(p-1))$. This "explicit" formula, like most other of its ilk, is of limited practical value, since it involves little-understood cancellations. If one were to derive formula (4.4) from formula (4.5), rather than the other way around, the formula (4.4) would then probably seem rather marvelous and mysterious.

We observe that, in accord with remark c) of §3, the right hand side of formula (4.4) is independent of r and s, except for the restrictions on the ranks of the D_i imposed by r and s. If $r, s \geq p$, then these restrictions are non-binding, and everything depends only on p. We state this formally. We restrict to the range $r, s > p$ in order to take advantage of the characterization in terms of Gelfand-Kirillov dimension of the representations of $\tilde{U}_{r,s}$ arising from the pair $(U_{r,s}, U_p)$. Let $S(U_r \times U_s) = (U_r \times U_s) \cap SU_{r,s}$, where $SU_{r,s}$ is the special unitary group.

PROPOSITION 4.1. Suppose $r,s > p$. Then the $S(U_r \times U_s)$-types occurring in holomorphic unitary representations of $SU_{r,s}$ of Gelfand-Kirillov dimension $p(r+s-p)$ are of the form $(\det_r{}^{p/2}\sigma_r(D_1)) \otimes (\det_s{}^{p/2}\sigma_s(D_2))^*$, where the Young's diagrams D_i have rank at most p. The lowest $S(U_r \times U_s)$-types of these holomorphic representations are those where $\operatorname{rk} D_1 + \operatorname{rk} D_2 \leq p$. If these representations of $S(U_r \times U_s)$ are parametrized by the Young's diagrams D_1 and D_2, and if a holomorphic representation of $SU_{r,s}$ is parametrized by the Young's diagram of its lowest $S(U_r \times U_s)$-type, then the multiplicities of $S(U_r \times U_s)$ representations in these representations of $SU_{r,s}$ is independent of r and s.

REMARKS: a) Using algebraic techniques Parthasarathy [P] and Zuckerman [Ad][V] constructed certain irreducible representations which should include most, if not all, of the representations discussed here. In an effort to unitarize these representations, Rawnsley, Schmid, and Wolf [RSW] have made a parallel construction using Dolbeault cohomology. These authors give formulas for the K-multiplicities of their representations. Their formulas presumably can be seen to reduce to formula (4.5) for the representations involved there.

b) Proposition 4.1 has some obvious implications for the characters of the $\rho(\mu,\nu)$. These are discussed in [C].

5. THE STABLE CASE.

The formula (3.2) would evidently benefit from a more explicit description of the restriction of τ to $\tilde{G}$. In §4, this was given by formula (4.3), from which formulas (4.4),(4.5) and proposition 4.1 followed. There is a fairly interesting case when we can describe $\tau|\tilde{G}$ without reference to M. This will let us combine formula (3.2) with Frobenius Reciprocity. We can do this when (G,G') is a stable pair in the sense of [Ho3].

For convenience, we recall what stability means. Rather than give the general definition, we will simply specify what it means for the 7 classes of simple pairs, as listed in [Ho1]. If $(G,G') = (GL_m(F), GL_n(F))$ where $F = \mathbb{R}, \mathbb{C}$, or $\mathbb{H}$, the quaternions, then (G,G') is stable, with G the smaller member, if $2m \leq n$. If $(G,G') = (O_{p,q}, Sp_{2n}(\mathbb{R}))$, $(O_p(\mathbb{C}), Sp_{2n}(\mathbb{C}))$, $(U_{p,q}, U_{r,s})$ or $(Sp_{p,q}, O^*_{2n})$ then (G,G') is stable, with G the smaller member, if $p+q \leq n$, or $p \leq n$, or $p+q \leq \min(r,s)$ or $p+q \leq n$, respectively; and is stable with G' the smaller member if $2n \leq \min(p,q)$, or $2n \leq \frac{p}{2}$, or $r+s \leq \min(p,q)$ or $n \leq \min(p,q)$, respectively.

Let (G,G') be a stable simple dual reductive pair in Sp with G the smaller member. Let K' be the maximal compact subgroup of G', and M the centralizer of K' in Sp. As has been remarked, the group M, if it is non-compact, has a Hermitian symmetric structure, and the representations of M associated to the pair (M,K') are of holomorphic type. Let us pin this down a little more closely. Let U_n be the $n \times n$ unitary group, the maximal compact subgroup of Sp_{2n}. Let $\mathfrak{sp}$ be the Lie algebra of Sp. We have the Cartan decomposition of the complexification

$$\mathfrak{sp}_{\mathbb{C}} = (\mathfrak{u}_n)_{\mathbb{C}} \oplus \mathfrak{q}^+ \oplus \mathfrak{q}^-$$

where $\mathfrak{q}^{\pm}$ are the irreducible subspaces, orthogonal to $\mathfrak{u}_n$, under the conjugation action $\mathrm{Ad}\, U_n$ of U_n on $\mathfrak{sp}_{\mathbb{C}}$. We may assume that $K' \subseteq U_n$, and that the Cartan involution of G' is that of Sp. Then if $\mathfrak{m}$ is the Lie algebra of M, we have

$$\begin{aligned} \mathfrak{m} &= (\mathfrak{m} \cap \mathfrak{u}_n) \oplus (\mathfrak{m} \cap \mathfrak{q}^+) \oplus (\mathfrak{m} \cap \mathfrak{q}^-) \\ &= \mathfrak{m}^{(1,1)} \oplus \mathfrak{m}^{(2,0)} \oplus \mathfrak{m}^{(0,2)} \end{aligned}$$

The subalgebra $\mathfrak{m}^{(1,1)}$ of $\mathfrak{m}$ is the Lie algebra of the maximal compact subgoup $M^{(1,1)}$ of M.

An irreducible representation ρ of $\tilde{M}$ is said to be holomorphic if there are non-zero $\tilde{M}^{(1,1)}$-finite vectors v in the space of ρ such that $\rho(\mathfrak{m}^{(0,2)})(v) = 0$. The space spanned by such vectors, i.e. $\ker \rho(\mathfrak{m}^{(0,2)})$ is clearly invariant by $M^{(1,1)}$, and it turns out that $\ker \rho(\mathfrak{m}^{(0,2)})$ is irreducible under the action of $M^{(1,1)}$. The representation of $\tilde{M}^{(1,1)}$ acting on $\ker \rho(\mathfrak{m}^{(0,2)})$ is called the lowest $M^{(1,1)}$-type of ρ. The holomorphic representation ρ is determined by its lowest $M^{(1,1)}$-type; if this is $\mu \in (\tilde{M}^{(1,1)})^{\wedge}$, we write $\rho = \rho(\mu)$.

By estimates of matrix coefficients like those in [Ho2], it is easy to establish the following lemma.

LEMMA 5.1. If $(G,G') \subseteq Sp$ is a stable pair, with G being the smaller member, and K' is the maximal compact subgroup of G', and M the centralizer of K' in Sp, then all the representations of $\tilde{M}$ arising from the dual pair (M,K') are holomorphic discrete series.

In view of lemma 5.1, the next result will describe the representations $\tilde{\tau}|\tilde{G}$.

THEOREM 5.2. Let (G,G') and (M,K') be as in lemma 5.1. Let $M^{(1,1)}$ be the maximal compact subgroup of M, and $K = M^{(1,1)} \cap G$, the maximal compact subgroup of G. Let $\rho(\mu)$, $\mu \in (\tilde{M}^{(1,1)})^\wedge$ be a holomorphic discrete series representation of $\tilde{M}$. Then the restriction of $\rho(\mu)$ to $\tilde{G}$ is the induced representation

$$\rho(\mu)|\tilde{G} \simeq \mathrm{Ind}_{\tilde{K}}^{\tilde{G}}(\mu|\tilde{K}) \tag{5.1}$$

REMARK. If G' is the isometry group of a (Hermitian) symmetric form (i.e., $G' = O_{p,q}, U_{p,q}$, or $Sp_{p,q}$), then G is of Hermitian symmetric type, and $M \simeq G \times G$. Hence a holomorphic representation $\rho(\mu)$ of $\tilde{M}$ is an (outer) tensor product $\rho(\mu_1) \otimes \rho(\mu_2)$ of holomorphic representations $\rho(\mu_i)$ of $\tilde{G}$. Further, $\tilde{G}$ is embedded in M in such a way that $\rho(\mu)|G$ is the (inner) tensor product $\rho(\mu_1) \otimes \rho(\mu_2)^*$ of the holomorphic $\rho(\mu_1)$ and the anti-holomorphic contragredient $\rho(\mu_2)^*$ of $\rho(\mu_2)$. Thus in this case, theorem 5.2 overlaps with the results of Repka [R2] on tensor products of holomorphic discrete series. The proof given here is basically the same as Repka's.

Before giving the proof of theorem 5.2, let us see how it affords a sharpening of formula (3.2). Since that formula deals with the discrete spectrum, and since when (G,G') is stable with G the smaller member, the representation of $\tilde{G}$ associated to the pair (G,G') is quasi-equivalent to the regular representation, the representation σ of $\tilde{G}$ will be a discrete series representation. Thus (5.1) and the appropriate form of Frobenius Reciprocity [Anh] implies

$$\begin{aligned} m(\sigma,\rho(\mu)|\tilde{G}) &= \dim \mathrm{Hom}_{\tilde{G}}(\sigma,\rho(\mu)) \\ &= \dim \mathrm{Hom}_{\tilde{K}}(\mu,\sigma) \end{aligned}$$

Plugging this into formula (3.2) yields the following statement.

Corollary 5.3. Let (G,G') be a stable dual pair, with G the small member, Let $\sigma \otimes \sigma'$ be a summand of the oscillator representation, where σ is a discrete series of $\tilde{G}$. Let K' be the maximal compact subgroup of G', and M the centralizer of K' in Sp. Let $\tau' \in (\tilde{K}')^\wedge$, and let τ be the corresponding representation of $\tilde{M}$, so that τ is in the holomorphic discrete series of $\tilde{M}$. Let $M^{(1,1)}$ be the maximal compact subgroup of M , and let $\tau_0 \in (\tilde{M}^{(1,1)})^\wedge$ be such that $\tau = \rho(\tau_0)$. Then

$$m(\tau',\sigma') = \dim \operatorname{Hom}_K(\tau_0,\sigma) \qquad (5.2)$$

REMARK. The multiplicities of $\tilde{K}$-types in discrete series of $\tilde{G}$ are in some sense known. Also it is in principle possible using Weyl's character formula to compute the $\tilde{K}$-decomposition of τ_0. (If $M = G \times G$, then $M^{(1,1)} = K \times K$, and K is a unitary group (or product of them) and we are in the same situation as in §4, decomposing tensor products for unitary groups.) Thus the right hand side is in some sense known, hence gives a formula for the left hand side, which is at the moment more mysterious. Eventually, many of the representations σ' should be identified with those constructed by Parthasarathy [P] and Zuckerman [Ad], [V], for which a multiplicity formula also exists. (This has already been done in some cases by Adams [A].) When this happens, formula (5.2) may be regarded as an interpretation of the multiplicity formula for singular representations, or as an identity between these formulas.

PROOF of theorem 5.2. We can realize the Hermitian symmetric space $X = M/M^{(1,1)}$ in its standard Harish-Chandra form [H1] as a bounded subset of $\mathfrak{m}^{(2,0)}$. Consider the holomorphic discrete series representation $\rho(\mu)$ of $\tilde{M}$, where $\mu \in (\tilde{M}^{(1,1)})^\wedge$. Let μ be realized on a vector space V . Then the space of $\rho(\mu)$ is the space of L^2 holomorphic sections of a certain Hermitian vector bundle $\mathcal{B}$ over X with fibre over the identity canonically isomorphic to V . More concretely, the space of $\rho(\mu)$ may be regarded as the space of holomorphic functions $f: X \to V$ whose norms are square-integrable with respect to a certain measure on X. When described in this fashion, the space of $\rho(\mu)$ is clearly invariant under multiplication by polynomial functions on $\mathfrak{m}^{(2,0)}$. The fact that $\rho(\mu)$ is in fact holomorphic discrete series guarantees that the functions f in the space of $\rho(\mu)$ have values which span V at every point of X .

Let $X_0 = G/K$ be the symmetric space of G . Since $K = M^{(1,1)} \cap G$, the inclusion $G \hookrightarrow M$ induces an embedding

$$X_0 \hookrightarrow X$$

The Fact 3, equations (3.4) and (3.5) of [Hol], show that X_0 is embedded in X as a "real form" of X. That is at any point of X_0, the tangent space to X_0 is a totally real subspace of $\mathfrak{m}^{(2,0)}$, whose complexification equals $\mathfrak{m}^{(2,0)}$.

The vector bundle $\mathcal{B}$ over X defining $\rho(\mu)$ may be restricted to a bundle $\mathcal{B}_0$ over X_0. The space of the induced representation $\mathrm{Ind}_{\tilde{K}}^{\tilde{G}}(\mu|\tilde{K}) = I(\mu)$ is simply the space of all measurable L^2-sections of $\mathcal{B}_0$ (modulo almost everywhere vanishing sections). Again, these may be regarded as measurable functions from X_0 to V which are square integrable with respect to an appropriate measure.

Let $f:X \to V$ define an $\tilde{M}^{(1,1)}$-finite element of the space of $\rho(\mu)$. Let $r(f):X_0 \to V$ be the restriction of f to X_0. Since f is holomorphic, the restriction $r(f)$ is well-defined. I claim

i) $r(f)$ is square integrable, so defines an element of the space of $I(\mu)$

ii) The map $r:\rho(\mu) \to I(\mu)$ is a densely-defined closed injective map which intertwines the $\tilde{G}$-action on these two spaces.

iii) The image of r is dense in $I(\mu)$.

From these claims and Schur's lemma [R1] the theorem follows directly. The claims are easily established. Perhaps the easiest way to prove claim i) is to notice that, if the elements of $\rho(\mu)$ are regarded as functions on $\tilde{M}$, transforming in a certain way under $\tilde{M}^{(1,1)}$, then the $\tilde{M}^{(1,1)}$-finite elements belong to the Schwartz space of $\tilde{M}$. The rate of decay required of a function in the Schwartz space of $\tilde{M}$ a fortiori entails its restriction to $\tilde{G}$ belong to $L^2(\tilde{G})$. But the square-integrability condition on functions in $I(\mu)$ simply amounts to the condition that their lifts to $\tilde{G}$ be in $L^2(\tilde{G})$. Thus claim i) follows.

The arguments for claims ii) and iii) are as in [R2]. Briefly, r is injective because X_0 is a real form of X and the elements of $\rho(\mu)$ are holomorphic. The map r is closed because the L^2-norm in $\rho(\mu)$ dominates the sup norm on compacta of X, by the maximum principle, so L^2-convergence of a sequence $\{f_m\} \subseteq \rho(\mu)$ guarantees uniform-on-compacta convergence of the $r(f_m)$. Our remarks above show that the image of r will be invariant under multiplications by polynomials on $\mathfrak{m}^{(2,0)}$. Evidently the polynomials on $\mathfrak{m}^{(2,0)}$ define, on restriction to X, an algebra of functions which separate points and contain the constants. Since X is a real form of X_0, this algebra will also be closed under complex conjugation. By the Stone-Weierstrass Theorem [N] , its norm closure is the algebra $\mathbb{C}(X_0)$ of all continuous bounded functions on X_0 . The closure of the image of r is therefore a $\mathbb{C}(X_0)$-module. Since we also know that elements of $\rho(\mu)$ have values which span V at every point, it follows easily that closure of the image of r contains all continuous functions of compact support from X_0 to V . Claim iii) is then evident.

6. HISTORICAL REMARKS

a) The notion of see-saw pair was introduced by Kudla [Ku] in order to explicate and generalize some computations of Hecke [Hc]. The phenomenon in question there was basically a certain concrete form of the reciprocity relation (1.5).

b) A case of equation (5.2) covered by the result of Repka [R2] was used by Adams [Ad] to identify some of the representations σ' with certain of the Parthasarathy-Zuckerman modules, thus establishing their unitarity.

The author was supported by the National Science Foundation.

REFERENCES

[Ad] J. Adams, Discrete Spectrum of the Oscillator Reparesentation and Reductive Dual Pairs, to appear.

[Anh] N. Anh, Restriction of the principal series of $SL(n,\mathbb{C})$ to some reductive subgroups, Pac. J. Math. 38(1971), 295-313.

[C] H. Chang, Character relations between singular holomorphic representations, these Proceedings.

[EHW] T. Enright, R. Howe and N. Wallach, Classification of Unitary Highest Weight Modules these Proceedings.

[EP] T. Enright and R. Parthasarathy, A proof of a conjecture of Kashiwara and Vergne, in Non commutative Harmonic Analysis and Lie Groups, Springer Lecture Notes in Math. 880, 74-90.

[HC] Harish-Chandra, Harmonic Analysis on Real Reductive Groups. II, Inv. Math. 36 (1976), 1-55.

[Hc] E. Hecke, Zur Theorie der elliptischen Modulfunktionen, Math. Annalen 97(1926), 210-242.

[Hl] S. Helgason, Differential Geometry and Symmetric Spaces, Academic Press, New York, 1962.

[Ho1] R. Howe, Transcending Classical Invariant Theory, preprint.

[Ho2] R. Howe, On a notion of rank for unitary representations of the classical groups, C.I.M.E. conference on Non-abelian Harmonic Analysis, Cortona, July 1980, to appear.

[Ho3] R. Howe, L^2-duality for stable reductive dual pairs, preprint.

[Hu] J. Humphreys, Introduction to Lie Algebras and Representation Theory, Graduate Texts in Math. 9, Springer Verlag, New York, Heidelberg, Berlin, 1972.

[Jc] N. Jacobson, Lie Algebras, Wiley-Interscience, New York, 1962.

[Jk] H. Jakobsen, On singular holomorphic representations, Inv. Math. 62 (1980), 67-78.

[KV] M. Kashiwara and M. Vergne, On the Segal-Shale-Weil representation and harmonic polynomials, Inv. Math. 44(1978), 1-44.

[Ku] S. Kudla, Holomorphic Siegel modular forms associated to SO(n,1), preprint.

[N] M. Naimark, Normed Rings, P. Noordhoff N.V., Groningen, Netherlands, 1964.

[P] R. Parthasarathy, A generalization of the Enright-Varadarajan modules, Comp. Math, v. 36(1978), 53-73.

[RSW] J. Rawnsley, W. Schmid and J. Wolf, Singular unitary representations and indefinite harmonic theory, preprint.

[R1] J. Repka, Tensor products of unitary representations of $SL_2(\mathbb{R})$, Am. J. Math, v.100(1978), 747-774.

[R2] J. Repka, Tensor products of holomorphic discrete series representations, Can. J. Math, v.XXXI (1979), 836-844.

[S] D. Shale, Linear symmetries of free boson fields, T.A.M.S. 103 (1962), 149-167.

[V] D. Vogan, Representations of Real Reductive Lie Groups, Birkhauser, Boston, Basel, Stuttgart, 1981.

[W] A. Weil, Sur certains groupes d'operateurs unitaires, Acta Math.111 (1964), 143-211.

CHARACTERS OF THE DISCRETE SERIES FOR PSEUDO-RIEMANNIAN SYMMETRIC SPACES

by Thongchai Kengmana

Let G be a connected semisimple Lie group. For simplicity we shall assume that G is linear (this is only necessary for defining relative Cartan subgroups). Let τ be an involutive automorphism of G, H_1 the subgroup of elements fixed by τ, and H its identity component. Let $X = G/H$ and $n = \dim X$. Those irreducible representations of G that appear discretely in $L_2(X)$ will be called the relative discrete series representations of G attached to X. We shall assume that H is non-compact, since otherwise there are no relative discrete series representations.

Suppose $(\pi,\mathcal{H})$ is a relative discrete series representation. Let $P\colon L_2(X) \longrightarrow \mathcal{H}$ be the G-invariant projection map onto $\mathcal{H}$ viewed as a closed invariant subspace. If $f \in C_c^\infty(X)$, then Pf is smooth, and we may define a distribution Θ on X by

$$\langle\Theta,f\rangle = Pf(eH) .$$

<u>Proposition 1</u>: Θ satisfies the following properties

1) Θ is H-invariant, i.e., $\langle\Theta,h\cdot f\rangle = f$, for any $h \in H$ and $f \in C_c^\infty(X)$

2) Θ transforms finitely under $D(X)$, the algebra of G-invariant differential operators on X.

A distribution on X that satisfies the properties in the proposition will be called an invariant $D(X)$-finite distribution. One that comes from a relative discrete series representation $\mathcal{H}$ as above will be referred to as a relative discrete series character of G. This generalises the usual discrete series character which arises in the case $G = G_1 \times G_1$, H = diagonal subgroup, $G/H = G_1$ where G_1 is semisimple. We shall refer to this example as the absolute case.

A number of rank one cases (see below for definition), though not all of them, have been studied case by case using explicit models of the space X (cf. [4,9,10,11,14]; some of these contain small errors). In this note we shall state some generalizations of results that are known in the absolute case. We shall consider the rank one case in more detail in the last section, and give sketches of uniform proofs that have some chance of extending to the general situation. In the course of the proof, we find some remarkable differences to the absolute case; the characters are almost never locally L_1 and in some cases, they are actually supported entirely on the singular set. Examples of this are given in the final remarks.

Oshima and Matsuki have recently announced in [12] quite general results about relative discrete series attached to a semisimple symmetric space $X = G/H$ of arbitrary rank. Their arguments apparently are based on the Flensted-Jensen duality [5] and boundary value properties as in [8] rather than a direct analysis of the characters. Nevertheless an understanding of the properties of these characters is essential for a number of reasons. Firstly, they give rise to the projection map onto a closed irreducible subspace in $L_2(X)$. Secondly, there are many properties of the global characters of a semisimple Lie group (as defined by Harish-Chandra) that should be extendable in some sense to these relative discrete series characters, such as the connection between these characters and the asymptotics of the "matrix coefficients".

Let σ be a Cartan involution of G commuting with τ. The differentials and their linear extensions to $\mathfrak{g}$, the complexification of the real Lie algebra $\mathfrak{g}_0$ of G, will also be denoted σ and τ respectively. As in [5], we have

$$\mathfrak{g} = \mathfrak{k} + \mathfrak{p} = \mathfrak{h} + \mathfrak{q} = \mathfrak{k} \cap \mathfrak{h} + \mathfrak{p} \cap \mathfrak{h} + \mathfrak{k} \cap \mathfrak{q} + \mathfrak{p} \cap \mathfrak{q} .$$

The Orbits of H on X

Denote $(x^{\tau})^{-1}$ by $\bar{x}$. Let $Q_1 = \{y \in G: y = \bar{y}\}$, and let Q be its identity component. Q is a closed submanifold of G of dimension n. The map φ: $G/H \longrightarrow Q$ defined by $\varphi(xH) = x\bar{x}$ is a finite covering with fibre H_1/H.

For $y \in Q$, let $\det(\mathrm{Ad}\, y - (t+1)I) = \sum_{k=r}^{\dim G} a_k(y)t^k$, where $a_r(y) \not\equiv 0$ on Q. We say $x \in G$ is τ-regular semisimple if $a_r(x\bar{x}) \neq 0$. If $S \subseteq G$, we will denote the τ-regular semisimple elements in S by S'. By definition, a (real) relative Cartan subalgebra of $\mathfrak{g}_0$ is a maximal abelian subalgebra of $\mathfrak{q}_0$ whose elements are semisimple.

Lemma 1: i) If $a_r(y) \neq 0$, $y \in Q$, then y is semisimple and $\mathfrak{q}_0^y$, its centralizer in $\mathfrak{q}_0$, is a relative Cartan. All relative Cartans arise in this way. In particular, we can define rank $G/H = r =$ dimension of a relative Cartan.

ii) Any relative Cartan is conjugate under H to one which is σ-invariant.

iii) If $\mathfrak{a}_0$ is a relative Cartan, then $Z_Q(\mathfrak{a})$, its centralizer in Q is an abelian subgroup of G. Call it the relative Cartan subgroup of G corresponding to $\mathfrak{a}_0$.

The following theorem is analogous to Harish Chandra's decomposition of the regular semisimple elements.

Theorem 1: The set of τ-regular semisimple elements in G is the complement of a real algebraic subvariety in G. We have a decomposition into disjoint open subsets:

$$G' = \coprod_{J,w_i} H\cdot(Jw_i)'\cdot H$$

where the union is taken over distinct H-conjugacy classes of σ-invariant relative Cartan subgroups J in G, and for each J, finitely many w_i's such that $w_i\bar{w}_i \in J$.

General Properties of Characters

As in the case of the characters of a semisimple Lie group, only invariant D(X)-finite distributions with certain decay properties can be characters (cf. [1]). Define the k-th Sobolev space of X by

$$S_k(X) = \{f \in L_2(X):\ Zf \in L_2(X),\ \ Z \in \mathcal{U}(\mathfrak{g}) \text{ of order} \leq k\} .$$

Proposition 2: If Θ is a relative discrete series character, then Θ extends continuously from $C_c^\infty(X)$ to $S_k(X)$, as a linear functional, for sufficiently large k.

Let Θ be a relative discrete series character. Since X has a G-invariant measure, it makes sense to say that a distribution on X is given by a function. As noted earlier, it will turn out that Θ need not be locally L_1. However as in [6] we have

Theorem 2: The restriction of Θ to the set of τ-regular semisimple elements is given by an analytic function.

The Rank One Case

We now assume rank X = 1. In this case D(X) is generated by the Casimir operator, hence a relative discrete series character is actually an eigendistribution, i.e., D(X) acts on it via scalars.

Up to conjugacy by H there are exactly two relative Cartans, one in $\mathfrak{p}$ and one in $\mathfrak{k}$, denoted $\mathfrak{a}_{\mathfrak{p}_0}$ and $\mathfrak{a}_{\mathfrak{k}_0}$ respectively. Let $Y_{\mathfrak{p}}$ (respectively $Y_{\mathfrak{k}}$) be the element of $\mathfrak{a}_{\mathfrak{p}_0}$ (resp. $\mathfrak{a}_{\mathfrak{k}_0}$) whose nonzero eigenvalues under ad are ± 1 and possibly ± 2 (resp. $\pm i, \pm 2i$). We have a root space decomposition corresponding to ad $Y_{\mathfrak{p}}$:

$$\mathfrak{g} = \mathbb{C}Y_{\mathfrak{p}} + \mathfrak{m} + \mathfrak{g}_1 + \mathfrak{g}_{-1} + \mathfrak{g}_2 + \mathfrak{g}_{-2}$$

where $\mathfrak{m} = z_{\mathfrak{h}}(Y_{\mathfrak{p}})$, and $\mathfrak{g}_j$ is the eigenspace of ad $Y_{\mathfrak{p}}$ corresponding to eigenvalue j. Here $\mathfrak{g}_{\pm 2}$ may be empty. Let $m_j = \dim \mathfrak{g}_j$, $j = 1,2$. Also let $n_{\mathfrak{p}} = \dim \mathfrak{q}\cap\mathfrak{p}$, $n_{\mathfrak{k}} = \dim \mathfrak{q}\cap\mathfrak{k}$. So $n = n_{\mathfrak{p}} + n_{\mathfrak{k}} = m_1 + m_2 + 1$.

Let Ω be the Casimir operator and let $\Omega\Theta = \lambda_0\Theta$. Write $\lambda_0 = \xi^2 - \rho_0^2$ where $\operatorname{Re}\xi \geq 0$ and $\rho_0 = \frac{m_1}{2} + m_2$. Θ restricted to the regular set is an analytic function, call it T. Define a function F(s) on part of the real line as follows:

Case i) $m_2 \neq 0$, F(s) is defined for $s \neq 0,1$

$$F(-\sinh^2 t) = T(\exp(tY_{\mathfrak{p}})H) \qquad \text{for } t > 0$$
$$F(\sin^2 t) = T(\exp(tY_{\mathfrak{k}})H) \qquad \text{for } 0 < t < \pi/2$$
$$F(1+\sinh^2(t/2)) = T(y'\exp(tY'_{\mathfrak{p}})H), \qquad t > 0$$

where $y' = \exp(\frac{\pi}{2} Y_{\mathfrak{k}})$, and $Y'_{\mathfrak{p}} \in \mathfrak{q}_0^{y'}$ such that $\mathrm{ad}\, Y'_{\mathfrak{p}}$ restricted to $\mathfrak{q}^{y'}$ has eigenvalues $\pm 1, 0$.

Case ii) $m_2 = 0$, $F(s)$ is defined for $s \neq 1,-1$

$$F(\cosh t) = T(\exp(tY_{\mathfrak{p}})H), \qquad t > 0$$
$$F(\cos t) = T(\exp(tY_{\mathfrak{k}})H), \qquad 0 < t < \pi$$
$$F(-\cosh t) = T(\exp(\pi Y_{\mathfrak{k}})\exp(tY_{\mathfrak{p}})H), \qquad t > 0 .$$

By computing the "radial component" of Ω, we find that in case i), $F(s)$ satisfies the hypergeometric equation corresponding to the parameters $a = \frac{\rho_0+\xi}{2}$, $b = \frac{\rho_0-\xi}{2}$, and $c = n/2$. In case ii), $(s^2-1)^{\frac{1}{2}\mu}F(s)$ satisfies the Legendre's equation with parameters $\mu = \frac{n}{2} - 1$, $\nu = \xi - \frac{1}{2}$. Here notations are as in [3].

In either case the fact that Θ is defined on some Sobolev space implies that F decays at ∞ (more precisely, $|s|^{\frac{1}{2}\rho_0}F(s) \longrightarrow 0$ in case i) and $|s|^{\rho_0}F(s) \longrightarrow 0$ in case ii) as $|s| \longrightarrow \infty$), This determines F up to a constant on each of the unbounded components of $\mathbb{R}$ on which it is defined and also requires that $\mathrm{Re}\, \xi > 0$.

An analysis similar to [4,9,15] at the singular points eH, $\exp(\pi Y_{\mathfrak{k}})H$ and, in case i), at $\exp(\frac{\pi}{2} Y_{\mathfrak{k}})H$ gives a "matching condition" which must be satisfied at each of the two singular points of F. By using a coordinate system similar to [2] on the "nilpotent stratum" we obtain

<u>Lemma 3</u>: Assume rank $(G/H) = 1$. An invariant eigendistribution on G/H supported on a union of H-orbits of codimension >1 is 0.

Via the Harish-Chandra isomorphism we have $\gamma\colon D(X) \xrightarrow{\simeq} I(\mathfrak{a}_{\mathfrak{k}})$. Each $\lambda \in \mathfrak{a}_{\mathfrak{k}}^*$ defines a character χ_λ of $D(X)$ by $\chi_\lambda(D) = \gamma(D)(\lambda)$ (cf. [7], ch. X). Pick a positive restricted root system $\Phi^+(\mathfrak{g},\mathfrak{a}_{\mathfrak{k}})$ and define $\rho \in \mathfrak{a}_{\mathfrak{k}}^*$ to be one-half the sum of positive restricted roots.

<u>Theorem 3</u>: Assume rank $(G/H) = 1$ and H is noncompact. If Θ is a relative discrete series character then $D(X)$ acts on Θ via the character χ_λ for some $\lambda \in \mathfrak{a}_{\mathfrak{k}}^*$ satisfying:

$$\langle\lambda,\alpha\rangle > 0 \quad \text{and} \quad \frac{\langle\lambda-\rho,\alpha\rangle}{\langle\alpha,\alpha\rangle} \in \mathbb{Z}, \qquad \forall\alpha \in \Phi^+(\mathfrak{g},\mathfrak{a}_{\mathfrak{k}}) .$$

Remarks:

1) It is known that relative discrete series representations exist iff there exists a compact relative Cartan subgroup (cf. [5,12]). However, in a remarkable contrast to the global characters, a relative discrete series character is not determined by its restriction to relative Cartans. In fact, it is possible for a nontrivial character Θ to be entirely supported on the singular set. This happens, for example, when $G = SO_0(p,q+1)$, $H = SO_0(p,q)$ with p,q even and $\lambda_0 < 0$, where $\Omega\Theta = \lambda_0\Theta$. The proof of theorem 3 gives the necessary and sufficient conditions for this to occur in general.

2) In the cases that were studied using case by case arguments, we find that all the possible χ_λ's as stated in theorem 3 actually occur. (Note that in some of those papers H is not connected.)

3) A close look near eH shows a sharp difference in the description of the character between the case $\langle\lambda-\rho,\alpha\rangle \geq 0$ and the case $\langle\lambda-\rho,\alpha\rangle < 0$ in the above parametrization. It would be interesting to see how the corresponding relative discrete series representations differ in the two cases.

Partially supported by NSF.

References

[1] M. Atiyah and W. Schmid, A Geometric Construction of the Discrete Series for Semisimple Lie Groups, Inventiones Math. 42 (1977), 1-62

[2] ______________________, Characters of semisimple Lie Groups, unpublished note

[3] A. Erdèlyi et al., Higher Transcendental Functions, vol. I, McGraw-Hill, New York, 1953

[4] J. Faraut, Distributions Sphériques sur les Espaces Hyperboliques, Journ. de Math. 58 (1979), 369-444

[5] M. Flensted-Jensen, Discrete Series for Semisimple Symmetric Space, Math. Ann. 228 (1977), 65-92

[6] Harish-Chandra, Discrete Series for Semisimple Lie Groups II, Acta Math. 116 (1966), 1-111

[7] S. Helgason, Differential Geometry and Symmetric Spaces, Academic Press, New York and London, 1962

[8] M. Kashiwara, A. Kowata, K. Minemura, K. Okamoto, T. Oshima and M. Tanaka, Eigenfunctions of invariant differential operators on a symmetric space, Annals of Math. 107 (1978), 1-39

[9] M.T. Koster, Spherical distributions on rank one Symmetric Spaces, thesis

[10] V.F. Molcanov, Harmonic Analysis on a Hyperboloid of One Sheet, Soviet Math. Dokl. vol. 7 (1966), No. 6, 1553-1556

[11] ____________, Analogue of Plancherel Formula for Hyperboloids, Soviet Math. Dokl. vol. 9 (1968), 1382-1385

[12] T. Oshima and T. Matsuki, A complete description of discrete series for semisimple symmetric spaces, preprint.

[13] W. Rossman, Analysis on Real Hyperbolic Spaces, J. Func. Anal. vol. 30 (1978), 448-477

[14] R.S. Strichartz, Harmonic Analysis on Hyperboloids, J. Func. Anal. vol. 12 (1973), 341-383

[15] A. Tengstrand, Distributions Invariant under an Orthogonal Group of Arbitrary Signature, Math. Scand. 8 (1960), 201-218

ALL SUPERCUSPIDAL REPRESENTATIONS OF SL_ℓ OVER A P-ADIC FIELD ARE INDUCED

P.C. Kutzko & P.J. Sally, Jr.

1. INTRODUCTION

Let F be a p-adic field (a finite extension of $\mathbb{Q}_p$), and let $G = GL_n(F)$. Then, it is predicted by Langlands that the set of n-dimensional representations of the absolute Weil group W_F of F should parameterize naturally the admissible, irreducible (non-special) representations of G, and that, in particular, the irreducible, n-dimensional representations of W_F should correspond under this parameterization to the irreducible supercuspidal representations of G.

If $(n,p) = 1$ (the tame case), then the irreducible n-dimensional representations of W_F are all monomial so that, given such a representation σ of W_F, there is an extension E/F of degree n and a character θ of $E^\times$ such that $\sigma = \mathrm{Ind}_{E/F}\theta$. Since the compact (modZ) Cartan subgroups of G are just embeddings of the multiplicative groups of such extension, the Langlands parameterization (in the tame case) may be viewed as an analogue of the parameterization of the discrete series for real groups.

From another perspective, one expects in general that irreducible supercuspidal representations of G should be constructed by inducing from subgroups of the form TB_n where T is an embedding of $E^\times$, E as above, and B_n is an appropriate congruence subgroup of some compact open subgroup in G. In the tame case, it follows from Hensel's lemma that any Cartan subgroup $T' \subset TB_n$ is, in fact, conjugate to T in G. This led Howe [H1] to conjecture that the parameterization of supercuspidal repreesentations obtained by induction should yield the Langlands' perameterization, a conjecture which, in slightly modified form, has been recently verified by Moy [M1].

If $p|n$ (the wild case), the group TB_n does not, in general, determine a unique extension of degree n over F. This explains, at least heuristically, the existence of supercuspidal representations paramterized by non-monomial representations of W_F (see Kutzko [Kl]).

Another view of the contract between the tame and the wild case may be seen in the consideration of the restriction of supercuspidal representations of G to the subgroup $\overline{G} = SL_2(F)$. Suppose $\sigma = \mathrm{Ind}_{E/F}\theta$ where E/F is Galois of degree n. Let $G_{E/F}$ be the subgroup of G consisting of elements whose determinants lie in $N_{E/F}E^{\times}$. Then, one expects that the restriction to $G_{E/F}$ of the representation $\pi(\sigma)$ parameterized by σ should decompose into n G-conjugate irreducible components, and that, conversely, if this decomposition occurs for a representation π of G, then π should be of the form $\pi(\sigma)$ where σ is induced from W_E.

In the tame case, one has $\det(TB_n) = N_{E/F}E^{\times}$ so that, if π is induced from TB_n, it follows from Mackey's theorem that $\pi|G_{E/F}$ does indeed decompose into n irreducible components. However, in the wild case, if the exponent of the different is large compared to n, then $\det(TB_n) = F^{\times}$ and the behavior of $\pi|_{G_{E/F}}$ is more difficult to predict.

In what follows, we consider the restriction to $\overline{G}$ of supercuspidal representations of G in the case when $n = \ell$, a prime. In Section 2, we summarize the construction of the supercuspidal representations of G as given by Carayol [C]. In Section 3, we consider a preliminary decomposition and show, in particular, that all irreducible supercuspidal representations of G are induced from certain compact open subgroups. In this development, we use ideas contained in the fundamental paper of Howe [H2]. In Section 4, we consider the tame case, and compare our results to those of Moy-Sally [MS].

2. SUPERCUSPIDAL REPRESENTATIONS OF $GL_\ell(F)$

In this section, we summarize the construction of the supercuspidal representations of $G = GL_\ell(F)$ (see Carayol [C]). We first define some subgroups of G and $M_\ell(F)$ which are required for this construction.

Let

(2.1) $K = GL_\ell(\mathcal{O}_F)$, a maximal compact subgroup G;

(2.2) $$B = \begin{bmatrix} \mathcal{U}_F & \mathcal{O}_F & \cdots & \mathcal{O}_F \\ \mathcal{P}_F & \mathcal{U}_F & & \\ \vdots & & \ddots & \\ \mathcal{P}_F & & & \mathcal{U}_F \end{bmatrix}$$, an Iwahori subgroup of G contained in K;

(2.3) $K^{ram} = Z'B = BZ'$, where Z' is the subgroup of G generated by

$$\pi' = \begin{bmatrix} 0 & 1 & \cdots & 0 \\ 0 & 0 & \cdots & 0 \\ \vdots & & & \vdots \\ & & & 1 \\ \varpi_F & 0 & \cdots & 0 \end{bmatrix}.$$

We observe that K^{ram} is the normalizer of B in G. Also, let

(2.4) $$\mathfrak{h} = \begin{bmatrix} \mathcal{O}_F & \mathcal{O}_F & \cdots & \mathcal{O}_F \\ \mathcal{P}_F & \mathcal{O}_F & & \\ \vdots & & & \\ \mathcal{P}_F & \cdots\cdots & & \mathcal{O}_F \end{bmatrix}$$, a subring of $M_\ell(F)$

which we call the <u>Iwahori subring</u>.

We define a filtration for $\mathfrak{h}$ as follows

(2.5) $$\mathfrak{h}_k = (\pi')^k \quad , \quad k \geq 0.$$

<u>Remarks 2.6</u>. (1) $\mathfrak{h}_\ell = \varpi_F \mathfrak{h}_0$

(2) The definition (2.5) can be extended so that $\mathfrak{h}_k$ is defined for any integer k.

(3) If $b \in \mathfrak{h}_k$, then $\nu_F(\det b) \geq k$.

(4) B is the group of units of $\mathfrak{h}$.

The filtration of $\{\mathfrak{h}_k\}_{k\geq 0}$ for $\mathfrak{h}$ yields a filtration of B (and K^{ram}) defined by

(2.7) $\quad B_k = I_\ell + \mathfrak{h}_k, \quad k > 0.$

We now fix a character $\psi \in \hat{F}^+$ with $\mathrm{cond}\psi = P_F$. For $b \in \mathfrak{h}_{1-n}$, we set

(2.8) $\quad \psi_b(x) = \psi(\mathrm{tr}\ b(x-1)),\ x \in B_r, \quad r \geq \frac{n+1}{2}.$

It is easy to see that ψ_b is a character on B_r/B_n.

Lemma 2.9. ([H2]) The map $b \to \psi_b$ induces an isomorphism from $\mathfrak{h}_{1-n}/\mathfrak{h}_{1-r}$ to $(B_r/B_n)^\wedge$.

The character ψ_b of greatest importance are those which are determined by generic elements (defined below). It is these characters which play a direct role in the construction of supercuspidal representation of G.

Definition 2.10. Let $b \in M_\ell(F)$, and let n be a positive integer such that $\ell \nmid n$. We say that b is generic of level n if

(1) $F[b]$ is totally ramified of degree ℓ over F;

(2) $\nu_F[b] \cap \mathfrak{h}_0 = \mathcal{O}_{F[b]}$.

Remarks 2.11. (1) To be precise, we should use the term ramified generic in the above definition. We shall define generic elements for unramified extensions later in this section.

(2) If $\mathfrak{h}'_n$ denotes the generic elements of level n ($\ell \nmid n$), then $\mathfrak{h}'_n + \mathfrak{h}_{n+1} = \mathfrak{h}'_n$.

(3) It is a fundamental property of generic elements that, if b is generic and xbx^{-1} is also generic for some $x \in \mathfrak{h}$ then $x \in K^{ram}$ (see [K2]).

We now outline the construction of the ramified supercuspidal representations of G as induced representations.

Definition 2.12. Let σ be an irreducible representation of K^{ram}. We say that σ has level n if $B_n \subset \ker\sigma$ and $B_{n-1} \not\subset \mathrm{Ker}\sigma$. We say that σ has minimal level n if n is the minimum value among the levels of the representations $\sigma \otimes (\chi \cdot \det)$ where χ runs through $\hat{F}^\times$.

For the remainder of this section, we assume that the minimal level of σ is equal to the level of σ. We note that this assumption is true if and only if $\ell \nmid n-1$ where n is the level of σ.

Lemma 2.13. ([C]) Let σ be an irreducible representation of K^{ram}. Assume that σ has level $n(\ell \nmid n-1)$. If $\sigma|B_{n-1}$ contains ψ_b, b generic of level $1-n$, then

(1) $\sigma|B_{n-1} = c \oplus \psi_b$ where b runs through one K^{ram}/B_1 orbit in $\mathfrak{h}'_{1-n}/\mathfrak{h}_{2-n}$, c is the common multiplicity of ψ_b in $\sigma|B_{n-1}$;

(2) $\mathrm{Ind}_{K^{ram}}^{G} \sigma$ irreducible and supercuspidal;

(3) Any irreducible supercuspidal representation π of G may be induced from either K^{ram} or $K^{ram} = F^{\times}GL_n(\mathcal{O}_F)$. If π is induced from K^{ram}, then π is induced either by a representation σ satisfying the conditions above or by $\sigma \otimes (\chi \circ \det)$, $\chi \in \hat{F}^{\times}$.

Remark 2.14. The irreducible supercuspidal representations induced from K^{ram} are called ramified supercuspidal representations.

In order to construct the supercuspidal representations induced from K^{un} (Lemma 2.13(3)), we proceed as follows. Take the usual filtration on K given by

$$(2.15) \qquad K_n = I + \varpi_F^n M_\ell(\mathcal{O}), \qquad n \geq 1.$$

Here, the analogue of the Iwahori subring is just $M_0 = M_\ell(\mathcal{O}_F)$, and we define

$$(2.16) \qquad M_r = \varpi_F^r M_\ell(\mathcal{O}_F), \qquad r \in \mathbb{Z}$$

This yields a filtration $\{M_r\}_{r \geq 1}$ for $M_\ell(\mathcal{O}_F)$ which leads naturally to (2.15).

In the present case, we take a character $\psi \in \hat{F}^{+}$ such that $\mathrm{cond}\psi = \mathcal{O}_F$. For $b \in M_{-n}$, we set

$$(2.17) \qquad \psi_b(x) = \psi(\mathrm{tr}\, b(x-1)), \ x \in K_r, \ r \geq \frac{n+1}{2}.$$

It is easy to see that ψ_b is a character on K_r/K_n.

Lemma 2.18. ([H2]). The map $b \to \psi_b$ induces an isomorphism from M_{-n}/M_{-r} to $(K_r/K_n)^{\wedge}$.

In analogy with the ramified case, we make the following definition.

Definition 2.19. Let $b \in M_0 = M_\ell(O_F)$. We say that b is (unramified) generic of level 0 if

(1) b is irreducible in $M_\ell(O_F/P_F)$ so that, in particular, $F[b]$ is unramified of degree ℓ over F and

$$\nu_{F[b]}(b) = 0;$$

(2) $F[b] \cap M_0 = O_{F[b]}$.

Definition 2.20. We denote the set of generic elements of level 0 by M_0'. We say that an element $b \in M_\ell(F)$ is (unramified) generic level r if $b \in \varpi_F^r M_0'$. We denote this set by M_r'.

Definition 2.21. Let σ be an irreducible representation of K^{un}. We say that σ has level n if $K_n \subset \ker\sigma$ and $K_{n-1} \not\subset \ker\sigma$. We say that σ has minimal level n if n is the minimum value amoung the levels of the representations $\sigma \otimes (\chi \circ \det)$ where χ runs through $\hat{F}^\times$.

As in the ramified case, we assume that the minimal level of σ is equal to the level of σ.

Lemma 2.22. ([C]) (a) Let σ be an irreducible representation of K^{un} of level $n > 1$. If $\sigma|K_{n-1}$ contains ψ_b, b generic of level $-n$, then

(a.1) $\sigma|K_{n-1} = c \oplus \psi_b$ where b runs through one K^{un}/K_1 orbit in M_{-n}'/M_{1-n}, c is the common mult. of ψ_b in $\sigma|K_{n-1}$.

(a.2) $\mathrm{Ind}_{K^{un}}^G \sigma$ is irreducible and supercuspidal.

(b) Let σ be an irreducible representation of K^{un} of level 1. Assume that $\sigma|K$, considered as a representation of

$GL_\ell(\mathcal{O}_F/P_F)$, is a cuspidal representation. Then $\mathrm{Ind}_{K^{un}}^{G}\ \sigma$ is irreducible and supercuspidal.

Remarks 2.23. (1) The irreducible supercuspidal representations induced by a representation σ of K^{un} satisfying the above conditions or by $\sigma \otimes (\chi \circ \det)$, $\chi \in \hat{F}^{\times}$, are called unramified supercuspidal representations.

(2) As pointed out in Lemma 2.13(3), all irreducible supercuspidal representations of G are obtained by induction from either K^{ram} or K^{un}. The irreducible supercuspidal representations induced from K^{un} are given by Lemma 2.23 and Remark (1) above.

3. RESTRICTION TO $SL_\ell(F)$.

The goal of this section is to prove the following theorem.

Theorem 3.1. Let $\bar{\pi}$ be an irreducible, supercuspidal representation of $\bar{G} = SL_\ell(F)$. Then $\bar{\pi}$ is induced from either $\bar{B}$, the Iwahori subring of $SL_\ell(\mathcal{O}_F)$

or

$$(\bar{K})^{w}, \quad \text{where } \bar{K} = SL_\ell(\mathcal{O}_F)$$

and

$$w \in \left\{ \begin{bmatrix} \varpi_F^{r} & & & 0 \\ & 1 & & \\ & & \ddots & \\ 0 & & & 1 \end{bmatrix} \;\middle|\; r = 0, 1, \ldots, \ell - 1 \right\}$$

We note that the set

$$\left\{ \begin{bmatrix} \varpi_{F_1} & & 0 \\ & \ddots & \\ 0 & & 1 \end{bmatrix} \quad r = 0, 1, \ldots, \ - 1 \right\} \text{ is a collection}$$

of double coset representatives for $\bar{G}\backslash G/K$ our appraoch will be to decompose the restriction of a supercuspidal representation using Mackey's theorem. We begin with the ramified supercuspidal representations.

Consider the pairing defined by the maps

$< \cdot, \cdot > : \ M_\ell(F) \times M_\ell(F) \to F$

(3.2) $\langle x,y\rangle = \mathrm{tr}\,(xy)$.

Remarks 3.3. (1) $\langle \cdot,\cdot \rangle$ is a non-degenerate, G-invariant pairing.

(2) If H is an $\mathcal{O}_F$ submodule of $M_\ell(F)$ then we denote by $H^\perp$ the submodule

$$\{k \in M_\ell(F) \mid \langle k,H \rangle \subset P_F\}.$$

It is easy to see that $\mathfrak{h}_n^\perp = \mathfrak{h}_{1-n}$, and, if $x \in G$, $(\mathfrak{h}_n \cap (\mathfrak{h}_n)^x)^\perp = \mathfrak{h}_{1-n} + (\mathfrak{h}_{1-n})^x$ where $(\mathfrak{h}_n)^x = x\mathfrak{h}_n x^{-1}$.

(3) The pairing $\langle\cdot,\cdot\rangle$ is used to implement the isomorphisms given in Lemma 2.9 and Lemma 2.18.

We now fix an irreducible representation σ of K^{ram}. We assume that σ has level n and that $\sigma|B_{n-1}$ contains ψ_b, b generic. Let $\pi(\sigma) = \mathrm{Ind}_{K^{ram}}^{G}\,\sigma$, a ramified, irreducible representation of G.

Lemma 3.4. $\pi(\sigma) \mid \overline{G} = \mathrm{Ind}_{\overline{B}}^{\overline{G}}\,(\sigma|\overline{B})$.

Proof. This follows from Mackey's theorem using the fact that $K^{ram}\overline{G} = G$.

Proposition 3.5. Let $\overline{\sigma}$ be an irreducible component of $\sigma|\overline{B}$. Then $\mathrm{Ind}_{\overline{B}}^{\overline{G}}\,\overline{\sigma}$ is an irreducible supercuspidal representation of $\overline{G}$.

Proof. This result follows from standard Mackey theory given the following claim.

Claim. Let $x \in \overline{G}\backslash\overline{B}$. Then $\dim \mathrm{Int}(\overline{\sigma}, (\overline{\sigma})^x) = 0$ on $\overline{B} \cap (\overline{B})^x$. To prove the claim, we suppose the contrary. We have $\overline{\sigma}|\overline{B}_{n-1} = c \oplus \psi_b$,

b generic, where b runs through one $\overline{B}/\overline{B}$, orbit in $\mathfrak{h}'_{1-n}/\mathfrak{h}_{2-n}$.
Thus, the existence of a non-trivial element in $\mathrm{Int}(\overline{\sigma}, (\overline{\sigma})^x)$ implies that there exist elements $b_1, b_2 \in \mathfrak{h}'_{1-n}$ such that $\psi_b = (\psi_{b_2})^x$ on $\overline{B}_{n-1} \cap (\overline{B}_{n-1})^x$. Since $\ell \nmid n-1$, we have $B_n \overline{B}_{n-1} = B_{n-1}$ so that $\psi_{b_1} = (\psi_{b_2})^x$ on $B_{n-1} \cap (B_{n-1})^x$. Thus, $b_1 - (b_2)^x \in \mathfrak{h}_{2-n} + (\mathfrak{h}_{2-n})^x$.
This means that there are elements $c_1, c_2 \in \mathfrak{h}$ such that

$$b_1 - (b_2)^x = c_1 - (c_2)^x \quad \text{on} \quad b_1 - c_1 = (b_2 - c_2)^x.$$

But this is impossible by Remarks 2.11 (2) and (3).

We note that the above proof is a modification of a proof given by Howe [H2] in a different context.

We now turn to the unramified supercuspidal representations.

Lemma 3.6. (Preliminary decomposition).

Let σ be an irreduicble representation of $K^{un} = F^x GL_\ell(\mathcal{O}_F)$ satisfying the conditions of Lemma 2.22. Let $\pi(\sigma) = \mathrm{Ind}_{K^{un}}^{G}$.
Then $\pi(\sigma)|\overline{G} = \bigoplus_W \mathrm{Ind}_{\overline{K}}^{\overline{G}} (\sigma|\overline{K})^w$,

$$\text{where} \qquad w \in \left\{ \begin{bmatrix} \varpi_F^r & & 0 \\ & 1 & \\ 0 & & \ddots\, 1 \end{bmatrix} \;\middle|\; r = 0\ 1\ ,\ldots,\ -1 \right\}$$

Proof. Mackey's theorem (see the observation after Theorem 3.1).

Proposition 3.7. Let $\overline{\sigma}$ be an irreducible component of $(\sigma|\overline{K})$. Then $\mathrm{Ind}_{\overline{K}}^{\overline{G}} \sigma$ is an irreducible supercuspidal representation of $\overline{G}$.

Proof. If σ has level $n > 1$, then the proof is identical to that in the ramified case (Proposition 3.5). If σ has level 1, the proof follows from the fact that irreducible cuspidal representations of $SL_\ell(\mathcal{O}_F/P_F)$, viewed as representations of $SL_\ell(\mathcal{O}_F)$ induce irreducible supercuspidal representations of $SL_\ell(F)$. This fact was known already to Mautner.

To conclude this section, we observe that Theorem 3.1 is an immediate consequence of Proposition 3.5, Proposition 3.7, and the classification of supercuspidal representations of $GL_{\ell}(F)$ given by Carayol [C].

4. COMPARISION WITH THE TAME CASE

It is instructive to compare the results in the previous section with the corresponding facts in the tame case, that is, the case when $(\ell,p) = 1$. Here, the results are quite explicit. We content ourselves with a statement of the relevant theorem. Full details may be found in [MS]. As is already illustrated by $SL_2(F)$, the tame case is consideralby simpler than the wild case (see [KS]).

Theorem 4.1. Suppose $(\ell, q-1) = 1$. Then

(1) if π is a ramified supercuspidal representation of G, $\pi|\overline{G}$ is irreducible;

(2) if π is an unramified supercuspidal representation of G, $\pi|\overline{G}$ decomposes into ℓ inequivalent, irreducible supercuspidal representations.

Theorem 4.2. Suppose $\ell|q-1$. Then

(1) if π is a ramified supercuspidal representation of G, $\pi|\overline{G}$ decomposes into ℓ inequivalent, irreducible supercuspidal representations;

(2) if π is an unramified supercuspidal representation of G such that π (or the inducing representation σ) has level greater than one, then $\pi|\overline{G}$ decomposes into ℓ inequivalent, irreducible supercuspidal representations.

Remarks 4.3. (1) In all of the cases considered in Theorem 4.1 and Theorem 4.2, the inducing representations for the irreducible supercuspidal representations of $\overline{G}$ which are obtained by restriction are given explicitly by decomposing the restriction of the corresponding inducing representation for π.

(2) In the wild case, the decomposition of the restriction of the inducing representations involved complicated arithmetic problems which do not arise in the tame case. For an illustration of this, see [KS].

Finally, we consider the case of unramified supercuspidal representations of level one when $\ell | q-1$. Here, the inducing representation σ may be regarded as a discrete series representation of $GL_\ell(\mathcal{O}_F/P_F)$. The decomposition of $\pi(\sigma)|\bar{G}$ is completely controlled by the decomposition of $\sigma|SL_\ell(\mathcal{O}_F/P_F)$. In fact, $\sigma|SL_\ell(\mathcal{O}_F/P_F)$ is either irreducible or has ℓ irreducible components.

Theorem 4.4. (1) If $\sigma|SL_\ell(\mathcal{O}_F/P_F)$ has ℓ irreducible components then $\pi(\sigma)|\bar{G}$ has ℓ^2 inequivalent, irreducible supercuspidal components.

(2) If $\sigma|SL_\ell(\mathcal{O}_F/P_F)$ is irreducible, then $\pi(\sigma)|\bar{G}$ has ℓ inequivalent, irreducible supercuspidal components.

Remarks 4.5 . (1) In a recent paper [M2], Moy has given explicit formulas for the characters of the irreducible componets of $\sigma|SL_\ell(\mathcal{O}_F/P_F)$.

(2) In the wild case, we always have $(\ell, q-1) = 1$. Thus, we have

$$GL_\ell(\mathcal{O}_F/P_F) = (\mathcal{O}_F/P_F)^\times \; SL_\ell(\mathcal{O}_F).$$

It follows that every irreducible rerpesentation of $GL_\ell(\mathcal{O}_F/P_F)$ restricts to an irreducible representation of $SL_\ell(\mathcal{O}_F/P_F)$. Consequently, Theorem 4.4(1) does not arise in the wild case.

(3) As shown by the results for $SL_2(F)$ [KS], there are always supercuspidal representations of $GL_\ell(F)$ which decompose into ℓ^2 irreducible components when restricted to $SL_\ell(F)$. As indicated in Remark (2) above, this does not occur for unramified supercuspidal representations of level one in the wild case. This phenomenon creates a substantial problem in obtaining an explicit decomposition.

Research of both authors supported by the National Science Foundation.

BIBLIOGRAPHY

[C] H. Carayol, Représentations cuspidales du groupe lineaire, preprint.

[H1] R. Howe, Tamely ramified supercuspidal representations of GL_n, Pacific J. Math. 73(1977), 437-460.

[H2] R. Howe, Some qualitative results on the representation theory of GL_n over a p-adic field, Pacific J. Math. 73(1977), 479-538.

[K1] P. Kutzko, The Langlands conjecture for GL_2 of a local field, Annals of Math. 112(1980), 381-412.

[K2] P. Kutzko, Characters of supercuspidal representations of GL_ℓ, preprint.

[KS] P. Kutzko and P.J. Sally, Jr., Supercuspidal representations of SL_2, preprint.

[M1] A. Moy, Local Constants and the Tame Langlands Correspondence, Thesis, University of Chicago, 1982.

[M2] A. Moy, An application of the Gel'fand-Graev representation to the computation of the character table of $SL_\ell(\mathbb{F}_q)$, preprint.

[MS] A. Moy and P.J. Sally, Jr., Supercuspdial representations of SL_n over a p-adic field, preprint.

A NOTE ON INVARIANT FORMS ON LOCALLY SYMMETRIC SPACES

BIRGIT SPEH

1. INTRODUCTION

Given a discrete subgroup Γ of a connected real semisimple Lie group G with finite center, there is a natural homomorphism

$$j^q_\Gamma: I^q_G \to H^q(\Gamma,\mathbb{C}),\ q = 0, 1,\ldots$$

where I^q_G denotes the space of G-invariant harmonic q-forms on the symmetric space $X = G/K$. Here K is a maximal compact subgroup of G. If Γ is cocompact, this homomorphism is injective in all dimensions. If G/Γ is not compact there exists a constant $c_G \leq \text{rank } G$ so that if $q \leq c_G$ then j^q_Γ is injective (and in fact is bijective) [1]. On the other hand, the cohomological dimension of $\Gamma\backslash X$ is $\dim X\text{-rank } G$ [2]. So j^q_Γ is trivial for $q > \dim X\text{-rank } G$.

The purpose of this note is to discuss the injectivity of the map j^q_Γ in the framework of representation theory. Using this setup we show that if $G_n = SL(n,\mathbb{R})$ then

$$\dim j^q(I^q_{G_n}) \leq \dim (I^q_{G_{n-1}}).$$

So in particular we conclude that for G_{2n} the map j^n_Γ fails to be injective.

We are grateful to Mark Steinberger for helpful remarks.

1.1 Let G be a simple connected Lie group with finite center and with maximal compact subgroup K. The Lie algebra of a subgroup $G_0 \subset G$ is denoted by the corresponding small German letter, its complexification by $\mathfrak{g}_{0,\mathbb{C}}$, its complex dual by $\mathfrak{g}_0'$ and the connected component of the identity by G_0^0. The enveloping algebra of $\mathfrak{g}_0$ is denoted by $U(\mathfrak{g}_0)$, the Cartan involution by θ and the Cartan decomposition by $\mathfrak{g} = \mathfrak{k} \oplus \mathfrak{p}$.

Suppose $\Gamma \subseteq G$ is a discrete finitely generated torsion-free subgroup of G. Then [5]

$$H^*(\Gamma,\mathbb{C}) \cong H^*(\mathfrak{g},K,C^\infty(G/\Gamma)).$$

So if Π is a $(\mathfrak{g},K)$-module and

$$\mathrm{Hom}_{\mathfrak{g},K}(\Pi,C^\infty(G/\Gamma)) \neq 0$$

then

$$\{E_\Pi^* H^*(\mathfrak{g},K,\Pi),\ E_\Pi \in \mathrm{Hom}_{\mathfrak{g},K}(\Pi,C^\infty(G/\Gamma)\}$$

is the contribution of Π to $H^*(\mathfrak{g},\mathbb{C})$.

Now suppose Π is the trivial representaion Id. We have

$$\dim \mathrm{Hom}_{\mathfrak{g},K}(\mathrm{Id},C^\infty(G/\Gamma)) = 1,$$

since the constant function is the only function in $C^\infty(G/\Gamma)$ which is invariant under the action of $U(\mathfrak{g})$. So if

$$E \in \mathrm{Hom}_{\mathfrak{g},K}(\mathrm{Id},C\ (G/\Gamma)),\ E \neq 0$$

then

$$E^*H^*(\mathfrak{g},K,\mathrm{Id})$$

is the contribution of Id to $H^*(\Gamma,\mathbb{C})$. On the other hand $H^*(\mathfrak{g},K,\mathrm{Id}) \cong \mathrm{Hom}_K(\Lambda\mathfrak{p}^*,\mathrm{Id})$ [3], and so it is isomorphic to the space I_G of G-invariant harmonic forms on $X = K\backslash G$. Every form in I_G defines a unique harmonic form on X/Γ and every class in

$E^*H^*(\mathfrak{g},K,Id)$ can be represented by such a form. Conversely if a G-invariant form represents a nontrivial cohomology class ω $H^*(\mathfrak{g},K,C^\infty(G/\Gamma))$, then $\omega \in E^*H^*(\mathfrak{g},K,Id)$. So the homomorphism

$$j^q_\Gamma\colon I^q_G \to H^q(\Gamma,\mathbb{C})$$

is injective in degree q, iff E^q is injective.

To obtain information concerning E^* we will proceed as follows: We will construct a representation Π and an embedding $E_\Pi\colon \Pi \to C^\infty(G/\Gamma)$ so that E factors through E_Π, i.e.,

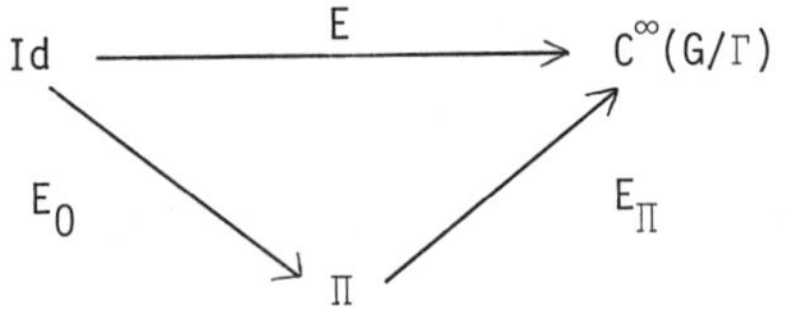

The $(\mathfrak{g},K)$-cohomology of Π is described by a long exact sequence (1.4) and it is possible to obtain some information about the kernel of E^*_Π as well. If $G = SL(n,\mathbb{R})$ we give a bound on $\dim E^qH^q(\mathfrak{g},K,Id)$.

1.2 Let $Q = L_QN_Q$ be a rational parabolic subgroup of G. Then $L_Q = M_QA_Q$ where A_Q is a maximal abelian split subgroup in the center of L_Q.

Let $\Sigma(\mathfrak{a}_Q,\mathfrak{g})$ be weights of $\mathfrak{a}_Q$ on $\mathfrak{g}$, $\Sigma^+(\mathfrak{a}_Q,\mathfrak{g})$ the weights of $\mathfrak{a}_Q$ on $\mathfrak{n}_Q$, C^+_Q the corresponding dominant Weyl chamber and $2\rho_Q$ the sum of roots in $\Sigma^+(\mathfrak{a}_Q,\mathfrak{g})$.

Put $S_Q = M_QN_Q$, $\Gamma_S = S \cap \Gamma$ and write Γ_M for the image of Γ_S under the map $S \to S/N$.

We write Id_M for the trivial representation of M_Q and we consider Id_M as the action of M_Q on the constant function on M_Q/Γ_M.

For an indecomposable representation

$$\nu_Q\colon A_Q \to \operatorname{End} \mathbb{C}^\ell \qquad \ell \geqslant 1$$

we define the space

$$U(Q,\nu_Q) = \{\phi: G/\Gamma_S N_Q \to \mathbb{C}^\ell\}$$

so that i) ϕ is integrable mod Q and is in $C^\infty(G/\Gamma_S)$

ii) ϕ is K-finite

iii) $\phi\ (gma) = \nu(a^{-1})e^{-\rho_Q(\log a)}\ \phi(g)$, $m \in M_Q$, $a \in A_Q$

As a $(\mathfrak{g},K)$-module $U(Q,\nu)$ is isomorphic to the induced representation

$$\mathrm{ind}_Q^G \mathrm{Id}_M \otimes \nu \otimes \mathrm{id},$$

where induction means normalized induction with $U(\mathfrak{g})$ acting on the left

For a character ν of A_Q and $\phi \in U(Q,\nu)$ put

$$E(Q,\phi,\nu,g) = \sum_{\gamma \in \Gamma_S \backslash \Gamma} \phi(g\gamma).$$

This Eisenstein series converges for $\mathrm{Re}\,\nu$ sufficiently large [4]. Here we identify a character of A_Q with its differential at the identity. For fixed $g \in G$ this function has a meromorphic continuation to all of $\mathfrak{a}_Q'$. The poles lay in certain hyperplanes [4].

Suppose $\nu_0 \in \mathfrak{a}_Q'$ with $\mathrm{Re}\,\nu_0 \in C_Q^+$ and suppose that for all $\nu \in C_Q^+$ with $\mathrm{Re}\,\nu \in \nu_0 + C_Q^+$ and for all $\phi \in U(Q,\nu)$ the functions $E(Q,\phi,\nu)$ are defined. Then the map

$$E_{Q,\nu}: U(Q,\nu) \to C^\infty(G/\Gamma)$$

$$\phi \to E(Q,\phi,\nu)$$

is an intertwining operator [4].

1.3 Now suppose $\dim A_Q = 1$ and suppose that the function $E(Q,\phi,\nu,g)$ has a pole at $\nu = \rho_Q$ for some $\phi \in U(Q,\rho_Q)$. The residue of $E(Q,\phi,\nu,g)$ at ρ_Q, which we denote by $\mathrm{res}_{\rho_Q} E(Q,\phi,\nu,g)$, is a square integrable function of g [6], and

$\{\text{res}_{\rho_Q} E(Q,\phi,\nu,g),\ \phi \in U(q,\rho_Q)\}$ is a unitary $U(\mathfrak{g})$-module. By [3] $U(Q,\nu)$ has no unitary quotient for $\text{Re}\ \nu > \rho_Q$, so $E(Q,\phi,\nu,g)$ is defined for $\text{Re}\ \nu > \rho_Q$ and we have an intertwining operator

$$U(Q,\nu) \to \{\text{res}_{\rho_Q} E(Q,\phi,\nu,g),\ \phi \in U(Q,\rho_Q)\}\ .$$

The trivial representation is the unique **unitarizable** quotient of $U(Q,\rho_Q)$ [3]. Hence

$$\dim\{\text{res}_{\rho_Q} E(Q,\phi,\nu,g),\ \phi \in U(Q,\nu) = 1.$$

So to obtain an explicit embedding of the trivial representation, it remains to show that the function $E(Q,\phi,\nu,g)$ actually has a pole for $\nu = \rho_Q$ if ϕ is the K-invariant vector in $U(Q,\nu)$. But this follows from [6, Chapter 5, 6] since the trivial representation always occurs in the residual spectrum if G/Γ has finite volume.

1.4 We continue to assume that $\dim A = 1$. Let H be a generator of $\mathfrak{a}_R$. We write $\tilde{H}$ if we consider H as a differential operator in the variable $\nu \in \mathfrak{a}_Q'$. For $\nu \in C_Q^+$ put

$$E_m(Q,\nu) = \text{span}\ \{\tilde{H}^i((\nu-\rho_Q)E(Q,\phi,\nu)),\ 0 \leqslant i \leqslant m,\ \phi \in U(Q,\nu)\}\ .$$

If $\nu \in \rho_Q + C_Q^+$ then $E_m(Q,\nu)$ is as a $(\mathfrak{g},K)$ module isomorphic to $U(Q,\nu_n)$ where ν_n is the n-dimensional indecomposable representation of $\mathfrak{a}_Q$ with unique subrepresentaion ν [7] and $E_m(Q,\rho_Q)$ is isomorphic to a quotient $\overline{U}(Q,\rho_{Q,m})$ of $U(Q,\rho_{Q,m})$.

Since Id_G is a subrepresentation of $\overline{U}(Q,\rho_{Q,m})$ we obtain a factorization

$$\begin{array}{ccc} \text{Id}_G & \xrightarrow{\quad E \quad} & C^\infty(G/\Gamma) \\ & {\scriptstyle E_0} \searrow \qquad \swarrow {\scriptstyle E_m} & \\ & \overline{U}(Q,\rho_{Q,n}) & \end{array}$$

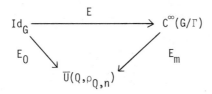

So we proved

1.4.1 THEOREM. Let

$$j^q_\Gamma:\ I^q_G \to H^q(\Gamma,\mathbb{C}),\ q = 0, 1, \ldots$$

be the homomorphism of the invariant harmonic q-forms on $X = K\backslash G$ into the cohomology of Γ with complex coefficients, then

$$\dim j^q_\Gamma(I^q_G) \leqslant \dim E^q_0 H^q(g,K,Id_G).$$

It is easy to see that we have a short exact sequence

$$0 \to Id_G \to U(Q,\rho_{Q,m}) \to U(Q,\rho_{Q,m-1}) \to 0\ .$$

Both $H^*(\mathfrak{g},K,U(Q,\rho_{Q,m-1}))$ and $H^*(\mathfrak{g},K,Id_G)$ are computable [3], [10]. So we can use a long exact sequence to estimate the dimension of the image of $H^q(\mathfrak{g},K,Id_G)$ in $H^q(\mathfrak{g},K,\overline{U}(Q,\rho_{Q,m}))$

2.1 We will now discuss $U(Q,\rho_{Q,m})$ and E^*_m in the case $SL(n,\mathbb{R})$. So from now on G_n stands for $SL(n,\mathbb{R})$ and if no confusion is possible we will drop the subscript n. Fix a maximal parabolic subgroup $Q = MAN$ of G_n with $M^0 \cong G_{n-1}$. By Frobenius reciprocity every K-type of $U(Q,\nu)$ has an $M \cap K$ invariant vector, i.e., it has an $O(n-1)$-invariant vector. Using a branching law we deduce that every K-type has multiplicity one and that all K-types are parametrized by natural numbers. We may choose this parametrization so that if K-types with index i and $i+\ell$, $\ell > 0$ are K-types of a subquotient then so are the K-types with index $i+j$, $1 < j < \ell$ [9]. Since finite-dimensional inequivalent representations have different infinitesimal characters, $U(Q,S_Q)$ has an infinite-dimensional irreducible subrepresentation Π_Q, so that

$$U(Q,\rho_Q)/\Pi_Q = \overline{U}(Q,\rho_Q)$$

and in particular

$$U(Q,\rho_Q)/\Pi_Q \cong Id_G\ .$$

Since by Frobenius reciprocity

$$\dim \mathrm{Hom}_{U(\mathfrak{g})}(U(Q,\rho_Q),\ U(Q,\rho_{Q,m})) = 1\ ,$$

and by [7]

$$\dim \mathrm{Ext}^1_{U(\mathfrak{g})}(\mathrm{Id}_G,\Pi_G) = 1$$

we conclude that

$$U(Q,\rho_{Q,m})/\Pi_Q$$

has a unique subrepresention. This subrepresentation is isomorphic to Id_G. So the argument in [7] section 4.5 shows that $\overline{U}(Q,\rho_{Q,m})$ is, in fact, a subrepresentation of $U(Q,\rho^{-1}_{Q,m+1})$. So if $m > 1$, then $U(Q,\rho_{Q,m})/\Pi_Q$ has a subrepresentation isomorphic to $U(Q,\rho_Q^{-1})$. Hence in 1.4 we may replace $U(Q,\rho_{Q,m})/\Pi_Q$ by the induced representation $U(Q,\rho_Q^{-1})$.

FORMULA 2.2 We have

$$\begin{aligned} H^*(\mathfrak{g},K,U(Q,\rho_Q^{-1}) &\cong H^*(\mathfrak{m},K\cap M,\mathrm{Id}_M)\otimes \Lambda^*\mathfrak{a}_Q \\ &\cong H^*(\mathfrak{g}_{n-1},O(n-1),\mathrm{Id}_{G_{n-1}})\otimes\Lambda^*\mathfrak{a}_Q \end{aligned} \qquad [3]$$

and for $m > 1$

$$\ker E_m^* H^*(\mathfrak{g},K,U(Q,\rho_Q^{-1})) \supset H^*(\mathfrak{m},K\cap M,\mathrm{Id}_{G_{n-1}})\otimes\mathfrak{a}_Q\,. \qquad [8]$$

So we proved

2.2.1 <u>THEOREM</u>. <u>Suppose</u> $G_n = SL(n,\mathbb{R})$ <u>and let</u>

$$j^q_\Gamma\colon I^q_{G_n} \to H^q(\Gamma,\mathbb{C})\quad q = 0,1,\ldots$$

<u>be the homomorphism of the invariant harmonic q-forms on</u> $X = K_n\backslash G_n$ <u>into the cohomology of</u> Γ <u>with complex coefficients. Then</u>

$$\dim j_\Gamma^q(I^q_{G_n}) \leq \dim I^q_{G_{n-1}} \quad .$$

To compute $\dim I^q_{G_n}$ we use that

$$\dim I^q_{G_n} = \dim H^q(SU(n)/SO(n)).$$

Standard topological arguments yield.

2.2.2 PROPOSITION. a) Suppose $n = 2k+1$. Then I_G is the exterior algebra with k generators χ_{4i+1} of degree $4i+1$, $1 \leq i \leq k$.

b) Suppose $n = 2k$. Then I_G is the exterior algebra with k generators χ_{4i+1}, $1 \leq i \leq k$ of degree $4i+1$ and a generator χ of degree $2k$.

2.2.3 COROLLARY. Suppose $G = SL(2n,\mathbb{R})$. Then

$$i^q_\Gamma : \; I^q_G \to H^*(\mathfrak{g},K,C^\infty(G/\Gamma))$$

is not injective for $q = 2n$.

PROOF: This follows from 2.2.1 and 2.2.2.

2.2.4 COROLLARY. Suppose $G = SL(n,\mathbb{R})$. Then

$$\dim j^q_\Gamma(I^q_G) \leq 1$$

if $q = \dim X\text{-rank } G = \text{coh.dim } \Gamma$.

PROOF: This follows 2.2.1 and 2.2.2.

REMARKS. a) It would be interesting to determine the kernel of j^q_Γ for $q = n = 2k$ explicitly and to check if the class χ corresponding to the Euler class of $SO(2n)$ is in the kernel.

b) The same methods can be applied to study the contribution to the cohomology of Γ of other representations in the residual spectrum of G/Γ.

c) Using another parabolic subgroup the same argument shows that if $G = SL(4,\mathbb{R})$, then $\dim j^q_\Gamma(I^q_G) = 0$ if $q > 4$.

The author was supported by the National Science Foundation.

REFERENCES

[1] A. Borel, Stable real cohomology of arithmetic groups II, Manifolds and Lie groups, Progress in Mathematics, Birkhäuser 1981, 21-55.

[2] A. Borel and J. P. Serre , Corners and arithmetic groups, Comm. Math. Helv. 48, 436-491 (1973).

[3] A Borel and N. Wallach, Continuous cohomology, discrete subgroups and representations of reductive groups, Ann. of Math. Studies 94, Princeton University Press 1980.

[4] R. P. Langlands, On the functional equations satisfied by Eisenstein series. Lectures Notes in Math. 544, Springer-Verlag, 1976.

[5] M. S. Raghunathan, Discrete subgroups of Lie groups, Ergebnisse der Mathematik und ihrer Grenzgebiete 68, Springer-Verlag 1972.

[6] M. S. Osborne and G. Warner, The theory of Eisenstein systems, Academic Press 1981.

[7] B. Speh, Indecomposable representations of semisimple Lie groups, Trans. Am. Math. Soc. 265 (1981), 1-33.

[8] B. Speh, Induced representations and the cohomology of discrete subgroups, preprint 1982.

[9] D. Vogan, Jr., Representations of real reductive Lie groups, Birkhäuser, 1981

[10] J. W. Milnor, J. Stasheff, Characteristic classes, Ann. of Math. Studies 76, Princeton University Press 1974.

OSCILLATORY INTEGRALS AND THEIR APPLICATIONS TO HARMONIC ANALYSIS ON SEMISIMPLE LIE GROUPS

V. S. Varadarajan

1. INTRODUCTION

The results discussed here have been obtained jointly with J. J. Duistermaat and J. A. C. Kolk of Utrecht, Netherlands [DKV 2]. They grew out of our efforts to obtain good error terms in the asymptotics of the spectra of compact locally symmetric manifolds of negative curvature [DV 1]. However they also seem to have some independent interest of their own.

Among other things we are concerned with the asymptotics of matrix coefficients of irreducible unitary representations of real semisimple Lie groups when the parameters defining the representations go to infinity. These matrix coefficients may be expressed as oscillatory integrals on the flag manifolds of the groups with phase functions that are intimately related to the group structure. The classical method of stationary phase is then applicable with the representations parameters as frequency variables. Substantial modifications of the classical method are however necessary to obtain estimates that are uniform in all representation parameters, because of the presence of caustics. That uniform estimates can be obtained at all is due to the remarkable and highly nongeneric properties of the phase functions, as reflected in the rigidity of their critical sets, the transversal nonsingularity of the Hessians, and the geometric simplicity of the caustic sets.

Although analytical questions concerning spectra are the source of the present investigations we hope the results and ideas in [DKV 2] will have wider applicability, especially in situations where one is interested in the behaviour of Fourier transforms of distributions on G at infinity in its dual $\hat{G}$. As an illustration of this we mention the problem of analysing the singularities of the distributions that enter the Poisson Summation Formula for compact locally symmetric manifolds of negative curvature [DKV 1].

2. OSCILLATORY INTEGRALS AND THE METHOD OF STATIONARY PHASE [D1] [G-S]

The term "oscillatory integral" refers to an integral of the form

$$I(\psi:a:\tau) = \int_X e^{i\tau\psi(x)} s(x)dx. \tag{1}$$

Here X is a smooth manifold of dimension n; dx is a smooth density on X; ψ is a smooth real function on X, called the <u>phase function</u>; and the integral, as a function of the amplitude $a \in C_c^\infty(X)$, is viewed as a distribution on X depending on the parameter τ which is real. The problem is to study the behaviour of this distribution as $\tau \to +\infty$. Integrals such as (1) occur in high frequency optics with τ representing the frequency and I representing the intensity. We shall refer to the parameter τ in (1) as the <u>frequency</u>.

The principle of stationary phase tells us that the main contributions to the asymptotic expansion of $I(\psi:a:\tau)$ come from the points in X at which ψ is stationary (= critical), i.e., $d = 0$. Let $x_0 \in X$ be a critical point of ψ and let us assume that it is <u>nondegenerate</u>, i.e., that the Hessian form is nonsingular. Then x_0 is an isolated critical point and there is an open neighborhood U of x_0 such that the following asymptotic expansion holds for $\tau \to +\infty$ and amplitudes $a \in C_c^\infty(U)$:

$$I(\psi:a:\tau) \sim \tag{2}$$
$$\left(\frac{2\pi}{\tau}\right)^{n/2} e^{\frac{i\pi}{4}\operatorname{sgn} H(\psi:x_0)} |\det H(\psi:x_0)|^{-\frac{1}{2}} e^{i\tau\psi(x_0)} \sum_{r=0}^{\infty} c_r(a)\tau^{-r}$$

where $H(\psi:x_0)$ is the Hessian, sgn refers to its signature, the determinant is calculated in frames with respect to which the density dx is 1, and the c_r are distributions supported at x_0; c_0 is the Dirac delta measure at x_0, and more generally, c_r is a derivative of the delta measure at x_0 of order $\leq 2r$.

If all critical points of ψ are nondegenerate (ψ is then called a <u>Morse function</u>) we can sum the expansions (2) coming from the various critical points to obtain global asymptotic expansions for I.

In particular,

$$I(\psi:a:\tau) = \gamma_0(a)\tau^{-\frac{n}{2}} + O\left(\tau^{-\frac{n}{2}-1}\right) \tag{3}$$

where γ_0 is a linear combination of the Dirac measures at the various critical points of ψ.

In applications we generally have phase functions $\psi(\cdot:\theta)$ that depend on an auxiliary parameter θ varying in a manifold Θ. Typically $\psi_\theta = \psi(\cdot:\theta)$ will be Morse for $\theta \in \Theta\backslash C$ where C is a subvariety of Θ; and the coefficient γ_0 of $\tau^{-n/2}$ in the asymptotic expansion of I, which is now a function of θ in $\Theta\backslash C$, will blow up as $\theta \to C$. In optics where $\tau^{n/2}$ I represents the intensity of light this means that the intensity is infinite at the points of C, i.e., light "burns". The points of C are therefore known as caustics and C is known as the caustic set. If $\theta = \theta_0 \in C$, the decay of $I(\psi_{\varepsilon_0}:a:\tau)$ as $\tau \to +\infty$ will typically be less rapid than the decay of $I(\psi_\theta:a:\tau)$ for θ in a neighborhood of θ_0 and varying off C. The question of obtaining estimates (and expansions) in τ that are uniform for θ in a neighborhood of $\theta_0 \in C$ is therefore a natural one. For generic families (ψ_θ) such expansions can be obtained; however the expansions will not be in powers of $1/\tau$ but will be in terms of more complicated special functions of the "Airy" type [D1][G-S]. One of the simplest examples is obtained when we take $\psi(x:\theta) = x^3 + \theta x (x, \theta \in \mathbb{R})$. Then $\theta = 0$ is the caustic point. For θ small and <0, $I(\psi_\theta:a:\tau) \sim \text{const.}\ \tau^{-1/2}$ while for $\theta = 0$, $I(\psi_\theta:a:\tau)$ decays only like $\tau^{-1/3}$. The determination of uniform asymptotics near a caustic is thus a basic problem whenever we have oscillatory integrals with respect to phase functions depending on parameters.

Our concern is with integrals of the form

$$\int_X e^{i(\tau_1\psi_1 + \dots + \tau_r\psi_r)}\, a\, dx \tag{4}$$

where $\underset{\sim}{\tau} = (\tau_1,\dots,\tau_r) \in \mathbb{R}^r$ and $\psi_1, \dots, \psi_r$ are phase functions on X. If we write $\tau = |\underset{\sim}{\tau}|$ and $\theta = \tau^{-1}\underset{\sim}{\tau}$, we have $\tau_1\psi_1 + \dots + \tau_r\psi_r = \tau\psi_\theta$ where $\psi_\theta = \theta_1\psi_1 + \dots + \theta_r\psi_r$ leading to possible caustics on the unit sphere on which θ varies. Thus studying integrals such as (4) with more than one frequency parameter will also in general involve questions of uniform estimates around caustics.

3. THE PHASE FUNCTIONS

Let G be a connected semisimple Lie group with finite center; $K \subset G$ a maximal compact subgroup; and $G = KAN$ an Iwasawa decomposition. We denote the Lie algebras by the corresponding lower case german letters so that $\mathfrak{g} = \mathrm{Lie}(G)$, $\mathfrak{k} = \mathrm{Lie}(K)$, $\mathfrak{a} = \mathrm{Lie}(A)$, $\mathfrak{n} = \mathrm{Lie}(N)$. We have a well-defined analytic map $H(x \to H(x))$ ("Iwasawa projection") of G into $\mathfrak{a}$ such that $x \in K \exp H(x)N$. We denote the Killing form on $\mathfrak{g} \times \mathfrak{g}$ by $\langle \cdot , \cdot \rangle$. For any $\lambda \in \mathfrak{a}^*$ let H_λ be the unique element of $\mathfrak{a}$ such that $\lambda(X) = \langle H_\lambda , X \rangle$ for all $X \in \mathfrak{a}$.

<u>FLAG MANIFOLDS</u>. For $x \in G$, $\lambda \in \mathfrak{a}^*$ we write $F_{x,\lambda}$ for the function on K defined by

$$F_{x,\lambda}(k) = \lambda(H(xk)) \qquad (k \in K) \tag{5}$$

It is clear that $F_{x,\lambda}(k)$ depends only on the coset kM so that $F_{x,\lambda}$ may be viewed as a function on the flag manifold $K/M \approx G/MAN$. Since $F_{k_1ak_2,\lambda}(k) = F_{a,\lambda}(k_2k)$ for $k_1, k_2 \in K$, $a \in A$, it is usually enough to work only with the $F_{a,\lambda}$, $a \in A$, $\lambda \in \mathfrak{a}^*$. The matrix coefficients of the unitary principal series of representations of the group G (associated to the minimal psgrp $P = MAN$) are integrals of the form

$$\int_K e^{(i\lambda-\rho)(H(xk))} g(k)dk$$

for suitable $g \in C^\infty(K)$. Their asymptotic behaviour (when x is bounded for instance) in λ is thus essentially the asymptotics in λ of the oscillatory integrals

$$\int_K e^{iF_{a,\lambda}(k)} g(k)dk.$$

It is also useful to introduce phase functions $f_{X,\lambda}(X \in \mathfrak{a}^*)$ which are "infinitesimal" versions of the $F_{a,\lambda}$. Let

$$f_{X,\lambda}(k) = \frac{d}{dt} F_{\exp tX,\lambda}(k)\Big|_{t=0} \qquad (k \in K). \tag{6}$$

then

$$f_{X,\lambda}(k) = \langle H_\lambda, X^{k^{-1}} \rangle \tag{7}$$

where X^x is written in place of $\mathrm{Ad}(x) \cdot X$. The oscillatory integrals with $f_{X,\lambda}$ as phase functions are essentially the matrix coefficients for the Cartan motion groups [Gi].

Since $K \simeq G/AN$, K becomes a G-space. Let $x, k \to \theta_x(k)$ denote the action. The "global" phase functions $F_{a,\lambda}$ can be obtained from the $f_{X,\lambda}$ by integrating along the flow lines of the action of A on K:

$$F_{\exp X,x}(k) = \int_0^1 f_{X,\lambda}(\theta_{\exp sX}(k))ds \quad (k \in K,\ X \in \mathfrak{a},\ \lambda \in \mathfrak{a}^*) \tag{8}$$

The fundamental result concerning these phase functions is the following. In what follows we denote by K_X (resp. K_λ) the centralizer of X (resp. H_λ) in K; $\mathfrak{w}$ is the Weyl group of (G,A) and for $w \in \mathfrak{w}$ we write $K_X w K_\lambda$ instead of $K_X x_w K_\lambda$ where x_w is a representative of w in the normalizer of A in K (permissible as $K_X w K_\lambda$ depends only on $x_w M$).

THEOREM. (1) *Both* $f_{X,\lambda}$ *and* $F_{\exp X,\lambda}$ *have the same critical set. This critical set is*

$$K_X \mathfrak{w} K_\lambda \underset{\mathrm{dfn}}{=} \coprod_{\mathfrak{w}_X \backslash \mathfrak{w} / \mathfrak{w}_\lambda} K_X w K_\lambda$$

In particular it is smooth.

(2) *The Hessians of* $f_{X,\lambda}$ *and* $F_{\exp X,\lambda}$ *are transversally non-singular to the critical set everywhere on it.*

COROLLARY. *If* X *and* λ *are both regular*, $F_{\exp X,\lambda}$ *and* $f_{X,\lambda}$ *are both Morse functions on* K/M *with the Weyl group points constituting the set of critical points.*

Remarks 1. The above theorem is only a part of more complete results concerning the $F_{a,\lambda}$ and $f_{X,\lambda}$. In particular the Hessians can be explicitly calculated. Fix $w \in \mathfrak{w}$ and let

$$\Delta_w^+ = \Delta_w^+(X,\lambda) = \{\alpha \in \Delta^+ \mid \langle\alpha,\lambda\rangle \cdot \langle w\alpha, X\rangle \neq 0\} \tag{9}$$

where Δ^+ is the set of positive roots of $(\mathfrak{g},\mathfrak{a})$. If $a = \exp X$ and k is a critical point for $F_{a,\lambda}$, we write $L_{a,\lambda,k}$ for the endormorphism of $\mathfrak{k}$ ($\simeq$ tangent space to K at k) which is symmetric with respect to $-\langle\cdot,\cdot\rangle$ and whose associated quadratic form is the Hessian of $F_{a,\lambda}$ at k. We then have the formula (with $x_w \in K$ a representative of $w \in \mathfrak{w}$)

$$L_{a,\lambda,x_w} = -\frac{1}{2} \sum_{\alpha\in\Delta^+} \langle\alpha,\lambda\rangle \left(1 - e^{-2w\alpha(\log a)}\right) F_\alpha \tag{10}$$

where F_α is the orthogonal projection $\mathfrak{k} \to \mathfrak{k}_\alpha = (\mathfrak{g}_\alpha + \mathfrak{g}_{-\alpha}) \cap \mathfrak{k}$.

Formula (10) gives the Hessian at all points of $K_X wM$ since $F_{\exp X,\lambda}$ is (trivially) left K_X and right M-invariant. For $f_{X,\lambda}$ a similar formula is enough to give the Hessian everywhere on $K_X wK_\lambda$ since $f_{X,\lambda}$ is left K_X and right K_λ invariant. On the other hand we have the remarkable

THEOREM. *If $\lambda \in \mathfrak{a}^*$ is dominant, i.e., is in the closure of the positive chamber of $\mathfrak{a}^*$, $F_{a,\lambda}$ is right K-invariant for all $a \in A$.*

Hence for dominant λ the formula (10) gives the Hessian of $F_{\exp X,\lambda}$ everywhere on $K_X wK_\lambda$, and hence the determination of the Hessian is complete. Even if λ is not dominant, the critical value as well as the rank, index, and signature of the Hessian of $F_{\exp X,\lambda}$ are constant on $K_X wK_\lambda$; they are given by the following formulae:

$$\begin{cases} \text{critical value} & : \langle w\lambda, X\rangle \\ \text{rank } (= n_w) & : \sum_{\alpha\in\Delta_w^+} \dim(\mathfrak{g}_\alpha) \\ \text{signature } (= \sigma_w) & : -\sum_{\alpha\in\Delta_w^+} \dim(\mathfrak{g}_\alpha)\cdot \operatorname{sgn}(\langle\lambda,\alpha\rangle \cdot \langle w\alpha, X\rangle) \\ \text{index } (= i_w) & : -\sum_{\alpha\in\Delta^+,\ \langle\alpha,\lambda\rangle\cdot\langle w\alpha,X\rangle > 0} \dim(\mathfrak{g}_\alpha) \end{cases} \tag{11}$$

2. The simplest case is $G = SL(2,\mathbb{R})$. For $x = \begin{pmatrix}\alpha & \beta \\ \gamma & \delta\end{pmatrix}$ one that $H(x) = \frac{1}{2}\log(\alpha^2 + \gamma^2)$. If $a = \begin{pmatrix} e^t, & 0 \\ 0, & e^{-t}\end{pmatrix}$, $k = \begin{pmatrix}\cos\theta, & \sin\theta \\ -\sin\theta, & \cos\theta\end{pmatrix}$

then $H(ak) = \frac{1}{2}\log(e^{2t}\cos^2\theta + e^{-2t}\sin^2\theta)$. $\begin{pmatrix}1 & 0\\ 0 & -1\end{pmatrix}$. The verification of the theorems stated is completely trivial. The Weyl group points correspond to $\theta = 0$ and $\theta = \frac{\pi}{2}$.

3. We see from these results that when X and λ vary there are only finitely many possibilities for the critical sets. In particular, when the variation of X and λ is "equisingular", the critical variety is rigid. This rigidity is a highly nongeneric phenomenon. Usually, in a generic family ψ_θ of phase functions where ψ_θ is Morse for generic θ, the critical set depends smoothly on θ; and when θ approaches a singular value, two or more of the critical points coalesce with infinite velocity. In our case the singular set is the union of root hyperplanes; when (X,λ) enters one of these, the critical set jumps to a new one which consists of smooth manifolds connecting some of the original points, the phenomenon repeating when (X,λ) becomes "more singular".

4. Although the systematic study of $F_{a,\lambda}$ is new, the $f_{X,\lambda}$ have been investigated for a much longer time. We refer to the papers cited in [DKV 2], especially the work of Bott [B], Takeuchi [T], and Takeuchi-Kobayashi [T-K] for a Morse theoretic study of the topology of the flag manifolds.

5. Let $\bar{N} = \theta N$ be the "opposite" nilpotent group and let γ be the map $\bar{n} \to \kappa(\bar{n})M$ of $\bar{N}$ into K/M; here, for $x \in G$, $\kappa(x)$ is the element of K such that $x \in \kappa(x)AN$. It is then easy to see that

$$F_{a,\lambda}(\gamma(\bar{n})) = \lambda(\log a) + \psi(\lambda:a:\bar{n}),\ \psi(\lambda:a:\bar{n}) = \lambda(H(\bar{n}^a) - H(\bar{n})).$$

Let us write $a \to +\infty$ if $\alpha(\log a) \to +\infty$ for all positive roots α of $(\mathfrak{g},\mathfrak{a})$. Then

$$\lim_{a\to+\infty} \psi(\lambda:a:\bar{n}) = -\lambda(H(\bar{n})) \qquad (\bar{n} \in \bar{N}) \tag{12}$$

giving a family of phase functions on $\bar{N}$. The associated oscillatory integrals are obviously closely related to the Harish-Chandra C-functions. A study of the C-functions from the point of view of oscillatory integrals with phase functions (12) was carried out by

Cohn [C]. Cohn however worked in a domain of $\mathfrak{a}_c^*$ off the real space $\mathfrak{a}^*$ and used Laplace's method instead of stationary phase.

6. One can show that $dF_{\exp X,\lambda}$ and $df_{X,\lambda}$, regarded as functions on the tangent bundle of K, are equivalent under a suitable diffeomorphism of the tangent bundle. Indeed, we have the formula

$$F_{\exp X,\lambda}(k;Y) = f_{X,\lambda}(\theta_{\exp X}(k);Z) \tag{13}$$

if $Z \in \mathfrak{k}$ and $Y = \mathrm{Ad}(k^{-1}) \cdot (\mathrm{ad}\, X/\sinh\, \mathrm{ad}\, X) \cdot \mathrm{Ad}\, \theta_{\exp X}(k)\ (Z)$; here we use the notation $g(k;R)$ for $\frac{d}{dt}\, g(k \exp t R))_{t=0}$ for $k \in K$, $R \in \mathfrak{k}$, $g \in C^\infty(K)$. These and other relations between F and f suggest the existence of a diffeomorphism $g_{X,\lambda}(K \tilde{\to} K)$ such that $F_{\exp X,\lambda} = f_{X,\lambda} \cdot g_{X,\lambda}$. If one can construct such $g_{X,\lambda}$ depending smoothly on X,λ, some of the present treatment would be simplified quite a bit.

CONJUGACY CLASSES. For the theory of asymptotics of spectra of compact locally symmetric manifolds it is important to study oscillatory integrals on the conjugacy classes of G with respect to the phase functions which are restrictions of $x \to \lambda(H(x))$. Fix $\gamma \in G$ and let

$$F_{\lambda,\gamma}(x) = \lambda(H(x)) \qquad (x \in C_\gamma = \text{conjugacy class of } \gamma). \tag{14}$$

THEOREM. Let G_λ be the centralizer of H_λ in G. Then the critical set of $F_{\lambda,\gamma}$ is $G_\lambda \cap C_\gamma$ which is smooth. The Hessian of $F_{\lambda,\alpha}$ is transversally nonsingular everywhere on the critical set.

Remark. The smoothness of the critical set follows from its description on taking into account results of Richardson [R]. Here again the Hessian can be determined explicitly; see [DKV 2] for details.

4. ASYMPTOTIC EXPANSIONS AND UNIFORM ESTIMATES

The calculations on $F_{a,\lambda}$ lead at once to

THEOREM. *Fix* $a \in A, \lambda \in \mathfrak{a}^*$. *Then the function* $k \to e^{i\tau\lambda(H(ak))}$ i.e., $e^{iF_{a,\tau\lambda}}$ *regarded as a distribution on* K, *has the following asymptotic expansion as* $\tau \to +\infty$:

$$e^{iF_{a,\tau\lambda}} \sim \sum_{w \in \mathfrak{w}_a \backslash \mathfrak{w}/\mathfrak{w}_\lambda} e^{i\tau w\lambda(\log a)} \sum_{r=0}^{\infty} \tau^{-\frac{1}{2}n_w - r} c_{w,r}$$

Here n_w *is the transversal rank of the Hessian of* $F_{a,\lambda}$ *at* w; $c_{w,r}$ *is a distribution supported on* $K_a w K_\lambda$ *of order* $\leq 2r$; $c_{w,0}$ *is a measure on* $K_a w K_\lambda$ *with a density (relative to the obvious measure) of the form*

$$\prod_{\alpha \in \Delta_w^+} \left| \langle\alpha,\lambda\rangle \sinh w\alpha(\log a) \right|^{-\frac{1}{2}\dim(\mathfrak{g}_\alpha)} \cdot \delta_{a,\lambda}$$

where $\delta_{a,\lambda}$ *is smooth. The expansion is uniform for local equisingular variations in* a *and* λ.

COROLLARY. *Fix* $a \in A, \lambda \in \mathfrak{a}^*$. *Then there is a neighborhood* ω *of* a *in* A *and a conical neighborhood* Γ *of* λ *in* $\mathfrak{a}^*$, *and a continuous seminorm* ν *on* $C^\infty(K)$, *such that for all* $a' \in A$, $\lambda' \in \Gamma$, $g \in C^\infty(K)$,

$$\left| \int_K e^{i\lambda'(H(a'k))} g(k)dk \right| \leq \nu(g) \sum_{\mathfrak{w}_a \backslash \mathfrak{w}/\mathfrak{w}_\lambda} \prod_{\alpha \in \Delta_w^+} (1 + |\langle\alpha,\lambda\rangle|)^{-\frac{1}{2}n(\alpha)}$$

where $n(\alpha) = \dim(\mathfrak{g}_\alpha)$.

These estimages are sharp as long as (a',λ') is equisingular with (a,λ); but when (a',λ') vary along neighboring generic rays they are poorer. Let us now fix $a \in A$ and regard λ as the parameter. The caustic set is now a union of hyperplanes in $\mathfrak{a}^*$. The oscillating integral decays like $\lambda^{-1/2\dim(N)}$ when $\lambda' = \tau\lambda$ and λ is regular; but the top coefficient blows up as a function of λ when λ approaches the root hyperplanes. So there is a nontrivial problem of obtaining uniform estimates. It is remarkable that such uniform estimates and asymptotic expansions can be obtained using only products of functions of the form $1 + |\langle\alpha,\lambda\rangle|$; the reader should contrast this with the situation for generic families of phase functions. The following theorem is typical.

THEOREM. Let $\omega \subset A$ be a compact set, and for $w \in \mathfrak{w}$ let $\Delta_w^+(\omega) = \{\alpha \in \Delta^+ \mid w\alpha(\log a) \neq 0$ for all $a \in \omega\}$. Then

$$\left|\int_K e^{i\lambda(H(ak))} g(k)dk\right| \leqslant \nu(g) \sum_{w \in \mathfrak{w}} \prod_{\alpha \in \Delta_w^+} (1 + |\langle\alpha,\lambda\rangle|)^{-\frac{1}{2}n(\alpha)}$$

for all $\lambda \in \mathfrak{a}^*$, $a \in \omega$, $g \in C^\infty(K)$; here ν is a continuous seminorm on $C^\infty(K)$.

The proof is rather complicated and we shall just sketch the main lines of the argument. For simplicity we consider a fixed $a \in A$. We consider at first only the λ in the closure of the positive chamber in $\mathfrak{a}^*$. Let $\{\alpha_1,\ldots,\alpha_r\}$ be an ordering of the simple roots in Δ^+ and $\{\ddot{\alpha}_1,\ldots,\ddot{\alpha}_r\}$ the corresponding coroots, i.e., $\langle\alpha_i,\ddot{\alpha}_j\rangle = \delta_{ij}$. Write $\lambda = \sum_i \tau_i\ddot{\alpha}_i$ so that we are working on the cone $\tau_1 \geqslant 0, \ldots, \tau_r \geqslant 0$. It is enough to prove the estimates around each point of K. The typical case is around $1 \in K$. Write $\psi_j = F_{a,\alpha_j}$, $1 \leqslant j \leqslant r$, and let K_m denote the centralizer in K of $H_{\alpha_1}, \ldots, H_{\alpha_m}$. We then have the filtration

$$K = K_0 \supseteq K_1 \supseteq \ldots \supset K_r = (1)$$

and the phase function ψ_j is right K_j-invariant. For the restriction to K_{j-1} of ψ_j, 1 is a critical point and the Hessian has rank equal to $n_j = \sum n(\alpha)$ where the sum is over all $\alpha \in \Delta^+$ for which $\alpha(\log a) \neq 0$ and α is a linear combination of $\alpha_j, \alpha_{j+1}, \ldots, \alpha_r$ with the coefficient of $\alpha_j > 0$. If X_j is a local section through 1 for K_{j-1}/K_j we see that locally, around 1, $(\psi_1,\ldots,\psi_r)$ have the remarkable property of <u>trigonalizability</u>: $(\psi_1,\ldots,\psi_r) \approx (f_1,\ldots,f_r)$ where the f_j are defined on $X_1 \times \ldots \times X_r$, with (a) f_j depending only on the variables $(x_1,\ldots,x_j) \in X_1 \times \ldots \times X_j$ (b) $x_j \to f_j(1,1,\ldots,1,x_j)$ has $x_j = 1$ as critical point with Hessian rank n_j. The classical Morse lemma with parameters in combination with the method of stationary phase may now be applied to $X_r, X_{r-1}, \ldots, X_1$ in succession. The final result is the validity of (16) (locally around 1) in the cone

$$\tau_1 \geqslant \gamma\tau_2 \geqslant \gamma^2\tau_3 \geqslant \ldots \quad \gamma^{r-1}\,\tau_r \geqslant 0$$

for a suitable $\gamma > 0$. This region is only a small part of the positive chamber in $\mathfrak{a}^*$; however, this type of argument may be used relative to any ordered partition $\pi: S_1 \cup S_2 \cup \ldots \cup S_m$ of the set of simple roots to obtain (16) (locally) in conical regions of the form $C(\pi:\mu:\gamma)$ $(\mu \geqslant 1, \gamma > 0)$ defined as follows: $\lambda = \tau_1\alpha_1 + \ldots + \tau_r\alpha_r$ belongs to $C(\pi:\mu:\gamma)$ if and only if

(a) $\tau_j \geqslant 0$ for all j
(b) If j, k belong to the same S_p, $\lambda_j \leqslant \mu\tau_k$
(c) If $j \in S_p$, $k \in S_q$ with $p < q$, $\tau_j \geqslant \gamma\tau_k$

This will suffice to get (16) (locally) on the whole positive chamber; for, the latter can be written as a union of finitely many of the $C(\pi:\mu:\gamma)$.

If the point of K, say k_0, around which the amplitudes g in (16) are localized, is such that only some of the ψ_j are critical, we use the following observation to come down to the earlier type of situation: if $\psi_1, \ldots, \psi_s$ are critical at k_0 but not $\psi_{s+1}, \ldots, \psi_r$, we can find $Z \in \mathfrak{i}$ tangent at k_0 to the critical manifolds of $\psi_1, \ldots, \psi_s$ and such that $\psi_m(k_0;Z) > 0$ for $s+1 \leqslant m \leqslant r$.

Finally there remains the problem of extending (16) to all of $\mathfrak{a}^*$. The method of proof is still as outlined above and is based on the "trigonalization" of $\psi_1, \ldots, \psi_r$. But the argument for trigonalization is now much more subtle since we no longer have right invariance properties for $F_{a,\lambda}$. The idea is to use (13) to transfer the question of trigonalizing to the $f_{X,\lambda}$, and then exploit the right invariance of $f_{X,\lambda}$ with respect to K_λ which is valid for all λ.

Uniform estimates and asymptotic expansions for the integrals

$$\int_{C_\gamma} e^{i\lambda(H(x))} g(x)d\dot{x} \qquad (g \in C_c^\infty(G),\ d\dot{x} = \text{invariant measure on } C_\gamma)$$

over semisimple conjugacy classes may be obtained in similar fashion. We refer to [DKV 2] for details.

5. APPLICATIONS

We indicate briefly some applications of the foregoing results.

(a) Conjugacy of maximal abelian subspace of $\mathfrak{s}$ and maximal tori. The argument goes back to Hunt [Hu]. Let $\mathfrak{g} = \mathfrak{k} \oplus \mathfrak{s}$ be the Cartan decomposition of $\mathfrak{g}$. If $X \in \mathfrak{s}, \lambda \in \mathfrak{a}^*$, $k \in K$ is critical for $f_{X,\lambda}$ if and only if $[X^{k^{-1}}, H_\lambda] = 0$. Choosing a regular λ, this becomes $X^{k^{-1}} \in \mathfrak{a}$.

(b) Convexity theorems. The typical result is a well-known theorem of Kostant [K]: If $X \in \mathfrak{a}$, the Iwasawa (resp. orthogonal) projection of the K-orbit of $\exp X$ (resp. X) under inner automorphisms (resp. Ad(K)-action) is the convex hull of the set of points wX ($w \in \mathfrak{w}$). In his 1980 Leiden thesis Heckhman [H] gave a proof of this and other theorems of the same nature, whose point of departure was the calculation of critical points and Hessians of $f_{X,\lambda}$ and $F_{\exp X,\lambda}$. We now know very much more general convexity theorems (cf. Atiyah [A], Diustermaat [D2]).

(c) Asymptotics of the Harish-Chandra C-functions. The C-functions are oscillatory integrals on the "big" Bruhat cell (cf. (12)). We refer the reader to the work of Cohn [C] for the deatils. In [DKV 2] the critical set calculations of Cohn are completed and extended to include $\lambda \in i\mathfrak{a}^*$.

(d) Error estimates for spectra. This was the original motivation of the present study. Let $X = \Gamma \backslash G/K$ where Γ is a discrete co-compact torsion-free subgroup of G. The problem of the asymptotics of the spectrum of X is studied in detail in [DKV 1]. One of the main results of [DKV 1] is that if Ω is any bounded open subset of $i\mathfrak{a}^*$ with smooth boundary, the spectral multiplicities $m(\lambda)$ satisfy, for $t \to +\infty$, the asymptotic relation

$$\sum_{\lambda \varepsilon t\Omega,\ \lambda \varepsilon \mathrm{Spec}(L^2(X))} m(\lambda) = \text{const.} \int_{t\Omega} d\mu + O(t^{n-1}) \qquad (18)$$

where $d\mu$ is the Plancherel measure corresponding to $L^2(G/K)$; the main term on the right of (18) is $\sim$ const. t^n. The error estimate is however a poor one. The results of Section 4 are already enough to yield the sharpening where $O(t^{n-1})$ gets replaced by $o(t^{n-1})$.

For further improvements it is necessary to use estimates of the form (16) where $a \in A$ is allowed to go to infinity. It appears that the methods of [DKV 2] are already capable of yielding (16) where ω is a canonical set in $C\ell(A^+)$ and there is in addition a factor of the form $e^{\text{const}\cdot\|\log a\|}$ that indicates the dependence on a. Such a generalization of (16) would allow us to improve the error estimate in (18) to $O(t^{n-1}/\log t)$. We hope to take these questions up in a future publication.

The fundamental question now is to find the "true" asymptotic behaviour of the integrals

$$\int_K e^{i\lambda(H(ak)) - \rho(H(ak))} g(k)dk \qquad (g \in C^\infty(K)) \tag{19}$$

when $a \in A$ and $\lambda \in \mathfrak{a}^*$ both go to infinity. Calculations when G is complex or of real rank 1 suggest the general pattern of the results to be expected. There are however a few difficulties to be overcome.

(3) Structure of the distribution T_λ of the Poisson formula for X. In [DKV 1] a Poisson formula was derived expressing the sum $\sum m(\lambda)e^{\lambda(\log a)}$ as the sum of distributions $\sum v_\gamma T_\gamma$ (cf. Theorem 5.1, loc. cit). If G has real rank 1, T_γ is a delta-function located at the point $\ell(\gamma)$ which is the length of the closed geodesic corresponding to $\gamma \in \Gamma(\gamma \neq 1)$. In the higher rank case it would be of interest to investigate the singular spectrum of T_γ (see [Ho], p. 5). Fix a semisimple element $\gamma \neq 1$ in G; then T_γ is the Weyl group invariant distribution on A defined by

$$<T_\gamma, f> = \int_{G/G_\gamma} (\mathbb{A}^{-1}f)(x\gamma x^{-1})d\dot{x} \qquad (f \in C_c^\infty(A)^{\mathfrak{w}}) \tag{20}$$

where $\mathbb{A}$ is the Abel transform. The idea is now to replace f by $fe^{i\tau\lambda}$ $(\lambda \in \mathfrak{a}^*)$ and let $\tau \to +\infty$. Expressing $\mathbb{A}^{-1}$ as the composition of Fourier transform (on A) followed by the inverse Harish-Chandra transform one reduces this to the study, as $\tau \to +\infty$, of integrals of the form

$$\int_{\mathfrak{a}^*} \hat{f}(-\nu)\beta(i(\tau\beta + \nu)) \left[\int_{C_\gamma} \psi(x)e^{(i\nu-\rho)(H(x))}e^{i\tau\lambda(H(x))}d\dot{x}\right] d\nu \tag{21}$$

where $\beta(\nu)d\nu$ is the Plancherel measure and $\psi \in C_c^\infty(G)$ while $\hat{f}$ is the Fourier transform of $f \in C_c^\infty(A)$. This leads to a full asymptotic expansion of $<T_\gamma; fe^{i\tau\lambda}>$ $(f \in C_c(A))$; see Theorem 10.4 of [DKV 2]. Let x_j $(1 \leq j \leq m)$ be a complete set of representatives of the G -conjugacy classes in $C_\lambda \cap G_\lambda$. We may assume that $x_j \in$ a θ-stable CSG L_j with CSA $\mathfrak{l}_j$ such that $\mathfrak{l}_{j,R} (= \mathfrak{l}_j \cap \mathfrak{s}) \subset \mathfrak{a}$. Then, using the identification of the cotangent bundle of $\mathfrak{a}$ with $\mathfrak{a} \oplus \mathfrak{a}^* \simeq \mathfrak{a} \oplus \mathfrak{a}$, we find that the singular spectrum of T_γ is contained in the union of affine spaces $\cup_j (E_j \times F_j)$ where $E_j = {}^*\mathfrak{l}_j + \log x_{j,R}$ (${}^*\mathfrak{l}_j$ is the orthogonal complement of $\mathfrak{l}_{j,R}$ in $\mathfrak{a}$, and $x_{j,R}$ is the projection of x_j in A mod $L \cap K$) while $F_j = \mathrm{Ker}(\mathrm{ad}(x_j) - I) \cap \mathfrak{a}$.

(f) The topology of real flag manifolds. We have already referred to the papers of Bott, Takeuchi, and Kobayashi. For further results (for example to tight imbeddings of flag varieties) and discussion the reader is referred to [DKV 2], Section 4.

6. ACKNOWLEDGEMENT

It is a pleasure to thank Peter Trombi, Henryk Hecht, and many other members of the Department of Mathematics of the University of Utah for their efforts which created a wonderful atmosphere of warmth and hospitality during the conference. Thanks are also expressed to Ann Reed who looked after our varied needs with unfailing courtesy.

Research partially supported by NSF Grant MCS 79-03184.

REFERENCES

[A] M. F. Atiyah, Convexity and commuting Hamiltonians, Preprint, 1981.

[B] R. Bott, On torsion in Lie groups, Proc. Nat. Acad. Sci. U.S.A., 40, 586-588 (1954).

[C] L. Cohn, Analytic theory of the Harish-Chandra C-function, Lecture notes in Mathematics No. 429, Springer-Verlag, Berlin, 1974.

[D 1] J. J. Duistermaat, Oscillatory integrals, Lagrange immersions, and unfolding of singularities, Comm. Pure. Appl. Math. 27, 207-281 (1974).

[D 2] J. J. Duistermaat, Convexity and tightness for restrictions of Hamiltonian functions to fixed point sets of an antisymplectic involution, preprint, 1981.

[DKV 1] J. J. Duistermaat, J. A. C. Kolk, and V. S. Varadarajan, Spectra of compact locally symmetric manifolds of negative curvature, Invent. Math. 52, 27-93 (1979).

[DKV 2] J. J. Duistermaat, J. A. C. Kolk, and V. S. Varadarajan, Functions, flows, and oscillatory integrals on flag manifolds and conjugacy classes in real semisimple Lie groups, preprint, 1981.

[Gi] S. G. Gindikin, Unitary representations of groups of automorphisms of Riemannian symmetric spaces of null curvature, Funcional Anal. i. Prilozen 1, 1, 32-37 (1967); English transl. Functional Anal. Appl. 1, 28-32 (1967).

[G-S] V Guillemin and S. Sternberg, Geometric Asymptotics, Amer. Math. Soc. Math. Surveys No. 14, Providence, R. I., 1977.

[H] G. J. Heckman, Projections of orbits and asymptotic behaviour of multiplicities for compact Lie groups, Thesis, Leiden (1980).

[Hö] L. Hörmander, Seminar on singularities of solutions of linear partial differential equations, Ann. Math. Studies. No. 91, Princeton, 1979.

[Hu] G. A. Hunt, A theorem of Elie Cartan, Proc. Amer. Math. Soc. 7, 307-308 (1956).

[K] B. Kostant, On convexity, the Weyl group, and the Iwasawa decomposition, Ann. Sci. Ecole. Norm. Sup. (4) 6, 413-455 (1973).

[R] R. W. Richardson, Jr., Conjugacy classes in Lie algebras and algebraic groups, Ann. of Math. 86, 1-15 (1967).

[T] M. Takeuchi, Cell decompositions and Morse equalities on certain symmetric spaces, J. Fac. of Sci. Univ. of Tokyo, 12, 81-192.

[T-K] M. Takeuchi and S. Kobayashi, Minimal imbeddings of R-spaces, J. Diff. Geo., 2, 203-215 (1968).

THE KAZHDAN-LUSZTIG CONJECTURE FOR REAL REDUCTIVE GROUPS

David A. Vogan, Jr.

1. INTRODUCTION

Let G be a reductive linear real Lie group with abelian Cartan subgroups. The Kazhdan-Lusztig conjecture of [11] provides an algorithm for computing explicitly the distribution characters of the irreducible (admissible) representations of G. The history and status of this conjecture will not be related here (see [6], [7], [1], [2], and [11]); suffice it to say that there is (at least) a very detailed program for proving it, although there is no complete account in print. Our purpose here is simply to state the conjecture in as elementary a way as possible. There are at least two motivations for this, both a little tenuous. First, the industry of computing irreducible characters was created largely to assist in the study of unitary representations. It may therefore be useful to have the Kazhdan-Lusztig conjecture written down without the ponderous baggage of its proof. There are no examples of applications in this direction as yet, however. Second, the existing proof of the conjecture is (to a narrow-minded group representer) unsatisfactory. In section 8, we explain what kind of serious theorems must be combined with the formal results to give a proof of the conjecture. They are tantalizingly simple; but they have resisted all attempts at representation-theoretic proof for several years.

Here is a rough outline of the argument. Using results from [10], (see section 7) one can reduce to the case of representations with nonsingular infinitesimal character. Write $\mathcal{D}$ for the set of equivalence classes of standard representations with a fixed non-singular infinitesimal character λ^a. These are the representations induced from discrete series representations on parabolic subgroups of G, in the usual way; they may therefore be regarded as analytic continuations of the representations appearing in Harish-Chandra's Plancherel formula. We will not distinguish between standard representations having the same distribution character. The representations in $\mathcal{D}$ are not irreducible, but they have finite Jordan-Holder series. To each $\gamma \in \mathcal{D}$, Langlands has associated in [8] a particular irreducible subquotient $\overline{\gamma}$ of γ. It may be characterized as the subquotient whose matrix coefficients have the largest growth at infinity ([8]); or as the one whose restriction to a maximal compact subgroup K contains the smallest representation of K ([12]). Langlands shows that every irreducible admissible representation of G of infinitesimal character λ^a is equivalent to some $\overline{\gamma}$, for a unique $\gamma \in \mathcal{D}$. We may therefore regard $\mathcal{D}$ as parametrizing the irreducible representations of infinitesimal character λ^a.

Suppose γ and δ are in $\mathcal{D}$. Write $m(\overline{\gamma},\delta)$ for the multiplicity of γ as a subquotient of δ: formally

$$\delta = \sum_{\gamma \in \mathcal{D}} m(\overline{\gamma},\delta)\overline{\gamma} . \qquad \text{(a)} \qquad (1.1)$$

This may be interpreted as an identity of distribution characters. The matrix m is unipotent upper triangular in an appropriate ordering of $\mathcal{D}$, as was observed by Speh and others; so its inverse matrix M has integer entries:

$$\overline{\delta} = \sum_{\gamma \in \mathcal{D}} M(\gamma,\overline{\delta})\gamma . \qquad \text{(b)} \qquad (1.2)$$

This formula may also be interpreted as an identity of distribution characters. It gives the character of the irreducible representation $\overline{\delta}$ in terms of the integers $M(\gamma,\overline{\delta})$, and the characters of standard representations. The latter are fairly well known; in principle by the work of Harish-Chandra, and in practice by the formulas of R. Herb ([4]). The problem is therefore to compute the integers $M(\gamma,\overline{\delta})$. This can be phrased a little more conveniently. Consider the lattice $\mathbb{Z}[\mathcal{D}]$; this is the group of all formal expressions

$$\sum_{\gamma \in \mathcal{D}} a_\gamma \gamma \qquad (a_\gamma \in \mathbb{Z}) \ .$$

(It may be identified with the lattice of distributions generated by the characters of standard representations.) We seek a second distinguished basis $\{\overline{C}_\delta\}_{\delta \in \mathcal{D}}$ of $\mathbb{Z}[\mathcal{D}]$; $\overline{C}_\delta$ will be

$$\sum_{\gamma \in \mathcal{D}} M(\gamma,\overline{\delta})\gamma \ .$$

The idea is to try to characterize $\overline{C}_\delta$ by some formal properties, which will allow us to compute it.

The first extra structure needed for characterizing $\overline{C}_\delta$ is the integral Weyl group W defined by the infinitesimal character λ^a. (It will be discussed more carefully in section 2.) Write S for the standard generating set of reflections in W, so that (W,S) is a Coxeter group. The group W acts on the lattice $\mathbb{Z}[\mathcal{D}]$ in a computable way (the <u>coherent continuation</u> representation of W). Since Jantzen's work (e.g. [5]), it has been clear that the $\overline{C}_\delta$ are closely related to this action. For example, if $s \in S$, and $\delta \in \mathcal{D}$, then either

$$s \cdot \overline{C}_\delta = - \overline{C}_\delta \qquad \text{(a)} \qquad (1.2)$$

or

$$s \cdot \overline{C}_\delta = \overline{C}_\delta + \sum_{\gamma \in \mathcal{D}} \mu(s,\gamma,\delta) \ \overline{C}_\gamma$$

Here $\mu(s,\gamma,\delta)$ is a non-negative integer; and one can say a lot about the value of $\mu(s,\gamma,\delta)$. Such results are very powerful for small groups, but they are apparently not enough to determine $\overline{C}_\delta$ completely. The idea of Kazhdan and Lusztig is to introduce an indeterminate q: instead of working over $\mathbb{Z}$, we work over the ring $\mathbb{Z}[q^{\frac{1}{2}},q^{-\frac{1}{2}}]$ of Laurent polynomials. Set

$$M = \mathbb{Z}[q^{\frac{1}{2}},q^{-\frac{1}{2}}] \ [\mathcal{D}] \ ; \qquad (1.3)$$

this is the set of all formal expressions

$$\sum_{\gamma \in \mathcal{D}} a_\gamma \gamma \qquad\qquad (a_\gamma \in \mathbb{Z}[q^{\frac{1}{2}}, q^{-\frac{1}{2}}]) .$$

We will describe certain elements

$$C_\delta = \sum_{\gamma \in \mathcal{D}} P_{\gamma,\delta}(q)\gamma \in \mathcal{M} . \tag{1.4}$$

Here $P_{\gamma,\delta}$ will be an ordinary polynomial in q , and we will have

$$C_\delta(1) = \overline{C}_\delta \qquad \text{up to signs;}$$

that is,

$$M(\gamma,\delta) = \pm P_{\gamma,\delta}(1) . \tag{1.5}$$

(The signs are specified precisely in (5.8).)

There are at least two ways of thinking about the definition of C_δ . From the first point of view (Lemma 5.7), the elements C_δ will be characterized by various formal properties, of which the critical one is a kind of self-duality. The $\mathbb{Z}[q^{\frac{1}{2}}, q^{-\frac{1}{2}}]$ module $\mathcal{M}$ carries a certain "duality"

$$D: \mathcal{M} \rightarrow \mathcal{M},$$

which is analogous to the operation of passing from a representation to a dual representation. That operation does not affect distribution characters (up to an automorphism of G); so it is not surprising that if $m \in \mathcal{M}$,

$$(Dm)(1) = m(1):$$

the operation D is invisible on the level of $\mathbb{Z}[\mathcal{D}]$. The main property of C_δ is

$$DC_\delta = q^{-\ell(\delta)} C_\delta ; \tag{1.6}$$

here $\ell(\delta)$ is a certain half integer. This requirement has no analogue at all for C_δ (which is why the indeterminate q was introduced). It corresponds simply to the fact that the irreducible representation $\overline{\delta}$ must be self-dual (up to an automorphism of G).

Computationally, this first approach to C_δ comes down to computing D . Here we need the analogue for M of the W action on $\mathbb{Z}[\mathcal{D}]$. This involves the Hecke algebra of W (whose definition is recalled in section 2), but we can think of it in a simple way. For each $s \in S$ (the generators of W), there will be a $\mathbb{Z}[q^{\frac{1}{2}},q^{-\frac{1}{2}}]$-linear map

$$T_s : M \to M ,$$

which (up to some simple twists) lifts the action of s on $\mathbb{Z}[\mathcal{D}]$. Now $s^2 = 1$; but T_s satisfies instead the q-analogue

$$T_s{}^2 = (q-1)T_s + q .$$

It is better to think of this formula as

$$(T_s + 1)^2 = (q + 1)(T_s + 1) ,$$

corresponding to the formula

$$(s + 1)^2 = 2(s + 1)$$

in the group algebra of W . At any rate, T_s is defined very explicitly on the basis $\mathcal{D}$ of M (section 5). This definition may be motivated by thinking of $T_s + 1$ as the "wall crossing" translation functor $\phi_\alpha\psi_\alpha$ considered in [10], [12], and elsewhere. (These are just some of the Jantzen-Zuckerman functors, of tensoring with finite dimensional representations and localizing with respect the center of the enveloping algebra.) This intuition suggests that $T_s + 1$ should essentially commute with the duality D; and in fact we have

$$D[(T_s+1)m] = q^{-1}(T_s+1)(Dm) \qquad (m \in M,\ s \in S)$$

Since we know T_s explicitly, this formula amounts to a computable constraint on D . Together with some formal properties, it will allow us to give recursion formulas for computing D ; and then (1.6) will essentially compute C_δ .

The second way of computing C_δ is closer to Jantzen's original ideas, but harder to motivate. It is based on a result which gives analogues of (1.2) for M (Lemma 6.7). The main point is that one gets a formula for $\mu(s,\gamma,\delta)$: in the difficult cases, it is just a certain coefficient of the polynomial $P_{\gamma,\delta}$. Naturally such a formula does not make sense in $\mathbb{Z}[\mathcal{D}]$, which sees only the sum $P_{\gamma,\delta}(1)$ of all the coefficients. This leads directly to recursion formulas for the polynomials $P_{\gamma,\delta}$.

Section 2 introduces the group W and some related notation. Section 3 recalls the Langlands classification in a convenient form. Section 4 defines the Cayley transforms needed to define T_s . Section 5 defines the length function and Bruhat order on $\mathcal{D}$, and the operators T_s; and states the formal properties defining D and the C_δ . Section 6 is a list of the explicit recursion formulas underlying the two computations of $P_{\gamma,\delta}$ sketched above. As an example, it treats the case of $Sp(2,\mathbb{R})$. Section 7 explains how to deal with singular infinitesimal character; and section 8 discharges my duty to those interested in giving representation-theoretic proofs of the Kazhdan-Lusztig conjecture.

2. GENERAL NOTATION

Recall that G is a real reductive linear group (not necessarily connected) with abelian Cartan subgroups. Write G_0 for the identity component of G , $\mathfrak{g}_0$ for its Lie algebra, and $\mathfrak{g} = \mathfrak{g}_0 \otimes_{\mathbb{R}} \mathbb{C}$. Analogous notation is used for other groups. Write $Ad(\mathfrak{g})$ for the identity component of the automorphism group of $\mathfrak{g}$. It is very convenient to have a fixed way of comparing various Cartan subalgebras of $\mathfrak{g}$. This we do by means of the <u>abstract Cartan subalgebra</u> $\mathfrak{h}^a$ of $\mathfrak{g}$. There are two ways to think of $\mathfrak{h}^a$. We will generally think of it as an honest Cartan subalgebra of $\mathfrak{g}$, fixed once and for all. A more satisfactory definition is

$$\mathfrak{h}^a = \{Ad(\mathfrak{g})\text{-conjugancy classes of pairs } (X,\mathfrak{b}) \mid \mathfrak{b} \text{ is a Borel subalgebra of } \mathfrak{g},\ X \in \mathfrak{b} \text{, and } X \text{ is semisimple}\} .$$

The reader may check that the two definitions can be related in a simple way, by fixing also a Borel subalgebra $\mathfrak{b}^a \subseteq \mathfrak{h}^a$ in the first definition.

If $\mathfrak{h} \subseteq \mathfrak{g}$ is any Cartan subalgebra, we have a Harish-Chandra isomorphism

$$\xi: \mathfrak{Z}(\mathfrak{g}) \to S(\mathfrak{h})^{W(\mathfrak{g},\mathfrak{h})} \qquad (2.1)$$

Here $\mathfrak{Z}(\mathfrak{g})$ is the center of $U(\mathfrak{g})$, and $W(\mathfrak{g},\mathfrak{h})$ is the Weyl group of $\mathfrak{h}$ in $\mathfrak{g}$. Suppose $\lambda \in \mathfrak{h}^*$. Define

$\xi_\lambda: \mathfrak{Z}(\mathfrak{g}) \to \mathbb{C}$, $\xi_\lambda(z) = \xi(z)(\lambda)$ (the _infinitesimal character_ λ)

$R(\lambda) = \{\alpha \in \Delta(\mathfrak{g},\mathfrak{h}) \mid \langle\check{\alpha},\lambda\rangle \in \mathbb{Z}\}$ (the _integral roots for_ λ)

$W(\lambda)$ = Weyl group of $R(\lambda)$ (the _integral Weyl group_)

(2.2)

(Here and throughout, $\langle,\rangle$ is (the complexified dual of the restriction to $\mathfrak{h}_0$ of) an invariant bilinear form on $\mathfrak{g}_0$ induced by a faithful finite dimensional representation ρ of G:

$$\langle X,Y\rangle = tr(\rho(X)\rho(Y))$$

for $X, Y \in \mathfrak{g}_0$. The symbol $\check{\alpha}$ denotes the coroot $2\alpha/\langle\alpha,\alpha\rangle$.) We call λ (or ξ_λ) _nonsingular_ if $\langle\alpha,\lambda\rangle$ is not zero for any root α. If λ is nonsingular, put

$$\begin{aligned} R^+(\lambda) &= \{\alpha \in R(\lambda) \mid \langle\check{\alpha},\lambda\rangle > 0\} \\ \Pi(\lambda) &= \text{simple roots of } R^+(\lambda) \subseteq R^+(\lambda) \\ S(\lambda) &= \{s_\alpha \mid \alpha \in \Pi(\lambda)\} \subseteq W(\lambda). \end{aligned} \qquad (2.3)$$

Now fix once and for all a nonsingular weight

$$\lambda^a \in (\mathfrak{h}^a)^*, \qquad (2.4)$$

and define

$$\begin{aligned} R = R(\lambda^a) &\supseteq R^+ = R^+(\lambda^a) \supseteq \Pi = \Pi(\lambda^a) \\ W = W(\lambda^a) &\supseteq S = S(\lambda^a) \end{aligned} \qquad (2.5)$$

Let $\mathfrak{h}$ be any Cartan subalgebra, and $\lambda \in \mathfrak{h}^*$ a weight. Assume that the infintesimal characters defined by λ and λ^a are the same: $\xi_\lambda = \xi_{\lambda^a}$. It follows that there is an element $g \in Ad(\mathfrak{g})$ such that

$$Ad(g)(\mathfrak{h}^a) = \mathfrak{h}$$
$$[{}^tAd(g)](\lambda) = \lambda^a$$

Now g is not unique; but since λ^a is assumed to be nonsingular, the map

$$i_\lambda = Ad(g)|_{\mathfrak{h}^a} \quad , \quad i_\lambda = \mathfrak{h}^a \to \mathfrak{h} \tag{2.6}$$

is independent of the choice of g. We also write

$$i_\lambda = (\mathfrak{h}^a)^* \to \mathfrak{h}^*$$

for the inverse transpose of i_λ; and for the induced isomorphism between W and $W(\lambda)$, and so on. If $w \in W$ and $\alpha \in R$, write

$$\begin{aligned} w_\lambda &= i_\lambda(w) \in W(\lambda) \\ \alpha_\lambda &= i_\lambda(\alpha) \in R(\lambda) \; . \end{aligned} \tag{2.7}$$

We may as well recall here the defintion of the Hecke algebra of W. Recall that W is generated by S, subject to the relations

$$\begin{array}{lll} s^2 = 1 & & s \in S \\ \underset{n(s,s')\text{factors}}{ss'ss'\ldots} = & \underset{n(s,s')\text{ factors}}{s's\,s's\ldots} & s,s' \in S \end{array}$$

Here $n(s,s')$ is a symmetric function on $S \times S$ taking the values 1 (if $s=s'$) 2 (if s and s' commute), 3, 4, and 6. The <u>Hecke algebra</u> H of W is the $\mathbb{Z}[q^{\frac{1}{2}},q^{-\frac{1}{2}}]$ algebra with unit, generated by elements $\{T_s | s \in S\}$, subject to

$$(T_s + 1)(T_s - q) = 0$$

$$\underbrace{T_s T_{s'} T_s \cdots}_{n(s,s') \text{ factors}} = \underbrace{T_{s'} T_s T_{s'} \cdots}_{n(s,s') \text{ factors}}$$

Of course this definition make sense over any ring containing $\mathbb{Z}[q]$, but $\mathbb{Z}[q^{\frac{1}{2}},q^{-\frac{1}{2}}]$ is most convenient for us. Although we do not need them, some facts about H may help to set the tone. If $w \in W$, choose a reduced expression

$$w = s_1 \ldots s_r \qquad (s_i \in S,\ r = \ell(w));$$

we have written ℓ for the length function on W. Then the element

$$T_w = T_{s_1} T_{s_2} \ldots T_{s_r} \in H$$

is independent of the choice of reduced expression. It turns out that H is a free $\mathbb{Z}[q^{\frac{1}{2}},q^{-\frac{1}{2}}]$ module with basis $\{T_w | w \in W\}$. (Again this would work over $\mathbb{Z}[q]$ as well.) We can therefore think of H as a q-analogue of the group algebra of W; and in fact specialization to $q=1$ gives a surjective homomorphism

$$H \to \mathbb{Z}[W]\ , \quad T_w \to w$$

from H to the group algebra of W.

3. THE LANGLANDS CLASSIFICATION

Let $P = MAN$ be a parabolic subgroup of G, $\sigma \in \hat{M}$ a discrete series representation of M, and $\nu \in \hat{A}$ a (possibly non-unitary) character of A. The induced representation

$$\gamma = \mathrm{Ind}_P^G (\sigma \otimes \nu \otimes 1) = I_P(\sigma \otimes \nu) \tag{3.1}$$

(normalized induction) is a standard representation of G; for this paper we regard two such representations as equivalent if and only if they have the same distribution character. Put

$$\mathcal{D} = \{\text{equivalence classes of standard representations with infinitesimal character } \lambda^a\} \qquad (3.2)$$

As was explained in the introduction, each $\gamma \in \mathcal{D}$ has a special irreducible subquotient

$$\overline{\gamma} = \text{irreducible Langlands subquotient of } \gamma . \qquad (3.3)$$

We need to understand $\mathcal{D}$ very concretely as a set. The main problem is the parametrization of discrete series. If $P = MAN$ as above, then the existence of a discrete series representation σ implies that M has a compact Cartan subgroup T ; and $H = TA$ is a θ-stable Cartan subgroup of G . The restriction of σ to M_0 will be a finite sum of discrete series for M_0 ; fix one of them, say σ_0 . Harish-Chandra's general theory associates to σ_0 a weight

$$\overline{\phi} \in \mathfrak{t}^*$$

which takes purely imaginary values, and is nonsingular with respect to the roots of $\mathfrak{t}$ in $\mathfrak{m}$. The pair

$$\lambda = (\overline{\phi}, \nu) \in \mathfrak{t}^* + \mathfrak{a}^* \cong \mathfrak{h}^*$$

defines the infinitesimal character of γ , and is therefore conjugate to λ^a under $Ad(\mathfrak{g})$ whenever $\gamma \in \mathcal{D}$ (see (2.4)). Since M is not connected in general, $\overline{\phi}$ does not necessarily determine σ . Set

$$\begin{aligned} \rho^I &= \text{half sum of roots of } \mathfrak{t} \text{ in } \mathfrak{m} \text{ which are positive on } \overline{\phi} \\ \rho^{I,c} &= \text{half sum of roots of } \mathfrak{t} \text{ in } \mathfrak{m} \cap \mathfrak{k} \text{ which are positive on } \overline{\phi} . \end{aligned} \qquad (3.4)$$

Here I stands for imaginary, and c for compact. Schmid has shown in [9] that the representation of $M_0 \cap K$ of highest weight $\overline{\phi} + \rho^I - 2\rho^{I,c}$ occurs in σ_0 . We can therefore find a character

Φ of T such that

$$d\Phi = \overline{\phi} + \rho^I - 2\rho^{I,c} \tag{3.5}$$

Φ is an extremal weight of an $M \cap K$ - type of σ

The pair $(\Phi,\overline{\phi})$ determines ϕ; and σ determines $(\Phi,\overline{\phi})$ up to conjugacy under $W(M,T)$.

From σ and ν, we have therefore produced

A θ-stable Cartan subgroup $H = TA$ of G
A character $\nu \in \hat{A} \cong \mathfrak{a}^*$ (3.6)(a)
A character $\Phi \in \hat{T}$
A weight $\overline{\phi} \in \mathfrak{t}^*$,

satisfying

$(\overline{\phi},\nu)$ is $\mathrm{Ad}(\mathfrak{g})$-conjugate to λ^a
$d\Phi = \overline{\phi} + \rho^I - 2\rho^{I,c}$ (notation (3.4). (3.6)(b)

PROPOSITION 3.7. (Harish-Chandra, Langlands - see [10]). Every four-tuple $(h,\Phi,\overline{\phi},\nu)$ satisfying (3.6) arises from a standard representation $\gamma = I_p(\sigma,\nu)$ in $\mathcal{D}$ by the construction just described. Two such four-tuples define the same element of $\mathcal{D}$ if and only if they are conjugate under K.

It is conjugacy by K rather than by G which matters, since we have required H to be θ-stable. The point of this proposition is that it allows us to manipulate standard representations (at least formally) using purely structural ideas about Cartan subgroups. To begin with, it allows us to parametrize $\mathcal{D}$ very explicitly as soon as we understand the Cartan subgroups of G, their Weyl groups, and their component groups. For example, if $\lambda^a - \rho^a$ is a sum of roots, we have

$$\#\mathcal{D} = \sum_{\substack{\text{conjugacy}\\ \text{classes of Cartan}\\ \text{subgroups } H}} \#(W(\mathfrak{g},\mathfrak{h})/W(G,H))\ \#\ (H/H_0). \tag{3.8}$$

4. CAYLEY TRANSFORMS AND THE CROSS ACTION

The first ingredient in the definition of the T_s operators of the introduction is an action of the integral Weyl group W on $\mathcal{D}$.

DEFINITION 4.1 (the cross action). Suppose $\gamma \in \mathcal{D}$ corresponds to $H = TA$, $\Phi \in \hat{T}$ and $(\overline{\phi},\nu) \in \mathfrak{h}^*$ as in (3.6). We will define a new four-tuple

$$w \times (H,\Phi,\overline{\phi},\nu) = (H,\Phi',\overline{\phi}',\nu') \tag{4.1)(a}$$

as follows. Define $w_\lambda \in W(\mathfrak{g},\mathfrak{h})$ (with $\lambda = (\overline{\phi},\nu)$) by (2.7). Since w_λ is in the integral Weyl group for $(\overline{\phi},\nu)$, we can write

$$\begin{aligned} w_\lambda^{-1}(\overline{\phi},\nu) &= (\overline{\phi},\nu) + \sum_{\alpha \in \Delta(\mathfrak{g},\mathfrak{h})} n_\alpha \alpha \qquad (n_\alpha \in \mathbb{Z}) \\ &= (\overline{\phi}',\nu') . \end{aligned} \tag{4.1)(b}$$

Define $(\rho^I)'$, $(\rho^{I,c})'$ with respect to $\overline{\phi}'$ as in (3.4), and write

$$(\rho^I)' - 2(\rho^{I,c})' = \rho^I - 2\rho^{I,c} + \sum_{\alpha \in \Delta(\mathfrak{m},\mathfrak{t})} m_\alpha \alpha \quad (m_\alpha \in \mathbb{Z}) \tag{4.1)(c}$$

Any root may be regarded as a character of H by the adjoint action of H on the root space; so we may define

$$\Phi' = \Phi + \sum_\alpha (n_\alpha + m_\alpha)(\alpha|_T), \tag{4.1)(d}$$

with n_α and m_α specified by (4.1)(b), (c). Finally, let <u>$w \times \gamma$</u> (<u>w cross γ</u>) be the element of $\mathcal{D}$ corresponding to (H,Φ',ϕ',ν') by Proposition 3.7.

It is essentially obvious that (H,Φ',ϕ',ν') satisifies (3.6). The integers n_α and m_α are not unique, however, so one must verify that Φ' does not depend on their choice. This is done in [12], Lemma 0.4.5. It is fairly easy to see that we have defined an action of W on $\mathcal{D}$. The main subtlety is that if w_λ happens to belong to $W(G,H)$, then it can happen that

$$w \times (H,\Phi,\phi,\nu) \neq w_\lambda^{-1} (H,\Phi,\phi,\nu) ;$$

more precisely, that $\Phi' \neq w^{-1}(\Phi)$. The simplest example is $G = GL(2,\mathbb{R})$, H=split Cartan subgroup, Φ=trivial character of T, ν=half sum of positive real roots, $w = s$ (the simple reflection) Then Φ' is the restriction to T of a root, and $w_\lambda^{-1}(\Phi)$ is trivial. In this case the original standard representation γ has the trivial representation as its Langlands subquotient; but that of $s \times \gamma$ is the representation

$$g \to \mathrm{sgn}(\det g).$$

The cross action captures some of the coherent continuation representation of W; but we know from the Hecht-Schmid character identities that this representation sometimes changes the underlying Cartan subgroup as well.

DEFINITION 4.2 (Cayley transforms). Fix an abstract simple integral root $\alpha \in \Pi$. The domain of the Cayley transform c^α consists of those $\gamma \in \mathcal{D}$ with the following property. Fix a four-tuple (H,Φ,ϕ,ν) corresponding to γ as in (3.6), and write $\lambda = (\overline{\phi},\nu)$. Then we require that α_λ be a noncompact imaginary root of $\mathfrak{h}$ in $\mathfrak{g}$ (or of $\mathfrak{t}$ in $\mathfrak{m}$). Suppose this is this case. The root vectors for $\pm\alpha_\lambda$ generate a subgroup L of G which is locally isomorphic to $SL(2,\mathbb{R})$. Choose a split θ-stable Cartan subalgebra $\mathfrak{a}^1$ of ℓ_0, and define

$$\begin{aligned} \mathfrak{a}^\alpha &= \mathfrak{a}^1 + \mathfrak{a} \\ \mathfrak{t}^\alpha &= \text{kernel of } \alpha_\lambda \text{ in } \mathfrak{t} \\ T^\alpha &= \text{centralizer of } (\mathfrak{t}^\alpha + \mathfrak{a}^\alpha) \text{ in } K \\ H^\alpha &= T^\alpha A^\alpha \end{aligned} \qquad (4.2)(a)$$

Then H^α is a θ-stable Cartan subgroup of G. Fix a weight

$$\lambda^\alpha = (\overline{\phi}^\alpha,\nu^\alpha) \in (\mathfrak{t}^\alpha)^* + (\mathfrak{a}^\alpha)^* \qquad (4.2)(b)$$

such that λ^α is conjugate under $Ad(\mathfrak{g})$ to λ^a, and

$$\lambda^\alpha|_{\mathfrak{h} \cap \mathfrak{h}^\alpha} = \lambda|_{\mathfrak{h} \cap \mathfrak{h}^\alpha} \qquad (4.2)(c)$$

(These conditions may also be summarized by saying that λ^α is conjugate to λ under $Ad(\ell)$. There are two choices for λ^α, which are conjugate by the reflection in $W(L,A^1)$.)
The Cayley transform of γ through α, $c^\alpha(\gamma)$, consists of those elements of $\mathcal{D}$ which correspond to four-tuples $(H^\alpha, \Phi^\alpha, \phi^\alpha, \nu^\alpha)$, such that

$$\Phi^\alpha|_{T^\alpha \cap T} = \Phi|_{T^\alpha \cap T} \qquad (4.2)(d)$$

It is easy to check that $c^\alpha(\gamma)$ does not depend on the choices in its definition. What is slightly less obvious is that if H^α, $\bar{\phi}^\alpha$, and ν^α are defined as above, and Φ^α is <u>any</u> character of T^α satisfying (4.2)(d), then $(H^\alpha, \Phi^\alpha, \bar{\phi}^\alpha, \nu^\alpha)$ satisfies (3.6). In particular,

$$\text{cardinality of } c^\alpha(\gamma) = \text{index of } T^\alpha \cap T \text{ in } T^\alpha \qquad (4.3)$$

This follows from a result of Schmid ([12], Lemma 5.3.4) relating the terms (3.4) on $\mathfrak{t}$ and $\mathfrak{t}^\alpha$. The index of $T^\alpha \cap T$ in T^α is either one or two. To describe the situation precisely, we need a little notation.

DEFINITION 4.4. In the setting and notation of Definition 4.2, we say that α (or α_λ) is <u>type I</u> if $T^\alpha \subseteq T$. In this case we write

$$\gamma^\alpha = \text{unique element of } c^\alpha(\gamma).$$

Otherwise we say α is <u>type II</u>, and write

$$c^\alpha(\gamma) = \{\gamma_+^\alpha, \gamma_-^\alpha\}$$

PROPOSITION 4.5. ([12], section 8.3) Suppose $\gamma \in \mathcal{D}$, and $\alpha \in \Pi$ is an abstract simple integral root. Assume that γ is in the domain of c^α, and use the notation of Definitions 4.2 and 4.4.

Write $\alpha_1 \in \Delta(\mathfrak{g},\mathfrak{h})$ for α_λ ; $\alpha_2 \in \Delta(\mathfrak{g},\mathfrak{h}^\alpha)$ for $\alpha_{(\lambda^\alpha)}$; and s_1, s_2 for the corresponding reflections in the Weyl groups. Finally put $s = s_\alpha$.

Assume α is type I. Then

(Ia) $s_1 \notin W(G,H)$

(Ib) α_2: $T^\alpha \to \{\pm 1\}$ is not surjective

(Ic) $s \times \gamma \neq \gamma$ (Definition 4.1)

(Id) $(c^\alpha)^{-1}(\gamma^\alpha) = \{\gamma, s \times \gamma\}$; that is, γ and $s \times \gamma$ are the only elements δ of $\mathcal{D}$ such that $\gamma^\alpha \in c^\alpha(\delta)$.

(Ie) $s \times \gamma^\alpha = \gamma^\alpha$

Next, assume α is type II. Then

(IIa) $s_1 \in W(G,H)$

(IIb) α_2: $T^\alpha \to \{\pm 1\}$ is surjective

(IIc) $s \times \gamma = \gamma$

(IId) $(c^\alpha)^{-1}(\gamma_\pm^\alpha) = \{\gamma\}$

(IIe) $s \times \gamma_\pm^\alpha = \gamma_\mp^\alpha$

Notice that α_2 is a real root of $\mathfrak{h}^\alpha$ in $\mathfrak{g}$, so α_2 is real-valued on H^α . Since T^α is compact, $\alpha_2(T^\alpha) \subseteq \{\pm 1\}$. Parts (a) and (b) are purely structural results about G, and are fairly easy. Parts (c) - (e) then follow by careful inspection of the definitions. We refer to [12] for details.

We also need an inverse Cayley transform.

DEFINITION 4.6. Fix an abstract simple integral root $\alpha \in \Pi$. The domain of the inverse Cayley transform c_α is the range of the Cayley transform c^α. If γ is in this range, we define

$$c_\alpha(\gamma) = \{\delta \in \mathcal{D} \mid \gamma \in c^\alpha(\delta)\} .$$

In this case we call a <u>type I</u> if it is type I for some $\delta \in c_\alpha(\gamma)$ (Definition 4.4), and <u>type II</u> otherwise. By Proposition 4.5, $c_\alpha(\gamma)$ has two elements $\{\gamma_\alpha^\pm\}$ if α is type I, and one element $\{\gamma_\alpha\}$ if α is type II. Suppose γ corresponds to $(H,\Phi,\bar{\phi},\nu)$ as in (3.6). Clearly a necessary condition for γ to be in the domain of c_α is that α_λ must be a real root of $\mathfrak{h}$ in $\mathfrak{g}$. This is not sufficient, however (as one sees for $SL(2, \mathbb{R})$). A precise condition, which is a little messy to state, is given in [12],

Definition 8.3.11. A direct description of $c_\alpha(\gamma)$ (without reference to c^α) is also given there.

Although we will make no direct use of it, we may as well conclude this section with a description of the coherent continuation representation of W on $\mathbb{Z}[\mathcal{D}]$, mentioned in the introduction. One terminological convention is useful. Suppose $\gamma \in \mathcal{D}$ corresponds to $(H,\Phi,\overline{\phi},\nu)$, and $\lambda = (\overline{\phi},\nu) \in \mathfrak{h}^*$. An abstract integral root $\alpha \in R$ is called <u>real</u>, <u>compact</u>, <u>complex</u>, and so on <u>for γ</u> if the root $\alpha_\lambda \in \Delta(\mathfrak{g},\mathfrak{h})$ has the property in question. We will not recall here the definition of the coherent continuation representation ([12], Definition 7.2.28); but here is how to compute it.

PROPOSITION 4.7 ([12], Chapter 8) Write $w \to t_w$ for the coherent continuation representation of W on $\mathbb{Z}[\mathcal{D}]$. Fix $\gamma \in \mathcal{D}$, and $s \in S$; let $\alpha \in \Pi$ be the corresponding simple root.

a) If α is complex or real for γ, then
$t_s(\gamma) = s \times \gamma$

b) If α is compact imaginary for γ, then
$t_s(\gamma) = -\gamma$

c) If α is type I noncompact imaginary for γ, then
$t_s(\gamma) = \gamma^\alpha - s \times \gamma$
(Definitions 4.4 and 4.1)

d) If α is type II noncompact imaginary for γ, then
$t_s(\gamma) = \gamma_+^\alpha + \gamma_-^\alpha - \gamma$.

5. HECKE OPERATORS AND THE BRUHAT ORDER

To define the operators T_s, one more bit of notation is useful. Fix $\gamma \in \mathcal{D}$, and an associated four-tuple $(H,\Phi,\overline{\phi},\nu)$ as in (3.6); set $\lambda = (\overline{\phi},\nu)$. By [12], Lemma 8.2.5, θ preserves $R(\lambda)$. Put

$$\theta_\gamma = (i_\lambda)^{-1}\, \theta(i_\lambda), \tag{5.1}$$

an automorphism of the abstract integral roots. Recall from (1.3) the $\mathbb{Z}[q^{\frac{1}{2}},q^{-\frac{1}{2}}]$ module M.

DEFINITION 5.2. Fix $s \in S$, and let $\alpha \in \Pi$ be the corresponding simple root. The Hecke operator

$$T_s : M \to M$$

is the unique $\mathbb{Z}[q^{\frac{1}{2}}, q^{-\frac{1}{2}}]$-linear map defined on a basis element $\gamma \in \mathcal{D}$ as follows.

a) If α is compact imaginary (for γ), then
$T_s\gamma = q\gamma$.

b) If α is noncompact type I imaginary, then
$T_s\gamma = s \times \gamma + \gamma^\alpha$

(Definitions 4.1 and 4.4).

c) If α is noncompact type II imaginary, then
$T_s\gamma = \gamma + \gamma_+^\alpha + \gamma_-^\alpha$.

d) If α is complex, and $\theta_\gamma\alpha \in R^+$ (notation (5.2), (2.5)), then
$T_s\gamma = s \times \gamma$.

e) If α is complex and $\theta_\gamma\alpha \notin R^+$, then
$T_s\gamma = q(s \times \gamma) + (q - 1)\gamma$.

f) If α is type I real, and γ is in the domain of c_α , then
$T_s\gamma = (q - 2)\gamma + (q-1)(\gamma_\alpha^+ + \gamma_\alpha^-)$.

(Definition 4.6).

g) If α is type II real, and γ is in the domain of c_α, then
$T_s\gamma = (q-1)\gamma - s \times \gamma + (q-1)(\gamma_\alpha)$.

h) If α is real, and γ is not in the domain of c_α , then
$T_s\gamma = -\gamma$.

Notice that T_s is actually defined on $\mathbb{Z}[q][\mathcal{D}]$. Although we make no use of the fact, it is of interest that the operators T_s define a representation of the Hecke algebra H (cf.(2.8)) on M . This is proved in [14], Proposition 12.5.

To do anything with the Hecke operators, we need the Bruhat order on $\mathcal{D}$.

DEFINITION 5.3. Suppose $\gamma \in \mathcal{D}$. The length of γ is

$$\ell(\gamma) = \tfrac{1}{2}\,\#\{\alpha \in R^+ \mid \theta_\gamma(\alpha) \notin R^+\} + \tfrac{1}{2}\dim(-1 \text{ eigenspace of } \theta_\gamma).$$

The <u>abstract τ-invariant of γ</u> is the subset of Π given by

$$\tau(\gamma) = \{\alpha \in \Pi | \alpha \text{ is compact imaginary; or } \alpha \text{ is complex, and } \theta_\gamma(\alpha) \notin R^+ \text{ ; or } \gamma \text{ is in the domain of } c_\alpha\} .$$

We may regard $\tau(\gamma)$ as a subset of S .

DEFINITION 5.4. Suppose $\gamma, \gamma' \in \mathcal{D}$, and $s \in S$. We write

$$\gamma \overset{s}{\rightarrow} \gamma'$$

if and only if $\ell(\gamma') = \ell(\gamma) - 1$, and γ' appears in $T_s\gamma$. Equivalently, we require that either

a) α is complex for γ' , $\theta_\gamma(\alpha) \in R^+$, and $\gamma = s \times \gamma'$; or

b) α is noncompact imaginary for γ', and $\gamma \in c^\alpha(\gamma')$.

DEFINITION 5.5. The <u>Bruhat $\mathcal{G}$-order</u> on $\mathcal{D}$ is the smallest partial order $<$ on $\mathcal{D}$ with the following property. Fix $\gamma', \gamma, \delta \in \mathcal{D}$, $s \in S$ with $\gamma \overset{s}{\rightarrow} \gamma'$. Suppose that either

a) $\delta < \gamma'$, or

b) there is a $\delta' \in \mathcal{D}$ with $\delta \overset{s}{\rightarrow} \delta'$, and $\delta' < \gamma'$.

Then we require that $\delta < \gamma$.

By way of motivation, we recall the analogous definitions for W.

DEFINITION (5.3)' Suppose $w \in W$. The length of w is

$$\ell(w) = \# \{\alpha \in R^+ | w^{-1}\alpha \notin R^+\}$$

The τ-invariant of w is

$$\tau(w) = \{\alpha \in \Pi | w^{-1}\alpha \in R^+\}$$
$$\leftrightarrow \{s \in S | \ell(sw) = \ell(w) - 1\}$$

DEFINITION (5.4)' Suppose $w_1, w_2 \in W$, $s \in S$. We write

$$w_1 \overset{s}{\rightarrow} w_2$$

if and only if $\ell(w_2) = \ell(w_1) - 1$, and $w_2 = sw_1$.

DEFINITION (5.5)' The <u>Bruhat order</u> on W is the smallest partial order $<$ on W with the following property. Fix $y', y, w \in W$, $s \in S$, with $y \overset{s}{\to} y'$. Suppose that either

a) $w < y'$, or

b) there is a $w' \in W$ with $w \overset{s}{\to} w'$, and $w' < y'$.

Then we require that $w < y$.

Of course Definition 5.5 is usually stated as a consequence of some other definition of the Bruhat order; but for applications to Verma modules or Schubert varieties, this is perhaps the most convenient form. We will not repeat here the discussions in [13] or [14] of why this order on $\mathcal{D}$ is called the G-order, and its relation to a more natural Bruhat order.

LEMMA 5.6 ([13], Lemma 6.8) There is a unique $\mathbb{Z}$-linear map

$$D: M \to M$$

with the following properties. Define $R_{\gamma,\delta} \in \mathbb{Z}[q^{\frac{1}{2}}, q^{-\frac{1}{2}}]$ by

$$D\delta = q^{-\ell(\delta)} \sum_{\gamma \in \mathcal{D}} (-1)^{\ell(\gamma) - \ell(\delta)} R_{\gamma,\delta}(q)\gamma .$$

Then we require

a) $D(q^{\frac{1}{2}}m) = q^{-\frac{1}{2}} D(m)$, all $m \in M$

b) $D((T_s+1)m) = q^{-1}(T_s+1) D(m)$, all $m \in M$, $s \in S$

c) $R_{\delta,\delta} = 1$

d) $R_{\gamma,\delta} \neq 0$ only if $\gamma < \delta$ (Definition 5.5).

The various $R_{\gamma,\delta}$ are (as a consequence of these conditions) polynomials in q .

LEMMA 5.7 ([13], Corollary 6.12 and Theorem 7.1) For each $\delta \in \mathcal{D}$, there is a unique element

$$C_\delta = \sum_{\gamma \in \mathcal{D}} P_{\gamma,\delta}(q)\gamma \qquad (P_{\gamma,\delta} \in \mathbb{Z}[q^{\frac{1}{2}}, q^{-\frac{1}{2}}]$$

of M , with the following properties.

a) $DC_\delta = q^{-\ell(\delta)}C_\delta$

b) $P_{\delta,\delta} = 1$

c) $P_{\gamma,\delta} \neq 0$ only if $\gamma \leq \delta$

d) If $\gamma \neq \delta$, then $P_{\gamma,\delta}$ is a polynomial in q , of degree at most $\frac{1}{2}(\ell(\delta) - \ell(\gamma) - 1)$.

The Kazhdan-Lusztig conjecture asserts that, in the notation of (1.1), we have

$$M(\gamma,\delta) = (-1)^{\ell(\gamma) - \ell(\delta)}P_{\gamma,\delta}(1) \tag{5.8}$$

Pretty neat, huh?

6. RECURSION FORMULAS

In this section, we will explain how to compute explicitly the various objects defined in section 5. This is a surprisingly subtle problem, although the only technique used is to write out the equations of Lemmas 5.6 and 5.7 using Definition 5.2.

DEFINITION 6.1 **Let $\sim$ be the smallest equivalence relation on $\mathcal{D}$ such that $s \times \gamma \sim \gamma$ whenever $\gamma \in \mathcal{D}$, $s \in S$, and s is real for γ . Write $G(\gamma)$ for the equivalence class of γ .**

Suppose $\gamma,\delta \in \mathcal{D}$, $\alpha \in \Pi$ and $c^\alpha(\delta) = \{\delta^\alpha_\pm\}$. By Proposition 4.7, $\delta^\alpha_- \in G(\delta^\alpha_-)$. The techniques of [6] lead to formulas for (say) $R_{\gamma,\delta^\alpha_+} + R_{\gamma,\delta^\alpha_-}$ (see Lemma 5.6); but it is difficult to get formulas for the two terms separately. The main idea is to compute $R_{\gamma,\delta}$ (or $P_{\gamma,\delta}$) by induction on $\ell(\delta)$; and for fixed $\ell(\delta)$, by downward induction on $\ell(\gamma)$. The following structural result will serve to guarantee the effectiveness of our recursion formulas.

LEMMA 6.2. ([13], Lemma 6.7). Suppose $\gamma,\delta \in \mathcal{D}$, and $\gamma < \delta$. Then there is a root $\alpha \in \Pi$ satisying at least one of the following conditions.

a) α is complex for δ, and $\theta_\delta(\alpha) \notin R^+$; or

b) there is a $\delta' \in G(\delta)$ such that

i) δ' is in the domain of c_α;

ii) $\alpha \notin \tau(\gamma)$ (notation 5.3); and

iii) α is not real for γ.

The analogous result for W is

LEMMA (6.2)' Suppose $y, w \in W$, and $y < w$. Then there is a root $\alpha \in \Pi$ such that $\alpha \in \tau(w)$.

This is the analogue of Lemma 6.2(a); nothing like (b) can happen in W. Roughly speaking, case (b) arises when δ is an ordinary principal series representation of a split group. In that case, the assertion is roughly that non-split Cartan subgroups of G must admit noncompact imaginary roots.

The recursion formulas are of three kinds. (We confine our discussion to the formulas for R; those for P are structurally similar.) Fix γ and δ in $\mathcal{D}$, $s \in S$, and let $\alpha \in \Pi$ be the corresponding simple root. Assume first that α is complex for δ, and $\theta_\delta(\alpha) \notin R^+$. Then we will write formulas

$$R_{\gamma,\delta} = \sum_{\mu \in \mathcal{D}} c(\mu)\, R_{\mu, s \times \delta} . \tag{6.3)(a}$$

(In fact the sums on the right will have at most three terms.) Since

$$\ell(s \times \delta) = \ell(\delta) - 1 \tag{6.3)(b}$$

this fits into our inductive procedure very well. Formulas of type (6.3) are given in [6]. For the second kind of formula, assume δ is in the domain of c_α, that $\alpha \notin \tau(\gamma)$, and that α is not compact imaginary for γ. If α is type I for δ, we will get formulas like (6.3) again, and all is well. So assume α is type II for δ. Then we will get formulas

$$R_{\gamma,\delta} = \sum_{\gamma' \overset{s}{\rightarrow} \gamma} R_{\gamma', s \times \delta} + \sum_{\mu} c(\mu) R_{\mu,\delta_\alpha} . \tag{6.4)(a}$$

Since $\gamma' \overset{s}{\to} \gamma$ implies that

$$\begin{aligned} \ell(\gamma') &= \ell(\gamma) + 1 \\ \ell(s \times \delta) &= \ell(\delta) \\ \ell(\delta_\alpha) &= \ell(\delta) - 1 , \end{aligned} \tag{6.4)(b}$$

such formulas can again be used in our proposed induction.

Now whenever $\gamma < \delta$, Lemma 6.2 provides an element $\delta' \in G(\delta)$ such that the first two types of recursion formulas compute $R_{\gamma,\delta'}$. The third type of formula allows one to compute $R_{\gamma,\delta''}$ for all $\delta'' \in G(\delta)$ once a single one is known. Specifically, assume again that α is type II real for δ, but make no restriction on γ. This will give a formula of the form

$$R_{\gamma,\delta} = -R_{\gamma,\, s \times \delta} + \sum_{\mu} c(\mu) R_{\mu,\delta_\alpha} \tag{6.5)(a}$$

$$\ell(\delta_\alpha) = \ell(\delta) - 1 \tag{6.5)(b}$$

which evidently does what we want.

Since the third kind of recursion formula is a fairly serious computational nuisance, it is worth remarking that it is never needed in real forms of $SL(n)$.

Without further ado, let us list the formulas. Always we will have fixed two elements γ, δ in $\mathcal{D}$, and a simple reflection $s \in S$; we write α for the simple root corresponding to s. The notation of section 4 is used freely.

FIRST TYPE. General hypothesis: α is complex for δ, and $\theta_\delta(\alpha) \notin R^+$. Therefore $\ell(s \times \delta) = \ell(\delta) - 1$. The general form of the recursion relation is

$$R_{\gamma,\delta} = \sum_{\mu \in \mathcal{D}} (-1)^{\ell(\gamma) - \ell(\mu)} [\text{multiplicity of } \gamma \text{ in } (q-1-T_s)_\mu] \; R_{\mu,\, s \times \delta}$$

(For brevity, we write the expression in brackets as $[\gamma\colon (q-1-T_s)\mu]$ and use analogous notation henceforth.) Specifically

α compact imaginary for γ

$$R_{\gamma,\delta} = -R_{\gamma,s\times\delta}$$

α type I noncompact for γ

$$R_{\gamma,\delta} = (q-1)R_{\gamma,s\times\delta} - R_{s\times\gamma,\,s\times\delta} + (q-1)\,R_{\gamma^{\alpha},s\times\delta}$$

α type II noncompact for γ

$$R_{\gamma,\delta} = (q-2)R_{\gamma,s\times\delta} + (q-1)(R_{\gamma_+^{\alpha},s\times\delta} + R_{\gamma_-^{\alpha},s\times\delta})$$

α complex for $\gamma, \theta_\gamma(\alpha) \in R^+$

$$R_{\gamma,\delta} = (q-1)R_{\gamma,s\times\delta} + q\,R_{s\times\gamma,\,s\times\delta}$$

α complex for γ, $\theta_\gamma(\alpha) \notin R^+$

$$R_{\gamma,\delta} = R_{s\times\gamma,\,s\times\delta}$$

α type I real for γ, $s \in \tau(\gamma)$

$$R_{\gamma,\delta} = R_{\gamma,s\times\delta} + R_{\gamma_\alpha^+,s\times\delta} + R_{\gamma_\alpha^-,s\times\delta}$$

α type II real for γ, $s \in \tau(\gamma)$

$$R_{\gamma,\delta} = R_{s\times\gamma,\,s\times\delta} + R_{\gamma_\alpha,s\times\delta}$$

α real for γ, $s \notin \tau(\gamma)$

$$R_{\gamma,\delta} = q\,R_{\gamma,\,s\times\delta}$$

SECOND TYPE: Case I

General hypothesis: α is type I real for δ (and $s \in \tau(\delta)$). Therefore there are two elements $\delta_\alpha^\pm$, with $\ell(\delta_\alpha^\pm) = \ell(\delta)-1$. Each of them gives a recursion formula, of the general form

$$R_{\gamma,\delta} = qR_{\gamma,\delta_\alpha^\mp} + \sum_\mu (-1)^{\ell(\gamma)-\ell(\mu)}\,[\gamma\colon (q-1-T_s)\mu]\,R_{\mu,\delta_\alpha^\pm}$$

Except in the first special case below, combining these two formulas does not seem to lead to simplifications; so in general we have listed only one.

α compact for γ

$$R_{\gamma,\delta} = (q-1)R_{\gamma,\delta_\alpha^\pm}$$

α type I noncompact for γ

$$R_{\gamma\,\delta} = qR_{\gamma,\delta_\alpha^-} + (q-1)R_{\gamma,\delta_\alpha^+} - R_{s\times\gamma,\delta_\alpha^+} + (q-1)R_{\gamma^\alpha,\delta_\alpha^+}$$

α type II noncompact for γ

$$R_{\gamma,\delta} = qR_{\gamma,\delta_\alpha^-} + (q-2)R_{\gamma,\delta_\alpha^+} + (q-1)(R_{\gamma_+^\alpha,\delta_\alpha^+} + R_{\gamma_-^\alpha,\delta_\alpha^+})$$

α complex for γ $\theta_\gamma(\alpha) \in R^+$

$$R_{\gamma,\delta} = qR_{\gamma,\delta_\alpha^-} + (q-1) R_{\gamma,\delta_\alpha^+} + qR_{s\times\gamma,\delta_\alpha^+}$$

α complex for $\gamma,\theta_\gamma(\alpha) \notin R^+$

$$R_{\gamma,\delta} = qR_{\gamma,\delta_\alpha^-} + R_{s\times\gamma,\delta_\alpha^+}$$

α type I real for γ, $s \in \tau(\gamma)$

$$R_{\gamma,\delta} = qR_{\gamma,\delta_\alpha^-} + R_{\gamma,\delta_\alpha^+} + R_{\gamma_\alpha^+,\delta_\alpha^+} + R_{\gamma_\alpha^-,\delta_\alpha^+}$$

α type II real for γ, $s \in \tau(\gamma)$

$$R_{\gamma,\delta} = qR_{\gamma,\delta_\alpha^-} + R_{s\times\gamma,\delta_\alpha^+} + R_{\gamma_\alpha,\delta_\alpha^+}$$

α real for γ, $s \notin \tau(\gamma)$

$$R_{\gamma,\delta} = q(R_{\gamma,\delta_\alpha^+} + R_{\gamma,\delta_\alpha^-})$$

SECOND TYPE: Case II

General hypothesis: α is type II real for δ (and $s \in \tau(\delta)$). Therefore $\ell(s \times \delta) = \ell(\delta)$, and $\ell(\delta_\alpha) = \ell(\delta) - 1$. The general formula with which one works is

$$\sum_\mu [\gamma: T_s\, \mu](-1)^{\ell(\gamma) - \ell(\mu)} R_{\mu,\delta} = -qR_{\gamma,\, s\times\delta} + q(q-1)R_{\gamma,\delta_\alpha}$$

This is manipulated in each case to try to get an effective recursion formula, in the inductive setting described earlier. This is not always possible.

α compact for γ

no recursion formula available

α type I noncompact for γ

$$R_{\gamma,\delta} = -R_{\gamma^\alpha,\delta} + q(R_{\gamma,\delta_\alpha} + R_{\gamma^\alpha,\delta_\alpha})$$

α type II noncompact for γ

$$R_{\gamma,\delta} = -R_{\gamma_+^\alpha,\delta} - R_{\gamma_-^\alpha,\delta} + q(R_{\gamma,\delta_\alpha} + R_{\gamma_+^\alpha,\delta_\alpha} + R_{\gamma_-^\alpha,\delta_\alpha})$$

α complex for $\gamma,\theta_\gamma(\alpha) \in R^+$

$$R_{\gamma,\delta} = R_{s\times\delta,\, s\times\delta} + (q-1)R_{\gamma,\delta_\alpha}$$

α complex for $\gamma,\theta_\gamma(\alpha) \notin R^+$

no recursion formula available

α real for γ, $s \in \tau(\gamma)$

no recursion formula available

α real for γ, $s \notin \tau(\gamma)$

$R_{\gamma,\delta} = qR_{\gamma,\delta_\alpha}$

THIRD TYPE

General hypothesis: α is type II real for δ (and $s \in \tau(\delta)$). The general form of the formula we want is

$$R_{\gamma,\delta} + R_{\gamma,\ s\times\delta} = \sum_\mu [\gamma:(2q-T_s-1)\mu](-1)^{\ell(\gamma)-\ell(\mu)} R_{\mu,\delta_\alpha} .$$

Explicitly, we get the following formulas for the right side:

α compact for γ

$(q-1)R_{\gamma,\delta_\alpha}$

α type I noncompact for γ

$(2q-1)R_{\gamma,\delta_\alpha} - R_{s\times\gamma,\delta_\alpha} + (q-1)R_{\gamma^\alpha,\delta_\alpha}$

α type II noncompact for γ

$(q-1)(2R_{\gamma,\delta_\alpha} + R_{\gamma_+^\alpha,\delta_\alpha} + R_{\gamma_-^\alpha,\delta_\alpha})$

α complex for $\gamma, \theta_\gamma(\alpha) \in R^+$

$(2q-1)R_{\gamma,\delta_\alpha} + qR_{s\times\gamma,\delta_\alpha}$

α complex for $\gamma, \theta_\gamma(\alpha) \notin R^+$

$qR_{\gamma,\delta_\alpha} + R_{s\times\gamma,\delta_\alpha}$

α type I real for γ , $s \in \tau(\gamma)$

$(1+q)R_{\gamma,\delta_\alpha} - R_{\gamma_\alpha^+,\delta_\alpha} - R_{\gamma_\alpha^-,\delta_\alpha}$

α type II real for γ, $s \in \tau(\gamma)$

$qR_{\gamma,\delta_\alpha} + R_{s\times\gamma,\delta_\alpha} - R_{\gamma_\alpha,\delta_\alpha}$

α real for γ, $s \notin \tau(\gamma)$

$2qR_{\gamma,\delta_\alpha}$

As indicated above, these formulas (or even a proper subset of them) are enough to compute the $R_{\gamma,\delta}$. However, one can get effective recursion formulas in more cases, which can be used to reduce the number of applications of the awkward third type of formula. Some of these follow.

AUXILIARY FORMULAS

General hypothesis: α is real for δ, and $s \notin \tau(\delta)$. There is a general formula

$$\sum_{\mu} [\gamma : (T_s+1)\mu](-1)^{\ell(\gamma) - \ell(\mu)} R_{\mu,\delta} = 0 .$$

which we try to manipulate to get a recursion formula in each case.

α compact for γ

$R_{\gamma,\delta} = 0$

α type I noncompact for γ

no recursion formula available

α type II noncompact for γ

$R_{\gamma\ \delta} = (q-1)R_{\gamma_+^\alpha,\delta}$

α complex for γ, $\theta_\gamma(\alpha) \in R^+$

$R_{\gamma,\delta} = qR_{s\times\gamma,\delta}$

α complex for γ, $\theta_\gamma(\alpha) \notin R^+$

no recursion formula available

α real for γ

no recursion formula available

Once all the R polynomials are computed, the $P_{\gamma,\delta}$ can be determined as in [6]: for $\gamma < \delta$, Lemma 5.7 gives

$$P_{\gamma,\delta} = \text{terms in } \{-\sum_{\gamma < \mu \leqslant \delta} (-q)^{\ell(\mu) - \ell(\gamma)} R_{\gamma,\mu}(q-1)P_{\mu,\delta}(q)\}$$
$$\text{of degree} < \frac{\ell(\gamma) - \ell(\delta)}{2}$$

For δ fixed, this computes $P_{\gamma,\delta}$ by downward induction on γ.

The second method of computing the P polynomials bypasses the R polynomials entirely; the penalty for this is that the recursion formulas are more complicated.

DEFINITION 6.6. Suppose $\gamma, \delta \in \mathcal{D}$. Define

$$\mu(\gamma,\delta) = \text{coefficient of } q^{\frac{1}{2}(\ell(\delta) - \ell(\gamma) - 1)} \text{ in } P_{\gamma,\delta} .$$

(Thus $\mu(\gamma,\delta) = 0$ unless $\gamma < \delta$ and $\ell(\delta) - \ell(\gamma)$ is odd.)

LEMMA 6.7. ([13], (6.15) and (6.16)). Suppose $\delta \in \mathcal{D}$ and $s \in S$.

a) If $s \notin \tau(\delta)$, then

$$(T_s+1)C_\delta = \sum_{\delta' \overset{s}{\to} \delta} C_{\delta'} + \sum_{\substack{\xi < \delta \\ s \in \tau(\xi)}} \mu(\xi,\delta)\, q^{\frac{1}{2}(\ell(\delta) - \ell(\xi)+ 1)} C_\xi$$

b) If $s \in \tau(\delta)$, then

$$(T_s - u)\, C_\delta = 0$$

This is the Hecke algebra version of (1.2). Here are the corresponding recursion formulas. One additional definition is helpful: whenever $\gamma,\delta \in \mathcal{D}$, $s \in S$, and $s \notin \tau(\delta)$, define

$$U^s_{\gamma,\delta} = \sum_{\substack{\xi \in \mathcal{D} \\ s \in \tau(\xi) \\ \gamma \geqslant \xi > \delta}} \mu(\xi,\delta)\, q^{\frac{1}{2}(\ell(\delta) - \ell(\xi) + 1)} P_{\gamma,\xi} .$$

FIRST TYPE

General hypothesis: α is complex for δ, and $\theta_\delta(\alpha) \notin R^+$

α compact for γ

$$P_{\gamma,\delta} \doteq (q+1)\, P_{\gamma,\, s\times\delta} - U^s_{\gamma,s\times\delta}$$

α type I noncompact for γ

$$P_{\gamma,\delta} = P_{\gamma,s\times\delta} + P_{s\times\gamma,s\times\delta} + (q-1)P_{\gamma^\alpha,s\times\delta} - U^s_{\gamma,s\times\delta}$$

α type II noncompact for γ

$$P_{\gamma,\delta} = (q-1)(P_{\gamma^\alpha_+,s\times\delta} + P_{\gamma^\alpha_-,s\times\delta}) + 2P_{\gamma,s\times\delta} - U^s_{\gamma,s\times\delta}$$

α complex for γ, $\theta_\gamma(\alpha) \notin R^+$

$$P_{\gamma,\delta} = P_{\gamma,s\times\delta} + qP_{s\times\gamma,s\times\delta} - U^s_{\gamma,\delta}$$

α complex for $\gamma, \theta_\gamma(\alpha) \notin R^+$

$$P_{\gamma,\delta} = qP_{\gamma,s\times\delta} + P_{s\times\gamma,\, s\times\delta} - U^s_{\gamma,s\times\delta}$$

α type I real for γ, $s \in \tau(\gamma)$

$$P_{\gamma,\delta} = (q-1)P_{\gamma,s\times\delta} + P_{\gamma^+_\alpha,s\times\delta} + P_{\gamma^-_\alpha,s\times\delta} - U^s_{\gamma,\, s\times\delta}$$

α type II real for γ, $s \in \tau(\gamma)$

$$P_{\gamma,\delta} = qP_{\gamma,s\times\delta} - P_{s\times\gamma,s\times\delta} + P_{\gamma_\alpha,\delta} - U^s_{\gamma,s\times\delta}$$

α real for γ, $s \notin \tau(\gamma)$

$$P_{\gamma,\delta} = 0$$

SECOND TYPE: Case I

General hypothesis: α is type I real for δ (and $s \in \tau(\delta)$). The recursion formulas are identical to those of the first type, with δ^+_α (or δ^-_α) replacing $s\times\delta$ everywhere.

SECOND TYPE: Case II

General hypothesis: $s \in \tau(\delta)$. (In particular, the case when α is type II real for δ, and $s \in \tau(\delta)$, is included.)

α compact for γ

no recursion formula available

α type I noncompact for γ

$$P_{\gamma,\delta} = P_{\gamma^\alpha,\delta}$$

α type II noncompact for γ

$$P_{\gamma,\delta} = P_{\gamma^\alpha_+,\delta} + P_{\gamma^\alpha_-,\delta}$$

α complex for $\gamma, \theta_\gamma(\alpha) \in R^+$

$$P_{\gamma,\delta} = P_{s\times\gamma,\delta}$$

α complex for $\gamma, \theta_\gamma(\alpha) \notin R^+$

no recursion formula available

α real for γ, $s \in \tau(\gamma)$

no recursion formula available

α real for γ, $s \notin \tau(\gamma)$

$$P_{\gamma,\delta} = 0$$

THIRD TYPE

General hypothesis: α is type II real for δ (and $s \in \tau(\delta)$). If we replace $s\times\delta$ by δ_α on the right side in the formulas of the first type, we get in all cases formulas for $P_{\gamma,\delta} + P_{\gamma,s\times\delta}$.

As an example of a calculation with these formulas, let us consider the group $G = PSp(2,\mathbb{R})$. By this we mean the group of symplectomorphisms of a four dimensional symplectic vector space, modulo its two element center. G has four conjugacy classes of Cartan subgroups; we write H_c for a compact one, H_s for a split one, and H_1, H_2 for the two others. Call α_1 the long (abstract) simple root, and α_2 the short one; we write s_1, s_2 for the corresponding reflections. We may choose the labeling so that the real and imaginary roots of H_1 are long, and those for H_2 are short. By explicit calculation or general theory, we find

$$|W(G,H_c)| = |W(G,H_1)| = 2$$

$$|W(G,H_2)| = 4$$

$$|W(G,H_s)| = 8$$

$$|H_s/(H_s)_0| = 2 , \ |H_i/(H_i)_0| = 1 \qquad (i = 1, 2, c) .$$

We take λ^a to be half the sum of a system of positive roots; so we consider representations with the same infinitesimal character as the trivial representation. By (3.8), $\mathcal{D}$ has twelve elements; we will call them A, B, ... L. Table 1 lists these elements, together with some of the other structure defined in sections 3-5. (We have not explicitly shown Cayley transforms and the cross action of W, since these can be read off from the Hecke algebra action.) Using this structural information, one calculates the G-order on $\mathcal{D}$ (Figure 1). Using these two things and the recursion formulas, one can complete Table 2: here the γ, δ entry is $R_{\gamma,\delta}$ if $\gamma \leqslant \delta$, and $P_{\delta,\gamma}$ if $\gamma \geqslant \delta$. Now the formal characters of Langlands quotients (also entered in Table 1) can be written down using (5.8). These formulas can easily be inverted to get the composition series of the standard representations. Perhaps the most interesting of the resulting formulas is

$$L = \overline{L} + \overline{H} + \overline{I} + \overline{J} + \overline{E} + 2\overline{F} + \overline{G} + \overline{A} + \overline{B} + \overline{C} + \overline{D} ,$$

showing multiplicity in the composition series of the spherical principal series representation. The formulas for $R_{\gamma,\delta}$ will appear terrible to those familiar with the original Kazhdan-Lusztig R polynomials on the Weyl group. For example, the relation $R_{\gamma,\delta} \neq 0$ is not transitive: $R_{A,I}$ and $R_{I,K}$ are non-zero, but $R_{A,K} = 0$. (In W , $R_{y,w} \neq 0$ if and only if $y \leq w$.) Other results from [6] whose analogues fail in this example are Lemma 2.1 (i), (iii), and Lemma 2.6(i).

TABLE 1. Some Representations of $PSP(2,\mathbb{R})$

Element of $\mathcal{D}$	Description of Langlands Quotient	Nature of Simple Roots		Associated Cartan	Hecke Algebra Action		Formal Character of Langlands Quotient	Length
		α_1 (long)	α_2 (short)		T_{s_1}	T_{s_2}		
A	holomorphic discrete series	nc I	cpt	H_c	B+E	qA	A	0
B	non-holomorphic discrete series	nc I	nc I	H_c	A+E	C+F	B	0
C	non-holomorphic discrete series	nc I	nc I	H_c	D+G	B+F	C	0
D	anti-holomorphic discrete series	nc I	cpt	H_c	C+G	qD	D	0
E	non-tempered, unitary, highest weight	real I	cplx, $\theta > 0$	H_1	(q-2)E+(q-1)(A+B)	H	E-A-B	1
F	non-tempered, unitary, not highest weight	cplx, $\theta > 0$	real I	H_2	I	(q-2)F+(q-1)(B+C)	F-B-C	1
G	non-tempered, unitary, lowest weight	real I	cplx, $\theta > 0$	H_1	(q-2)G+(q-1)(C+D)	J	G-C-D	1
H	non-unitary, highest weight	nc I	cplx, $\theta < 0$	H_1	J+L	qE+(q-1)H	H-E-F+A+B+C	2
I	no properties	cplx, $\theta < 0$	nc II	H_2	qF+(q-1)I	I+K+L	I-E-F-G+A+B+C+D	2
J	non-unitary, lowest weight	nc I	cplx, $\theta < 0$	H_1	H+L	qG+(q-1)J	J-F-G+B+C+D	2
K	no properties	real, not in τ	real II	H_s	-K	(q-1)K-L+(q-1)I	K-I-A-D	3
L	trivial	real I	real II	H_s	(q-2)L+(q-1)(J+H)	(q-1)L-K+(q-1)I	L-H-I-J+E+F+G-A-B-C-D	3

TABLE 2. $R_{\gamma,\delta} \backslash P_{\delta,\gamma}$

$\delta \backslash \gamma$	A	B	C	D	E	F	G	H	I	J	K	L
A	1	0	0	0	1	0	0	1	1	0	q	1
B	0	1	0	0	1	1	0	1	1	1	0	1
C	0	0	1	0	0	1	1	1	1	1	0	1
D	0	0	0	1	0	0	1	0	1	1	q	1
E	q-1	q-1	0	0	1	0	0	1	1	0	0	1
F	0	q-1	q-1	0	0	1	0	1	1	1	0	1
G	0	0	q-1	q-1	0	0	1	0	1	1	0	1
H	1-q	$(q-1)^2$	1-q	0	q-1	q-1	0	1	0	0	0	1
I	1-q	$(q-1)^2$	$(q-1)^2$	1-q	q-1	q-1	q-1	0	1	0	1	1
J	0	1-q	$(q-1)^2$	1-q	0	q-1	q-1	0	0	1	0	1
K	0	$q(q-1)^2$	$q(q-1)^2$	0	q(q-1)	q(q-1)	q(q-1)	0	q-1	0	1	0
L	$-(q-1)^2$	$(q-1)^3$	$(q-1)^3$	$-(q-1)^2$	$(q-1)^2$	(q-1)(2q-1)	$(q-1)^2$	q-1	q-1	q-1	0	1

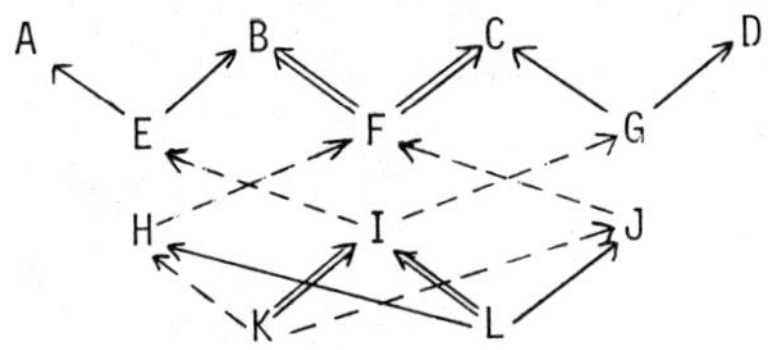

Figure 1 The Bruhat G-order on $\mathcal{D}$

$\longrightarrow$: denotes $\xrightarrow{s_1}$

$\Longrightarrow$: denotes $\xrightarrow{s_2}$

$\dashrightarrow$: other relations in the order

7. SINGULAR INFINITESIMAL CHARACTER

We summarize here the results of [10] which reduce the problem of computing characters in general to the case of regular infinitesimal character. This requires backtracking to before (2.4) (when a nonsingular infinitesimal character was fixed). Now we fix a weight (possibly singular)

$$\lambda_0^a \in (\mathfrak{h}^a)^* \tag{7.1}$$

and define

$$\begin{aligned} &R = R(\lambda_0^a) \\ &R_0 = \{\alpha \in R \mid \langle \alpha\, \lambda_0^a \rangle = 0\} \subseteq R \\ &W = W(R) \supseteq W_0 = W(R_0)\ . \end{aligned} \tag{7.2}$$

Fix also a finite dimensional representation F of G, and an extremal weight

$$\mu^a \in (\mathfrak{h}^a)^* \tag{7.3)(a}$$

of $\mathfrak{h}^a$ on F. Assume that for all $\alpha \in R$,

$$\langle \alpha, \lambda_0^a \rangle > 0 \Longrightarrow \langle \alpha, \lambda_0^a + \mu^a \rangle > 0 \tag{7.3)(b}$$

and that

$$\lambda^a = \lambda_0^a + \mu^a \text{ is nonsingular.} \tag{7.3)(c}$$

We can now use all the notation previously established with respect to λ^a; and we also set

$$\Pi_0 = \Pi \cap R_0, \qquad S_0 = S \cap W_0 \tag{7.4}$$

(cf. (2.5)).

DEFINITION 7.5 ([15], [10]) Suppose Θ is an invariant eigendistribution on G with infinitesimal character λ^a. We define a new invariant eigendistribution $\psi\Theta$ on G, with infinitesimal character λ_0^a, as follows. Fix a Cartan subgroup H of G, and a regular element $h_0 \in H$. Choose $\lambda \in \mathfrak{h}^*$ conjugate to λ^a under $\mathrm{Ad}(\mathfrak{g})$, and put $\mu = i_\lambda(\mu^a)$ (cf.(2.6)). For $X \in \mathfrak{h}_0$ small, we have

$$\Theta(h_0 \exp X) = \Delta(h_0 \exp X)^{-1}\Big[\sum_{w \in W(\mathfrak{g},\mathfrak{h})} a(w,h_0) \exp(w\lambda(X))\Big];$$

here Δ is the Weyl denominator, and $a(w,h_0) \in \mathbb{C}$. Put

$$(\psi\Theta)(h_0 \exp X) = \Delta(h_0 \exp X)^{-1} \Big[\sum_w a(w,h_0) \exp(w\lambda(X))(w\mu)^{-1}(h_0 \exp X)\Big].$$

Here $w\mu$ is a weight of the finite dimensional representation F of G, and so may be regarded as a character of the group H. Essentially we have just replaced λ^a by $\lambda^a - \mu^a = \lambda_0^a$ in the formula for Θ. That this defines an invariant eigendistribution is verified in [10] or [15]; the result is due to Schmid.

THEOREM 7.6 ([10], Section 6). With notation as above, suppose $\delta \in \mathcal{D}$; that is, that δ is a standard representation with nonsingular infinitesimal character λ^a. Write $\Theta(\overline{\delta})$ for the distribution character of its Langlands quotient. Recall from Definition 5.3 the τ-invariant $\tau(\delta) \subset S$.

a) If $\tau(\delta) \cap S_0 \neq \emptyset$ (cf.(7.4)), then $\psi(\Theta(\overline{\delta})) = 0$.
b) If $\tau(\delta) \cap S_0 = \emptyset$, then $\psi(\Theta(\overline{\delta}))$ is the character of an irreducible representation of G, having infinitesimal character λ_0^a. Every irreducible representation of infinitesimal character λ_0^a arises in this way, from a unique $\delta \in \mathcal{D}$.

Although this result solves the problem of explicitly computing characters, it is rather unsatisfactory in various ways: for example, the representation in (b) is not specified in the Langlands classification. Any serious discussion of these issues leads quickly to the study of reducibility of unitary standard representations. All the necessary bookkeeping has been done, mostly by Knapp; but the results do not seem to lend themselves to easy summary. We will therefore drop the subject at this point (but see [10] for further information).

8. POSSIBILITIES FOR A REPRESENTATION - THEORETIC PROOF.

There are several approaches to the Kazhdan-Lusztig conjectures within representation theory. The first is by the theory of Jantzen filtrations of standard representations ([3]). The second is by the theory of U_α ([11]; see (8.8) below). Both of these are thoroughly explained elsewhere; and in any case, they no longer seem as promising as when they first appeared. There is a third approach, however, which is a closer analogue of the easiest algebraic geometry proof. It begins in the same way as the theory of the U_α, so we will recall the ingredients of that. Fix an abstract simple root $\alpha \in \Pi$ (cf. (2.5)). After passing to a covering group of G if necessary, we can find a weight $\lambda_0^a \in (\mathfrak{h}^a)^*$ with the following properties.

$$\begin{aligned} &\lambda^a - \lambda_0^a = \mu^a \quad \text{is an extremal weight of a finite dimensional representation } F \text{ of } G . \\ &\langle\alpha,\lambda_0^a\rangle = 0 \qquad\qquad\qquad\qquad\qquad\qquad\qquad\qquad\qquad\qquad (8.1)\\ &\text{If } \beta \in R^+ - \{\alpha\} \text{, then } \langle\beta,\lambda_0^a\rangle > 0 . \end{aligned}$$

Define, for all $\lambda \in (\mathfrak{h}^a)^*$,

$$\begin{aligned} &F = F(\mathfrak{g}, K) = \text{category of } (\mathfrak{g}, K) \text{ modules of finite length} \\ &F(\lambda) = F(\mathfrak{g}, K)(\lambda) = \text{full subcategory generated by irreducibles of infinitesimal character } \lambda \qquad (8.2)\\ &P(\lambda) = \text{the "localization functor" from } F \text{ to } F(\lambda). \end{aligned}$$

(Any finite length $(\mathfrak{g}, K)$ module X can be written

$$X = \bigoplus_{\lambda \in (\mathfrak{h}^a)^*/W(\mathfrak{g},\mathfrak{h}^a)} X(\lambda) ,$$

with $X(\lambda)$ having generalized infinitesimal character λ. Then $P(\lambda)(X)$ is just $X(\lambda)$.) We need two of the Jantzen-Zuckerman translation functors:

$$\begin{aligned}
&\psi_\alpha \text{ from } \mathcal{F}(\lambda^a) \text{ to } \mathcal{F}(\lambda_0^a)\\
&\phi_\alpha \text{ from } \mathcal{F}(\lambda_0^a) \text{ to } \mathcal{F}(\lambda^a)\\
&\psi_\alpha X = P(\lambda_0^a)(X \otimes F^*) \quad (X \in \mathrm{Ob}(\mathcal{F}(\lambda^a)))\\
&\phi_\alpha Y = P(\lambda^a)(Y \otimes F) \quad (Y \in \mathrm{Ob}(\mathcal{F}(\lambda_0^a)))
\end{aligned} \tag{8.4}$$

(Here F is defined by (8.1).)

PROPOSITION 8.5 ϕ_α and ψ_α are exact functors, and each is the left and right adjoint of the other.

This is elementary - see [15].

As it is now very easy we may as well recall the U_α approach to the Kazhdan-Lusztig conjecture. Fix an irreducible X in $\mathrm{Ob}(\mathcal{F}(\lambda^a))$. Since ϕ_α is a left and right adjoint of ψ_α, the identity map on $\psi_\alpha X$ induces maps

$$X \overset{d_1}{\to} \phi_\alpha \psi_\alpha X \overset{d_2}{\to} X\ . \tag{8.6}$$

This is a chain complex (the composite map is zero) - see [10], or [12], Proposition 7.3.14. Define

$$\begin{aligned}
U_\alpha(X) &- \text{cohomology of (8.6)}\\
&= (\ker d_2)/(\mathrm{im}\ d_1)\ .
\end{aligned} \tag{8.7}$$

By [11], the Kazhdan-Lusztig conjecture is equivalent to

For all irreducible X of infinitesimal character λ^a, and all $\alpha \in \Pi$, the $(\mathfrak{g}, K)$ module $U_\alpha(X)$ is completely reducible. (8.8)

Since this is hard to prove even by algebraic geometry, it is perhaps not the best representation-theoretic approach, however.

Fix an automorphism τ of G, preserving K, and sending any semisimple element x to a conjugate of x^{-1}. (Such automorphisms always exist). Since τ acts on $\mathfrak{g}$ and K, it acts on $F(\mathfrak{g}, K)$; write $X \to \tilde{X}$ for this action. Obviously this is a covariant exact functor on $F(\mathfrak{g}, K)$. On the other hand, there is a contravariant exact functor $X \to X^c$, the "K-finite dual" functor. Since

$$\Theta(X^c)(g) = \Theta(X)(g^{-1})$$

for all regular semisimple g, we have

$$\Theta(X^c) = \Theta(\tilde{X}) .$$

Therefore, the functor

$$\overline{D}X = (\tilde{X})^c \tag{8.9}$$

from $F(\mathfrak{g}, K)$ to $F(\mathfrak{g}, K)$ is contravariant, exact, and satisfies

$$\begin{aligned} &\overline{D}X \cong X \qquad (X \text{ irreducible}) \\ &\overline{D}^2 = \text{identity}. \end{aligned} \tag{8.10}$$

By the first formula, D acts on each $F(\lambda)$ (see (8.2)). Write

$$\overline{F}_s = \phi_\alpha \, \psi_\alpha \quad \text{from } F(\lambda^a) \text{ to } F(\lambda^a); \tag{8.11}$$

here $s \in S$ corresponds to α. We have (obviously)

$$\overline{D}\,\overline{F}_s \cong \overline{F}_s\,\overline{D} \tag{8.12}$$

The action of $\overline{F}_s$ on the standard representations can be described fairly explicitly, by the following refinement of Proposition 4.7.

PROPOSITION 8.13 ([12], Propositions 8.2.7, 8.4.3, 8.4.5, and 8.4.9). Suppose $\gamma \in \mathcal{D}$. If the standard representations are chosen so that their Langlands subquotients are actually subrepresentations, then $\overline{F}_s\gamma$ has the following structure (with cases labelled as in Definition 5.2).

a) $\overline{F}_s\gamma = 0$

b) There are a $(\mathfrak{g}, K)$ module $Y = Y(s,\gamma)$, and short exact sequences

$$0 \to \gamma \to \overline{F}_s\gamma \to Y \to 0$$

$$0 \to Y \to \gamma_\alpha \to s\times\gamma \to 0$$

c) There are a $(\mathfrak{g}, K)$ module Y and short exact sequences

$$0 \to \gamma \to \overline{F}_s\gamma \to Y \to 0$$
$$0 \to Y \to \gamma_\alpha^+ \oplus \gamma_\alpha^- \to \gamma \to 0$$

d) $0 \to \gamma \to \overline{F}_s\gamma \to s\times\gamma \to 0$

e) $0 \to s\times\gamma \to \overline{F}_s\gamma \to \gamma \to 0$

f) There are Y and Z with
$$0 \to Y \to \overline{F}_s\gamma \to \gamma \to 0$$
$$0 \to \gamma_\alpha^+ \oplus \gamma_\alpha^- \to Y \to Z \to 0$$
$$0 \to Z \to \gamma \to \gamma_\alpha^+ \oplus \gamma_\alpha^- \to 0$$
Alternatively, $\overline{F}_s\gamma = \overline{F}_s\,\gamma_\alpha^+ + \overline{F}_s\,\gamma_\alpha^-$

g) There are Y and Z with
$$0 \to Y \to F_s\gamma \to s\times\gamma \to 0$$
$$0 \to \gamma_\alpha \to Y \to Z \to 0$$
$$0 \to Z \to \gamma \to \gamma_\alpha \to 0 \ .$$
Alternatively, $\overline{F}_s\gamma = \overline{F}_s\gamma_\alpha$.

h) $0 \to \gamma \to \overline{F}_s\gamma \to \gamma \to 0$.

The idea of the third representation theory approach to Kazhdan-Lusztig is that $\overline{F}_s$ and $\overline{D}$ behave very much like $(-T_s+q)$ and D . The difficulty is that the category $F(\lambda^a)$ (or at least its Grothendieck group) is too crude to see the fine structure of $\overline{F}_s$ and $\overline{D}$. We therefore seek an abelian category C (to be thought of as a thicker version of $F(\lambda^a)$) with the following properties (or something like them).

1) There is an exact functor ε from C to $F(\lambda^a)$.
2) The Grothendieck group $G(C)$ is isomorphic to M (cf.(1.3)); and the induced map

$\varepsilon: \ G(C) \to G(F(\lambda^a))$

from $\mathbb{Z}[q^{\frac{1}{2}}, q^{-\frac{1}{2}}][\mathcal{D}]$ to $\mathbb{Z}[\mathcal{D}]$ is evaluation at 1 .

3) C has exact functors F_s and D (covariant and contravariant, respectively) satisfying

$D(q^{\frac{1}{2}}m) = q^{-\frac{1}{2}}Dm$ on $G(C)$

$D\,F_s = q^{-1}F_s\,D$ on $G(C)$

$\varepsilon D = \overline{D}\varepsilon,\ \varepsilon F_s = \overline{F}_s\varepsilon$

4) For each irreducible $\overline{\delta}$ in $\mathrm{Ob}(F(\lambda^a))$, there is an X in $\mathrm{Ob}(C)$ satisfying

$\varepsilon X = \overline{\delta}$

$DX = q^{-\ell(\delta)}\,X$ in $G(C)$

5) Define $\tilde{T}_s$ on $M \cong G(C)$ to be $-F_s+q$. Then $\tilde{T}_s$ is given by the formulas of Definition 5.2, with each term δ multiplied by $(-1)^{\ell(\gamma)-\ell(\delta)}$

Ideally, C should be constructed from $F(\lambda^a)$ in some fairly straightforward way; then (1) - (5) should be consequences of (8.10) - (8.12) and Proposition 8.13. To prove the Kazhdan-Luztig conjectures, one would have to show that D defines the map of Lemma 5.6 on $G(C)$, and that (in (4) above) X corresponds to C_δ in $G(C)$ (Lemma 5.7). Because of (1) - (5), this would come down to some vanishing statements of a kind which are usually easy to prove in representation theory. (In the algebraic geometry proof, the vanishing statements amount to the Gabber-Deligne "purity" theorem for intersection cohomology; that is, to an appropriate generalization of part of the Weil conjectures.) We wish the ambitious reader luck with this program.

The author was supported by the National Science Foundation.

REFERENCES

[1] A. Beilinson and J. Bernstein, "Localisation de $\mathfrak{g}$-modules," C.R. Acad. Sc. Paris, t. 292(1981), Serie 1, 15-18.

[2] J.L. Brylinski and M. Kashiwara, "Kazhdan-Lusztig conjecture and holonomic systems, "Inventiones Math. 64 (1981), 387-410.

[3] O. Gabber and A. Joseph, "Towards the Kazhdan-Lusztig conjecture," preprint.

[4] R. Herb, "Fourier inversion and the Plancherel theorem," in Non-commutative Harmonic Analysis and Lie Groups, Lecture Notes in Mathematics 880, Springer-Verlag, Berlin-Heidelberg-New York, 1981.

[5] J. C. Jantzen, "Zur Charakter formel gewisser Darstellungen halbeinfacher Lie-Algebren," Math. Ann. 226(1977), 53-56.

[6] D. Kazhdan and G. Lusztig, "Representations of Coxeter groups and Hecke algebras," Inventiones Math. 53 (1979), 165-184.

[7] D. Kazhdan and G. Lusztig, "Schubert varieties and Poincare duality," in Geometry of the Laplace Operator, Proc. Symp. Pure Math. XXXVI, American Mathematical Society, Providence, Rhode Island, 1980.

[8] R. P. Langlands, "On the classification of irreducible representations of real algebraic groups," mimeographed notes, Institute for Advanced Study, Princeton, New Jersey, 1973.

[9] W. Schmid, "Some properties of square-integrable representations of semisimple Lie groups," Ann. of Math. 102 (1975), 535-564.

[10] B. Speh and D. Vogan, "Reducibility of generalized principal series representations," Acta Math. 145 (1980), 227-299.

[11] D. Vogan, "Irreducible characters of semisimple Lie groups II," Duke Math. J. 46 (1979), 805-859.

[12] D. Vogan, Representations of Real Reductive Lie Groups, Birkhauser, Boston-Basel-Stuttgart, 1981.

[13] D. Vogan, "Irreducible characters of semisimple Lie groups III," to appear in Inventiones Math.

[14] D. Vogan, "Irreducible characters of semisimple Lie groups IV," to appear in Duke Math. J. (1982).

[15] G. Zuckerman, "Tensor products of finite and infinite dimensional representations of semisimple Lie groups." Ann. of Math 106 (1977), 295-308.

COMPLETENESS OF POINCARÉ SERIES FOR AUTOMORPHIC FORMS ASSOCIATED TO THE INTEGRABLE DISCRETE SERIES

Nolan R. Wallach and Joseph A. Wolf

1. INTRODUCTION

A couple of years ago, Wolf [11] studied the Poincaré series operator ϑ for a homogeneous holomorphic vector bundle $\mathbb{E} \to D$ over a flag domain $D = G/V$ and an arbitrary discrete subgroup $\Gamma \subset G$. He showed that if $\mathbb{E} \to D$ is nondegenerate (see below), and if G acts on the square integrable cohomology space $H_2^s(D; \mathbb{E})$ by an integrable discrete series representation, where s is the complex dimension of the maximal compact subvariety K/V in D, then every Γ-automorphic L_p cohomology class $\psi \in H_p^s(\Gamma\backslash D; \mathbb{E})$, $1 \leq p \leq \infty$, is represented by a Poincaré series

$$\psi = \vartheta(\phi) = \sum_{\gamma\in\Gamma} \gamma^*\phi \quad \text{with} \quad \phi \in H_p^s(D; \mathbb{E}). \tag{1.1}$$

The purpose of this note is to shift the context from L_p bundle-valued harmonic forms over flag domains G/V to eigenspaces of the Casimir operator of G on L_p sections of bundles over symmetric spaces G/K. This lets us drop the nondegeneracy condition of [11], where it was used to ensure that every K-finite element of $H_2^s(D; \mathbb{E})$ is in $H_1^s(D; \mathbb{E})$, using [10]. This allows sharp estimates on the L_p behavior, $1 \leq p \leq \infty$, of the reproducing kernel for $H_2^s(D; \mathbb{E})$ inside the space of all $\mathbb{E}$-valued square integrable $(0,s)$-forms on D. These estimates replaced the explicit calculations of Bers [3,4] and Ahlfors [1,2] for classical automorphic forms over the unit disc. Here, over G/K, those sharp L_p estimates are obtained very easily. Once we have them, everything proceeds as in [11].

For simplicity we work with the case of a connected semisimple Lie group G in this paper. However, all the results go through in the same way for the larger class of reductive Lie groups considered in [12].

We thank the University of California at San Diego for its hospitality during Winter, 1981, at which time this note was written.

2. THE BUNDLES

G is a connected real semisimple Lie group, θ is a Cartan involution of G, and $K = G^{\theta}$ is its fixed point set. So K is the Ad_G^{-1} image of a maximal compact subgroup of $\mathrm{Ad}(G)$. We assume that $\mathrm{rank}\, K = \mathrm{rank}\, G$, so G has relative discrete series representations, and we choose a Cartan subgroup $T \subset K$ of G. Write

$$\begin{aligned} &\mathfrak{g}_0, \mathfrak{k}_0, \mathfrak{t}_0 &&: \text{ Lie algebras of } G, K, T;\\ &\mathfrak{g}, \mathfrak{k}, \mathfrak{t} &&: \text{ complexifications of } \mathfrak{g}_0, \mathfrak{k}_0, \mathfrak{t}_0; \qquad (2.1)\\ &\Phi, \Phi_K, \Phi_{G/K} &&: \mathfrak{t}\text{-roots of } \mathfrak{g},\ \mathfrak{t}\text{-roots of } \mathfrak{k},\ \Phi\backslash\Phi_K, \end{aligned}$$

If necessary, replace by G a double covering group so that in some (hence every) positive root system Φ^+, $\rho = \frac{1}{2}\sum_{\Phi^+}\alpha$ exponentiates to a character on T. G has center $Z \subset T \subset K \subset G$.

Let $\lambda \in \mathfrak{t}^*$ be $\mathfrak{g}$-regular and K-integral. Denote the corresponding (Harish Chandra parameterization) relative discrete series representation of G by π_λ, its class by $[\pi_\lambda] \in \hat{G}$. Then

$$\Phi^+ = \{\alpha \in \Phi: (\lambda,\alpha) > 0\},\ \Phi_K^+ = \Phi_K \cap \Phi^+,\quad \Phi_{G/K}^+ = \Phi_{G/K} \cap \Phi^+ \qquad (2.2)$$

are the positive roots systems with which we work. Denote

$$\rho = \frac{1}{2}\sum_{\Phi^+}\alpha,\quad \rho_K = \frac{1}{2}\sum_{\Phi_K^+}\alpha,\quad \rho_{G/K} = \frac{1}{2}\sum_{\Phi_{G/K}^+}\alpha. \qquad (2.3)$$

Then $\lambda - \rho_K + \rho_{G/K}$ is Φ_K^+-dominant and K-integral. Denote the irreducible representation of K with that highest weight by

$$\tau = \tau_{\lambda-\rho_K+\rho_{G/K}},\ \text{representation space } E = E_{\lambda-\rho_K+\rho_{G/K}}. \qquad (2.4)$$

It is (see Schmid [7] or Wallach [9]) the lowest K-type of π_λ, in the sense that all others have highest weights obtained by adding elements of $\Phi^+_{G/K}$ to $\lambda - \rho_K + \rho_{G/K}$, and it has multiplicity 1 in π_λ.

Consider the associated homogeneous hermitian C^∞ vector bundle

$$\mathbb{E} = G \times_K E \to X = G/K, \text{ typical fibre } E. \tag{2.5}$$

Denote its space of L_p sections by

$$L_p(X, \mathbb{E}) = \{f: G \to E: f(gk) = \tau(k)^{-1} f(g), \|f(\cdot)\| \in L_p(X)\}. \tag{2.6}$$

Let Ω be the Casimir element of the universal enveloping algebra $\mathfrak{U}(\mathfrak{g})$, $\tilde{\Omega}$ its closure as operator on $L_p(X, \mathbb{E})$. Then, for $1 \leqslant p \leqslant \infty$,

$$H_p(X, \mathbb{E}) = \{f \in L_p(X, \mathbb{E}): \tilde{\Omega} f = (\|\lambda\|^2 - \|\rho\|^2) f\} \tag{2.7}$$

is a closed subspace of $L_p(X, \mathbb{E})$ on which G acts continuously and isometrically. In particular G acts on $H_2(X, \mathbb{E})$ by a unitary representation. The point is that (Hotta [6])

the representation of G on $H_2(X, \mathbb{E})$ is equivalent to π_λ. (2.8)

If $[\pi] \in \hat{G}$ and H is the representation space of π, we have the <u>coefficients</u>

$$f_{u,v}: G \to \mathbb{C} \text{ by } f_{u,v}(x) = (u, \pi(x)v)_H \text{ for } u, v \in H. \tag{2.9}$$

We recall that $[\pi]$ is said to be L_p if its K-finite coefficients satisfy $|f_{u,v}| \in L_p(G/Z)$ where Z is the center of G. So $[\pi]$ is in the relative discrete series if it is L_2, is in the <u>integrable relative discrete series</u> if it is L_1. The Trombi-Varadarajan-Hecht-Schmid condition for a relative discrete series class $[\pi_\lambda]$ to be integrable is ([5], [8])

$$|\langle\lambda,\gamma\rangle| > \frac{1}{2} \sum_{\alpha \in \Phi^+} |\langle\alpha,\gamma\rangle| \text{ for all } \gamma \in \Phi^+_{G/K}. \tag{2.10}$$

Finally, we note that

if $[\pi_\lambda]$ is L_p and $f \in H_2(X, \mathbb{E})$ is K-finite then $\|f\| \in L_p(G/Z)$. (2.11)

For $f \in H \otimes H^* \otimes E$, $H = H_{\pi_\lambda}$, and $H \otimes H^*$ is the L_2-closure of the space of coefficients of π_λ. We are assuming f left-K-finite. $f(gk) = \tau(k)^{-1}f(g)$ forces it to be right K-finite. That proves (2.11).

3. THE REPRODUCING KERNEL

The K-type (τ,E) occurs with multiplicity 1 in π_λ. Denote the isometric K-equivalent inclusion which is adjoint to evaluation at $1 \in G$, by

$$i\colon E \to \mathcal{E} = H_2(X, \mathbb{E})_\tau. \tag{3.1}$$

Denote also

$$e\colon L_2(X, \mathbb{E}) \to \mathcal{E}, \text{ orthogonal projection, and} \tag{3.2}$$

$$\Xi\colon G \to GL(E) \text{ by } \Xi(x)v = i^{-1} \cdot e \cdot \pi_\lambda(x) \cdot i(v). \tag{3.3}$$

We are going to prove that

$$K_\lambda(x,y) = d_\lambda \cdot \text{trace } \Xi(y^{-1}x),\ d_\lambda = \text{formal degree of } [\pi_\lambda], \tag{3.4}$$

is the reproducing kernel for $H_2(X, \mathbb{E})$ inside $L_2(X, \mathbb{E})$.

Let $\{v_1, \ldots, v_\ell\}$ be an orthonormal basis of E and $\{\phi_j = i(v_j)\}$ the corresponding orthonormal basis of $\mathcal{E}$. We have K-finite coefficients of π_λ,

$$f_j = f_{\phi_j,\phi_j}\colon x \to (\phi_j, \pi_\lambda(x)\phi_j), \tag{3.5}$$

and we note from the definition (3.4) that

$$K_\lambda(x,y) = d_\lambda \sum_{j=1}^{\ell} (\pi_\lambda(y^{-1}x)\phi_j,\phi_j) = d_\lambda \sum_{j=1}^{\ell} f_j(x^{-1}y). \tag{3.6}$$

We assert that $i\colon E \to H_2(X, \mathbb{E})$ is given by

$$i(v)(x) = d_\lambda^{1/2} \cdot \Xi(x^{-1})v \quad \text{for} \quad v \in E,\ x \in G. \tag{3.7}$$

To see this, let $\phi: G \to E$ be given by $\phi_v(x) = \Xi(x^{-1})v$. Then $\phi_v(xk) = \Xi(k^{-1}x^{-1})v = i^{-1} \cdot e \cdot \pi_\lambda(k)^{-1} \cdot \pi_\lambda(x^{-1}) \cdot i(v) = i^{-1} \cdot \pi_\lambda(k)^{-1} \cdot e \cdot \pi_\lambda(x^{-1}) \cdot i(v) = \tau(k)^{-1} \cdot i^{-1} \cdot e \cdot \pi_\lambda(x^{-1}) \cdot v = \tau(k)^{-1}\phi_v(x)$ for $k \in K$, so ϕ is a section of $\mathbb{E} \to X$. Also, writing H for $H_2(X, \mathbb{E})$,

$$\begin{aligned}
\int_X \|\phi_v(x)\|_E^2 d(xK) &= \int_X \|e \cdot \pi_\lambda(x^{-1}) \cdot i(v)\|_H^2 d(xK) \\
&= \int_X \Big\| \sum_{j=1}^{\ell} (\pi_\lambda(x^{-1}) \cdot i(v), \phi_j)_H \phi_j \Big\|_H^2 d(xK) \\
&= \int_X \sum_{j=1}^{\ell} |(i(v), \pi_\lambda(x)\phi_j)_H|^2 d(xK) \\
&= \sum_{j=1}^{\ell} \|f_{i(v),\phi_j}\|_{L_2(G/Z)}^2 = d_\lambda^{-1} \|i(v)\|_H^2 = d_\lambda^{-1}\|v\|_E^2
\end{aligned}$$

so $\phi_v \in L_2(X, \mathbb{E})$. Further

$$\begin{aligned}
\Omega\phi_v(x) &= i^{-1} \cdot e \cdot d\pi_\lambda(\Omega) \cdot \pi_\lambda(x^{-1}) \cdot i(v) \\
&= (\|\lambda\|^2 - \|\rho\|^2) i^{-1} \cdot e \cdot \pi_\lambda(x^{-1}) \cdot i(v) = (\|\lambda\|^2 - \|\rho\|^2)\phi_v(x)
\end{aligned}$$

so $\phi_v \in H_2(X, \mathbb{E})$. Finally, if $k \in K$ then

$$\begin{aligned}
\phi_{\tau(k)v}(x) &= \Xi(x^{-1})\tau(k)v = \Xi((k^{-1}x)^{-1})v \\
&= \phi_v(k^{-1}x) = (\pi_\lambda(k)\phi_v)(x)
\end{aligned}$$

so $v \to \phi_v$ is K-equivariant. As $\|\phi_v\|^2 = d_\lambda^{-1}\|v\|_E^2$, now $v \to d^{1/2}\phi_v$ coincides with $i: E \to E$ up to multiplication by a scalar of absolute value 1. Now (3.7) follows by our choice of i as adjoint to evaluation $E \to E$ at $1 \in G$.

<u>3.8. THEOREM</u>. If $f \in L_2(X, \mathbb{E})$, then its orthogonal projection to $H_2(X, \mathbb{E})$ is given by an absolutely convergent integral

$$Hf(x) = \int_{G/Z} K_\lambda(x,y)f(y)d(yZ) \tag{3.9}$$

<u>PROOF</u>. Let $\zeta \in \hat{Z}$ such that $\tau(kz) = \zeta(z)\tau(k)$ for $k \in K$ and

$z \in Z$. Then the action $\tilde{\pi}$ of G on $L_2(X, \mathbb{E})$ satisfies

$$\tilde{\pi}(z)f(x) = f(z^{-1}x) = f(xz^{-1}) = \tau(z) \cdot f(x) = \zeta(z)f(x),$$

so $\tilde{\pi}$ and its subrepresentation π_λ have central character ζ. Now $K_\lambda(x, yz) = \zeta(z)^{-1}K_\lambda(x,y)$, so $K_\lambda(x,yz)f(yz) = K_\lambda(x,y)f(y)$, and the integrand in (3.9) is well defined.

In (3.5) we have $|f_j| \in L_2(G/Z)$, so (3.6) shows that $|K_\lambda(x,y)|$ is in $L_2(G/Z)$ for each variable separately. Thus the integral (3.9) converges absolutely. Now compute

$$\begin{aligned} Hf(xk) &= \int_{G/Z} d_\lambda \cdot \text{trace } \Xi(y^{-1}xk)f(y)d(yZ) \\ &= \int_{G/Z} d_\lambda \cdot \text{trace } \Xi(ky^{-1}x)f(y)d(yZ) \\ &= \int_{G/Z} d_\lambda \cdot \text{trace } \Xi(y^{-1}x)f(yk)d(yZ) \\ &= \int_{G/Z} d_\lambda \cdot \text{trace } \Xi(y^{-1}x) \cdot \tau(k)^{-1}f(y)d(yZ) \\ &= \tau(k)^{-1}Hf(x). \end{aligned}$$

Thus Hf is a well defined section of $\mathbb{E} \to G/K$.

Denote $\langle u, v \otimes a\rangle_H = (u,v)_H a$ for $u, v \in H$ and $a \in E$. If $f \in L_2(X, \mathbb{E})$ and $u, v \in H$ then

$$f_{u,v} \otimes f\colon x \to (u,\pi(x)v)_H f(x)$$

is integrable over G/Z. That defines a map $\Pi(f)\colon H \to H \otimes E$ by

$$\langle u,\Pi(f)v\rangle_H = \int_{G/Z} (u,\pi(x)v)_H f(x)d(xZ).$$

As $\|f_{u,v}\|_{L_2(G/Z)} = d_\lambda^{-1/2}\|u\|_H\|v\|_H$, now

$$|\langle u,\Pi(f)v\rangle_H| \leq d_\lambda^{-1/2}\|u\|_H\|v\|_H\|f\|_{L_2(X)},$$

so the operator norm

$$\|\Pi(f)\| \leq d_\lambda^{-1/2}\|f\|_{L_2(X)}.$$

The calculation just above, will allow us to estimate

$$\|Hf\|^2_{L_2(X)} = \int_X \|Hf(x)\|^2_E d(xK) = \int_{G/Z} \|Hf(x)\|^2_E d(xZ)$$

$$= \int_{G/Z} \left\| \int_{G/Z} d_\lambda \sum_{j=1}^{\ell} f_j(x^{-1}y)f(y)d(yZ) \right\|^2_E d(xZ).$$

For the inner integral, note

$$\int_{G/Z} f_j(x^{-1}y)f(y)d(yZ) = \int_{G/Z} (\pi(x)\phi_j, \pi(y)\phi_j)_H f(y)d(yZ)$$

$$= \langle\pi(x)\phi_j, \Pi(f)\phi_j\rangle_H.$$

Thus

$$\|Hf\|^2_{L_2(X)} = \int_{G/Z} \|d_\lambda \sum_{j=1}^{\ell} \langle\pi(x)\phi_j, \Pi(f)\phi_j\rangle_H\|^2_E d(xZ)$$

$$= d_\lambda^2 \int_{G/Z} \sum_{j,k} (\langle\pi(x)\phi_j, \Pi(f)\phi_j\rangle_H, \langle\pi(x)\phi_k, \Pi(f)\phi_k\rangle_H)_E d(xZ)$$

$$= d_\lambda^2 \sum_{j,k} d_\lambda^{-1} (\phi_j, \phi_k)_H (\Pi(f)\phi_k, \Pi(f)\phi_j)_{H\otimes E}$$

$$= d_\lambda \sum_j \|\Pi(f)\phi_j\|^2_{H\otimes E}$$

$$\leqslant d_\lambda \cdot \dim E \cdot \|\Pi(f)\|^2$$

$$\leqslant (\dim E)\|f\|^2_{L_2(X)}.$$

Thus $Hf \in L^2(X, \mathbb{E})$ with $\|H\| \leqslant (\dim E)^{1/2}$. Finally,

$$(\tilde{\Omega} \cdot Hf)(x) = \int_{G/Z} d_\lambda \cdot \operatorname{trace}(\tilde{\Omega}_x \Xi(y^{-1}x))f(y)d(yZ)$$

$$= \int_{G/Z} d_\lambda \cdot d\pi_\lambda(\Omega)\operatorname{trace} \Xi(y^{-1}x)f(y)d(yZ)$$

$$= (\|\lambda\|^2 - \|\rho\|^2)Hf(x),$$

showing $Hf \in H_2(X, \mathbb{E})$. Now the integral operator (3.9) is a bounded operator $H: L_2(X, \mathbb{E}) \to H_2(X, \mathbb{E})$.

Next, we prove that H is a projection. It is hermitian because

$$(Hf,\ f')_{L_2(X)}$$

$$= \int_{G/Z}\left(\int_{G/Z} d_\lambda \cdot \sum_{j=1}^{\ell} f_j(x^{-1}y)f(y)d(yZ),\ f'(x)\right)_E d(xZ)$$

$$= \int_{G/Z}\int_{G/Z} d_\lambda \cdot \sum_{j=1}^{\ell} f_j(x^{-1}y)(f(y),\ f'(x))_E d(yZ)d(xZ) \qquad (3.10)$$

$$= \int_{G/Z} (f(y),\ \int_{G/Z} d_\lambda \cdot \sum_{j=1}^{\ell} f_j(y^{-1}x)f'(x)d(xZ))_E d(yZ)$$

$$= (f,\ Hf')_{L_2(X)}.$$

And H is idempotent because

$$H^2f(g) = \int_{G/Z} K_\lambda(g,x)\int_{G/Z} K_\lambda(x,y)f(y)d(yZ)d(xZ)$$

$$= \int_{G/Z}\int_{G/Z} d_\lambda^2 \sum_{j,k} f_j(g^{-1}x)f_k(x^{-1}y)f(y)d(yZ)d(xZ)$$

$$= \int_{G/Z} d_\lambda^2 \sum_{j,k}\left\{\int_{G/Z} f_{\tilde{\pi}(g)\phi_j,\phi_j}(x)f_{\tilde{\pi}(y)\phi_k,\phi_k}(x)d(xZ)\right\}f(y)d(yZ)$$

$$= \int_{G/Z} d_\lambda \cdot \sum_{j,k} (\tilde{\pi}(g)\phi_j,\tilde{\pi}(y)\phi_k)(\overline{\phi_j,\phi_k})f(y)d(yZ)$$

$$= \int_{G/Z} d_\lambda \sum_{j=1}^{\ell} f_i(g^{-1}y)f(y)d(yZ) = Hf(g).$$

The projection H is G-equivalent because

$$(\pi_\lambda(g) \cdot Hf)(x) = Hf(g^{-1}x) = \int_{G/Z} K_\lambda(g^{-1}x,y)f(y)d(yZ) =$$

$$\int_{G/Z} K_\lambda(g^{-1}x,g^{-1}y)f(g^{-1}y)d(yZ) = \int_{G/Z} K_\lambda(x,y)f(g^{-1}y)d(yZ) = H(\tilde{\pi}(g)f)(x).$$

Thus its range is a G-invariant subspace of the G-irreducible space $H_2(X, \mathbb{E})$. Let $v \in E$ and $\phi_v = d_\lambda^{-1/2} i(v)\colon x \to \Xi(x^{-1})v$ as in (3.7) and its proof. Then

$$\phi_v(x) = i^{-1} \cdot e \cdot \pi_\lambda(x^{-1}) \cdot i(v) = \sum_{j=1}^{\ell} (\pi_\lambda(x^{-1}) \cdot i(v),\phi_j)_H v_j.$$

Thus

$$H\phi_v(x) = \int_{G/Z} d_\lambda \cdot \sum_{j=1}^{\ell} f_{\phi_j,\phi_j}(x^{-1}y) \sum_{k=1}^{\ell} f_{i(v),\phi_k}(y)v_k d(yZ)$$

$$= d_\lambda \sum_{j,k} (f_{i(v),\phi_k} * f_{\phi_j,\phi_j})(x)v_k \quad \text{convolution over } G/Z$$

$$= \sum_{j,k} (i(v),\phi_j)_H f_{\phi_j,\phi_k}(x)v_k$$

$$= \sum_{j,k} (v,v_j)_E(\pi_\lambda(x^{-1})\phi_j,\phi_k)v_k$$

$$= \sum_j (v,v_j)\Xi(x^{-1})v_j$$

$$= \Xi(x^{-1})v = \phi_v(x).$$

In particular $H \neq 0$. This completes the proof of Theorem 3.8. q.e.d.

4. PROJECTION TO $H_p(X, \mathbb{E})$

We now assume that the relative discrete series representation π_λ of G on $H_2(X, \mathbb{E})$ is integrable, i.e., that λ satisfies (2.10).

4.1. LEMMA. $|K_\lambda(x,y)|$ is in $L_p(G/Z)$ in each variable, for $1 \leqslant p \leqslant \infty$, with L_p norms $\| K_\lambda(x,\cdot)\|_{L_p(G/Z)} = \| K_\lambda(\cdot,y)\|_{L_p(G/Z)}$ independent of $x, y \in G$.

PROOF. By (3.6), $x \to |K_\lambda(x,1)|$ is a finite sum of K-finite coefficients of π_λ, hence is $L_p(G/Z)$ for $1 \leqslant p \leqslant \infty$. If $y \in G$ and $1 \leqslant p < \infty$ then

$$\| K_\lambda(\cdot,y)\|^p_{L_p(G/Z)} = \int_{G/Z} |K_\lambda(x,y)|^p d(xZ)$$
$$= \int_{G/Z} |K_\lambda(y^{-1}x,1)|^p d(xZ) = \| K_\lambda(\cdot,1)\|^p_{L_p(G/Z)} < \infty$$

and

$$\| K_\lambda(\cdot,y)\|_{L_\infty(G/Z)} = \operatorname{ess\,sup}_{x\in G} |K_\lambda(x,y)|$$
$$= \operatorname{ess\,sup}_{x\in G} |K_\lambda(y^{-1}x,1)| = \| K_\lambda(\cdot,1)\|_{L_\infty(G/Z)} < \infty.$$

The same argument works in the other variable. q.e.d.

Now define a constant $b = b(G,K,\lambda)$ by

$$b = \| K_\lambda(x,\cdot)\|_{L_1(G/Z)} = \| K_\lambda(\cdot,y)\|_{L_1(G/Z)}. \tag{4.2}$$

4.3. THEOREM. Assume $[\pi_\lambda]$ integrable. Let $1 \leqslant p \leqslant \infty$. If $f \in L_p(X, \mathbb{E})$, then

$$Hf(x) = \int_{G/Z} K_\lambda(x,y)f(y)d(yZ) \tag{4.4}$$

converges absolutely to an element of $H_p(X, \mathbb{E})$. Furthermore, $H: L_p(X, \mathbb{E}) \to H_p(X, \mathbb{E})$ has norm $\|H\| \leqslant b$, and if $\phi \in H_p(X, \mathbb{E})$ then $H\phi = \phi$.

PROOF. Convergence and the bound on H are clear for $p = \infty$:

$$\begin{aligned}\| Hf\|_\infty &\leqslant \operatorname*{ess\,sup}_{x\in G} \int_{G/Z} \| K_\lambda(x,y)f(y)\|_E d(yZ) \\ &\leqslant \sup_{x\in G} \int_{G/Z} |K_\lambda(x,y)|d(yZ) \cdot \operatorname*{ess\,sup}_{y\in G} \| f(y)\|_E \\ &= b\|f\|_\infty.\end{aligned}$$

If f is continuous with support compact modulo K, it is in $L_\infty(X, \mathbb{E})$ so Hf converges absolutely, as just seen, and of course

$$\begin{aligned}\| Hf\|_1 &= \int_{G/Z} \left\| \int_{G/Z} K_\lambda(x,y)f(y)d(yZ)\right\|_E d(xZ) \\ &\leqslant \int_{G/Z} \int_{G/Z} |K(x,y)|\| f(y)\|_E d(yZ)d(xZ) \\ &\leqslant b \int_{G/Z} \| f(y)\|_E d(yZ) = b\| f\|_1.\end{aligned}$$

Extend H to $L_p(X, \mathbb{E})$ by continuity for $1 \leqslant p < \infty$. The Riesz-Thorin Theorem gives convergence of (4.4) and shows that $H: L_p(X, \mathbb{E}) \to L_p(X, \mathbb{E})$ has norm $\|H\| \leqslant b$. Also,

$$(\tilde{\Omega} \cdot Hf)(x) = \pi_\lambda(\Omega)Hf(x) = (\|\lambda\|^2 - \|\rho\|^2)Hf(x)$$

for $1 \leqslant p \leqslant \infty$, so in fact $H: L_p(X, \mathbb{E}) \to H_p(X, \mathbb{E})$.

If $p, q \geqslant 1$ with $\frac{1}{p} + \frac{1}{q} = 1$, then we have a sesquilinear pairing

$$L_p(X, \mathbb{E}) \times L_q(X, \mathbb{E}) \to \mathbb{C} \quad \text{by} \quad (f,f')_X = \int_{G/Z} (f(x),f'(x))_E d(xZ).$$

We assert that it satisfies

$$(Hf,f')_X = (f,Hf')_X \quad \text{for} \quad f \in L_p,\ f' \in L_q,\ \frac{1}{p} + \frac{1}{q} = 1. \tag{4.7}$$

If one of f, f' is in the space $C_c(X, \mathbb{E})$ of continuous compactly supported sections, and the other is in $C_c(X, \mathbb{E})$ or $L_\infty(X, \mathbb{E})$, then this follows by the calculation (3.10). As H is L_p, L_q bounded, it now follows when one is in the closure of $C_c(X, \mathbb{E})$ in its $L_r(X, \mathbb{E})$, and the other is L_∞ or also in the closure of C_c in its $L_r(X, \mathbb{E})$. This covers all cases, so we have (4.7).

Now let $f \in H_p(X, \mathbb{E})$. If $f' \in C_c(X, \mathbb{E})$ then (4.7) applies, so $((1-H)f,f')_X = (f,(1-H)f')_X$. Let

$$D = \tilde{\pi}(\Omega) - (\|\lambda\|^2 - \|\rho\|^2).$$

The L_2 range of D is dense in $(1-H)L_2(X, \mathbb{E})$. The same follows for the L_q range, $\frac{1}{p} + \frac{1}{q} = 1$. Thus $(1-H)f' = \lim_{n\to\infty} Df_n$ in $L_q(X, \mathbb{E})$, and

$$\begin{aligned} ((1-H)f,f')_X &= \lim_{n\to\infty}(f,Df_n)_X \\ &= \lim_{n\to\infty}(Df,f_n)_X = 0. \end{aligned}$$

We have shown that $f = Hf$ as distribution section of $\mathbb{E} \to X$. It follows that $Hf = f$. q.e.d.

5. PROJECTION TO $H_p(X/\Gamma, \mathbb{E})$

Fix a discrete subgroup $\Gamma \subset G$ that acts discontinuously on $X = G/K$, i.e., such that ΓZ is closed in G. Let F be a fundamental domain for the action of Γ on X. Then we have

$$L_p(X/\Gamma, \mathbb{E}): \begin{cases} \text{all measurable } \Gamma\text{-invariant sections } f \\ \text{of } \mathbb{E} \to X \text{ with } \|f|_F(\cdot)\| \in L_p(F) \\ \text{and norm } \|f\|_{\Gamma,p} = \|f|_F(\cdot)\|_{L_p(F)} \end{cases} \tag{5.1}$$

and its closed subspace

$$H_p(X/\Gamma, \mathbb{E}) = \{f \in L_p(X/\Gamma, \mathbb{E}) : \tilde{\Omega} f = (\|\lambda\|^2 - \|\rho\|^2) f\}. \tag{5.2}$$

As in (4.6), for $\frac{1}{p} + \frac{1}{q} = 1$ these Banach spaces have a nondegenerate sesquilinear pairing

$$L_p(X/\Gamma, \mathbb{E}) \times L_q(X/\Gamma, \mathbb{E}) \to \mathbb{C} \quad \text{by} \quad (f,f')_\Gamma = \int_F (f(x), f'(x))_E d(xK).$$

The arguments of Wolf [11, §5] now apply without any modification. The result is

5.4. THEOREM. Assume $[\pi_\lambda]$ integrable. Let $1 \leqslant p \leqslant \infty$. If $f \in L_p(X/\Gamma, \mathbb{E})$ then Hf is well defined by

$$Hf(x) = \int_{G/Z} K_\lambda(x,y) f(y) dy \quad \text{for} \quad p = \infty,$$

L_p limits from $C_c(X/\Gamma, \mathbb{E})$ for $1 \leqslant p < \infty$.

Furthermore,

$$H: L_p(X/\Gamma, \mathbb{E}) \to H_p(X/\Gamma, \mathbb{E}) \quad \text{with} \quad \|H\| \leqslant b, \tag{5.5}$$

$$\text{if} \quad f \in H_p(X/\Gamma, \mathbb{E}) \quad \text{then} \quad Hf = f, \text{ and} \tag{5.6}$$

$$\text{if } f \in L_p(X/\Gamma, \mathbb{E}) \text{ and } f' \in L_q(X/\Gamma, \mathbb{E}) \text{ with } \frac{1}{p} + \frac{1}{q} = 1, \text{ then } (Hf, f') = (f, Hf'). \tag{5.7}$$

In effect, if $p = \infty$ then (5.5) is a computation and (5.6) follows from Theorem 4.3. If $p = 1$, then (5.7) is proved by approximation, and (5.5) and (5.6) are extracted in the distributional sense from the case $q = \infty$. If $1 < p < \infty$ the assertions extend from C_c to L_p by Riesz-Thorin.

Proceeding exactly as in Wolf [11,§6] we obtain

5.8. THEOREM. Assume $[\pi_\lambda]$ integrable. Let $1 \leqslant p < \infty$ and $\frac{1}{p} + \frac{1}{q} = 1$. Then the pairing (5.3) establishes a conjugate-linear isomorphism between $H_q(X/\Gamma, \mathbb{E})$ and the dual space of $H_p(X/\Gamma, \mathbb{E})$. If $f' \in H_q(X/\Gamma, \mathbb{E})$ corresponds to the linear functional ℓ, then

$b^{-1}\|f'\|_{\Gamma,q} \leqslant \|\ell\| \leqslant \|f'\|_{\Gamma,q}.$

5.9. COROLLARY. Let $f \in L_p(X/\Gamma, \mathbb{E})$ and $f' \in L_q(X/\Gamma, \mathbb{E})$. Then $Hf = 0$ if and only if $(f, H_q(X/\Gamma, \mathbb{E}))_\Gamma = 0$, and $f' \in H_q(X/\Gamma, \mathbb{E})$ if an only if $((1-H)L_p(X/\Gamma, \mathbb{E}), f')_\Gamma = 0$.

6. THE POINCARÉ SERIES OPERATOR

The Poincaré series of a section f of $\mathbb{E} \to X$, relative to a discrete subgroup $\Gamma \subset G$, is defined by

$$\vartheta(f)(x) = \sum_{\gamma\in\Gamma} f(\gamma^{-1}x) \quad \text{for} \quad x \in G \tag{6.1}$$

whenever the right hand side converges in some suitable sense. In that case, $\vartheta(f)$ is a Γ-invariant section of $\mathbb{E} \to X$.

For example, if $f \in L_1(X, \mathbb{E})$ then $\vartheta(f)$ converges absolutely a.e. because $\int_{G/Z} \|f(x)\|_E d(xZ) = \sum_{\gamma\in\Gamma} \int_F \|f(\gamma^{-1}x)\|_E d(xK) = \|f\|_1$, $\vartheta(f) \in L_1(X/\Gamma, \mathbb{E})$ with $\|\vartheta(f)\|_{\Gamma,1} \leqslant \|f\|_1$ because

$$\int_F \|\vartheta(f)(x)\|_E d(xK) = \int_F \Big\| \sum_{\gamma\in\Gamma} f(\gamma^{-1}x) \Big\|_E d(xK)$$
$$\leqslant \int_F \sum_{\gamma\in\Gamma} \|f(\gamma^{-1}x)\|_E d(xK) = \sum_{\gamma\in\Gamma} \int_F \|f(\gamma^{-1}x)\|_E d(xK) = \|f\|_1,$$

and if $f \in H_1(X, \mathbb{E})$ then $\vartheta(f) \in H_1(X/\Gamma, \mathbb{E})$ because

$$\tilde{\Omega} \cdot \vartheta(f)(x) = \sum_{\gamma\in\Gamma} \tilde{\Omega}_x \cdot f(\gamma^{-1}x) = \vartheta(\Omega f)(x) = (\|\lambda\|^2 - \|\rho\|^2)\vartheta(f)(x).$$

In brief, using ellipticity of Ω on X,

$$\vartheta: H_1(X, \mathbb{E}) \to H_1(X/\Gamma, \mathbb{E}) \text{ with } \|\vartheta\| \leqslant 1, \text{ and} \tag{6.2}$$

here each $\vartheta(f)$ converges absolutely and uniformly on compact sets.

If $f \in L_1(X, \mathbb{E})$ and $f' \in L_\infty(X/\Gamma, \mathbb{E})$ we compute

$$(\vartheta(f),f')_\Gamma = \sum_{\gamma\in\Gamma} \int_F (f(\gamma^{-1}x),f'(x))_E d(xK)$$
$$= \sum_{\gamma\in\Gamma} \int_{\gamma F} (f(x),f'(\gamma x))_E d(xK)$$
$$= \sum_{\gamma\in\Gamma} \int_{\gamma F} (f(x),f'(x))_E d(xK) = \int_X (f(x),f'(x))_E d(xK)$$
$$= (f,f')_X.$$

Thus $\vartheta: L_1(X, \mathbb{E}) \to L_1(X/\Gamma, \mathbb{E})$ has adjoint

$$\vartheta^*: L_\infty(X/\Gamma, \mathbb{E}) \to L_\infty(X, \mathbb{E})$$

which is continuous inclusion of a closed subspace. This says that $\vartheta: L_1(X, \mathbb{E}) \to L_1(X/\Gamma, \mathbb{E})$ is surjective. The case $p = 1$ of Theorem 5.8 lets us specialize this to H_1, as in (6.2). Thus

<u>6.3. PROPOSITION</u>. The Poincaré series map $\vartheta: H_1(X, \mathbb{E}) \to H_1(X/\Gamma, \mathbb{E})$ is continuous and surjective, and its adjoint is the inclusion $\vartheta^*: H_\infty(X/\Gamma, \mathbb{E}) \to H_\infty(X, \mathbb{E})$.

One now continues just as in Wolf [11, §7]. ϑ converges on the dense subspace $H_1(X, \mathbb{E}) \cap H_p(X, \mathbb{E})$ of $H_p(X, \mathbb{E})$ -- dense because it contains all K-finite elements -- so $\vartheta \circ H$ converges on

$$J_F = \{\chi f: f \in C_c(X/\Gamma, \mathbb{E})\} \tag{6.4}$$

where χ is the indicator function of the fundamental domain F of Γ and $C_c(X/\Gamma, \mathbb{E})$ is the space of Γ-invariant sections of $\mathbb{E} \to X$ with support compact modulo Γ from X, i.e., compact modulo ΓZ from G.

If $f \in L_1(X/\Gamma, \mathbb{E})$, then $\chi f \in L_1(X, \mathbb{E})$, so $H(\chi f) \in H_1(X, \mathbb{E})$ and thus $\vartheta(H(\chi f)) \in H_1(X/\Gamma, \mathbb{E})$. If $f' \in H_\infty(X/\Gamma, \mathbb{E})$ then

$$(Hf,f')_\Gamma = (f,f')_\Gamma \quad \text{by Corollary 5.9}$$

and, using the calculation just after (6.2),

$$(\vartheta H(\chi f),f')_\Gamma = (H(\chi f),f')_X = (\chi f,f')_X = (f,f')_\Gamma.$$

Thus, from Theorem 5.8 with $p = 1$,

$$\vartheta H(\chi f) = Hf \quad \text{for all} \quad f \in L_1(X/\Gamma, \mathbb{E}). \tag{6.5}$$

In particular, if $\eta = \chi f \in J_F$ then (5.5) says $\|\vartheta H(\eta)\|_{\Gamma,p} = \|\vartheta H(\chi f)\|_{\Gamma,p} = \|Hf\|_{\Gamma,p} \leqslant b\|f\|_{\Gamma,p} = b\|\eta\|_p$. That is the L_p bound on ϑH in

6.6. PROPOSITION. Let $1 \leqslant p < \infty$. If $\eta \in J_F$ then $\vartheta H(\eta)$ converges absolutely, uniformly on compact subsets of X, to an element of $H_p(X/\Gamma, \mathbb{E})$, and $\|\vartheta H(\eta)\|_{\Gamma,p} \leqslant b\|\eta\|_{L_p(X)}$. So ϑH extends by continuity to a linear map

$$\vartheta H: (L_p\text{-closure of } J_F) \to H_p(X/\Gamma, \mathbb{E})$$

of norm $\leqslant b$. This extension is surjective: if $\phi \in H_p(X/\Gamma, \mathbb{E})$ then $\chi\phi$ is in the L_p-closure of J_F and $\vartheta H(\chi\phi) = \phi$.

The case $p = \infty$ is slightly different. If $f \in L_\infty(X/\Gamma, \mathbb{E})$ then H is absolutely convergent on $\vartheta(\chi f)$ because

$$\int_X \sum_{\gamma \in \Gamma} |K_\lambda(x,y)| \cdot \|(\chi f)(\gamma^{-1}y)\|_E d(yZ) \leqslant b\|\chi f\|_\infty .$$

Since $\vartheta(\chi f) = f$ now $\vartheta(H(\chi f)) = H(\vartheta(\chi f)) = Hf$. Thus

6.7. PROPOSITION. If $\eta \in H(\chi \cdot L_\infty(X/\Gamma, \mathbb{E}))$ then $\vartheta(\eta)$ converges absolutely to an element of $H_\infty(X/\Gamma, \mathbb{E})$. The map $\vartheta: H(\chi \cdot L_\infty(X/\Gamma, \mathbb{E})) \to H_\infty(X/\Gamma, \mathbb{E})$ is surjective: if $\phi \in H_\infty(X/\Gamma, \mathbb{E})$ then $\vartheta(H(\chi\phi)) = \phi$.

In summary, now, we have completeness of Poincaré series for the bundles $\mathbb{E} \to X$.

6.8. THEOREM. Suppose that $[\pi_\lambda]$ is integrable. Let $1 \leqslant p \leqslant \infty$. Then the Poincaré series operator is defined on

$p = 1$: all of $\mathcal{H}_1(X, \mathbb{E})$ as in (6.2);

$1 < p < \infty$: $H(\chi \cdot L_p(X/\Gamma, \mathbb{E}))$ as in Proposition 6.6;

$p = \infty$: $H(\chi \cdot L_\infty(X/\Gamma, \mathbb{E}))$ as in Proposition 6.7;

and maps that space onto $\mathcal{H}_p(X/\Gamma, \mathbb{E})$. In fact, if $\phi \in \mathcal{H}_p(X/\Gamma, \mathbb{E})$ then $\|H(\chi\phi)\|_p \leqslant b\|\phi\|_p$ and $\vartheta H(\chi\phi) = \phi$.

The authors were supported by the National Science Foundation.

REFERENCES

[1] L. V. Ahlfors, Finitely generated Kleinian groups, Am. J. Math. 86 (1964), 413-429.

[2] L. V. Ahlfors, Finitely generated Kleinian groups, Am. J. Math. 87 (1965), 759.

[3] L. Bers, Completeness theorems for Poincaré series in one variable , Proc. Internat. Symp. on Linear Spaces, Jerusalem, 1960, 88-100.

[4] L. Bers, Automorphic forms and Poincaré series for infinitely generated Fuchian groups, Am. J. Math. 87 (1965), 196-214.

[5] H. Hecht and W. Schmid. On integrable representations of a semi-simple Lie group, Math. Ann. 220 (1976), 147-150.

[6] R. Hotta, On realization of the discrete series for semisimple Lie groups, J. Math. Soc. Japan 23 (1971), 384-407.

[7] W. Schmid, Some properties of square integrable representations of semisimple Lie groups, Ann. of Math. 102 (1975), 535-564.

[8] P. C. Trombi and V. S. Varadarajan, Asymptotic behavior of eigenfunctions on a semisimple Lie group: The discrete spectrum, Acta Math. 129 (1972), 237-280.

[9] N. R. Wallach, On the Enright-Varadarajan modules: A construction of the discrete series, Ann. Sci. Ec. Norm. Sup. (4) 9 (1976), 81-102.

[10] R. O. Wells Jr. and J. A. Wolf, Poincaré series and automorphic cohomology on flag domains, Ann. of Math. 105 (1977), 397-448.

[11] J. A. Wolf, Completeness of Poincaré series for automorphic cohomology, Ann. of Math. 109 (1979), 545-567.

[12] J. A. Wolf, The action of a real semisimple group on a complex flag manifold, II: Unitary representations on partially holomorphic cohomology spaces, Memoirs Am. Math. Soc., No. 138, 1974.

GEOMETRIC METHODS IN REPRESENTATION THEORY

Gregg J. Zuckerman

This lecture is a brief introduction to the relationship between the algebraic geometry of flag varieties and the representation theory of reductive Lie algebras and real reductive Lie groups. The author would like to thank the organizers of this conference for the opportunity to make a presentation.

1.

We begin with a quick introduction to the theory of local cohomology, for which the standard references are Grothendieck-Hartshorne [5], and Kempf [6]. (Local cohomology also arises in Sato's work on hyperfunctions.) Let X be a topological space and let F be a sheaf of abelian groups over X. Suppose at first that Y is a closed subset of X. Denote by $\Gamma_Y(F)$ the sections of F that are supported in Y. Then $\Gamma_Y(-)$ is a left exact functor from sheaves to abelian groups, and we can form the right derived functors $H^*_Y(X,-)$ of $\Gamma_Y(-)$. Thus, if we resolve F by a complex I^* of injective sheaves (or even flabby sheaves), then the cohomology of the complex $\Gamma_Y(I^*)$ will be $H^*_Y(X,F)$, the local cohomology of X along Y with coefficients in F.

If more generally Y is locally closed in X, then by definition we can surround Y by an open set $U \supseteq Y$ such that Y is closed in U. In this case we define local cohomology by

$$H^*_Y(X,F) = H^*_Y(U,F/U) .$$

The above groups are independent of the choice of U.

Now suppose X is a filtered space, i.e. $X \supseteq X_0 \supseteq X_1 \supseteq \cdots \supseteq X_i \supseteq \cdots$, where each X_i is closed in X. The difference set $X_i \setminus X_{i+1}$ will be locally closed in X (it is closed in the open set $X \setminus X_{i+1}$).

1.1. THEOREM. There exists a spectral sequence, natural in the sheaf F, whose E_1 - term is given by

$$E_1^{p,q} = H^{p+q}_{X_q \setminus X_{q+1}}(X,F),$$

and which abuts to

$$H^*_{X_0}(X,F) .$$

The E_1 - differential is horizontal: $E_1^{p,q} \to E_1^{p,q+1}$.

We will apply the spectral sequence above to spaces with a finite filtration, i.e. X_i is eventually empty. We will also work only with spaces having finite dimension, so that the local cohomology groups will always vanish for sufficiently high degree. Under such conditions, the spectral sequence will converge after a finite number of terms.

2.

We specialize to the situation: X is the variety of Borel subgroups of a complex reductive connected algebraic group. Suppose Y is an algebraic subvariety of X, i.e. Y is locally the zero set of a collection of regular functions on X. Then Y is automatically locally closed in the Zariski topology on X. We assume further:

i) Y is smooth.

ii) Y is affinely embedded in X,
i.e. if $U \subseteq X$ is affine open, then $U \cap Y$ is affine.

Let c be the (complex) codimension of Y in X. Let L be a positive homogeneous line bundle over X and $O(L)$ the sheaf of regular sections in the Zariski topology on X. The Borel - Weil theorem asserts that $H^i(X,\mathcal{O}(L)) = 0$ for $i > 0$, and $H^0(X,\mathcal{O}(L))$ is nontrivial and realizes a finite dimensional irreducible representation of G.

2.1. THEOREM. (Bernstein - Beilinson[2]). Assuming all the above conditions, we have

$$H^i_Y(X,\mathcal{O}[L]) = 0 \quad \text{if} \quad i \neq c \ ,$$

and $H^c_Y(X,\mathcal{O}[L]) \neq 0$. The complex vector space $H^c_Y(X,\mathcal{O}[L])$ is canonically a module over the enveloping algebra $\mathcal{U}(\mathfrak{g})$ of the Lie algebra $\mathfrak{g}$ of G. Moreover, $H^c_Y(X,\mathcal{O}[L])$ has a finite composition series as a $\mathcal{U}(\mathfrak{g})$ module.

There is a particular proposition that nicely illustrates the term "geometric representation theory".

2.2. PROPOSITION. (Bernstein - Beilinson[2]). Suppose Y is a smooth, closed and irreducible subvariety of the flag variety X. Then, for $i \neq c$, $H^i_Y(X, \mathcal{O}[L]) = 0$, and for $i = c$,

$H^c_Y(X, \mathcal{O}[L])$ is a nontrivial irreducible $\mathcal{U}(\mathfrak{g})$ module.

REMARK. If Y is an orbit on X of some Borel subgroup B in G, then the above theorem and proposition was known to G. Kempf[6]. Kashiwara and Brylinski improved Kempf's work by showing that for a B orbit Y, $H^c_Y(X,\mathcal{O}[L])$ is isomorphic to the B-finite dual of a Verma module (see [3]).

3.

As in the last section, let X be the flag variety of G, and L a positive homogeneous line bundle. Consider a filtration $X \supseteq X_0 \supseteq \cdots \supseteq X_q \supseteq \cdots$ of X such that:

i) each X_i is a closed subvariety;
ii) codim $X_i = c + i$ for some fixed nonnegative integer c, and for all i;
iii) $X_i \setminus X_{i+1}$ is smooth and affinely embedded in X;
iv) X_0 is smooth.

3.1. PROPOSITION. Under the above conditions, the spectral sequence for calculating $H^*_{X_0}(X,\mathcal{O}[L])$ collapses to a resolution of $H^c_{X_0}(X,\mathcal{O}[L])$ by a (cohomology) complex whose i - th term is

$$H^{c+i}_{X_i \setminus X_{i+1}}(X,\mathcal{O}[L]) .$$

Thus, the differential goes from the i - th term to the (i + 1) - th term, and the resolution is a long exact sequence of finite length $\mathcal{U}(\mathfrak{g})$ - modules.

Example 1. X_i = the union of all B orbits of codimension $\geq i$. We obtain Kempf's resolution of $H_0(X,\mathcal{O}[L])$, a finite dimensional $\mathfrak{g}$ module in this case. Kempf's resolution is dual (in the sense of the duality in category $\mathcal{O}$ (see [3])) to the Bernstein - Gelfand - Gelfand homology resolution of a finite dimensional $\mathfrak{g}$ - module (see [6]).

Example 2. Let θ be an automorphism of order two of G , and let K be G^θ . K is a closed algebraic subgroup of G. Let X_i = the union of K orbits of codimension $\geq i$. These K orbits are affinely embedded in X (see [2]), and there are finitely many K orbits on X. Proposition 3.1 gives a new resolution of $H_0(X,\mathcal{O}[L])$ by finite length $(\mathfrak{g},K)$ modules, since K acts canonically on $H^*_Y(X,\mathcal{O}[L])$ if Y is K - stable. Vogan's recent book [8] describes a correspondence between K orbits on X (more generally K orbits equipped with K - equivariant flat bundles) and certain $(\mathfrak{g},K)$ modules known as the standard modules in Langlands' classification theory. We can always construct a real reductive group G_0 inside G so that $G_0(\mathbb{C})$ = G , G_0 is Θ-stable, and G_0^θ is a maximal compact subgroup of G_0. The standard $(\mathfrak{g},K)$ modules are then the infinitesimal counterparts of G_0 representations induced from discrete series representations of cuspidal real parabolic subgroups of G_0 .

The punchline here is that Vogan has proved in [9] that the standard module he attaches to a K orbit Y (equipped with the trivial flat connection) is isomorphic to $H^i_Y(X,\mathcal{O}[L])$, i = codimension Y . Thus, our second resolution is a resolution of a finite dimensional module by standard $(\mathfrak{g},K)$ modules. When we apply the **Lefschetz** trick we obtain the global character of a finite dimensional module as an alternating sum of global characters induced from discrete series characters of real parabolic subgroups of G_0. This character identity was essentially proved for indefinite unitary groups in the author's thesis [10]. The author conjectured the identity for general real reductive groups some time ago. Vogan's book proves the identity directly, without recourse to geometry (see [8], Prop. 9.4. 16).

Example 3. We now fix a Borel subgroup B in G compatible with the subgroup $K = G^{\theta}$ in Example 2: thus we assume $K \cap B$ is a Borel subgroup of K. Let $X_0 = K$ orbit of B in X (X_1 is the set of all Borel subgroups in G; G acts by conjugation). Thus, let $c = \operatorname{codim} X_0$. Let X_i = the union of $K \cap B$ orbits lying in X_0 and having codimension $\geqslant c + i$ in X. Thus, $X_0 \supseteq X \supseteq X_2 \supseteq \cdots \supseteq X_i \supseteq \cdots$; each $K \cap B$ orbit in X_0 is an affine cell.

Propostion 3.1 now gives P. Trauber's resolution (unpublished) of $H^c_{X_0}(X, \mathcal{O}[L])$ by finite length $(\mathfrak{g}, K \cap B)$ modules.

Introduce again the real reductive group G_0 mentioned in example 2. The module $H^c_{X_0}(X, \mathcal{O}[L])$ is a standard $(\mathfrak{g}, K)$ module attached to the K orbit X_0. If rank (K) = rank (G), we get an infinitesimal discrete series module, depending on X_0 and L. As we run over all possible X_0 (exactly the set of closed K orbits), and all possible positive L, we exhaust the discrete series of the real group G_0. Historically, Schmid's thesis[7] was the first work to associate discrete series representations with closed K orbits in X, although not all details were understood at the time (1967). Schmid worked with a geometric construction dual to local cohomology: he considered the cohomology of a formal neighborhood of a closed K orbit with coefficients in the restriction of $\mathcal{O}[L]$ (see also [11]).

Enright and Varadarajan have constructed a series of $(\mathfrak{g}, K)$ modules associated to pairs (X_0, L) considered above (see [4]). Enright and Wallach have constructed a homology resolution of the Enright - Varadarajan module. It is now known that $H^c_{X_0}(X, \mathcal{O}[L])$ is dual to the Enright - Varadarajan - Wallach module (even when rank $(K) <$ rank (G)).

Conjecture 3.2. (P. Trauber): Trauber's resolution is dual to the Enright - Wallach resolution.

Example 4. Let Y be a K orbit in X such that the closure, X_0, of Y is <u>smooth</u>. Let the codimension of Y be c, and let X_i = the union of K orbits of codimension $\geqslant c + i$ and lying in X_0. Then, Proposition 3.1 gives a resolution of $H^c_{X_0}(X,\mathcal{O}[L])$ by standard $(\mathfrak{g}, K)$ modules. By construction X_0 is irreducible as a subvariety, so $H^c_{X_0}(X,\mathcal{O}[L])$ is an irreducible $(\mathfrak{g}, K)$ module, whose global character will be a sum of standard characters with coefficients plus or minus one.

Unfortunately, a K orbit need not have smooth closure. The corresponding statement in character theory is that the expansion of the irreducible character attached to Y into standard characters (see [2], [8]) may have some coefficients not equal to plus or minus one or zero. The geometry and representation theory required to understand the general K orbit is much deeper than we can indicate here (see [2], [9]).

Nevertheless, for any reductive group G, there are <u>some</u> K orbits on X having smooth closure. Let Q be a parabolic subgroup of G. Let Z be the variety of subgroups of G conjugate to Q. If B is any Borel subgroup of G, there is a unique subgroup Q' of G conjugate to Q and containing B. The map $\pi: B \to Q'$ is a smooth submersion of X onto Z. Let Z_0 be a closed K orbit in Z. Then $\pi^{-1}(Z_0)$ will be a closed smooth irreducible subvariety of X. Moreover, $\pi^{-1}(Z_0)$ will be K-stable. It follows that $\pi^{-1}(Z_0)$ is the closure of a single K orbit, Y. By construction, Y has smooth closure in X.

There are some especially interesting $(\mathfrak{g},K)$ modules associated to the smooth K orbits constructed above. Let Q be a θ - stable parabolic subgroup of G such that if L is the θ - stable Levi factor of Q, then L is the centralizer in G of a linear form λ in $\mathfrak{g}^*$ of elliptic type, i.e. under the G isomorphism of $\mathfrak{g}^*$ and $\mathfrak{g}$, λ maps to an element in $\sqrt{-1}\,\mathfrak{k}_0$. Suppose further that $\lambda + \rho_{\mathfrak{u}}$ lifts to a rational character of L, and hence to a character of Q trivial on the unipotent radical of Q. There will be an associated homogeneous line bundle $\tilde{L}$ on G/Q, which we can pull back to a homogeneous line bundle L over X, the variety of Borel subgroups of G. We can also construct the K orbit Y in X corresponding to Q, as in the previous paragraph.

3.3. PROPOSITION. Suppose λ is chosen so that L is positive. Then the irreducible $(\mathfrak{g},K)$ module $H_Y^c(X, \mathcal{O}[L])$ is isomorphic to the module $A(\mathfrak{q},\lambda)$ constructed by (among others) the author of this paper.

For an introduction to the $A(\mathfrak{q},\lambda)$ modules see J. Adams' thesis [1] and Vogan's book [8] (for a more general construction). We mention here the outstanding conjucture (see also [8] Conj. 6.5.17) on the $A(\mathfrak{q}, \lambda)$ modules.

Conjecture 3.4. For $\mathfrak{q}$ and λ as in the propostion, $A(\mathfrak{q},\lambda)$ is unitarizable.

Supported by NSF Grant MCS79-04473. The author is an Alfred P. Sloan Fellow.

REFERENCES

[1] J. Adams, "Some results on the dual pair (O(p,q), Sp(2m))." Yale University thesis (1981).

[2] A. Beilinson, J. Bernstein. Localisation de $\mathfrak{g}$-modules. C.R. Acad. Sc. Paris, T. 292 (1981), 15-18.

[3] J.L. Brylinski, M. Kashiwara. Kazhdan - Lusztig conjecture and holonomic systems. Inv. Math. 64, 387 - 410 (1981).

[4] T. Enright. On the fundamental series of a real semisimple Lie algebra: their irreducibility, resolutions, and multiplicity formulae. Ann. of Math. 110 (1979), 1-82.

[5] R. Hartshorne. "Local Cohomology." (Based on lectures of A. Grothendieck.) Lecture Notes in Math., Springer-Verlag, Berlin (1967).

[6] G. Kempf. The Grothendieck-Cousin complex of an induced representation. Adv. in Math. 29, 310-396 (1978).

[7] W. Schmid. "Homogeneous complex manifolds and representations of semisimple Lie groups." Univ. of Calif. at Berkeley thesis, (1967).

[8] D. Vogan. "Representations of real reductive Lie groups." Birkhauser, Boston (1981).

[9] D. Vogan. Irreducible characters of semisimple Lie groups III. Proof of the Kazhdan-Lusztig conjecture in the integral case. To appear in Inv. Math (1981).

[10] G.J. Zuckerman. Some character identities for semisimple Lie groups. Princeton University thesis, (1974).

[11] G.J. Zuckerman. Coherent translation of characters of semisimple Lie groups. "Proceedings of the International Congress of Mathematicians," Helsinki (1978).

Progress in Mathematics

Edited by J. Coates and S. Helgason

Progress in Physics

Edited by A. Jaffe and D. Ruelle

- A collection of research-oriented monographs, reports, notes arising from lectures or seminars
- Quickly published concurrent with research
- Easily accessible through international distribution facilities
- Reasonably priced
- Reporting research developments combining original results with an expository treatment of the particular subject area
- A contribution to the international scientific community: for colleagues and for graduate students who are seeking current information and directions in their graduate and post-graduate work.

Manuscripts

Manuscripts should be no less than 100 and preferably no more than 500 pages in length.

They are reproduced by a photographic process and therefore must be typed with extreme care. Symbols not on the typewriter should be inserted by hand in indelible black ink. Corrections to the typescript should be made by pasting in the new text or painting out errors with white correction fluid.

The typescript is reduced slightly (75%) in size during reproduction; best results will not be obtained unless the text on any one page is kept within the overall limit of 6x9½ in (16x24 cm). On request, the publisher will supply special paper with the typing area outlined.

Manuscripts should be sent to the editors or directly to:
Birkhäuser Boston, Inc., P.O. Box 2007, Cambridge, Massachusetts 02139

PROGRESS IN MATHEMATICS
Already published

PM 1 Quadratic Forms in Infinite-Dimensional Vector Spaces
Herbert Gross
ISBN 3-7643-1111-8, 432 pages, paperback

PM 2 Singularités des systèmes différentiels de Gauss-Manin
Frédéric Pham
ISBN 3-7643-3002-3, 346 pages, paperback

PM 3 Vector Bundles on Complex Projective Spaces
C. Okonek, M. Schneider, H. Spindler
ISBN 3-7643-3000-7, 396 pages, paperback

PM 4 Complex Approximation, Proceedings, Quebec, Canada, July 3-8, 1978
Edited by Bernard Aupetit
ISBN 3-7643-3004-X, 128 pages, paperback

PM 5 The Radon Transform
Sigurdur Helgason
ISBN 3-7643-3006-6, 207 pages, hardcover

PM 6 The Weil Representation, Maslov Index and Theta Series
Gérard Lion, Michèle Vergne
ISBN 3-7643-3007-4, 348 pages, paperback

PM 7 Vector Bundles and Differential Equations
Proceedings, Nice, France, June 12-17, 1979
Edited by André Hirschowitz
ISBN 3-7643-3022-8, 256 pages, paperback

PM 8 Dynamical Systems, C.I.M.E. Lectures, Bressanone, Italy, June 1978
John Guckenheimer, Jürgen Moser, Sheldon E. Newhouse
ISBN 3-7643-3024-4, 305 pages, hardcover

PM 9 Linear Algebraic Groups
T. A. Springer
ISBN 3-7643-3029-5, 314 pages, hardcover

PM 10 Ergodic Theory and Dynamical Systems I
A. Katok
ISBN 3-7643-3036-8, 346 pages, hardcover

PM 11 18th Scandinavian Congress of Mathematicians, Aarhus, Denmark, 1980
Edited by Erik Balslev
ISBN 3-7643-3040-6, 526 pages, hardcover

PM 12 Séminaire de Théorie des Nombres, Paris 1979-80
Edited by Marie-José Bertin
ISBN 3-7643-3035-X, 404 pages, hardcover

PM 13 Topics in Harmonic Analysis on Homogeneous Spaces
Sigurdur Helgason
ISBN 3-7643-3051-1, 152 pages, hardcover

PM 14 Manifolds and Lie Groups, Papers in Honor of Yozô Matsushima
Edited by J. Hano, A. Marimoto, S. Murakami, K. Okamoto, and H. Ozeki
ISBN 3-7643-3053-8, 476 pages, hardcover

PM 15 Representations of Real Reductive Lie Groups
David A. Vogan, Jr.
ISBN 3-7643-3037-6, 776 pages, hardcover

PM 16 Rational Homotopy Theory and Differential Forms
Phillip A. Griffiths, John W. Morgan
ISBN 3-7643-3041-4, 258 pages, hardcover

PM 17 Triangular Products of Group Representations and their Applications
S. M. Vovsi
ISBN 3-7643-3062-7, 142 pages, hardcover

PM 18 Géométrie Analytique Rigide et Applications
Jean Fresnel, Marius van der Put
ISBN 3-7643-3069-4, 232 pages, hardcover

PM 19 Periods of Hilbert Modular Surfaces
Takayuki Oda
ISBN 3-7643-3084-8, 144 pages, hardcover

PM 20 Arithmetic on Modular Curves
Glenn Stevens
ISBN 3-7643-3088-0, 236 pagers, hardcover

PM 21 Ergodic Theory and Dynamical Systems II
A. Katok, editor
ISBN 3-7643-3096-1, 226 pages, hardcover

PM 22 Séminaire de Théorie des Nombres, Paris 1980-81
Marie-José Bertin, editor
ISBN 3-7643-3066-X, 374 pages, hardcover

PM 23 Adeles and Algebraic Groups
A. Weil
ISBN 3-7643-3092-9, 138 pages, hardcover

PM 24 Enumerative Geometry and Classical Algebraic Geometry
Patrick Le Barz, Yves Hervier, editors
ISBN 3-7643-3106-2, 260 pages, hardcover

PM 25 Exterior Differential Systems and the Calculus of Variations
Phillip A. Griffiths
ISBN 3-7643-3103-8, 349 pages, hardcover

PM 26 Number Theory Related to Fermat's Last Theorem
Neal Koblitz, editor
ISBN 3-7643-3104-6, 376 pages, hardcover

PM 27 Differential Geometric Control Theory
Roger W. Brockett, Richard S. Millman, Hector J. Sussmann, editors
ISBN 3-7643-3091-0, 349 pages, hardcover

PM 28 Tata Lectures on Theta I
David Mumford
ISBN 3-7643-3109-7, 254 pages, hardcover

PM 29 Birational Geometry of Degenerations
Robert Friedman and David R. Morrison, editors
ISBN 3-7643-3111-9, 410 pages, hardcover

PM 30 CR Submanifolds of Kaehlerian and Sasakian Manifolds
Kentaro Yano, Masahiro Kon
ISBN 3-7643-3119-4, 223 pages, hardcover

PM 31 Approximations Diophantiennes et Nombres Transcendants
D. Bertrand and M. Waldschmidt, editors
ISBN 3-7643-3120-8, 349 pages, hardcover

PM 32 Differential Geometry
Robert Brooks, Alfred Gray, Bruce L. Reinhart, editors
ISBN 3-7643-3134-8, 267 pages, hardcover

PM 33 Uniqueness and Non-Uniqueness in the Cauchy Problem
Claude Zuily
ISBN 3-7643-3121-6, 185 pages, hardcover

PM 34 Systems of Microdifferential Equations
Masaki Kashiwara
ISBN 0-8176-3138-0
ISBN 3-7643-3138-0, 182 pages, hardcover

PM 35 Arithmetic and Geometry Papers Dedicated to I. R. Shafarevich on the Occasion of His Sixtieth Birthday Volume I Arithmetic
Michael Artin, John Tate, editors
ISBN 3-7643-3132-1, 373 pages, hardcover

PM 36 Arithmetic and Geometry Papers Dedicated to I. R. Shafarevich on the Occasion of His Sixtieth Birthday Volume II Geometry
Michael Artin, John Tate, editors
ISBN 3-7643-3133-X, 495 pages, hardcover

PM 37 Mathématique et Physique
Louis Boutet de Monvel, Adrien Douady, Jean-Louis Verdier, editors
ISBN 0-8176-3154-2
ISBN 3-7643-3154-2, 454 pages, hardcover

PM 38 Séminaire de Théorie des Nombres, Paris 1981-82
Marie-José Bertin, editor
ISBN 0-8176-3155-0
ISBN 3-7643-3155-0, 359 pages, hardcover

PM 39 Classical Algebraic and Analytic Manifolds
Kenji Ueno, editor
ISBN 0-8176-3137-2
ISBN 3-7643-3137-2, 644 pages, hardcover

PROGRESS IN PHYSICS
Already published

PPh 1 Iterated Maps on the Interval as Dynamical Systems
Pierre Collet and Jean-Pierre Eckmann
ISBN 3-7643-3026-O, 256 pages, hardcover

PPh 2 Vortices and Monopoles, Structure of Static Gauge Theories
Arthur Jaffe and Clifford Taubes
ISBN 3-7643-3025-2, 294 pages, hardcover

PPh 3 Mathematics and Physics
Yu. I. Manin
ISBN 3-7643-3027-9, 112 pages, hardcover

PPh 4 Lectures on Lepton Nucleon Scattering and Quantum Chromodynamics
W. B. Atwood, J. D. Bjorken, S. J. Brodsky, and R. Stroynowski
ISBN 3-7643-3079-1, 574 pages, hardcover

PPh 5 Gauge Theories: Fundamental Interactions and Rigorous Results
P. Dita, V. Georgescu, R. Purice, editors
ISBN 3-7643-3095-3, 406 pages, hardcover

PPh 6 Third Workshop on Grand Unification
University of North Carolina, Chapel Hill, April 15-17, 1982
P. H. Frampton, S. L. Glashow, and H. van Dam, editors
ISBN 3-7643-3105-4, 382 pages, hardcover